ISRAEL'S NUCLEAR DILEMMA

A volume in the series

CORNELL STUDIES IN SECURITY AFFAIRS

edited by Robert J. Art, Robert Jervis,
and Stephen M. Walt

ISRAEL'S NUCLEAR DILEMMA

Yair Evron

Cornell University Press

Ithaca, New York

To Ruti and Roi

© 1994 Yair Evron

Phototypeset in Baskerville by Intype, London
Printed in Great Britain

First published 1994 by Cornell University Press.

Library of Congress Cataloging in Publication Data

Evron, Yair.
  Israel's nuclear dilemma / Yair Evron.
      p.   cm. – (Cornell studies in security affairs)
  Includes bibliographical references and index.
  ISBN 0–8014–3031–3
  1. Israel–Military policy. 2. Nuclear weapons–Israel.
  3. Middle East–Military policy. 4. Nuclear weapons–Middle
  East. I. Title. II. Series.
  UA853.I8E863   1994
  327.1'74–dc20   93–42628
                                                         CIP

CONTENTS

INTRODUCTION

The nuclear issue in the Middle East has become increasingly more salient. Significant since the 1970s, it attained much more visibility during the Gulf Crisis and War and its aftermath. While several academic works have already dealt with various aspects of proliferation in the Middle East, a great deal is still open to analysis.

This book deals with Middle Eastern proliferation in general (to be specified below), and with some of the dimensions of Israel's nuclear policy in particular. My method here has been to present an historical-analytical investigation grounded in various theoretical frameworks, primarily that of deterrence theory, followed by an analytical and theoretical discussion of the possible implications of proliferation in the Middle East, and a policy-oriented analysis, viz. some recommendations for Israeli strategic behavior. These recommendations are based on the analyses preceding them.

The topics discussed are all connected by the following interrelated core issues: Israel's nuclear postures and Arab reactions to them; the role that nuclear weapons may already have played in the dynamics of the Arab–Israeli conflict; political and strategic implications of the spread of nuclear weapons; preferred Israeli strategies.

Chapter 1 discusses the nuclear status of Middle Eastern countries. As the subject of the book is primarily Israel's nuclear policy and dilemmas, these are presented in much greater detail than the Arab ones. The chapter focuses on the development of Israel's politico-strategic positions regarding nuclear weapons, the background for the initial decisions to develop that capability, and the early internal debate concerning the advisability of developing an Israeli capability and strategy. Because of the deep secrecy surrounding these subjects, their treatment here is based exclusively on open literature, and on interviews I have conducted concerning the early debate in the 1960s. Also, because of the element of secrecy, it is impossible to define the various stages in the Israeli nuclear program. I have relied, therefore, on various descriptions suggested by the international literature. Thus, this is an account based on secondary sources drawn from the international literature; it is not based on personal knowledge.

Israel's strategy of nuclear ambiguity came about as a result of circumstance and unintentional developments. Once it manifested itself, however, this ambiguity turned into a deliberate policy. The nature of this policy and the extent to which we can still consider the Israeli nuclear capability ambiguous (or opaque), form another part of Chapter 1.

Discussion of the nuclear status of the various Arab states is also problematic since no inside information is available about their decision-making processes. What is available are international reports about the Arab efforts in this field. And since it is not the purpose of this book to present and analyze in detail their decisions on nuclear issues, these reports serve as a basis for the description of the Arab nuclear status. Since Israel led the nuclear effort in the Middle East, Arab perceptions about the Israeli nuclear effort are important and relevant as background for Arab strategic decisions. An analysis of changes in Arab perceptions of Israeli capabilities and intentions is therefore included in the chapter.

The main policy-oriented issue with which I deal in the book (primarily in Chapter 7) is a comparison between conventional and explicit nuclear deterrence postures as preferred strategies for Israel. I lay the ground for that discussion by investigating, in Chapter 2, two main themes: the Israeli conventional deterrence posture, and the relevance to deterrence of Israel's emerging ambiguous nuclear posture, and its potential political impact on Arab states. This discussion is grounded in deterrence theory as it developed over the years. Apart from forming the background for the policy-oriented discussion, both themes are of central academic interest since they refer to important chapters in Middle Eastern political strategic history. They are also of much interest as part of the general literature on proliferation and on deterrence.

Israel's conventional posture was and remains the main pillar of her overall deterrence. The evolution, formulation, successes, and failures of this posture are the subject of an historical-analytical discussion. Five Arab–Israeli wars are assessed from this perspective.

International literature on proliferation has only rarely discussed the extent to which nuclear options or assumptions about the existence of nuclear capabilities have affected the dynamics of conflicts, particularly in the Middle East. The relevance of Israel's ambiguous nuclear posture as a deterrent or compellent is analyzed in Chapter 2 through the prism of the 1973 War and Sadat's peace initiative—because of their momentous impact on the Arab–Israeli conflict, and because several publications have advanced the argument that Israel's ambiguous nuclear posture profoundly affected both events—as well as by an assessment of Arab strategic behavior during the 1980s.

Chapter 3 deals with the potential strategic and political effects of proliferation on the Middle East. This subject has received considerable attention in the proliferation literature. An important contribution is Shai Feldman's *Israel's Nuclear Deterrence*, which recommends that Israel adopt an explicit nuclear doctrine as a basis for her national security, and argues that proliferation in the Middle East will stabilize the region. In this chapter I discuss the sources for the stability of the central balance of nuclear deterrence between the superpowers and assess the extent to which a nuclear Middle East could be a stable region. While accepting the view that the introduction of nuclear weapons into the Middle East may constrain decision-makers in their strategic choices, an analysis of the various political, strategic, and technical factors leads to the conclusion that proliferation alone cannot stabilize the region to the level where wars would be completely prevented. The probability of war would be much higher than that which pertained in the superpowers' relationship. Therefore, there are serious dangers that proliferation may result in escalation of violence to the point of nuclear exchanges.

The international nonproliferation regime which has developed since the 1960s was based primarily on the superpowers' opposition to proliferation. They considered global proliferation as seriously threatening their vital interests. Yet their ability, in the past, to uphold, let alone deepen, the nonproliferation regime had been constrained by their competition. Chapter 4 examines their respective policies on proliferation in general and in the Middle East in particular.

Since the end of the Cold War, the dissolution of the Soviet Union, and the emergence of the United States as the single leading global power, the prospects for a more effective nonproliferation policy by the international community have increased. On the other hand, paradoxically, the end of the bipolar system may enhance regional powers' motivations to equip themselves with independent nuclear capabilities. The reason for this is that precisely because of its overall competitive dynamics, bipolarity provided for the security of many states around the globe. This paradoxical situation is also referred to in this chapter. Based on this analysis, as well as on current American and other big powers' interests, Chapter 4 assesses their possible reaction were Israel to adopt an open and explicit nuclear strategy.

While the discussion in Chapters 1 to 4 is mostly historical-analytical, and partly, especially in Chapter 3, analytical and theoretical, the discussion in Chapters 5 and 7, though grounded in several conceptual and theoretical frameworks, is more policy-oriented. Much of the proliferation literature weighs the pros and cons of the attainment of a nuclear capability by new powers. But scant discussion is devoted to the *management* of a nuclear world if proliferation does take place. Based on the discussion in Chapter 3, it is my contention that proliferation will not significantly stabilize the Middle East and that it is therefore dangerous and should be prevented. If there is proliferation, however, there may be several ways to limit its potentially catastrophic consequences—until a more effective nonproliferation policy can be applied. In Chapter 5 several strategies designed to limit the destabilizing effects of nuclearization of the Middle East are proposed. Some of these are desirable as stabilizers in any case—under both nuclear and conventional conditions.

The Gulf Crisis and War were critically interlinked with proliferation issues and problems. First, Iraq's suspicions of United States policy, dating back to early 1990, were critically influenced by American activity against Iraq's nuclear developments. Similarly, as long ago as 1989 and certainly since April 1990, there evolved an Iraqi–Israeli deterrence "dialogue" in which Iraq sought to deter Israel, which she suspected of planning to attack her nuclear facilities. In this "dialogue," links appeared to have been created between chemical and nuclear weapons. Then again, Iraq's nuclear effort was among the causes for the American decision on war. Indeed, the Iraqi nuclear facilities were among the prime targets of the coalition air forces. Finally, during the crisis and more so during the war, Israeli deterrence was tested and at least partly failed. Was it a failure of an ambiguous nuclear threat? In Chapter 6, I analyze these questions and try to assess whether a nuclear posture, opaque or explicit, was relevant to the deterrence of Iraqi chemical attacks against Israel.

It is the contention of this book that a public and explicit strategic nuclear doctrine for Israel would inevitably cause wider proliferation in the Middle East, which would leave Israel sitting on the brink of probable catastrophe. From the narrow Israeli point of view, then, the question is whether she should rely on a purely conventional capability or on one backed by a limited ambiguous nuclear capability designed for a "last resort" mission only, or whether she should opt for an explicit nuclear doctrine with all its consequences. On the background of various themes discussed throughout the book, I propose in Chapter 7, a package of political and strategic measures comprising a conventional strategy for Israel and compare these to an explicit nuclear strategy. In addition, I analyze the possible functions and uses of Israel's putative nuclear capability. Finally, I discuss possibilities for nuclear arms control in the Middle East and various Israeli dilemmas connected with it.

The first version of this book was written in 1984–1985 and was published in Hebrew in 1987. Several major changes have taken place since then. First, Mordechai Vanunu's story dented Israel's nuclear ambiguity. While a measure of opacity was maintained, Israeli deterrence threats during the Gulf Crisis, interpreted as they were by the international media as partly referring to nuclear reaction, further eroded the ambiguous posture. Indeed, since then most academic works as well as the international media have tended to perceive Israeli nuclear weapons' capability as a fact of international life. However, major questions remain regarding the size and nature of Israel's actual capability, the extent to which it has been integrated into Israel's strategic doctrine, its relevance to strategic and political processes in the region, and its impact on Arab states. Thus, an important measure of ambiguity has been maintained even following these events. I have included these developments and their effects in the present edition.

While the original version included a description of Arab perceptions of Israeli nuclear developments, the effects of the latter as a deterrent or compellent were only partly covered. I have added a discussion of these effects and assessed the likely role of Israel's ambiguous nuclear posture as a deterrent to Arab-initiated hostilities, or as a political instrument, during the 1980s. This is included in Chapter 2.

Another major development since the publication of the Hebrew version has been the end of the Cold War, the dissolution of the Soviet Union, and the emerging (and as yet undefined) new structure of the international system. These changes are relevant to some of the main themes in the book: the superpowers' nonproliferation policies in general and in the Middle East in particular; the proneness of regional powers to proliferate because of the changes in their self-perceived relative security in a new international system, the relevance to the Gulf Crisis and to its dynamics, and in particular to its proliferation aspects; finally, the prospects for effective nuclear arms control in a new international system. Naturally, there are no clear and conclusive answers to most of these questions. Hence, their treatment in the book is tentative and reflective. They are discussed in this version, primarily in Chapters 4, 5, 6, and 7.

The study of the model of superpower nuclear relations, its emergence, its main features, dilemmas, and paradoxes as a basis of comparison with a possible model of relations in a nuclear Middle East, in Chapter 3, remains largely as it was in the original version. This is so because it serves by now as an historical model for a strategic relationship between two or more nuclear opponents within one specific set of conditions.

As has already been pointed out, the Gulf Crisis and the War required a special discussion, both as an historical event and a demonstration of some of the changes mentioned. This is included in Chapter 6. Finally, a brief presentation of possible nuclear arms control measures for the Middle East is included in Chapter 7.

In addition, following the excellent advice of my editor, Robert Art, the English edition of this book is structured in a different way from the Hebrew edition.

ACKNOWLEDGEMENTS

I am very grateful to Yad Tabenkin who sponsored and financed the research on which this book is based.

The late Yisrael Galili and Arnan Azariahu ("Sini") encouraged me to launch this project. Azariahu followed the various phases of writing the earlier Hebrew version of this book and continued to contribute from his knowledge to the ongoing research. His comments and advice were of great value.

I am particularly indebted to Robert Art who painstakingly reviewed the manuscript, commented on it and forced me to rethink ideas, concepts and formulations. His contribution was invaluable.

I would also like to thank Warwick Sharp for his considerable contribution in carefully editing and correcting the manuscript.

Yair Evron
Tel Aviv

1

THE NUCLEAR STATUS OF THE MIDDLE EAST STATES

ISRAEL AND THE DEVELOPMENT OF AN OPAQUE POSTURE

The development of nuclear technology in Israel has been the focus of intense interest. Both the press and professional publications have been rife with reports of the presumed existence of an Israeli nuclear capability.[1] The press coverage of the issue has come in waves. Since the mid-1980s, the number of reports has increased, some of them broaching aspects of the issue that had previously received little attention. Of late, the Vanunu story has led to a new round of speculation among specialists and observers regarding Israel's nuclear capability.[2] The overall consensus now is that Israel has, over the years, assembled an extensive arsenal of nuclear bombs. For her part, Israel continues to deny this, insisting that she will not be the first to introduce nuclear weapons into the Middle East. As will be shown below, this position helps to maintain a certain fiction which has its own utilities.

The focus of the present chapter is the political-strategic context surrounding the development of Israeli nuclear technology, the main policy alternatives as proposed by key decision-makers, and the difficulties and doctrinal problems attendant on the various policy proposals. Finally, against the background of repeated claims by international experts attributing to Israel a concealed nuclear capability, an attempt will be made to define the characteristics of the Israeli ambiguous posture. However, a brief description of Israel's nuclear status serves as an introduction. Since Israel maintains official silence on nuclear matters, this account is based on international literature, primarily on one source widely accepted as serious and credible—the annual publication of Leonard Spector.

According to foreign sources, Israeli nuclear research was initiated in 1948, soon after independence. The catalyst for this research program was the discovery of a uranium deposit in phosphates in the Negev. The issue gained momentum with the decision to send a number of young physicists on study programs in nuclear research centers throughout the world.

1

On June 13, 1952, the Israel Atomic Energy Commission was established within the Ministry of Defense. This Commission became the main supervisory body for all activities associated with nuclear development. The mandate of the Commission was limited to consultory and supervisory functions. Development activity accelerated in the early 1950s, and centers for nuclear research were established at the Hebrew University of Jerusalem and the Weizmann Institute. These were the first steps in the formation of an infrastructure that could support a nuclear program. An appropriate technological infrastructure is a necessary precondition for effective nuclear development.

One consequence of the educational effort was the emergence of close ties between Israeli scientists and French nuclear research institutes. These connections created a conducive context for the nuclear agreement signed with France in 1957 (a limited agreement on nuclear cooperation had preceded this major agreement). It should, of course, be noted that these links were formed within the broader context of strengthening ties between the Israeli and French defense establishments. The development of these ties had an uncertain start in 1953–1954, but markedly accelerated in 1955–1956. The architect of these developments was Shimon Peres, then director-general of the Ministry of Defense. As is well known, the background to the warming of French–Israeli relations was the two countries' shared interests concerning Egypt under Nasser. France, then heavily involved in her war in Algeria, had reached the conclusion that President Nasser was supporting the Algerian rebels. His removal, so it was claimed in Paris, might bring the collapse of the rebel front, or at least its weakening. Israel, for her part, perceived Nasser as a source of serious danger.

The coming to power of the socialist government of Guy Mollet in 1956 led to an unprecedented period of intense relations between Israel and France. This development was an outgrowth, in part, of the decision by Mollet to opt for an aggressive approach toward the rebellion in Algeria. While Mollet did feel a certain affinity to Israel, and in particular to her socialist leadership, the eventual catalyst of improved bilateral relations was a concurrent and parallel adjustment in the orientation of Israeli foreign policy. Since 1954, the Israeli leadership had been divided between, on the one hand, the "activists" led by Ben-Gurion, and his supporters, including the Chief-of-Staff, Moshe Dayan, the director-general of the Defense Ministry, Shimon Peres, and a small group of leaders from *Mapai* and *Achdut Ha'avodah*, and, on the other hand, the moderates under Moshe Sharett who served as Prime Minister from late 1953 until mid-1955 (while Ben-Gurion retreated to *Sde Boker* to contemplate the future of Israel and of his own role therein), supported by a group of senior members from *Mapai* and some other parties. The "activist" school urged firm military reprisals against the limited guerrilla activities conducted by border infiltrators. Moreover, certain supporters of the "activist" school saw these military actions as a vehicle in the pursuit of foreign policy ends. From 1955, the activists concentrated their efforts on emphasizing the dangers presented by Egypt. Some even favored a preemptive strike against Egypt, in order to weaken Nasser politically and militarily.

The differences between the moderates and the activists to a certain extent reflected variant international orientations. The moderates urged the centrality of Israel's relationship with the United States. The activists, on the other hand, while not denying the importance of the American connection, made a variety of claims as to the necessity of locating an alternative partner. It seems that on this issue, Ben-Gurion was more cautious than his advisers, and was certainly aware of the critical importance of maintaining a close relationship with the Americans. However, he was also ready to argue for undertaking an independent initiative, even were such an action likely to cause tension with the United States. Furthermore, it appeared that Washington was at that time ready to weaken her relations with Israel, as part of an attempt to improve her relations with the Arab world. It was against the background of this internal debate on her foreign policy orientation, that Israel's relations with France were tightened.

As her association with France deepened, Israel began to examine the possibility of establishing her own nuclear infrastructure. Shimon Peres, having obtained the support of Ben-Gurion, sought the purchase of a French research reactor. The negotiations were conducted between Peres and senior-level officials of the French defense ministry, and were linked with the lengthy negotiations that were proceeding between the two sides in planning for the attack on Egypt (operations *Musketeer* and *Kadesh*). During the meeting in Sevres in late October 1956, in which agreement was reached for French–British–Israeli cooperation in the planned war, Peres raised the issue of the nuclear reactor. However, at this point, the subject of discussion was a reactor of small scale.

At the conclusion of the 1956 war, the French–Israeli negotiations were resumed, with both sides expressing a certain hesitancy. Israeli fears focused on the adequacy of her technological capabilities for mounting such a project, and on the political wisdom of the undertaking as a whole. However, despite the existence of doubts on both sides, a secret agreement was signed on October 3, 1957. While earlier discussions had focused on a small reactor, the signed agreement was for a much larger one of 24 megawatt capacity. On the Israeli side, as was mentioned above, the chief instigator of the agreement was Peres. Among the French, the main supporter of the project was the then Defense Minister, Bourges-Manoury. For a time Jacques Soustelle, then Minister for Science and Energy, and a close friend of Israel, also lent his support.[3]

The agreement was at the governmental level. It was determined that the French and Israeli Atomic Energy Commissions would sign a technical agreement detailing the technological and scientific assistance to be supplied by France. Israel was obligated to consult France on all issues associated with the reactor. According to one report, France also extended Israel support in the construction of a plutonium separation plant. According to the same source, this point was not included in the agreement, but was nevertheless approved by the French government.[4]

Another source has reported four areas of cooperation that were included in the secret agreement: supply of the reactor, supply of a plutonium separation facility, cooperation in the development of a ground-to-ground missile carrying a nuclear warhead, and the provision of Israeli technological assistance to the French nuclear program.[5]

The extensive support given by France enabled Israel to initiate construction of the reactor in 1958. However, in 1960, a question mark hung over the future of the project when de Gaulle decided on changes in French nuclear policy toward Israel. For example, Israel was required to publicly declare that she was constructing a nuclear reactor, and to permit foreign, or even international surveillance. The policy change was transmitted to Israel on May 14, 1960. Israeli acceptance of the changes was set as a precondition for the French supply of uranium.[6] On June 13, Ben-Gurion went to Paris in an attempt to convince the French president to change his position. While the tensions that had been aroused were calmed somewhat by Ben-Gurion's visit, no policy changes of substance were obtained.[7] French pressure on Israel did not subside[8] until Peres eventually met with Couve de Merveille, Giomma and several of his assistants, and concluded with them a compromise agreement, whereby the French assistance would be continued, but Israel would publicly declare that the reactor serves only research purposes.[9] In the event, large-scale French support was granted to the Israeli nuclear project until the mid-1960s.

In the meantime the United States began to intervene. Whether the source of her information was French, a third party, or intelligence-gathering flights over Israeli territory, the first signs of American intervention were in late 1960. On December 9, 1960, Secretary of State Harter expressed the administration's concern over the revelation that Israel was building a nuclear reactor.[10] In the same period, reports that were at first vague,[11] and later became more specific,[12] started appearing in the press. This saw the onset of bilateral negotiations on the issue, as the United States sought to pressure Israel into allowing American scientists to check the reactor and its operation. Israel objected, and it was not until a meeting between Ben-Gurion and Kennedy in May 1961 that a compromise was reached, in which Israel agreed to allow a one-time inspection of the reactor by two American scientists.

In response to the repeated American demand that the nature of activity in the reactor be made clear, Israel declared that she had no intention of producing nuclear weapons. Israel stated, in what has become a familiar diplomatic standby, that she would not be the first to introduce nuclear weapons into the Middle East. However, this was not enough to ward off the American pressure. Finally, upon receipt of a firmly worded memorandum from President Kennedy in May 1963, Ben-Gurion agreed to an annual inspection of the Dimona reactor.[13]

Differences Among the Israeli Leadership

The nuclear issue was a main focus of dispute among Israeli decision-makers. One of the main protagonists in this argument was, of course, Ben-Gurion, who had become a firm supporter of Israeli development of a nuclear capability, apparently out of a pessimistic appraisal of future changes to the Israeli–Arab balance of power. As will be detailed in Chapter 3, his decision to undertake the Sinai (*Kadesh*) campaign derived to a large extent from his fears of Arab unification under Nasser's leadership, and a deterioration in the regional balance. The Israeli failure to reap political gains from the *Kadesh* campaign seems to have led Ben-Gurion to a number of conclusions: first, political goals cannot be achieved through the use of military force; second, a derivative of the first point, Israel ought to avoid wars—on the one hand by not initiating an offensive war, and on the other, by deterring the Arab states from launching war against Israel; and third, it affirmed his previously held view as to the importance of maintaining a close and special relationship with a superpower. The experience of the Sinai campaign was proof to him that only the two superpowers were possessed of political power sufficient to influence the outcome of crisis situations in the Middle East.

The *Kadesh* campaign demonstrated the Israeli military advantage. However, Ben-Gurion was not convinced that this conventional advantage would necessarily be long-standing. In his view, the Sinai military victory served only to earn Israel some breathing space, in that it sharpened the effectiveness of her conventional deterrence posture. It was necessary, however, to develop a deterrent of more permanent standing. Thus Ben-Gurion arrived at the nuclear solution.

It seems safe to assume that the other supporters of the nuclear development also saw it as an answer to problems of an unstable and possibly short-term deterrence advantage. It is also possible that certain decision-makers believed that political ends could be obtained by means of a nuclear strategy.

In opposition to the nuclear scheme, there developed a broad-based front comprising representatives of various political groupings. Within the leading decision-making group, the opposition to the development of a nuclear option was led by the leaders of *Achdut Ha'avodah*, Yisrael Galili and Yigal Allon. They were joined by veteran *Mapai* leaders, Golda Meir and Pinhas Sapir. It appears that Levi Eshkol also opposed the scheme, but on budgetary rather than strategic grounds. However, Eshkol's stand was far from consistent, and, unlike the others opposed to nuclear development, his position did not derive from principled disagreement. *Mapam* also opposed the development. In addition, a group of intellectuals and writers was organized, which strove for the denuclearization of the Middle East. In short, the opposition to the scheme derived from various corners of the political spectrum, and cut across party lines.

To the internal political debate was added the element of ongoing American pressure, and thus there arose a certain urgency in determining the shape of future Israeli strategy. According to the international professional literature,[14] the fate of future Israeli nuclear policy was essentially decided in a meeting in 1962 of a limited forum of the top leadership. At that meeting, opposition to a nuclear-based strategy was expressed by Allon and Galili. Galili's presentation was based on a memorandum written by his aide Arnan Azariahu ("Sini") who had conducted a close study of the nuclear issue. Allon argued that the conventional Israeli advantage showed no signs of diminishing. On the contrary, were Israel to introduce nuclear weaponry to the region, there was the possibility that Arab states would follow suit, and thereby overturn the very advantage that Israel had sought to preserve. Furthermore, emphasis on the nuclear dimension within the overall national strategy threatened to weaken the military, both in terms of resource allocation and in terms of its self-image as the hub of national security. Another issue raised by Galili and Allon related to the impact of nuclear deterrence on regional stability. Galili reasoned that in a nuclear environment the motivation to strike first and to deliver a decisive initial blow would increase, since each side fears that the other may be preparing to launch a nuclear attack. In the Israeli–Arab context, argued Galili, Nasser was the only one likely to consider initiating a nuclear attack. Regional tension would be increased since the mutual fear of being subject to attack was exacerbated. It was urged that account had also to be taken of the danger of a nuclear strike undertaken by "hotheads," such as might appear on the scene following some future revolution in Egypt.

Galili warned that nuclear armament may accelerate the regional arms race. It was also argued that because she occupied a small geographical area, Israel would not be able to develop a second strike capacity. Galili also referred to the dissimilarity between the conditions of the Arab–Israeli conflict and the context of nuclear deterrence between the United States and the Soviet Union. The superpowers were possessed of a far broader range of political interests, affording them greater maneuverability in military conflict situations, prior to the resort to nuclear weapons. Galili noted the ability of the two superpowers "to carefully measure the weight of the issue at stake, without exposing themselves to excessive risk—as they did in Cuba, Laos and Korea."

The supporters of accelerated nuclear development, Dayan and Peres, focused on the requirements of deterrence and on the possible diminution of resources allocated to defense. Surprisingly, Eshkol at first tended to side with the supporters of the nuclear program, on the grounds that it would reduce the monetary cost of deterrence.

According to the reports of this meeting, Ben-Gurion was ultimately convinced by the arguments of Galili and Allon. This had a number of far-reaching consequences: first, it was decided not to adopt a nuclear-based national strategy. Second, in the battle over the allocation of resources, greater emphasis was placed on the purchase of conventional weapons. In effect, the result of this meeting, without the participants being aware of it, was that Israel adopted an ambiguous nuclear strategy. This occurred because Israel decided to refrain from basing her strategy on nuclear deterrence but did not stop her nuclear effort. Although official financial resources allocated to this effort were diminished, the nuclear lobby succeeded in mobilizing alternative financial resources outside the Israeli budget. Thus, in fact, the development of the nuclear capability continued.

At this point it should be noted that Galili and Allon were not absolute in their opposition to nuclear development. Their opposition was rather to the attempt to base overall Israeli military strategy on a nuclear doctrine. Their opposition to this attempt was accepted, and has since served as a guidepost of Israeli strategic planning.

The internal debate on the nuclear issue was one of the main topics of debate within the innermost circle of the Israeli political elite in the late 1950s and early 1960s. However, it would be overstretching the point to claim that this difference influenced the shape of internal party politics. The critical split in *Mapai* between Ben-Gurion and a large portion of the veteran leadership, on the one hand, and the closer relations between the leadership of *Achdut Ha'avodah* and the group of veterans from Mapai, on the other, were two major events whose origins were entirely unrelated to the nuclear issue.[15] These processes were derivative of a complicated tangle of political and psychological factors, and internal and inter-party power struggles.

There is no necessary connection between stands taken on the nuclear issue and positions on other security questions. For example, after the Sinai campaign, Ben-Gurion became a "dove" on the territorial issue, and even abandoned the view that the actual use of Israeli military force could be instrumental in achieving Israeli political objectives. At this stage, Ben-Gurion's approach to the nuclear issue was purely as a deterrent. This approach was not defined by him publicly, in such terms, but one may surmise it from his overall policy. It might be added that he was apparently not explicitly aware of the distinctions between deterrence and "war fighting" postures, but as mentioned, his was most probably a deterrence approach. In contrast, Dayan, who also supported nuclear development, remained an "activist" on security policy issues even after the Sinai campaign. Indeed, in the years following the 1967 war, he indicated a preparedness to undermine any political initiative aimed at reaching an Israeli–Jordanian settlement involving the return of the West Bank to Jordanian sovereignty. As far as Egypt was concerned, while he was willing, in late 1970–early 1971, to enter negotiations for a partial agreement involving a limited Israeli withdrawal along the Suez Canal, his overall posture seemed to indicate readiness to risk another round of war, rather than allowing major concessions. Dayan moderated his position only after the 1973 War. For his part, Eshkol at first opposed nuclear development, changed his mind at the time of the 1962 meeting, and renewed his opposition some time later. However, Eshkol's stand was not a function of his overall views on security issues. Other *Mapai* leaders' opposition to the nuclear program was based on their generally "dovish" approach to security problems. This was especially the case with Pinhas Sapir.

Allon tended to be more of the "activist" school. But his overall security approach was rooted in strategic concepts that were essentially nonnuclear. For example, the system of *casus belli*, which he developed in the 1960s was explicitly based on conventional warfare. So was his famous "Allon Plan." Politically, this plan, which at the time of its formulation in 1967 may have appeared maximalist, has always stood as one of the moderate alternatives to those opposing any division of the Land of Israel. Indeed, over the years, the Allon Plan has tended to appear more and more moderate relative to an Israeli political climate that has moved to the right. All along, his positions on the nuclear question had remained essentially unchanged.[16]

Beyond the ranks of the decision-makers, the nuclear issue aroused only a relatively limited public debate. In the 1960s, for example, there was an intense debate in the Knesset on a proposed idea to seek the attainment of a treaty to keep the Middle East free of nuclear weapons. In this debate, the outstanding opponents of the Israeli nuclear effort were the leaders of *Mapam*, in particular their chief spokesman on security issues, Yaakov Chazan. Another source for criticism of the Israeli program was the "Committee for the Nuclear Demilitarization of the Middle East," two of whose members were also retired members of the official Atomic Energy Commission.[17]

When Levi Eshkol was elected as Prime Minister in 1963, following the resignation of Ben-Gurion, he continued the line that his predecessor had adopted in 1962, refraining from the adoption of a doctrine of nuclear deterrence. The nuclear development program continued, albeit at a reduced pace, and its share of budgetary resources was decreased.

Furthermore, the political leadership under Eshkol was characterized by the increased influence of Galili and Allon, and of the group of *Mapai* veterans that opposed the approach of Dayan and Peres. These factors created a political-strategic environment restrained in its support of the nuclear effort. This tendency was given clear expression in the oft-repeated claim that Israel would not be the first to introduce nuclear weapons into the Middle East. The claim was later changed somewhat by Allon, who added "nor will Israel be the second to introduce them to the region."

Eshkol's attention to the strengthening of ties with the United States contributed to the further amelioration of the nuclear issue. American concern over Israel's nuclear development had somewhat subsided. American officials visited the Dimona reactor in spring 1964, February 1965, and again in 1967, prior to the outbreak of the war. The improvement of relations with the United States in the period under Eshkol, led to speculation about a possible agreement between the two nations in which Israel would suspend her nuclear program in return for political concessions by the Americans, including arms supply arrangements.[18] It seems that no such agreement was ever obtained, but the general improvement in relations bettered mutual understanding.

As relations with the United States developed, the debate within the Israeli political elite on nuclear policy continued. The debate was sharpened with Ben-Gurion's resignation from *Mapai*, and his establishment of the breakaway party Rafi, with the participation of Dayan and Peres. One of the focuses of criticism by Rafi, whether openly or tacitly, was the failure of the Eshkol government to deal adequately with the nuclear issue. This criticism was, however, more than a little misleading since it had been the decision of a government under Ben-Gurion to refrain from the development of a nuclear strategic doctrine.

Following the Six Day War, there were changes in the Israeli decision-making environment, the most important of which was the appointment, just prior to the war, of Moshe Dayan as Defense Minister. Dayan had an enormous influence over all defense matters. It has been suggested that it was during his tenure between 1967 and 1974 that the critical decision to produce a small inventory of nuclear weapons was taken. Despite these changes, Galili and Allon prevented the adoption of a nuclear strategy for Israel. During this period, the United States decided to cease her periodic inspections of the Dimona reactor. According to one foreign observer, the background to the American decision may have been the suspicion that Israel had moved beyond the stage of possessing the mere option of developing a nuclear capability. Continued American surveillance of the reactor, in the absence of steps to compel termination of the nuclear armament program, was liable to be interpreted as an expression of tacit support for the program.[19] If this was indeed the case, it means that some critical decisions had been taken by Dayan in regard to nuclear developments.

The coming to power of the Likud in 1977 seems not to have altered the Israeli position on the nuclear question. If at all, Menachem Begin was even more doubtful of the benefits of an explicit nuclear doctrine. He also expressed his deep concern over the possible acquisition of nuclear arms by Arab states. The Israeli attack on the Iraqi reactor was the outstanding manifestation of this concern. Indeed since 1977, it seems that both political blocs, the Likud on the one hand and the Labor party under the leadership of Rabin and Peres, on the other, have shared approximately similar positions on the nuclear issue. Indeed, in his first speech in the Knesset in July 1992, after becoming Prime Minister, Rabin stated clearly that the threat of regional nuclear proliferation is one of the main reasons for his government's search for political settlements with the Arab neighbors (and see below in Chapter 7).

From this brief survey, it emerges that Israeli leaders across the political spectrum have tended to maintain a skeptical stance toward the proposal for adoption of an explicit nuclear doctrine, preferring an ambiguous posture.

Israeli Nuclear Developments[20]

While officially maintaining an ambiguous posture, Israel continued to develop her capability. According to various French reports, from the very beginning, the Dimona reactor had a far greater capability than the initial 24 megawatt size mentioned by Israeli and other sources. In addition, the Israeli–French agreement also called for the construction of a plutonium processing plant—a unit that was not completed before 1966.

Israel also purchased natural uranium from various sources, primarily in Africa. It may also have produced some uranium as a by-product of phosphate processing. This uranium was used in the reactor for the purpose of producing plutonium.

It is rumored that in order to increase her uranium reserves, Israel secretly obtained 200 tons of "yellow cake" by diverting a cargo presumably meant for another destination. In addition, it is widely believed, according to Spector, that Israel was able to obtain 100 kilograms of enriched uranium by stealing it from a uranium fabrication plant in Apollo, Pennsylvania, sometime during the mid-1960s.

Spector raises the possibility (following the London *Sunday Times* assessment based on the Vanunu story) that altogether Israel may have produced between 100 and 200 nuclear weapons. U.S. government specialists interviewed by Spector, however, argued that various indications about the Dimona reactor suggest that in fact the output was much smaller. Accordingly, Israel may have had (by 1987–1988) only 50–60 nuclear warheads. Spector adopts a middle of the road view, thus estimating that Israel may have about 100 nuclear warheads. Basing his assessments on Vanunu's story, Barnaby's study, and Pean and Peron's accounts, Spector also suggests that Israel may have been able to assemble "boosted" nuclear weapons, viz. fission bombs with enhanced destructive capability.

The Nature of the Israeli Threshold Posture

The status "threshold state" is an ambivalent and dynamic concept. In the absence of a generally accepted definition, I suggest that it relates to three elements: the nuclear capability of the threshold state, its nuclear policies and strategies, and finally domestic and international images, perceptions about and reactions to the nuclear status of the state.[21]

Altogether three states are continuously referred to as belonging to the threshold status—India, Pakistan and Israel. All three share some "threshold" characteristics, while differing in others.

Until the late 1980s, official Israeli denials contributed to the maintenance of some degree of ambiguity concerning its actual nuclear weapons capability. However, Vanunu's revelations and, more importantly, the emerging consensus among international experts analyzing his story, have made official Israeli denials less credible. Even so, these denials continue to play an important role, as will be outlined below.

One tangible demonstration of a nuclear capability is a nuclear test. A test may have two functions: first, to give to the tester a final proof as to the effectiveness of its nuclear weapons technology, and second, to demonstrate the nuclear capability of the state. Increasingly, however, experts argue that tests are not needed any more for the first function— the credibility of the weapons, as testing could be computer-simulated. In any case, the absence of an Israeli test adds a measure of opacity to the Israeli effort.[22]

The second set of factors relates to the observable policies, strategies, and related actions (or "non-actions") of the threshold state in the nuclear dimension. The first and most important factor is the existence or absence of a nuclear deterrence strategy. Needless to say, the absence of an open and clearly defined nuclear deterrence strategy makes this primary function a problematic one. In this sense, all three threshold states are genuinely nonnuclear. In the specific case of Israel, her ambiguous posture itself may have certain residual deterrence effects (see discussion below in this chapter and also in Chapters 6 and 7). However, the deterrence effect of an ambiguous posture is most probably more constrained than that of an unambiguous one. (The possibility that an

11

open nuclear deterrence posture may also have only limited effectiveness in the Israeli case is discussed in Chapters 6 and 7.)

It should be added that Israel herself continues to emphasize the need to rely on conventional forces for deterrence and for warfighting. Consequently, the Israeli planners are careful to maintain a conventional capability which should not fall below a certain quantitative ratio compared to Arab forces. When the quantitative ratio becomes impossible to maintain, Israel tries to compensate for that by acquisition of balancing advanced weapon systems. As will be discussed extensively in Chapter 6, the nuclear dimension surfaced during the Gulf Crisis and War. Yet even there, Israel did not officially make use of nuclear deterrence. However, it is not at all clear how seriously Israel's ambiguous nuclear threats influenced the Iraqis regarding the use of chemical weapons against Israel during the war.

Beyond testing and an explicit deterrence doctrine, there are other policy factors that can diminish the ambiguity surrounding a nuclear option. These relate to the incorporation of the nuclear component within the state's military framework. Most obvious would be the deployment of nuclear weapons and their involvement in military exercises. Another issue relates to the development of a separate command and control mechanism for the handling of the nuclear capability. The open professional literature contains no suggestions that Israel has indeed deployed nuclear weapons or created a mechanism of nuclear command and control (but for a speculative discussion of a possible control system, see later chapters). Occasionally, journalistic accounts have alluded to suspicions of Israeli nuclear deployments. But in the absence of more substantive evidence, no definitive conclusions can be reached.

Whatever her actual weapons capability, the most critical component of Israel's threshold status relates to the perceptions and images of that capability. One may divide these images into four different categories: domestic Israeli perceptions; Arab perceptions; the views held by international experts and aired in the world press; and the official reactions of the international community.

The Israeli public reacts in a very interesting way to the nuclear issue. According to the most comprehensive study to date of Israeli public attitudes on matters of national security, the majority of Israelis believe that Israel has nuclear weapons.[23] However, an even greater majority think that Israel should not base her national security on nuclear weapons. This study was conducted prior to the publication of the Vanunu story. More recent surveys have posed only the first question and the results have been similar to those obtained in the earlier study. The most revealing assessment of Israeli public opinion took place during the Gulf War itself. A Gallup poll conducted on February 15, 1991, included the following question. "Under what conditions, if any, should Israel use nuclear weapons?" Nine percent were against any use under any conditions; 41 percent said they were in favor only to prevent total annihilation of Israel; 8 percent were in favor in case Israel suffered very extensive casualties and 42 percent were in favor in case Iraq used such weapons first.[24] Furthermore, it should be noted that in the intensive (while admittedly not very enlightened) public debate about the future of the occupied territories and related security issues, the nuclear subject is hardly mentioned. The same holds for the rather frequent statements on security issues that come from military leaders. Similarly, feelings of military insecurity, which are usually more prevalent among "hawks" than among "doves", seem to have no redress in the commonly held belief in Israel's nuclear capacity.

These attitudes seem to invite at least one, or some combination of the following explanations:

1 The Israeli strategy of ambiguity is very successfully internalized by the majority of Israelis. They distinguish between what they believe Israel has in terms of hardware, and the uses to which this could be put.
2 Israelis are possessed of highly sophisticated views on security and therefore realize that nuclear weapons have, if at all, only very limited applicability in addressing most of Israel's security problems.
3 Israelis are horrified by the whole issue of nuclear weapons, and therefore opt to ignore it altogether. They may even suffer from a collective cognitive dissonance in regard to nuclear weapons.

The second explanation is less plausible—it is too much to claim that the Israeli public is well versed in the intricacies of nuclear strategy. Rather, the lack of public debate contributes to an ignorance that leads to a straightforward acceptance of the "official" line that is plied through the media. One tends therefore to assume that points (1) and (3) explain Israeli attitudes.

As for Arab perceptions, reactions, and policies, see below in this chapter and in Chapter 2. It will suffice, however, to note here that a measure of uncertainty still characterizes Arab perceptions about the actual Israeli nuclear capability. Moreover, although decision-makers and officials from several Arab states increasingly refer to Israel's nuclear capability as a justification for various policies they undertake, most Arab states still refrain from formulating explicit policies and strategies to deal with Israel's nuclear development. It could therefore be concluded that in terms of Arab reactions, the threshold status is still a useful definition describing Israel's nuclear posture. (For Egyptian arms control policy see Chapter 7.)

As far as the professional literature is concerned, it mostly tends to the view that Israel indeed has manufactured an arsenal of nuclear weapons.[25] Although even there some ambiguity persists,[26] the overall approach holds that Israel has gone beyond a certain threshold. At the same time, some of the observers do recognize that in the absence of some of the attributes of a nuclear capability, Israel cannot be fully defined as a nuclear power.

This latter position is manifest even more clearly in the approach taken by the superpowers. Both are offically inclined to view Israel as essentially a threshold state rather than a full-fledged nuclear power. Both, however, are increasingly calling for international measures to control nuclear proliferation in the Middle East (current U.S. and Russian positions on nuclear arms control are elaborated upon in greater detail in Chapter 4 below).

ARAB APPROACHES

Arab approaches to the nuclear issue have five clearly identifiable characteristics (except in the case of Iraq in the late 1970s–early 1980s, and again since 1987, which will be discussed separately).

1 Arab nuclear policies are in the main formulated in reaction to nuclear developments in Israel, and in the case of Iraq, to developments in both Iran and Israel.
2 There exists a substantial gap between the political motivation and financial resources backing the advancement of nuclear weaponry, as compared with the available technological and scientific infrastructure.
3 Generally speaking, the nuclear issue has not been perceived as sufficiently critical at the strategic level, for the leading Arab states to attribute it the highest priority. Consequently, they have not been sufficiently motivated to cooperate and share resources in order to achieve a nuclear option, let alone an actual capability.
4 The different Arab states differ widely in their policies and reactions to the nuclear issue.
5 The nuclear issue has been the focus of only a relatively limited debate in the Arab press, especially in comparison to the volume of comment addressed to the Arab–Israeli conflict in general. The issue has remained largely peripheral even during periods of peak interest in the nuclear question.

Iraq, for her part, differed from other Arab countries in that her nuclear policy was dictated by both the overall Iranian threat and by Israeli nuclear developments and political objectives. Consequently, she did invest very considerably in the nuclear effort.

Arab public reactions can be divided chronologically into several main phases. The first phase, which was triggered by the revelations in December 1960 concerning the establishment of a nuclear reactor in Dimona, extends from 1961 until the 1967 war.[27] This can be further divided into two sub-phases, the first terminating in 1965, with the publication of a series of articles on Israeli atomic policy authored by Muhamad Hassenin Heikal, the editor of *Al-Aharam* and a close confidant of Nasser. The second sub-phase ends with the 1967 war. A second phase can be identified between 1967 and 1973. The beginning of a third phase was marked by the 1973 War, and while the characteristics of that period persisted till the mid-1980s, the bombing of the Iraqi reactor in 1981 added a new variant to the discussion. Since the mid-1980s, certain changes in emphasis can be detected, and this may be defined as a new phase. In particular, there has been a growing tendency for observers to assert clearly that Israel possesses nuclear weapons, or is very close to so doing.

Surprisingly, but perhaps predictably, the Vanunu story has not, until recently, created a qualitative change in declared Arab positions. His story did strengthen suspicions that Israel has indeed assembled a nuclear arsenal. Nevertheless, some ambiguity and confusion still persists. This period will be the focus of a discussion later in the chapter. I now turn to a detailed description of each of the phases.

The Arab public debate of the nuclear issue originated in 1960 with the publication in the international press of reports on the Dimona reactor.[28] First reactions were mixed. On the one hand, Israel was suspected of intending development of a military nuclear capability. On the other hand, it was suggested that such rumors may have been spread by Israel in order to incite fear in the Arab world. At one stage President Nasser even raised the possibility that the "imperialist powers" were using the rumors of an independent Israeli capability as a cover for their provision of nuclear arms to Israel.[29]

The first official Arab forum to address the nuclear issue was the conference of Arab foreign ministers held in Baghdad in February 1961. The issue was also discussed in meetings of Arab chiefs-of-staff. However, in the Arab press, and, apparently, for decision-makers too, the nuclear question has played only a peripheral role in discussions of the Arab–Israeli conflict. Indeed, in the second Arab summit meeting of September 1964, the issue was not even raised. Public interest intensified somewhat with the publication in 1965 of the first of Heikal's articles. From his analysis of the Israeli nuclear effort, Heikal concluded that an appropriate Arab response was necessary. (Heikal's sudden interest in this topic probably resulted from his erstwhile visit to London, where he was exposed to the views of Western strategic analysts focusing on nuclear proliferation, and to their evaluation of the Israeli nuclear program.)

Salah Shibal, probably representing views mainly voiced in Syria, has classified Arab responses in the 1960s into five categories:[30]

1 Nuclear weapons are unusable, and thus Israel's sole intention in acquiring them is to induce Arab fear.

15

2 The Arab population advantage counterbalances the Israeli nuclear weaponry.
3 If Israel attains a nuclear capability, so too will the Arabs. The impact of the Israeli nuclear weaponry will be neutralized, thereby allowing conventional war to be conducted.
4 The liberation of Palestine is to be sought in any case by guerrilla warfare, against which nuclear weapons are ineffective.
5 The superpowers will prevent nuclear proliferation in the Middle East, so that neither Israel nor the Arab states will acquire nuclear weapons.

The Syrian Ba'ath regime tended to emphasize arguments along the lines of the fourth category, concerning the impotence of nuclear weapons against Palestinian guerrilla tactics.[31] One practical outcome of such views was Syrian support of the then recently established *Fatah* organization. The Syrian attitude resulted from a mix of two factors. Ideologically, the Ba'ath leadership, espousing its radical views, adopted the heritage of Communist Third World guerrilla warfare as well as that of the Algerian revolution. On the more pragmatic level, however, this leadership was all too aware of Syrian military inferiority vis-à-vis Israel. Consequently, the Syrians could contend that conventional warfare against Israel was unnecessary, thus freeing themselves from the need to undertake such a war. In addition, *Fatah* argued that an Israeli capability could not counter guerrilla tactics, but fears were expressed that such weapons might freeze the status quo.

The view of things in Egypt was very different, caused as it was by Egypt's being the leading Arab military power and perceiving of its army as the main instrument to counter Israel. According to some of the public Egyptian assessments, an actual Israeli nuclear capability would represent a dangerous threat to the Arab world, and it was necessary to undertake every possible effort to deal with that threat. Heikal, for example, identified a number of possible tactical alternatives:

1 delay taking action until Israel was equipped with nuclear weapons;
2 attempt to obtain a nuclear arms capability, while, in the meantime, the Palestinian cause would be indefinitely frozen;
3 wait for international action; or
4 undertake preventive action.

It is difficult to assess the priority that the Egyptians attached to the nuclear issue in this period. It can, however, be safely posited that until 1967 the Israeli development of a nuclear capability was perceived in Cairo as a rather remote possibility. To the extent that the nuclear issue was recognized as demanding an active response,[32] Egyptian policy was constrained by the failure of all initial tentative attempts to develop an independent nuclear capability, and by the determination to persist in

16

the conventional arms race with Israel in the hope of attaining superiority. Conventional superiority, so argued Heikal and others, would balance the Israeli nuclear capability were the latter to materialize. It should be noted, however, that the Egyptian participation in the arms race between Israel and the Arab states was essentially independent of the nuclear issue and not motivated by it. The Egyptian policy response was also characterized by a possible attempt to obtain nuclear guarantees from the Soviet Union. In addition, Cairo sought the creation of a nuclear-free zone in the Middle East.

There is no firm evidence of an Egyptian attempt to obtain Soviet guarantees in the event of Israel successfully acquiring a nuclear capability. At the time there was mention of such an Egyptian request, and of partial Soviet acquiescence, but these reports were later denied by Egyptian sources.[33] Egypt did seek to acquire nuclear weapons from the Soviets, or at least Soviet assistance in the development of the technological infrastructure that would enable Egyptian production of nuclear weapons, but Moscow rejected both requests.

President Nasser's warnings to the effect that Israel's attainment of a nuclear capability would be met by an Egyptian preemptive military strike obtained no practical manifestation. The 1967 War bore no connection to the nuclear issue, but was the outcome of other politico-strategic factors: the deterioration of the situation on the Syrian–Israeli border and the complex of inter-Arab relations. In the latter respect, an important underlying dynamic was provided by the Syrian–Egyptian defense pact, which was signed in November 1966, and which the Egyptians intended as a moderating force on Syria and as a deterrent against Israel. The pact failed to obtain either objective; on the contrary, it contributed to the 1967 prewar crisis.

Between 1967 and 1973, Arab pronouncements reflected a marked lowering of the profile on the nuclear issue. The 1967 War was decisive proof of Israel's *conventional* superiority. In view of their self perception of conventional inferiority Israel's attainment of, or progress toward, a nuclear capability seemed peripheral. Apart from anything else, indeed, as we shall see in Chapter 2, the nuclear question was of no relevance whatsoever in both the War of Attrition, and the 1973 War.

As of 1974, as circumstances changed, the nuclear issue did achieve greater prominence in Arab public debate. However, the fact remains that the nuclear question has never obtained a position of preeminence among the issues bearing on the Arab–Israeli conflict.

In the years of debate through to the mid-1980s, Arab opinion on the question of Israel's possession of an atomic bomb resolved into three salient categories. One opinion was that Israel possessed a nuclear weapons capability, a second opinion was that it did not, and a third opinion was that they did not know. The latter view was apparently the most widely shared among decision-makers and observers. It would seem then that the Israeli policy of ambiguity was largely successful, in the sense that Arab leaders and publicists had no clear estimate of Israel's actual capability.[34]

The following examples are illustrative of the uncertainty of Arab estimates: In his assessment of the situation, President Sadat remained largely undecided, but tended to favor the view that while Israel had no existent nuclear arsenal, a nuclear option was open to her.[35] President Assad stated in 1976 that Israel was only in the process of developing a nuclear weapon,[36] and similarly, in April 1977, he spoke of Israel's possession of nuclear weapons as a future possibility.[37] King Faisal of Saudi Arabia also said that he did not believe that Israel had nuclear arms.[38] Dr. Ibrahim Hammuda, head of the Egyptian Atomic Energy Commission, claimed that if a state has never conducted a nuclear test, her possession of a nuclear capability could not be determined with certainty.[39] Finally, President Mubarak of Egypt stated in 1983 that "Egypt does not contemplate the development of nuclear weapons. We hope to turn the Middle East into a nuclear-free zone. We have no reliable information as to whether Israel possesses a nuclear weapon or not."[40]

Since the mid-1980s there have been proportionally a growing number of Arab pronouncements indicating belief in Israel's possession of atomic weapons. This tendency would seem to result from the appearance of numerous reports in the international press attesting to an Israeli inventory of nuclear weapons among which and of importance was the Vanunu story, and from the somewhat lowered profile of official Israeli denials.

The various responses to Israeli nuclear development, as they have been expressed in Arab pronouncements since 1974, tend to reflect the arguments of the 1960s. Some have urged the Arab states to arm themselves with nuclear weapons. Others warn of the regional stability that would emerge following the introduction of nuclear weapons: this regional stability would undermine efforts to solve the Palestinian problem. Against this view it has been argued that even under conditions of regional nuclear proliferation, it would still be possible to deploy conventional forces against Israel. Finally, there are those who have gone one step further, suggesting that nuclear proliferation would in fact weaken Israel's position because her sensitivity and vulnerability to the prospect of nuclear warfare exceeds that of the Arab states.

Vanunu's story initially led to many reactions in the Arab press. However, within a very short time, the volume of reactions subsided considerably. The main themes represented in the Arab press were as follows:[41]

1 The story is a fabrication intended to strengthen Israeli deterrence and to demoralize the Arab world.
2 Israel has the bomb.

3 There is nothing new in the story. For years there have been leaks in the media concerning Israel's nuclear development. If Israel has not yet attained a nuclear weapons capability, she can do so within a short time.

4 The Arabs must build a nuclear capability as a counter to that possessed by Israel.

5 The muted reactions in the Arab world to Vanunu's story are disappointing.

6 The Israeli nuclear capability cannot be used in battle, nor can it serve as a bargaining card in negotiations.

While more voices have been suggesting that Israel has already produced nuclear weapons, one of the interesting features of Arab reactions has been the consistency of other commentators in maintaining that Israel has, in fact, not passed that threshold. Thus, for instance, Syrian Defense Minister Mustapha Tlas, said in an interview[42] that the Arabs (or Syria) know that Israel has the potential to produce nuclear weapons but there is no positive information that she actually has the bomb. The Syrian government, in a letter to the International Atomic Energy Agency (IAEA), pointed out that Israel has the capability to produce nuclear weapons within a short timespan. The letter demanded that Israel place her nuclear activity under international supervision and agree to leave the Middle East denuclearized. Syrian officials have also claimed that the Syrian effort in chemical weaponry is intended as a deterrent against the Israeli nuclear capability.

There may be different explanations for this persistent uncertainty. In assessing the Arab position, it is important to be aware of the deep divisions separating Arab states, and of the spectrum of opinion concerning Israel. This makes it difficult to draw general conclusions from public statements by Arab officials. Perhaps one central factor is a genuine disbelief in Israel's ability to develop a nuclear weapons capability. Further, some Arab observers appear convinced that Israel herself is interested in creating the image that she has succeeded in developing a nuclear weapons capability, either to deter an attack by hostile Arab states, or to compel them to reach a political accommodation with her. Another possibility is that Arab leaders actually believe that Israel has a nuclear weapons capability but, for various reasons, they prefer not to admit it. The leaders of the more extreme states prefer not to appear subject to an Israeli nuclear threat. In denying its existence, they signal that they are not concerned about it, are not deterred by it, and are therefore not exposed to possible future Israeli coercive threats. The denial of the existence of an Israeli nuclear capability also releases Arab leaders from certain difficult dilemmas. By proclaiming that Israel actually possessed a nuclear weapons capability, they would have been obliged to propose counterstrategies. Such strategies, however, are not readily available (for a detailed discussion see below).

Intensified Arab reactions to an assumed Israeli nuclear capability were manifest in the Paris conference on chemical weapons in January 1989. Some of the Arab delegations insisted that any measures restraining the use of chemical weapons should be linked to the problem of nuclear proliferation.

Israeli nuclear developments stirred the Arab states—not only into a discussion of the problem, but also into undertaking various practical actions. For those states that decided to pursue the attainment of a nuclear capacity, three options were available:

1 to acquire ready-made bombs, or components for bomb assembly. Such efforts on the part of Arab states have until now yielded no results.
2 to gradually develop an independent nuclear infrastructure. This option requires a very major investment of resources.
3 to provide financial assistance to a technologically equipped state that is attempting to develop a nuclear arms facility, in order that when that state eventually secures a nuclear capability, it will furnish the investor with bombs in return for the original investment.

Bomb Basics

At this point it will be instructive to take account of certain technical details concerning nuclear reactors. There are basically two types of reactors—those whose main purpose is the production of electrical power, and those that are designed for research purposes and the production of plutonium. Both types of reactors produce plutonium, either as a by-product or as the main product. Beyond this initial division, reactors can be classified according to a number of additional categories.

Research reactors are categorized according to the types of fuel, cooling material, and moderator used. For the purposes of the present discussion, we will focus on the fuel variable. There are two main types of reactor fuel; enriched uranium and natural uranium.

In natural uranium, the percentage of the U–235 isotope is only 0.7 percent. Enriched uranium comprises processed natural uranium in which the proportion of the U–235 isotope has been increased to up to 93 percent. The process of uranium enrichment is discussed in greater detail later.

A state that aspires to produce nuclear weapons must pass the following stages:

1 Obtain isotope Pu–239 of plutonium or enriched uranium. Both form the basis of the nuclear bomb. Plutonium can be produced in all the

various types of reactors, but enriched uranium produces far less plutonium than natural uranium.

2 The plutonium output from the reactor cannot be used directly in the construction of a bomb. The reactor output comprises the requisite Pu–239 isotope combined with other plutonium isotopes, and must undergo a refining process involving chemical separation, performed in a reprocessing plant.
3 Assembly of the bomb using the separated plutonium (or using enriched uranium).
4 Obtain appropriate weapon launch and delivery systems.

The usual process of uranium enrichment is very expensive, and can be undertaken only by large, developed states with the requisite scientific and technological infrastructure. The process is known as gaseous separation in which the natural uranium in the form of "yellow cake" is converted into a gaseous state, and then compressed into numerous membranes. A medium-sized enrichment facility using this method costs in the vicinity of U.S. $1 billion. Such a plant also consumes an enormous amount of electricity. For example, in the 1960s, the Chinese enrichment plant consumed a quarter of the country's electricity output. Thus, such facilities have been constructed by only the wealthiest and most advanced states.

In the past two decades, other enrichment processes have been developed. Of these, the most prominent has been centrifuge technology. After being heated and turned into gas (uranium hexafluoride, in a special plant) the uranium is introduced into a centrifuge rotating at very high speed. The uranium atoms are distanced from one another, and the different isotopes are thereby separated (for further details see Chapter 6). A combined German, Dutch, and British consortium (URENCO), constructed a facility of this type in Holland, and similar experimental facilities exist in the United States and Japan. As will be discussed below, Pakistan and Iraq have respectively adopted this process.

The difficulties associated with the uranium enrichment process have narrowed the options for less-industrialized nations seeking nuclear development.[43] They can choose to build a nuclear reactor that uses natural uranium, but, if they prefer to use enriched uranium, they must purchase it from foreign producers. A state that intends to apply its nuclear development for military purposes will usually choose a reactor based on natural rather than enriched uranium, for two main reasons:

1 Enriched uranium is rare, and for a state seeking a nuclear weapon capability, free of the restraints imposed by dependence on a limited number of foreign suppliers, it is preferable that it uses the much more widely available natural uranium.

2 Natural uranium, as we mentioned above, is a much more effective source for the production of plutonium than enriched uranium.

The construction of a nuclear reactor usually requires five or six years, and sometimes even longer. The Iraqi reactor—Osiraq for example, was built in five years. A reprocessing plant (for chemical separation) can be constructed more quickly, if there is a willing supplier. It should be noted that the development of a nuclear reactor is in itself no clear indication that a state is intending a military application. However, the establishment of a reprocessing facility is far more indicative of an intention to produce weapon-grade material. Thus, efforts to control nuclear proliferation have focused on this aspect of the nuclear cycle.

The design and assembly of a nuclear bomb is also highly complex. While the basic principles are relatively well known, numerous substantial technical problems remain. Indeed, even the most developed states have encountered serious difficulties in the design stage. Overcoming these problems is time-consuming and requires the development of an extensive team of scientists, engineers and technicians.

Egypt

By 1961, a small research reactor had been established in Egypt. The reactor was built in Inshas by the Soviet Union, and it is of the WWR-C type, utilizing a water-cooling system. The reactor uses 10 percent enriched uranium, and has an output of 2 megawatts. Because of its small size, it is of no military significance.[44]

In the past, Egypt sought Soviet assistance to broaden her nuclear infrastructure, but without success. She also developed relations with the Indian nuclear establishment, but nor was this connection of any substantive benefit. It should be borne in mind that Egypt lacks the scientific and technological reserves to develop an independent nuclear infrastructure, and will have to rely on extensive foreign assistance in order to achieve nuclear independence.

Negotiations over the purchase of two reactors from the United States have been conducted over a number of years.[45] The original intention was, and remains, to acquire two reactors from the Westinghouse Corporation, each with an output of 440 megawatts. In 1981, as a first step, Egypt granted parliamentary approval to the nuclear Non-Proliferation Treaty (which she had previously signed, but not approved). Similarly, in 1975, it was agreed that the reactors be under the close supervision of the United States and of the IAEA.

On August 5, 1976, Egypt and the United States signed a draft outline agreement on the purchase of the reactors.[46] A similar draft was sent to Israel with whom negotiations were also being conducted over the purchase of energy-producing reactors. From then until 1979, the negotiations did not progress, apparently because of the failure to obtain a parallel agreement with Israel. In 1979, following the signing of the Egyptian–Israeli peace agreement, the United States considered herself released from the obligation to pursue symmetrical reactor purchase agreements with both countries, and set about obtaining a separate agreement with Egypt. However, apart from the political problems that had delayed matters until 1979, there were several new obstacles now standing in the way of agreement. The major problem, to which no solution has yet been found, is finance. Egypt requested credit for the entire costs of construction of the reactors. The Export-Import Bank has consistently refused to provide any credit for these purchases, on the basis of its experts' advice that Egypt lacks adequate economic resources to return the loan. However, in the wake of heavy pressure applied by Secretary of State Shultz, the bank agreed to provide U.S. $250 million over 1985–1986 in order to realize the first stage of the purchase of the reactors.[47] In any case Egypt has not until now began to implement her nuclear power program and no construction of a nuclear power plant has started.

The economic feasibility of the project has been a topic of debate in Egypt. According to one school of thought, the purchase of the reactors represents a misplaced investment of valuable resources, that meets no pressing needs. Pointing to the unexploited potential of the Aswan Dam, and Egypt's oil reserves, the critics argue that the nuclear project can be justified on neither economic nor energy grounds.

In February 1981, while the negotiations over the American reactors were still in process, President Sadat signed a protocol agreement for nuclear cooperation with France. Within the framework of this cooperation, Egypt would purchase two nuclear power stations, each with a capacity of 900 megawatts. In this connection, Sadat also reported on his country's intention to build eight nuclear power reactors by the end of the century. By the time of writing, however, the French agreement has realized no tangible results. The opposition to the nuclear power project within Egypt appears—until the present—to have had the upper hand. Finally, Egypt also has nuclear technology exchange agreements with Germany, Canada, and India.

This brief survey of Egyptian nuclear policy has been indicative of differing tendencies among the Egyptian leadership. There is possibly the desire to obtain a nuclear capability in response to the Israeli capability. However, since the peace initiative, Egyptian efforts in this regard have been motivated not only by strategic but increasingly more by peaceful considerations.[48] In any event, Egypt still confronts major obstacles on the way to her development of a nuclear infrastructure. Even if she does begin construction of the nuclear reactors, almost two decades after the initial discussions, it will be many years until the reactors are active.

Moreover, if the reactors built are American, the supervision and control arrangements for the reactors will be far more stringent than those of the IAEA. Any infringement of these arrangements would doubtless lead to a major diplomatic crisis with the United States, and may make it difficult for the Egyptians to continue operation of the reactors. It should be noted, however, that if Israel does not accept some confidence-building measures in the nuclear field (see below a discussion in Chapter 7), and if other Arab countries and Iran pursue a nuclear weapons capability, there would be increasing pressure within Egypt to launch a nuclear program.

Libya

Libya is the state most frequently used as an example of the dangers of nuclear proliferation. Indeed, the Libyan ruler, Colonel Ghaddafi, has devoted intensive efforts to the acquisition of a nuclear capability. However, it hardly needs mentioning that Libya totally lacks the scientific and technological resources for the development of advanced industry, let alone a nuclear industry. There have been reports from different sources of Libyan attempts to attain nuclear weapons or assistance in the development of a military nuclear infrastructure from the Soviet Union, India, China, France, and Pakistan.[49] Rumors have even spoken of Libyan attempts to steal nuclear weapons. All of these various efforts have failed to produce any concrete results.

In 1975, Libya became a signatory to the Nuclear Non-proliferation Treaty. About a month later, she completed an agreement with the Soviet Union for the construction of a small research reactor with a capacity in the order of 2 megawatts, which can apparently be expanded to 10 megawatts.[50] International reaction was forbearing, because the reactor was not large enough to produce plutonium in militarily significant quantities. The reactor was eventually constructed in Tajoura and is subject to IAEA safeguards.

However, in March 1976, Libya signed a preliminary agreement with France concerning the establishment of a 600-megawatt reactor. Shortly afterward, France announced her withdrawal from the agreement. In December 1977, another agreement was signed with the Soviets, this time for the construction of a 300-megawatt reactor and a nuclear research center. The reactor was to be under the supervision of the IAEA.[51] Some time later, the two states also discussed the possibility of establishing two research reactors, each with a capacity of 440 megawatts.[52] Despite these agreements, the projects have shown no sign of progressing, and Libya has been forced to seek other sources of assistance. An approach was made to the Belgian firm Belgonicleaire, but following U.S. pressure, the Belgians declined the Libyan request.[53]

Also of interest was the Libyan financial support of the Pakistani nuclear development effort. The extent of the support actually provided and details of the exchange provisions have never been fully revealed, but various reports have noted that the Libyan support was generous, and in exchange she was to receive "full access to Pakistan nuclear technology."[54] The currently accepted view is that in the event, Pakistan did not transfer the technology to Libya. In any case, such technology would not have been sufficient for Libya to actually develop a nuclear weapon, in the absence of an adequate scientific and technological base. Indeed, it can quite safely be assumed that in exchange for the financial assistance, Libya had sought ready-made weapons. The outcome of the whole project for Libya was altogether very disappointing.

Iraq[55]

It would appear that of the Arab states Iraq has made the most significant progress toward the attainment of a nuclear capability. Her achievement in this regard suggests that excepting the direct transfer of nuclear devices, it is the Iraqi development strategy that other Arab states will have to emulate if they seek to realize their nuclear ambitions.

The background to the Iraqi decision to pursue a nuclear strategy is variegated. Following the meteoric rise in oil prices in 1973–1974, Iraq's financial resources were greatly expanded. Baghdad then decided to translate this financial growth into increased overall power. The Iraqi regime directed substantial resources toward strengthening the economy and improving the standard of living. In the tradition of the central Arab states, this economic development effort was paralleled by increased arms purchases, an expanded military, and attempts to improve her political position in the Middle East. Nuclear weaponry was perceived as an effective means of increasing political influence and of elevating her international status.[56] In the 1970s, Iraq set about obtaining dominance in the Persian Gulf and in the Arab world as a whole. In this respect, the regime of Saddam Hussein was giving practical expression to a traditional Iraqi ambition, and was following the policy of the Hashemite rulers of Iraq and of Iraq's Prime Minister, Nuri Sa'id, in the 1940s and 1950s. In the 1970s, the Iraqi dictatorship saw the country's oil resources as a new means to the realization of the traditional ambitions. It should however be added that apart from the pursuit of political influence, Iraqi nuclear policy was also informed by additional sets of strategic considerations: namely, the potential threats posed by Israeli nuclear development and Iranian plans for such. For these reasons Iraq undertook a policy of attaining nuclear weaponry, or at least a nuclear option, and for which her professions of peaceful purposes were only a cover.

As early as 1968 a small Soviet-built research reactor, of the IRT–2000 type, with a capacity of 2 megawatts, began operating in Iraq. However, in 1974, Iraq began negotiations with France for the establishment of a much larger reactor.[57] At first, Iraq sought the purchase of a power-product facility: a 500-megawatt natural-uranium/gas graphite reactor, with the capability of simultaneously producing both electricity and plutonium. The French rejected this request because of the enormous quantity of plutonium produced by this type of reactor, and, in any case, the manufacture of such reactors had been discontinued in the late 1960s. The agreement eventually signed in 1976 was for a research reactor of the Osiris type, with an output of 40 megawatts. The reactor was known in France as Osiraq, and its official name in Iraq was "Tamuz 1." It was also agreed to sell a small reactor of the "Isis" type.

The Osiraq reactor uses 93 percent enriched uranium, which France was committed to supply. Operation of the reactor require approximately 12 kilograms of enriched uranium as fuel. For a year's continual operation, several 12 kilogram loads are required.

The sale of the reactor aroused concern in the United States and certain pressure was applied on France from Washington.[58] Israel also used her diplomatic connections in both Paris and Washington in an attempt to obtain suspension of the project. In the face of these pressures, France sought a change in the agreement. It requested Iraqi acceptance of a different type of fuel, known as the "Caramel" type which operates on only 7–8 percent enriched uranium. Iraq was not ready to accept the change, and France decided to continue fulfillment of the original contract. The infrastructure was completed in the years 1976–1979, and in 1979 construction of the reactor itself commenced.

Osiraq operated, as stated, on enriched uranium, and, thus the quantity of plutonium that could be produced under normal operation of the reactor could not sustain any military purpose. Nevertheless, Iraq continued to press for attainment of a nuclear arms option. In reactors of the Osiris type, plutonium can be produced by introducing a change in the configuration of the reactor: the reactor core is coated with natural uranium, and this coating is bombarded with particles emitted in operation of the reactor. Plutonium can then be extracted from the external surface of the natural uranium. This is known as the "blanket" technique, and Iraqi intentions to apply it would seem to be evidenced by her large purchases of natural uranium from Brazil and Nigeria, and an attempted purchase of depleted uranium metal from the West German firm NUKEM.

Iraq joined the nuclear Non-proliferation Treaty in 1969 and accepted the IAEA's supervisory role. What would have been the reactions of France and the IAEA to the Iraqi change in the configuration of the reactor? The answer to this question is complex and relates to a labyrinth of international political considerations. It is quite possible that France

26

would have suspended the supply of enriched uranium, leaving Iraq the virtually impossible task of obtaining enriched uranium on the open market. Furthermore, and despite the contractual requirement that French technicians supervise operation of the reactor until 1989,[59] France may have withdrawn her technicians from the reactor, an action that would have made continued operation of the reactor difficult. However, it is also possible that given the appropriate political conditions, and sufficient financial inducement, the French may have been willing to turn a blind eye to the configuration change. This latter scenario is a rather remote possibility, especially under conditions of international pressure. Nevertheless, the "blanket" configuration was a theoretical possibility, even if it was clouded with considerable uncertainty.

The IAEA supervisory function centers on the report submitted by the agency representatives. The report carries certain political clout, but a state determined to use a reactor for military purposes can overcome this obstacle. However, a published statement by the IAEA as to the configuration change in the Iraqi reactor would have placed France in an embarrassing political situation, and would have contributed to the pressures on France to discontinue the supply of enriched uranium.

In Israel and elsewhere fears were expressed that Iraq might divert the enriched uranium that France was committed to supply to military purposes. However, as we have seen, the probability that the material could have served Iraq for the production of nuclear weapons was virtually nil. According to the terms of the agreement, Iraq was required to return all the waste uranium to France. Each load of uranium would be sufficient for the production of one bomb at most. But such an act would most certainly have led to the termination of the supply of enriched uranium. Furthermore, there is no strategic logic in the production of just one nuclear bomb. France had also announced her intention to apply radiation to the uranium prior to its transfer to Iraq. This treatment makes the uranium dangerous to handle, and would have effectively prevented its use for production of a bomb.[60]

Thus, if Iraq was to have used Osiraq in order to advance toward a nuclear arms capability, it could only have done so by changing the configuration of the reactor to allow application of the "blanket" technique. But this would be of course only a first step toward development of a bomb: Iraq would have then been required to establish a separation facility for the extraction of the Pu–239 isotope, and to obtain the knowledge and technology required for assembly of the bombs themselves. Each of these stages is enveloped by difficulties and uncertainties. Nevertheless, it is quite possible that by virtue of her substantial financial resources, and assuming the nonintervention of other international actors, Iraq could have obtained a nuclear capability and even built a number of primitive bombs. Indeed, Iraq took a first step in this direction when she acquired from Italy three "hot cells" in which small quantities of plutonium could be extracted from irradiated uranium. She also began negotiating with Italian companies for the purchase of a larger reprocessing facility.[61] Given the abovementioned difficulties, this process is likely to have extended over between six to ten years as of final completion of the reactor. In the event, the perceived dangers provoked Israel to attack and destroy the Osiraq reactor on June 6, 1981.

Shortly after the destruction of the reactor, Iraq set about the purchase of a new reactor, and Saudi Arabia announced her readiness to provide finance.[62] In mid-August 1981, the deputy Prime Minister, Tariq Aziz, visited Paris, and following two days of discussions, President Mitterrand declared France's in-principle agreement to rebuild the Baghdad reactor. Mitterrand emphasized the necessity of a surveillance system for the reactor. While France imposes this requirement on all purchases of her nuclear technology, it seems that she was adopting a more cautious approach than she had prior to the destruction of Osiraq. As shall be detailed in Chapter 7, Iraq decided to adopt an alternative route toward the acquisition of a nuclear weapons capability.

Iran

Under the leadership of the Shah, Iran had already begun developing an extensive nuclear infrastructure. While the official justification of the nuclear project was the development of peaceful nuclear energy, it appears likely that the Shah also had in mind a weapons option. Indeed, bearing in mind the enormous oil reserves of Iran, the need for nuclear energy appeared dubious. On the other hand, the Shah entertained very ambitious foreign policy aspirations. He aimed to make Iran the leading regional power in the Gulf area, projecting its influence first toward the "heart" of the Middle East and, then, in the direction of South Asia. Indeed, research on plutonium extraction and possibly even weapon design, had been conducted at the Teheran nuclear research center as early as the 1970s.

However, the Khomeini revolution put an end to the nuclear effort. The actual buildup of nuclear facilities was abandoned and agreements with nuclear suppliers were aborted. Thus, the construction of two partly completed German-supplied nuclear power plants at Bushehr was halted, as was a French project to build another pair of reactors in Darkhouin. Moreover, the war with Iraq, which broke out shortly after the revolution, forced Iran in any case to divert most of her efforts and resources to this critically demanding effort. Later, when Iran found the necessary means and tried to renew the work in Bushehr, West Germany balked, stating that nothing could be done as long as the war continued. It appears,

28

however, that some limited weapon-oriented research continued during the war.

At the end of the war and, perhaps under the influence of the Iraqi nuclear effort, Iran renewed her nuclear program on two fronts: the acquisition of power reactors, and further weapons-related research. Following diplomatic contacts with several countries, Iran eventually reached an agreement with China to complete the German reactors in Bushehr and to build an additional one. China may encounter difficulties in building these facilities, however. Many of the critical components of the reactors are produced in the West, and the producers (especially Germany) may be unwilling to assist in this project. It is also likely that the United States would apply pressure both on China and on the Western producers to desist.

In 1990 Iran also signed an agreement with the Soviet Union for the construction of two power reactors of 440 megawatts each. The reactors would operate on the basis of low-enriched uranium. Although the United States has asked Russia not to honor this Soviet agreement, Russia is, apparently ready to build the reactors. It is still unclear if, under increased American pressure, Russia will persist in this undertaking. In any case, building the reactors is a long-term project: the first would probably be finished only in about eight to ten years' time.

In addition to the production of plutonium (which would, by necessity, require some modifications in the reactors or in the method of operating them) the Iranians could use the low-enriched uranium supplied with the Russian reactors for further enrichment (provided they develop facilities for enrichment) at a quicker pace than if they used natural uranium.

The Iranian interest in nuclear development, most probably for weapons production, can be seen in the contacts they maintain with other technology suppliers. They have, for example, been negotiating with India and Argentina for the building of research reactors designed for the production of plutonium. In both cases, American intervention has either delayed or resulted in the termination of the negotiations.

Over the past years news has frequently appeared in the international press about Iranian research in plutonium reprocessing and uranium enrichment. It was reported, for example, that China transferred a calutron designed for research purposes to Iran. (Concerning the use of calutrons for uranium enrichment in Iraq, see Chapter 6 below.) In view of the aid apparently given to Iraq by China in the area of uranium enrichment based on calutrons, one suspects that this calutron may eventually serve as a prototype for the indigenous production of much larger calutrons.

Another avenue for uranium enrichment may be opened by the close cooperation between Pakistan and Iran. There have been some press reports suggesting that this cooperation has spilled over into the nuclear field. This suggestion, when added to Pakistani expertise in centrifuge technology, points to the possibility that Iran is aiming at developing an option for uranium enrichment based on this technology.

On the basis of continued reports on Iranian nuclear efforts, the following tentative conclusions may be reached. To begin with, Iran is clearly interested in attaining at least a high option for nuclear weapons. Second, this capability is probably intended, primarily as a counter to Iraqi nuclear capability. It is also possible that Iran is pursuing this capability for political and prestige purposes. After all, the revolutionary regime in Iran perceives itself as the vanguard of the worldwide Islamic revolution. Gaining a nuclear capability would strengthen such a posture. Finally, an Iranian nuclear capability may ultimately serve as a counter to the alleged Israeli nuclear capability, provided that Iran searches for a leading position in Middle East affairs.

Though these aspirations appear to fit the overall Iranian posture, it is still too early to assess with any certainty Iran's present state of nuclear development. As mentioned, apart from research work conducted in laboratories, no clear evidence has surfaced about the actual development of an infrastructure for either plutonium production or uranium enrichment. But, left to its own devices, it is likely that Iran would try to develop a nuclear weapons capability. Intensive international efforts could, however, put an end to or at least delay this endeavor.

The role of Pakistan

Will Pakistan transfer nuclear weapons to Arab states? While the issue cannot be determined with any certainty, at the present time it would appear that such an eventuality appears to be a remote possibility. Nevertheless, in the light of the close relations between Pakistan and various Arab states, it is worth briefly examining the Pakistan effort, and its relevance to possible nuclear development in the Middle East.

The Pakistan nuclear weapons development program has achieved considerable success.[63] A limited program was initiated in the 1950s and expanded in the 1960s. Pakistan has chosen to follow development strategies for the use of either plutonium or uranium. The program was greatly accelerated following the 1971 Indo-Pakistani war. According to some sources, Bhutto, the then new national leader, announced Pakistan's nuclear program at a conference of Pakistani nuclear scientists in January 1973. India's explosion of a nuclear device in 1974 further intensified the Pakistani effort. Pakistan possesses a series of nuclear installations. In Karachi she has a 135-megawatt power station of the Kendu type, that has been operational since 1972. For the separation of plutonium produced by this reactor, she purchased a separation plant from France. Pressure from the Carter administration led to delays in the transfer of components critical for completion of the reactor. However, it appears that Pakistan has since come to terms with the technology needed to complete the reactor. Nevertheless, it is still unclear whether the installation has been completed. A smaller pilot-scale separation plant has been established using equipment clandestinely obtained from a number of Western firms.

However, it seems that the main focus of Pakistan military nuclear development has been uranium enrichment. To this end, she has concentrated on application of centrifuge technology. Even though Pakistan has a well-established group of nuclear scientists, she was forced to adopt a rather unconventional approach to advance her development of the centrifuge technique: plans for a centrifuge plant in Elmells in Holland (a joint project of Britain, Holland, and West Germany) were stolen by a Pakistani scientist. Following this initial step, she set about the gradual accumulation, often through irregular sources, of various components required for such a plant. The plant under construction in Kahuta (the first phase was apparently completed in 1986) is of large capacity, and is theoretically capable of producing quantities of enriched uranium sufficient for up to five bombs a year. According to one source, by 1990, 14,000 centrifuges were already in place. However, because of machine failures only 1,000 of them were capable of operating simultaneously. A much smaller plant is also under construction, but is at a far more advanced stage. Pakistan has also purchased several hundred tons of natural uranium for the enrichment process.

U.S. officials believe that Pakistan began to produce weapons-grade uranium in 1986, and in the years since produced sufficient quantity for one weapon per year. They further believe that she is capable of rapidly deploying nuclear weapons in any future conflict, even if she does not "possess" fully assembled weapons. The evidence that Pakistan has in fact produced already several nuclear weapons has so accumulated that the Administration found it difficult in 1990 to provide Congress with the customary declaration connected with the Non-Proliferation Act (and see below the discussion in Chapter 4).

Pakistan's desire to produce nuclear weapons, or if she has already—which is most likely—produced them, to adopt an open nuclear strategy, is moderated by a number of constraints. Among these constraints, U.S. opposition is of overriding significance. Also critical is the inevitable acceleration of Indian nuclear weapon development that Pakistan's declared possession of a bomb would instigate. Nor should Pakistan's fears of a Russian reaction be discounted. Taking account of all these factors, it can be assumed that Pakistan will continue to adopt an ambiguous strategy. She is unlikely to adopt an open nuclear doctrine, unless India takes the lead in doing so.

If indeed Pakistan already succeeded in producing a hidden nuclear

31

capability, there are several sets of considerations that would probably prevent her from secretly transferring bombs to other states. First, there are the political and strategic considerations that hold for all nuclear states. The history of nuclear states shows that once they have reached the stage of weapons production, they tend to be averse to the transfer of these devices to other states. This tendency has been true even of states such as China, that prior to their achievement of a nuclear capacity have argued that nuclear proliferation poses no threat to the international system.[64]

Further to this general position, account should also be taken of the particular factors attending the Pakistani situation. Pakistan initiated her nuclear program in response to India, as an attempt to achieve a deterrent capability against Indian nuclear weaponry. For this purpose she needs to produce a full-scale inventory of weapons. It can be assumed that Pakistan will not start exporting bombs before accumulating a quantity that will meet her strategic needs.

Finally, one of the upshots of an ambiguous nuclear strategy is that states pursuing such a policy will prefer not to transfer nuclear weapons to other states, for fear that the transfer will be discovered, thus causing the disintegration of the ambiguous strategy. Indeed, under U.S. pressure, the Pakistani Foreign Minister declared, in February 1992, that Pakistan undertakes not to transfer sensitive nuclear technology or components to third countries (and see below in Chapter 4).

The Pakistani position on nuclear weapons transfer may possibly change if U.S. policy on nuclear proliferation is completely transformed, leading to a readiness to accept worldwide open proliferation. In such circumstances, the force of the constraints on Pakistan would be significantly weakened, and the possibility of earning politically and financially on a weapons deal might appear more attractive. Moreover, such financial gains would make the future production of additional weapons for her nuclear arsenal easier.

The route of Arab states to nuclear weapons

This short survey has pointed to the wide range of factors that influence the Arab nuclear effort. In this regard, one important consideration has been, at least until the 1980s Arab uncertainty concerning the Israeli possession of nuclear weapons, and, if she indeed does possess them, what are the strategic consequences of the Israeli ambiguous doctrine, and what would be the impact of an open doctrine.[65] To the extent that during the 1980s, they reached the conclusion that Israel does indeed have a weapons capability, they probably accepted the view that this capability has only two functions (to be elaborated in Chapter 4): for use as a last-resort weapon or deterrence against an Arab nuclear capability. Both functions did not pose a threat to them.

Uncertainty over the Israeli position has been one of the main factors preventing the Arab states from reaching categorical, unanimous and perhaps extreme policy conclusions on this issue. The Arab states most certainly did not consider the Israeli nuclear development, at least until recently, as a high-priority issue that demanded a salient response. Furthermore, due to the deep divisions in the Arab world, the progress of any Arab state toward the attainment of a nuclear capability, has been and will continue to be, a source of concern not only in Israel, but also in other Arab states. Similarly, inter-Arab divisions also *de facto* preclude the formation of a coalition whose objective would be to develop a nuclear weapons capability. Presumably, in such a coalition, a rich Arab state would be expected to provide financial assistance to a technologically advanced counterpart for the production of nuclear weapons. But, it appears unrealistic to expect such assistance unless the weapons would be put under joint control, something which appears to be difficult to attain in the deeply divided Arab world. Then again, the oil-rich countries (except Iraq), are strongly oriented toward the United States and tend to listen carefully to U.S. advice (unless it critically clashes with their national interest). Consequently, the U.S. antiproliferation policy will carry weight with them. Indeed, it is strongly believed that several years ago, Saudi Arabia began considering the establishment of a weapons-related nuclear infrastructure. Strong American diplomatic intervention convinced Riad to abandon this idea.[66]

Be that as it may, a number of Arab states have sought to create a nuclear capability in response to Israeli nuclear development. The Arab efforts have encountered serious difficulties, deriving on the one hand from the opposition of the international community to nuclear proliferation, and on the other, from the lack of scientific and technological expertise within the Arab societies. From the Arab nuclear experience, it has emerged that so long as the nuclear powers abstain from the transfer of nuclear weapons to third parties, the only way open to the latter is the gradual construction of a nuclear infrastructure, using either plutonium-oriented or uranium enrichment technologies. Both courses were chosen by Iraq. Limitations and difficulties also beset these routes, largely from the supervisory roles played by the suppliers of nuclear technology and the IAEA. In the absence of these limitations, the technological gap could probably be bridged by the use of the financial reserves of the various Arab states to purchase nuclear technology and to hire foreign scientists and technicians, enabling the production of nuclear weapons. The Iraqi experience with enrichment (to be discussed in Chapter 6) demonstrates that the inspection system of the IAEA is not sufficient to monitor even a major enrichment effort. It also demonstrates that, at least in Iraq, there is already a scientific infrastructure which probably could, with continued outside advice, develop a nuclear weapons capability. There is no reason to doubt that a country such as Egypt could also develop, over time, the indigenous scientific community which could—if financial resources were found and external advice and know-how were forthcoming—develop a nuclear weapons capability.

However, time is also an important factor: the construction of a reactor for plutonium production takes five to six years. A separation plant must also be established, although theoretically this could be achieved simultaneously with the construction of the plutonium facility, and a team of local technicians needs to be trained. Time must also be devoted to solving the problem of bomb assembly. Thus, even under ideal conditions, given the total absence of supervision over the reactor and allowing the possibility of hiring foreign expertise, an Arab state could expect to reach the stage of bomb production only some five to ten years after beginning reactor construction or enrichment facility. In the case of the centrifuge technology, the lead time may be even longer. The destruction of Iraqi nuclear facilities during the Gulf War, followed by the on-site UN inspection and demolishing teams, places Iraq at the same stage, with the mentioned difference of a scientific community which had already been created, as the other Arab states.

There exist, of course, two possible scenarios. International efforts to limit nuclear proliferation might be expanded, in which case the process of acquiring a nuclear capability would be slowed even further, and, indeed, the very possibility of Arab nuclear armament would be clouded in uncertainty. Alternatively, the relaxation of such supervisory functions would make the likelihood of accelerated proliferation more likely.

An Israeli decision to adopt a nuclear doctrine and completely erode the ambiguity surrounding her nuclear capability, would undoubtedly serve as a powerful stimulus to Arab efforts to obtain a military nuclear capability. It might be assumed, first, that the allocation of financial resources to nuclear development within Arab defense budgets could be expanded, thus easing the purchase of nuclear technologies. Second, in such circumstances, the nuclear suppliers such as France, other European states, China, India, Pakistan, and perhaps even Russia, would likely display a greater readiness to transfer nuclear technology, or even nuclear weapons. Third, an Israeli nuclear doctrine may be a negative influence on the overall international regime of nonproliferation, and may adversely affect American willingness to act against suppliers of nuclear technology and materials to Arab states or even to other states within the Third World.

2

THE DYNAMICS OF THE CONFLICT

Israel's Posture of Conventional Deterrence and the Limited Relevance of a Nuclear Capability

As discussed in Chapter 1, since the 1960s, Israel has persisted in nuclear development while maintaining an ambiguous posture. As a partial reflection of this ambiguous posture, Arab perceptions about Israel's nuclear capability have, until recently, remained somewhat uncertain. During this long period, Israel did apply a deterrence strategy, primarily based on her conventional capability. It is the contention of this book that conventional deterrence played a central role in Israel's overall strategy. This chapter focuses on an analysis of this posture, its successes and failures.

While the conventional relationship forms a central component in the Israeli–Arab strategic "dialogue," the nuclear issue has gradually penetrated the texture of relations. Some of the fascinating questions that emerge are: to what extent did Israel's assumed threshold posture or actual capability affect the dynamics of the conflict until recently? Did it contribute to Israel's deterrence during the 1970s and 1980s? Did it affect Arab readiness to reach peaceful relations with Israel? And did it contribute to the legitimization of Israel in the Middle East? These questions will be dealt with in this chapter.

THE ISRAELI CONVENTIONAL POSTURE OF DETERRENCE—SUCCESSES AND FAILURES

Most studies of deterrence focus on the nuclear relationship between the superpowers. However, as has been apparent to a growing body of scholars, deterrence also operates in conventional environments. In many respects deterrence in conventional environments is far more complex, uncertain and difficult to analyze than in nuclear environments.[1] This chapter analyzes the Israeli posture of deterrence in its development since 1948, within the context of deterrence theory.

Before proceeding to the specific Israeli context, we shall be detained at the outset by a brief outline of the concept of deterrence.[2] The discussion will primarily focus on those modalities of deterrence most relevant to the analysis of Israeli deterrence behavior. Deterrence has been defined in many different ways but the essence of these definitions might be summarized as follows: *Deterrence is the threat to use military force in a punishing mode or a denial-punishing mode in order to dissuade a challenger from undertaking a certain course of action involving the use of military force.*[3]

Some elaboration of the concept is necessary. First, deterrence should be distinguished from "compellence" which is the attempt to compel one's opponent to undertake positive political or military steps. Second, deterrence usually refers to situations of international conflict involving two (or more) states, but the concept can accommodate cases of a state matched against a substate organization. Third, both the challenger's intended action and the defender's deterrence threat must be of a military character. However, despite focusing on the military character of the deterrence relationship, this is not to imply that the outcome of this relationship will be decided on the pure military balance.

The formal theory of deterrence suggests that the success or failure of deterrence depends on a rational calculation by the challenger regarding the likely costs and benefits resulting from an intended military action. As such, theorists of deterrence have focused on the military balance between opponents, ignoring political factors. However, some deterrence theorists, but particularly critics of the theory, have pointed to the profound effect of political factors on the outcome of a deterrence relationship. Indeed, the Israeli experience of deterrence is ample illustration that the success or failure of deterrence depends to a large extent on complex political factors. This does not detract from the potency of deterring military threats. It does, however, mean that the success or failure of deterrence depends on a complex interaction between political and military factors.

For the purpose of analysis the deterrence process can be divided in a schematic way into two parallel streams: the calculus of the challenger and the calculus of the deterrer. The calculus of each side comprises roughly speaking the following elements:

1 An assessment of its own interests in the issue under contention,[4] and of the importance of that interest to the other side.
2 An assessment of the balance of military power between the two sides, and of the opposing side's perception of that balance.
3 An assessment of the resolve of the other side to carry out the intended action (in the case of the challenger) or the deterring threat (in the case of the deterrer).

Deterrence theory holds that the outcome of the deterrence process depends on the credibility of the deterrence threat. Beyond this initial formulation it appears, that once a commitment is made by the deterrer, the success or failure of deterrence depends on the three abovementioned balances and their perceptions by both sides: the "balance of military power," the "balance of interests," and the "balance of resolve." The "balance of military power" takes into account objective military capabilities, but also encompasses mutual perceptions of that power. The balance of interests refers to political and strategic interests directly involved in the issue under consideration—what Jervis called "intrinsic interests" or "primary interests," and "secondary interests," such as prestige and credibility.[5] The balance of resolve refers to the readiness of both sides to suffer for the defense of their interests. Although that readiness depends to a large extent on intrinsic interests, it also derives from other sources: the general values of the society and its elite, martial tradition, and the need to uphold prestige and credibility.[6]

When intrinsic interests are well established, deterrence commitments follow more clearly. However, the credibility of these commitments varies according to the challenger's perception of the value of the interests to the deterrer and the balance of military power.

The "art of commitment" so masterly analyzed by Thomas Schelling[7] is intended to harden one's own resolve as well as to project resolve to the other side. It is in a sense, a strategy aimed at bolstering images of resolve when the profile of intrinsic interests appears to be low.

While the relevance of political factors to the deterrence process has been noted in the literature, most writers on deterrence continue to focus primarily on perceptions of the military balance. In addition, the literature has as yet failed to address the distinction between the intrinsic interests (the balance of interests) and the political context (defining a broader set of interests) within which the challenger and the deterrer operate. The impact of these two distinct sets of factors on deterrence may differ both analytically and practically.

Two further distinctions developed in the deterrence literature have particular relevance in the study of deterrence in the Middle East (and in other deterrence situations). The first distinction refers to differences between "immediate" or "specific" deterrence and "general" deterrence. Specific deterrence refers to a situation in which the deterrer perceives a potential *specific* action by the challenger intended to change the status quo, and so issues a deterring threat. General deterrence denotes the buildup of military capabilities by the deterrer, for the ongoing deterrence of a whole range of potential moves by the challenger. General deterrence is, therefore, close to some aspects of the notion of "balance of power." It is, however, a much more limited concept. This distinction is inspired by a formulation suggested by Morgan.[8] He distinguished between "immediate" or "pure" deterrence, which refers to an imminent planned action by the challenger, and "general" deterrence. My definition of "specific" deterrence includes immediate deterrence but in addition encompasses other specific deterrence threats that might also pertain to potential future challenging acts. The obvious case of such threats are definitions of *casus belli.*

Another central distinction turns on the concepts "deterrence by punishment" and "deterrence by denial."[9] Deterrence by punishment, which has been more thoroughly treated in the literature, refers to the threat to punish the challenger's society if the challenger takes his action. Deterrence by punishment is more applicable to situations of nuclear deterrence. Deterrence by denial on the other hand, refers to the ability to deny the challenger victory on the battlefield, while raising costs that far outweigh the possible benefits. Deterrence by denial is therefore much more applicable to conventional deterrence.[10]

Deterrence theory has come under criticism for a number of reasons:[11] that it is a deductive theory with insufficient empirical testing; that it assumes a level of rationality rarely apparent in decisions taken by statesmen; that it ignored the cognitive context of decision-making processes; that it overlooks the emotional background of decisions; that it oversimplifies extremely complex relationships between states; that it ignores domestic political and bureaucratic factors and processes. Two diametrically opposed political schools of thought have also criticized deterrence theory as a useful guide to foreign policy formulation. At one end of the spectrum it has been argued that deterrence cannot and would not work. The proponents of this argument claim that the opponent is basically intent on aggression and war; that eventually, at an opportune time, the opponent will attack; and that it would not be deterred even by the threat of a nuclear war. Indeed an extreme American version of this school called in the 1950s for a preventive attack on the Soviet Union at a time convenient for the West. On the other side of the spectrum are those who argue that deterrence strategy is dangerous because it overemphasizes the military dimensions of conflict. Any deterrence strategy, be it ever cautious and moderate, leads not to restraint and stability, but to escalation and ultimately to war.[12] The real way to resolve or limit the conflict is through the diplomacy of conciliation.

The Israeli deterrence posture[13]

In the context of the Arab–Israeli conflict, Israel has generally taken a deterrence posture, since in most cases, although not without exception, the Arab states have adopted the role of the anti-status quo powers.

Needless to say, deterrence forms but one aspect of the overall Israeli strategic posture. No strategic posture in a conventional environment can depend exclusively, or even mainly, on deterrence. Deterrence constitutes only one element in an overall strategy. Since the end of the War of Independence in 1948, Israel has sought to deter two different types of military threats: low level violence such as infiltration and sabotage actions by irregulars, or small-scale military operations carried out by regular forces and full-scale wars.

Deterrence of low level violence

Infiltration has been a hindrance to Israel almost since the end of the 1948 War. Israeli military response to acts of infiltration was spasmodic in the first years after independence. However, the scope of terrorist infiltration widened in the first half of the 1950s. By late 1953, and more so from 1954, Israel had evolved a new more comprehensive strategy of response, identified primarily with the then Chief of Staff, General Moshe Dayan.[14] The new strategy had several objectives. The first objective could be defined as "third party (or indirect) deterrence,"[15] in which military pressure was applied on the Arab governments from whose territories the infiltration took place. The idea was that such military pressure, applied through military attacks on military targets and on villages where the infiltrators were based, would force the respective Arab governments to control the infiltrators and curtail hostile actions, each action serving as a signal that further "punishment" was imminent unless the infiltration ceased. Second, the strategy involved elements of "compellence," such as the attempts to force Arab acceptance of Israeli political demands which until the 1967 War, included acceptance of the 1949 territorial status quo and the signing of a peace treaty. A third objective was escalatory in nature. It seems that some Israeli decision-makers, in particular Dayan, were hoping that the dynamics of retaliation and counter-retaliation would ultimately lead to a general war. This objective became more salient during 1955–1956 in relation to Egypt. Needless to say, this escalatory function and, to a lesser extent, the function of "compellence" if accurately perceived by the target state, exert an influence on the latter that is diametrically opposed to the effect of deterrence.

The strategy of "third party deterrence" was partly successful when applied to Jordan against Jordanian-based infiltrators in the 1950s and again in the mid-1960s. The same policy was largely ineffective against Jordan in the late 1960s, and against Lebanon since the early 1970s. The use of the strategy against Egypt in 1955–1956, rather than deterring infiltration, led to a vicious circle of actions and counteractions that culminated in the 1956 War.[16] A similar, though not identical process took place along the Israeli–Syrian border in 1964–1967.

Deterrence Against Full-Scale War

The most important element in Israeli deterrence strategy has been to dissuade the initiation of a regular war by an Arab state or coalition of states. In analyzing this aspect of Israeli deterrence, account must be made of two important complexes: the actual deterrence posture, which is the outcome of both military capabilities and doctrine, and public references by decision-makers; and second, the success or failure of deterrence. The success or failure of deterrence is difficult to prove. For a deterrence threat to succeed, the following process must ensue: the challenger contemplates a military action which threatens a deterrer's interest; the deterrer is aware of this contemplated action and issues a deterrence threat; the threat is perceived by the challenger; the challenger reconsiders the cost/benefit balance of his intended action, including the deterrence threat in his calculations; and finally, the challenger decides to abandon his intended action in view of the deterrence threat. To state it differently, successful deterrence means that were it not for the threat, the challenger would have decided to proceed with the intended action. Recorded evidence for all these stages of a deterrence situation is not easily accessible. The analytic difficulties increase when one has to rely on public pronouncements by the challenger's decision-makers explaining their policy choices and decisions. Therefore, their actual actions or inactions may be a better guide.

Since the end of the 1948–1949 War, there have been five Arab–Israeli wars: 1956, 1967, 1969–1970, 1973, and 1982. The questions of the relevance and of the success or failure of Israeli deterrence will now be considered in regard to 1956, 1967, 1973, and 1982.[17] The 1969–1970 War of Attrition will be discussed only briefly because, in terms of the success or failure of general deterrence, it served as a prelude to the 1973 War.

The Israeli deterrence posture 1949–1956 and its relevance to the 1956 War

In the early 1950s, the then Chief of Staff, Yigael Yadin, formulated an *operational* military doctrine, but which encompassed some central strategic principles.[18] Yadin's doctrine comprised the following principles:

1 Israel would not be the first to initiate war.
2 If war nevertheless breaks out, the first task of the Israeli forces is to halt the enemy.
3 The next stage is to transfer the war to enemy territory.
4 Optimal use is to be made of Israel's short internal lines.
5 The war should be as brief as possible, primarily because of the economic constraints under which Israel operates.

The first principle according to which Israel will refrain from launching a war, defines a politico-strategic orientation favoring the status quo. This principle excludes notions urging the use of force to compel Arab acceptance of Israeli conditions for peace. The third principle also bears association with a strategy of deterrence. A doctrine of counterattack, to carry the war to the enemy's territory, is a possible basis for "deterrence by denial"; viz. Arab states should take into account that their initiation of an attack may entail costs beyond the mere failure of their attack.

However, a clear strategy of deterrence against all-out war did not evolve during the early 1950s, in the sense of forming an articulated salient element in the Israeli posture. This development had to await the aftermath of the 1956 Sinai campaign.

By late 1954–1955, Israel perceived a new critical threat emanating from the Arab side. For Israel's chief decision-maker, Ben-Gurion, the emergence of Nasser as a new, vigorous and apparently unifying leader of the Arab world, constituted a major long- term threat to Israel. According to this perception, once Nasser resolved his relationship with Britain, he would unite the Arab world and lead a major war against Israel. Indeed, already in 1953, in a secret overall report to the Cabinet about the long range security problems of Israel, Ben-Gurion pointed out the weaknesses in the Arab front, among them internal competition and mutual suspicions.[19] He added, however, that all these difficulties were surmountable and "if a blessed leader would emerge there [in the Arab world], he could transform all that and would hasten the process of unification and preparations, and the war might break out even earlier."

It seems likely that other decision-makers, in particular Dayan, were less alarmed about the long range military threat to Israel. Their endorsement of an escalatory strategy was derived from their confidence in Israel's ability to impose political conditions on her environment through the use of arms.

Notwithstanding Arab rhetoric calling for a "second round" against Israel, it could be argued that until late 1955 the Arab states were in fact almost entirely preoccupied with other sets of problems: domestic issues, the struggle against Britain, and inter-Arab competition. From early 1955, Egypt became more actively involved in the conflict with Israel due to the process of escalation along the Israeli border, caused initially to a large extent by Israel, and the acceleration in the arms race. It is not clear, however, to what extent Nasser was considering initiating hostilities. In any case, other Arab states and primarily Iraq and Jordan belonged to a different Arab bloc and were not allied to Egypt. Iraqi leaders would have welcomed a military defeat for Nasser, even at the hands of Israel. However, what counted most in the ensuing escalation were the Israeli perceptions.

The Israeli response to its perceived threat was not to adopt a deterrence strategy, but rather to seek an opportunity for a military action to destroy Egyptian arms, and if possible to undermine Nasser's regime.

Consequently, the period between 1954 and 1956 marked a change in the Israeli politico-strategic orientation. Initially, through the strategy of retaliation described above, there was an attempt to *compel* the Arab side and primarily Egypt to accept the territorial status quo and the Israeli conditions for a peace settlement. As stated above, nuances in the Israeli retaliatory strategy suggested that some of the leadership went beyond compellence and would have welcomed a process of military escalation leading to a full-scale war. With the accelerations of the arms race from late 1955, the trend toward a preventive war was set in motion. The emphasis on fighting a war, coupled with notions about the use of force for political compellence, undercut any development of a deterrence strategy.[20]

Israel did not apply a strategy of deterrence against Egypt in 1955–1956. Israel's was a strategy of escalation, and she was the party that ultimately launched the attack. Thus, in Ben-Gurion's view of it, the 1956 War was a preventive war.[21] The question of the success or failure of Israel's deterrence does not arise at all in relation to the 1956 War. Deterrence was in fact irrelevant.

1956–1967

The Israeli deterrence posture

In the wake of the 1956 War, changes were introduced into the Israeli politico-strategic approach. To a large extent these changes resulted from the realization on the part of the Israeli strategic leadership, of the tremendous political constraints on any Israeli military victory. The political gains which Nasser was able to snatch from his own military defeat, pointed to the lack of direct correlation between military victory and political gains in the Middle East, and in particular for Israel. The Israeli leadership concluded that the use of the military instrument would not secure Arab acceptance of the political and territorial status quo. On the other hand, there was general pessimism as to the possibility of a political breakthrough in her relationship with the Arabs, and especially with Egypt. An alternative strategy seemed to be the avoidance of war primarily through deterrence. Ben-Gurion continued to have a basically pessimistic outlook concerning the long-term balance of power between the two sides, and he turned to the nuclear option as a panacea. However, the realization of that endeavor lay in the distant future. In the meantime, and as is true until the present day, the Israeli deterrence posture remained based on conventional arms. In any case, the emphasis in Israeli strategy moved away from compellance and notions of preventive war, to defense and avoidance of war. Indeed, a more elaborate emphasis on conventional deterrence emerged in the late 1950s and early 1960s and was especially apparent after 1963 when Rabin became Chief of Staff, and Eshkol Prime Minister. Deterrence, however, remained only one element within the overall Israeli political and military conception. Moreover, although it received closer emphasis, its conceptual formulation suffered from various simplifications.

Due to the significant demographic, geographic and economic constraints operating on Israel, she has had to rely primarily on a reserve army. This reliance has dictated her endorsement of an offensive operational doctrine. Thus, on the one hand, Israel moved toward an emphasis on strategy of defense and deterrence, while on the other hand, she has had to rely on an offensive posture at the operational level. The link between the strategic and operational level was formed through the formulation of a system of *casus belli.*

Four basic principles constituted the context for the deterrence dimension of the Israeli strategic doctrine, each principle serving several functions besides deterrence: first, a genuine desire on the part of Israel to maintain the territorial status quo; second, the formulation of a system of *casus belli* that was tailored to the maintenance of the status quo and was not unduly provocative; third, the development of a superior military capability, but with the emphasis on not initiating wars; and fourth, insistence on limiting the scale of retaliatory strikes in response to Arab provocations.

Of particular interest was the system of *casus belli.* In distinction to *general deterrence,* which was central to the new posture, *casus belli* belongs to the category of *specific deterrence.*

The *casus belli* element in the Israeli strategic conception was not entirely new. For example, the Israeli warning that the introduction of foreign Arab troops into Jordan might serve as a *casus belli,* dates from before 1956. However, the new formulation was much more elaborate, and included several new tolerance thresholds. Nevertheless, there remained several profound ambiguities in regard to the *casus belli.* In the first place, some of them were not officially presented as such. Rather, they were mentioned in the writings of two leading strategists and decision-makers, Allon and Peres.[22] Others were presented in the *Knesset,* and as such received recognition as official policy. Second, all the Israeli formulations left some ambiguity as to how automatic would be the Israeli reaction. Usually the formulation was that Israel "would feel free to react" if a certain violation of the status quo was committed.

The *casus belli* mentioned prior to 1967, including those communicated through both official and unofficial channels, were as follows:[23]

1 The closure of the Straits of Tiran to Israeli shipping. This particular cause became the most "official" of all Israeli *casus belli*.
2 The introduction of foreign Arab troops into Jordan. One ambiguity in regard to this particular cause, was whether it pertained to the introduction of foreign troops only into the West Bank, or even into areas east of the river Jordan. These first two mentioned *casus belli* were repeatedly cited by Israeli decision-makers in official forums.
3 A major concentration of Arab forces close to the vital areas of Israel. This cause referred primarily to the massing of Egyptian forces in the Sinai close to the international border.
4 The diversion of the waters of the Jordan.
5 A major intensification of the Arab guerrilla campaign against Israel.

In addition, two further acts were mentioned as possible grounds for an Israeli action: an attack on the Israeli atomic installations; and a change in the domestic situation in Jordan, such as the formation of a pro-Nasserite regime.

The question of to what extent Israeli military reaction would be automatic, has two aspects. The first question is whether the Israeli leadership was itself fully committed to such a course of action, and the second is whether the Arab decision-makers were fully aware of the *casus belli* and of the seriousness of the Israeli commitment to them. The usual paradox about *casus belli* is that on the one hand, the deterrer tries to maximize his deterring threat by increasing the certainty of his reaction. On the other hand, decision-makers, prefer to maintain a high level of freedom of action. If deterrence fails, this freedom allows the decision-makers to control their response, and does not bind them to an automatic reaction. One of the costs of *not* implementing the deterrence threat, may be some loss of credibility of future deterrence threats.

Israeli decision-makers seem to have assumed that the element of perceived automatic response would be quite high, at least in two instances: the closure of the Straits of Tiran, and the massing of Egyptian forces close to the international border in Sinai. But one high ranking official, who probably was cognizant of the views held by the majority of decision-makers went even further and stated: "There are four Arab acts which would constitute an automatic *casus belli* for Israel: two are on water, two on land; north, south, east and west; one is the attempt to divert the waters of the Jordan, another the closing of the Straits of Tiran; a third is the control of the Jordan 'bulge' [meaning the 'West Bank'] by a state or united command more powerful than Amman; and the fourth is the concentration of Egyptian military power in the Sinai desert."[24]

The credibility of a deterrence threat, within the context of a *casus belli*, increases if it is clear that *not* reacting to a violation would carry very high costs for the deterrer. Credibility also increases to the extent that the strategic and operational doctrine of the deterrer, and his armed forces, are irrevocably committed to a reaction when deterrence fails. Credibility increases when the deterrer becomes so involved publicly and otherwise committed to the *casus belli*, that *non* implementation of the deterrence threat appears improbable, since inaction would carry very high costs to the deterrer. In these respects the massing of large concentrations of Egyptian forces near the international border, or of hostile forces in the Jordan "bulge" in the West Bank, were the most critical. Such eventualities would threaten the vital areas of Israel, especially in the case of a surprise attack. Hence, from the point of view of Israel's real *strategic* interests, the probability of an Israeli military reaction in the form of a preemptive strike, would have been very high.

The Effectiveness of the Israeli Deterrence Posture

During the period 1957–1967, the Israeli–Egyptian strategic relationship was remarkably stable. This stability resulted from a convergence of several factors, all relating to the three balances that affect the calculations of the challenger: the balances of perceived military power, political interests and resolve. These balances should be viewed within the broad political situation prevailing in the Middle East at the time.

To begin with, the balance of military power favored Israel. Moreover, the main Arab opponents, Egypt and Syria, perceived the military balance as such, and did not believe in their capacity to completely defeat Israel on the battlefield.[25] It is reasonable to assume that until the 1967 crisis, Egypt also was not entirely confident in her capacity to defend Sinai against an Israeli attack. The 1956 War, while ending with an Egyptian political success, demonstrated inherent Egyptian military weaknesses.

In terms of the balance of political interests, it seems most probable that the leading Arab countries did not perceive the Israeli–Arab conflict and the resolution of the Palestinian problem, as being the most urgent of their priorities. Despite their extreme anti-Israel rhetoric, there can be no other explanation of their all-engrossing involvement in the fierce inter-Arab competition, which accelerated in the first half of the 1960s. At that time, radical and conservative states were in conflict, and the radical camp itself was deeply divided. The Yemen War absorbed much Saudi and Egyptian energy, while Syria and Iraq were busy nibbling at Nasser's regional influence. Leadership of the Arab World appeared to be much more important than a war against Israel. Hence, the combination of the first two balances, and the ways in which they were perceived, contributed to the emergence of a credible posture of Israeli deterrence by denial.

Finally, was the deliberate projection of resolve relevant to successful Israeli deterrence? The balance of resolve seems to be of particular importance in two categories of conflict: for deterrence of an attack on allies ("extended deterrence"), and in some cases of specific deterrence. In both these categories, since a state's existence is not directly threatened, there may be a certain ambiguity about the vitality of intrinsic interests. The first category is most relevant to American policy and strategy—Washington's most perplexing strategic problem is the defense of allies.[26]

Credibility of extended deterrence became even more difficult to achieve under nuclear conditions. The nature of the military balance has been thrown into ambiguity, and no interests in the defense of allies would seem to justify suicide. Hence, the other balances partly nullified, the credibility of deterrence came to depend more on resolve.[27] On the other hand, in conventional environments the question of resolve is far less critical in contributing to credibility. Most states will fight when attacked in a general war. Their resolve to defend themselves is not at issue. Doubts about resolve might arise only when the aggression is for a limited specific objective. Even in such cases, states can be expected to fight back. This is especially so in the Middle East and particularly in the case of Israel. No Arab leader has ever assumed that the Israelis will not fight when directly attacked. Thus, within the context of the Israeli deterrence of war, the balance of resolve is in most cases identical with the balance of military power. Resolve becomes a factor only in three other *specific* instances: first, the readiness of Israel to preempt when one of her *casus belli* is violated; second, in her readiness to escalate the level of violence, for example, from a war of attrition initiated by the Arabs to an offensive mode; and finally, in certain cases when Israel became tacitly or explicitly committed to the defense of another state or community in the Middle East. In the period prior to 1967, the first two situations, preemption and escalation, were of particular importance.

It is interesting to note that Israeli thinking about deterrence has always tended to disregard the distinction between the differential applicability of demonstrations of resolve to successful deterrence in various situations. Demonstrations of resolve were seen as crucial in regard to all categories of deterrence—general war against Israel, as well as the three abovementioned cases—preemption, intended escalation, and commitment to a third party. In summary then, Israel perceived an intense need to demonstrate her resolve in order to achieve a successful deterrence posture against a regular Arab attack, though very probably objectively there was no need for such a demonstration.

One can infer from Egyptian behavior that generally speaking, during the period 1957–1967, Egypt viewed Israeli readiness to escalate hostilities as quite high. This was the source of Egyptian concern over Syrian plans for diversion of the Jordan River. Cairo was also worried about the escalatory outcome of small-scale Egyptian-based guerrilla operations against

Israel, and indeed Egypt put a stop to such infiltrations. Finally, she viewed seriously the dangers involved in a violation of the two Israeli *casus belli* that were related to her own behavior, that is, the massing of Egyptian forces in the eastern part of Sinai and the closure of the Straits of Tiran. Egypt clearly understood the major risk Israel would face were Egyptian forces to enter the Sinai and be deployed in mass along the Israeli border, and as a result refrained from deploying sizeable forces in the Sinai. Indeed, Sinai was to a large extent *de facto* demilitarized during 1957–1967. Egypt was also aware of the Israeli strategic doctrine calling for a preemptive strike in the case of a violation of that particular *casus belli*. In short, Israeli specific and general deterrence against Egypt was successful during this period, because of the way in which the three balances were perceived by Egypt.

Deterrence of a general Syrian attack was also successful. Syria was dissuaded by the balances of military power and political interests from the initiation of a major war against Israel. However, the balance of political interests affected her in another and somewhat contradictory direction: her ambitions to attain a more important and influential position in the Arab world, and to that end to embarrass Egypt, led her to adopt more forward and aggressive strategies vis-à-vis Israel, but with "catalytic" intentions. Syria searched for a situation which would involve Israel and Egypt in a direct confrontation.[28] She promoted small scale operations against Israel, and became involved in plans to divert the Jordan River. While Syria was genuinely (but mistakenly) concerned about the Jordan Water Project as a major Israeli aggressive action, she belittled Israeli readiness to escalate in response to low level Syrian provocations. Syrian behavior led to a process of escalation which ultimately involved Egypt as well.

It should be noted that Israel also contributed to the escalation along the Syrian border during that period. Israel was prepared to rapidly escalate limited clashes, and also to respond violently to Syrian attempts to divert the sources of the Jordan River. Israel also assumed that tough and escalatory reactions to Syrian activities would deter Egypt from joining Syria in a forward strategy against Israel.

However, when escalation along the Israeli–Syrian border reached threatening dimensions, Egypt was faced by a difficult dilemma: to refuse assistance to Syria and thus completely lose her claim to Arab leadership, or to assist Syria and thus face the possibility of confrontation with Israel. To resolve this dilemma, Egypt turned to the mechanism of defense treaty. The Egyptian–Syrian defense treaty of November 1966 was intended by Egypt to deter Israel, on the one hand, and to control the Syrian leadership (which in Egyptian eyes was irresponsible) on the other. The treaty failed in both respects. Syria was uncontrollable and Israel was not deterred.

The Egyptian decision to send forces into Sinai in May 1967, was primarily intended to deter Israel from initiating an attack on Syria. Whether or not Israel planned such an attack is not important in this context. What is important were the Egyptian leaders' perceptions at the time, and they clearly believed that an Israeli attack on Syria was probable.[29] In addition, Nasser probably believed that this move might better the Egyptian position in the Arab world, which had suffered due to the Yemen War and inter-Arab competition.

Thus, the Egyptian move, itself constituted an act of deterrence, and as such did not point to the failure of Israeli *general* deterrence. It did demonstrate a partial failure in regard to *specific* deterrence, viz. a violation of one *casus belli* concerning the massing of Egyptian troops in the Sinai desert.

The process of the 1967 crisis suggests that, beyond calculations relevant to the balance of interests, military power and resolve, stable deterrence can be maintained provided both sides are aware of the nature of their opponent's general *and* specific deterrence postures, and that both sides are careful not to adopt additional deterrence measures which might violate an opponent's tolerance thresholds concerning which she has already issued deterrence threats. The Israeli escalatory moves along the Syrian border, although partially justified by Syrian actions, nevertheless forced Egypt to adopt deterrence moves which violated essential Israeli tolerance thresholds. The general threat to stability resulting from conflicting deterrence postures, becomes even more ominous when the behavior of the two sides depends to a large extent on a third uncontrollable party.

Once the crisis began to escalate, the dynamics of deterrence were substituted by the dynamics of crisis. Egypt went beyond her initial deterrence action and sought to accomplish political objectives. In the first place, the status quo created after the war of 1956 allowing the presence of United Nations observers in Sinai collapsed, and Egypt insisted on the cancellation of this arrangement; there were allusions to the possible renewed closure of the Straits to Israeli shipping, and finally, demands were also mentioned concerning territorial changes, primarily in regard to Eilat and its immediate vicinity. The Egyptian side moved from a purely deterrence posture at the beginning of the crisis, to a deterrence-cum-compellence posture at a later point. In addition to the violation of the two *casus belli*—massing of troops and the threatened closure of the Straits of Tiran—Israel could have expected further Egyptian demands. This change in the nature of the crisis completely destabilized the strategic relationship between Israel and Egypt.

It might be speculated that even without the change in the Egyptian posture, Israel would have had to preempt because of the threat posed by the massing of Egyptian forces near the international border, and possibly in order to maintain the credibility of her deterrence in regard to specific threats. The change in Egyptian behavior nevertheless added to Israel's feeling of urgency in the crisis.

To summarize, the Egyptians were at first intent on deterrence, but then utilized the crisis for the achievement of political gains. In both these strategies, the underlying approach was *not* to initiate the actual use of force. It might be argued that had Israel not preempted, three possible scenarios might have eventuated: first, Israeli political concessions followed by the diffusion of the crisis and Egyptian withdrawal of forces; less probable was the continuation of the Egyptian deployment with no political achievements; the least likely scenario was an Egyptian attack on Israel. It is interesting to note that the Egyptian leadership refrained from referring to the latter alternative in diplomatic exchanges with the big powers. It is more plausible that Egypt would have been content with limited political successes and the defusion of the crisis. All this only underlines the basic point concerning the continued affectivity of the Israeli *general* deterrence posture even during the crisis itself. To state it succinctly: the two countries differed in their approach to the crisis and in their preferred strategic choices. Because of the primacy of strategic considerations, Israel decided to preempt, while Egypt would probably have preferred the management of the crisis (with some political achievement) without resort to military force.

The Israeli strategic doctrine during the 1960s until 1967 was remarkably coherent and internally logical. As such, it created an effective context for successful *general deterrence.* Were it not for a process of escalation with Syria (to which Israel contributed considerably) coupled with intensified competition in the Arab world, Egypt would not have initiated the crisis during which Israeli *specific deterrence* failed. This leads to another observation regarding Israeli deterrence: The system of *casus belli* and its attendant system of *specific* deterrence could have been more effective. But greater efficacy would have required a greater awareness by Israel of the politico-strategic context in which Egypt and Syria were operating. Consequently, Israel failed to consider Egyptian tolerance thresholds. Escalating border violence with Syria clearly violated these thresholds. Maintaining strategic stability with Egypt should have dictated more constrained military activity against Syria.

The period 1967–1973—Israeli perceptions of deterrence

The overwhelming Israeli victory of 1967 should have bolstered the Israeli deterrence posture in several profound ways. To begin with, the balance of military power was found to be in Israel's favor to a previously unimagined extent. Moreover, this Israeli superiority was perceived as such by the Arab world. In the second place, American political and military backing for Israel during and following the war, seemed to promise that the arms race ensuing after the war would not undermine the demonstrated Israeli military superiority. Finally, the new cease-fire borders appeared, at first glance, to further increase the said military gap. (That the new borders did *not* supply additional security was amply demonstrated during the 1973 War.) In summary then, the objective and mutually perceived balance of military power, should have enhanced the Israeli deterrence posture.[30] That deterrence ultimately failed was not related to the military balance.

It is interesting to note, however, that at first Israeli leaders did not necessarily recognize that deterrence could be maintained as an essential posture. Quite the contrary, there was a feeling that the 1967 War had demonstrated the failure of Israeli deterrence. This perception resulted from the assumption that Israel had no share of the responsibility for the escalation leading to the 1967 crisis. The 1967 crisis was seen as the failure of deterrence generally, and that failure resulted from the inevitable animosity of the Arab world toward Israel. To be sure, the role of Israel in the process leading to the crisis was at times acknowledged, but played only a limited role in the general perceptions of the leadership.

If deterrence had failed, so the argument went, then there were two ways that Israel should react to Arab threats: on the one hand, there should be less reliance on deterrence as a central organizing principle for the Israeli politico-strategic approach, while on the other hand, if at all—deterrence should be enhanced through continued strengthening of the Israeli military capability and maintenance of the new cease-fire borders.

To the extent that deterrence continued to play a role in Israeli strategic thinking, it was perceived by Israel to be a simple function of the balance of military power. The period saw Israel participating in an arms race with her Arab opponents. Israel increased her order of battle so as to maintain, and in some cases to better the ratios existing in 1967. More importantly, Israeli political and military decision-makers assumed that the new borders added considerably to Israeli deterrence.

In terms of the balance of political interests, a traditional major Israeli misperception persisted. Israel maintained that Arab animosity toward Israel was a constant, and primarily derived from the basic Arab refusal to legitimize Israel. This basic animosity, it was understood, leads to periodic eruptions for which the main, if not exclusive, responsibility lies with the Arabs. Little attention was paid to the fact that the consequences of the 1967 War, that is, the continued Israeli occupation of Egyptian and Syrian territories, transformed the nature of the conflict. The element of grievance, or as it were, the vitality of Egyptian and Syrian interests involved in the liberation of the Sinai and the Golan Heights far exceeded their traditional commitment to the Palestinian cause. From a general posture of hostility toward Israel, related to notions of general Arab nationalism, there had been a switch to respectively particularist Egyptian, Syrian, and Jordanian vital national interests. These particularist interests were much more important and central for Egypt, Syria and Jordan respectively, than the traditional Arab reasons for hostility against Israel. Hence, the balance of interests swung in a way that undermined Israeli deterrence. The Egyptian and Syrian motivation to launch a military strike in order to redress their grievance increased manifold following 1967. In order to balance this critical change in the balance of interests, the balance of military power had to become sufficiently favorable for Israel, that it would render the results of any potential Arab strike so painful to the Arab side as to make it totally unacceptable. It is doubtful whether such a superiority could have been achieved at all. Moreover, as shall be discussed in Chapter 4, war was seen by Egypt as a political instrument, and its military outcome less important than its political consequences.

The system of casus belli

An interesting change had taken place in regard to specific deterrence. The relevance of most, if not all of the Israeli *casus belli* disappeared. The massing of Egyptian forces along the international border in the Sinai became an impossibility as Israel herself occupied all of the Sinai. Israel controlled the Straits of Tiran, and hence its closure also became an impossibility. Once the Golan Heights came under Israeli occupation, the issue of the diversion of the Jordan River also lost its salience. Most interestingly, once Israel occupied the West Bank, she could hardly threaten to attack Jordan if foreign Arab troops were to be deployed there. After all, Israel believed and maintained that her border on the Jordan River gave her optimal security. If that was the case, then no serious threat could emanate from a concentration of Arab forces in Jordan. Furthermore, the Israeli deterrence threat against Jordan before 1967, had been Israeli occupation of the West Bank. After 1967, this ceased to be an effective threat as Israel already occupied that area. Indeed, for several years after 1967, Iraqi troops were deployed in Jordan and Israel did not consider it a *casus belli*. The disappearance of specific deterrence based on a system of *casus belli* adversely affected Israeli strategic thinking and posture. The false trust in "secure" and "deterring" borders diverted Israeli thinking from the important security threats which Israel faced, and was critical in the failures in the first days of the 1973 War.

The new borders were detrimental in yet another way concerning levels of Israeli deterrence: they created ample opportunities for limited military confrontations. Israeli forces along the Suez Canal faced the Egyptian forces directly. Such direct contact favored the Egyptian side as indeed was manifest in the "War of Attrition" 1969–1970. Ostensibly Israel could have deterred limited military operations or variants of attrition wars only by threatening punishment to the Egyptian civilian population or by crossing the Canal and attacking deep into Egypt. The first act would have brought Israel into direct confrontation with the Soviet Union, as was the case in 1970 following the "deep penetration" bombing. As a result the USSR extended its deterrence umbrella over Egypt. The second act would have led to very costly operations. As such Israel had lost her capability to deter these acts of hostility, or her ability to create a system of specific deterrence.

The 1973 War

The outbreak of the 1973 War demonstrated that the change in the balance of interests far outweighed the changes in the balance of military power. (For a more detailed account of the war, see below in this chapter.) In 1973, the Egyptians were convinced that Israel was far superior to them militarily, and they recognized that crossing the Canal would involve tremendous costs, but they were "forced" to attack because of political motivation, what Lebow and Stein have termed "need."[31] The failure of the Israeli general deterrence posture was related therefore, almost exclusively to the changes in the balance of interests. The main question which President Sadat faced was not the cost/benefit balance of a military attack, but rather the cost/benefit outcome of *not* attacking.[32] The continuation of the status quo became too much to bear, and it appeared that with each passing year, the costs became higher and more intolerable. A change in the political status quo became so urgent that the perceived negative balance of power could not balance the political costs involved in inaction.[33]

The logic of the military component in the deterrence equation declined in relation to the logic of political interest. This does not mean that the logic of military relations and punishment completely disappeared. The Israeli deterrence effect was sufficient to impress on Egypt and Syria the need for a specific strategy with only limited military objectives. They both opted for a limited war in concert with the objectives to be gained. The Egyptian plan had two stages: first, crossing the canal and securing a narrow strip along the eastern bank; second, and this stage was to be executed only after the first stage was completed and the anticipated Israeli counter attack defeated, a push toward the Sinai Passes, and in northern Sinai, a movement eastward up to Romani. The plan did not envisage even conquering the whole of Sinai, let alone areas in Israel itself.

Thus, the partial failure of deterrence resulted from the Israeli failure to understand the complex relationship between the balance of military power and the balance of interests. The failure had nothing to do with the balance of resolve. Deterrence failed not because the Israelis were perceived as lacking in determination or readiness to defend Sinai even though this was not declared specifically. On the contrary, Israel was seen as aggressive and threatening. Nor was deterrence failure, as discussed above, due to any dent in the credibility of overall Israeli military superiority.

Janice Stein[34] has pointed out that the Egyptian leadership miscalculated Israeli determination to cross the Canal in a counter attack—one variant of deterrence by punishment, and this affected the overall credibility of the Israeli deterrence posture. Although the Egyptians seem to have miscalculated Israeli resolve on that account, such was the pressure of their political grievance that even had they anticipated such an Israeli action, it seems that they would have in any case launched the operation to cross the Canal. Moreover, Egyptian confidence in her ability in defensive operations was quite high. Consequently, they may have estimated that they would be able to withstand an Israeli attempt to re-cross the Canal. Finally, the Egyptians might also have assumed that the Soviet Union could be relied upon to deter or halt such an escalatory Israeli move.

To sum up, it is true that Israel did not formulate a *specific* deterrence threat against the potential Egyptian move, and instead relied on her general deterrence posture.[35] It is, however, almost certain that by 1973 even the formulation of a specific deterrence threat would not have altered Egyptian plans.

Another Israeli misunderstanding concerned the perception of the post-1967 cease-fire borders as "deterring." In theory these new borders may have added to general deterrence against a military attempt to conquer the whole of Israel, in that they isolated vital areas of Israel from the direct threat of ground forces. However, that particular contingency ceased in any case to appear realistic in Arab perceptions following the 1967 War. On the other hand, the new borders supplied Egypt with easier military conditions for surprise attacks, as in 1973, and for the implementation of limited military campaigns, as in 1969–1970. In these senses Israeli failures in the first days of the 1973 War were not at all accidental, but were built into the Israeli military posture, resulting from Israeli occupation of the Sinai.

Two additional variables contributed to the failure of the Israeli deterrence, one in the political sphere, one in the military one. In the political sphere, the flourishing détente between the United States and the USSR, and the Russian unreadiness to demand the withdrawal of Israeli forces from the occupied territories as part of detente, affected Arab cost/benefit calculations in regard to future political developments.

International diplomacy did not seem to promise a change in the status quo. Similarly, the American caution, and even foot-dragging in reaction to the Egyptian feelers during 1972–1973 toward Washington, led to the same conclusion. The second variable was in the military area, where the assumed increased power of defensive systems, that is anti-tank and anti-air weapons, bolstered Egyptian confidence in regard to their ability to implement the first stage of their plan for crossing the Canal and withstanding the Israeli counteroffensive.

The Israeli deterrence posture 1974–1981

The partial failure of the Israeli deterrence posture in 1973, led to the decline of deterrence as an organizing principle in Israeli strategic thinking. It had been assumed, and it will be argued in the following that this was a wrong assumption, that the Arabs had concluded that they could strike again at Israel. As Rabin observed: "Because the Arabs no longer fear a military defeat, it seems to me that it is necessary for us to change our military doctrine so as to build the IDF with the aim of decisively subduing the enemy, rather than deterring him."[36]

In fact, however, the lessons that the Arab states gleaned from the war appeared to be different. They most probably realized that the balance of military power was still tipped heavily in favor of Israel. The war ended with a diplomatic victory for the Arabs, but with a military defeat that could not be denied. Thus, even a limited war seemed to be a very difficult proposition for them. Certainly there seemed to be no chance of destroying Israel in an unlimited war. There might be possibilities of securing political goals through limited campaigns, but even these seemed to be risky and uncertain. However, the pressure to mount such limited campaigns remained extremely high so long as the political grievances felt by the particular Arab states remained. The Egyptian grievance over Sinai could be redressed if Israel made the necessary political concessions. Tacitly this became the shared strategy of both Egypt and Israel. Through a long and protracted process beginning with the first disengagement agreement in 1974, through the second Sinai agreement of 1975, the contacts between the Rabin government and Egypt, the meetings between Dayan and Tohamy in Morocco under the first Begin government, and culminating with Sadat's visit to Jerusalem and the Peace Treaty between Israel and Egypt, the two countries changed the balance of political interests in such a way as to unwittingly recover the primacy of the military balance in the deterrence equation. Once Egyptian political grievances had diminished, the Israeli deterrence posture was considerably enhanced. Moreover, once Egypt abandoned her war intentions, and Israel was able to concentrate her forces against other threats, the balance of military power between her and the other Arab states, primarily Syria,

54

became even more positive. Israel's deterrence posture in regard to these states had also been enhanced.

In regard to the military balance *per se*, the arms race which raged in the Middle East following the 1973 War, initially favored Israel. Under the Rabin government specially, and while Gur served as the Chief of Staff, the IDF underwent a major process of quantitative growth. This was the result of the convergence of Israeli sensitivities and concerns resulting from the 1973 War, and American generosity in supplying large quantities of high-quality arms to Israel. By the end of the decade, the order of battle of Israel and the quality of its arms, increased at a higher rate than that of the Arab confrontation states. From the early 1980s onwards, this trend began to change somewhat. However, the balance of power still favored Israel, and certainly with respect to an Arab war coalition in which Egypt did not take a part.

While Israeli general deterrence was enhanced in this period, it is significant that from 1973 and up to 1981, Israel refrained from adding a system of specific deterrence to her general deterrence posture. The system of *casus belli*, so central before 1967, and which became blurred during the period 1967–1973, was not reintroduced.[37] The only exception was the system of "red lines" applied to the Syrian intervention in Lebanon.[38]

The Israeli–Egyptian relationship changed with the signing of the Peace Treaty in 1979. The new situation recreated the necessity to formulate a *casus belli* that related to Egyptian violation of the Sinai demilitarization. In a sense, this problem was partly dealt with in the military Annex to the Peace Treaty. However, it was not fully articulated as a *casus belli* in Israeli strategic thinking. This was probably a result of Israeli concern about Egyptian political sensitivity to Israeli declarations of intentions of war, in case of violations of the new treaty. It also appeared to run counter to the desire to build a new system of political relations with Egypt. In initially refraining from articulating this *casus belli*, Israel probably committed a mistake, although no harm has as yet come of it. The vitality of Israeli interests involved in the continued demilitarization of the Sinai is such, that it is certainly extremely important to define violations of the demilitarization as a *casus belli*.

One of the main concerns that has preoccupied Israeli strategic and military leaders since 1973, has been the threat of surprise attack. The Israeli–Egyptian Peace Treaty should have moderated that concern, but the Israeli strategic leadership remained obsessed with this threat. A reasonable and balanced system of *casus belli*, coupled with political concessions and moderation, could have ameliorated that concern. Although the relationship with Egypt was in fact moderated, the concern about surprise attacks continued to permeate Israeli thinking. During the 1970s, this concern was dealt with through the great emphasis placed on territorial defense. These policies reflected a basic misunderstanding of how a combination of political concessions affecting the balance of political interests, and the reintroduction of a system of *casus belli*, could considerably limit the threat of a surprise attack.

What about Syria?

As has already been noted in this chapter, the Israeli deterrence effect against a general war initiated by Syria remained high between 1949–1973. Syrian leaders have correctly estimated Israeli military superiority, and on this point all Syrian regimes have concurred. On another level, that of limited violence along the Syrian boarders, Syrian behavior until the early 1960s fell into well-defined patterns. Syrian decision-makers were ready to react toughly yet in a limited way, to what they perceived as Israeli provocations along the border. Some of them were also ready to cause provocations along the border. However, these were not intended simply to escalate the situation, but rather were caused by deeply conflicting interpretations concerning different clauses in the cease fire agreement between Israel and Syria. By the mid-1960s, Syrian behavior had changed. The "New Ba'th" regime began to extend support to the limited infiltration activities of the newly founded Fatah. This change came about either because of a more extreme ideological position, or because of the competition in the Arab world, in which Syria tried to back her opposition to Egyptian hegemonic tendencies by endorsing a belligerent posture against Israel. The Syrian activity had primarily a catalytic objective—to bring about an escalation between Israel and Egypt. Syria certainly had no desire to confront the Israeli army in open large-scale war. This was amply demonstrated in the first days of the 1967 War, when Syria avoided any significant military activity. Instead, she resigned herself to artillery bombardment of Israeli border settlements, together with one hesitant limited probe by a small military contingent which advanced toward one of the settlements.

While the loss of the Golan in 1967 created a deep political grievance for Syria, she refrained on the whole from a massive encounter with Israel, as long as she was militarily isolated. Syrian calculations changed only in 1973, when she became convinced that Egypt was ready to go to war. Even then, she planned only a limited operation designed to conquer the Golan or part of it in a surprise attack. She also counted on an immediate cease-fire which would save her from the expected Israeli counterattack.

Once Israel and Egypt began their dialogue in 1974, leading eventually to the peace treaty, Syria had to search for an alternative to her military alliance with Egypt. She adopted two strategies: a rapid increase of her order of battle, and a search for coalitions with other Arab states. Indeed,

Syria increased her forces by about a third between 1973 and 1982. She also modernized them (for details see Chapter 7). However, while the reconquering of the Golan Heights remains a very high Syrian priority, she has refrained from initiating any military operation, including limited ones, in order to implement that objective. This demonstrates that Syria perceives the military balance as unfavorable. The increase in her military capabilities (which continued at an accelerated pace following 1982—see Chapter 7) may have bolstered Syrian perception that she possesses a credible deterrence against an unprovoked Israeli attack, but clearly has not convinced her that she has a credible offensive capability.

The second strategy—a search for an alternate military alliance—failed completely. Following a limited and hesitant rapprochement with Iraq in the mid-1970s, relations between the two worsened again, deteriorated to a new low in the second half of the 1970s, and have not recovered since. Similarly, Syrian–Jordanian relations improved for several years, and then began deteriorating to the point where Syria resorted to military threats to preempt a Jordanian diplomatic move in 1980. Relations with Algeria and Libya were warm, but these countries could not be counted upon in a military round against Israel. In order to strengthen her deterrence posture against Israel, Damascus turned to the USSR and in 1980 signed with her a treaty for friendship and cooperation. For purposes of deterrence against a massive Israeli thrust into Syria, this was a credible instrument. However, for the purpose of a military initiative designed to regain the Golan, this was no substitute to a coalition with a strong Arab state (or states). Thus, Syria has had to postpone any such move.

When assessing Syrian motivation to regain the Golan Heights, account must also be taken of another important factor. Since the mid-1970s, deepening Syrian involvement in Lebanon has absorbed considerable quantities of military and political resources. It also required much decision-making energy. There was a consequent decline in the volume of such resources that could be directed toward the Golan. In addition, while Syria had to sustain considerable costs due to her involvement in Lebanon, she also obtained some important benefits: Syrian de facto annexation of parts of the Beqa appears as partial compensation for the loss of the Golan (although the motivation to regain the Golan remains very high). Moreover, in the period prior to 1981, and again since its renewal in 1984, Israel and Syria have shared a series of partial understandings regarding their mutual behavior in Lebanon. The existence of these understandings may have contributed to a Syrian assessment that the two states may eventually be able to reach an understanding, through the mediation of the United States concerning the Golan Heights. This factor probably added to Syrian caution in regard to a military operation on the Golan.

It was within the context of relations with Syria in Lebanon that Israel has developed, since 1976, a complex system of specific deterrence.[39] Here I shall only mention the main features of this system:

1 Beginning in early 1976, Israel and Syria began exchanging signals, mainly through the good offices of the United States, concerning Syrian military intervention in Lebanon and the limits on such an intervention. Washington was very active in promoting understandings between the two states in regard to such military activity. In addition, Israel also sent other tacit deterrence signals.

2 By March–April of that year, the two states succeeded in working out a system of mutually agreed "red lines" delimiting the scope of the intended Syrian military intervention in Lebanon. Accordingly, Syrian forces penetrated Lebanon toward the end of May, attacking the PLO and Muslim-radical militias. The limits imposed on the intervention by the Israeli deterrence signals related to the geographical area in which the Syrian forces were "allowed" to operate, the size of forces to be involved and the nature of their weapon systems. In general, Syria adhered to these limitations. Of the latter, the most important were the limitations on the operation of the Syrian air force in Lebanese air space, and on the introduction and deployment of air to surface missiles.

3 The Israeli–Syrian understandings, and the consequent strategic stability obtaining between these two countries in Lebanon, depended on several factors: First, Israeli recognition of the vitality of Syrian political interests in Lebanon. Israel also recognized that her own political interests in Lebanon were less vital to her than the Syrian interests were to Syria. Second, Syria perceived the balance of military power as favoring Israel. Third, the two states realized that they had shared or coincidental interests in Lebanon—the defeat of the PLO and the Muslim-radical coalition. Finally, the deep involvement of the United States was heavily instrumental in the achievement of these understandings.

It should be stressed that the strategic stability in Lebanon between Israel and Syria in the period 1976–1981, and that has been restored since 1984–1985, is dependent on Syrian caution—Damascus has refrained from violating the Israeli thresholds—as well as on Israel's caution in exercising her military capability. During the second Begin government (1981–1983) Ariel Sharon's appointment as Defense Minister in 1981 led to several changes in Israel's defense policy, the most important of which was the invasion of Lebanon in 1982. But prior to the war in Lebanon, another important change occurred in official Israeli strategic thinking— this was Sharon's interesting attempt to reintroduce a system of *casus belli* into the Israeli strategic posture. According to Sharon, "Israel intends to prevent any deterioration in the geographic and military status quo in the neighboring countries." Specifically Sharon formulated seven contingencies which would require an Israeli response:[40]

1 Any violation of the clauses concerning the demilitarization of the Sinai in the 1979 Peace Treaty.
2 Any violation of the demilitarization of strips of the Golan, according to the 1974 disengagement agreement with Syria. (The first two contingencies were included by Sharon in the same clause as if they were essentially similar.)
3 A massive introduction of Iraqi forces into south Syria or into Jordan, or the introduction of Syrian forces into Jordan.
4 The deployment of a SAM system along the Jordan River.
5 Movement of Syrian forces south of the line along which they were stationed in Lebanon.
6 The presence of nuclear weapons in an enemy Arab country or the capacity to produce a nuclear device in an enemy Arab country.
7 A campaign of terrorism from south Lebanon.

Sharon maintained some ambiguity as to the nature of the Israeli reactions to the acts mentioned. However, it was clear that these would involve some use of military force, even if not a full-scale war.

An analysis of the seven contingencies demonstrates that they belong to different categories. The contingency concerning nuclear weapons differs qualitatively from the others which refer to conventional scenarios. Violations of the demilitarization of Sinai refers to a formal peace treaty, where the others do not. This *casus belli* and the ones detailed in (2) and (3) do, however, represent vital strategic interests. Those noted in (4), (5) and (7) also relate to strategic concerns, but of a lower vitality compared to the first three.

The 1982 War and its effects on Israeli deterrence

At the time, it may have seemed that Sharon's formulation of a system of *casus belli* was intended to strengthen the Israeli deterrence effect. But further analysis of Israel's strategic behavior during his tenure as Defense Minister points in an opposite direction. Within Sharon's formulation the only *casus belli* concerning Syrian military behavior in Lebanon referred to the movement of Syrian forces south of the line along which they were deployed. Such a contingency was not infringed prior to Israel's invasion of Lebanon in 1982. As such, the strike at the Syrian forces was unrelated to any Syrian violation of defined Israeli *casus belli*. It did not conform to the criteria which Israel herself, through Sharon, had formulated for war with Syria.

Thus, the war decision demonstrates either Sharon's lack of

understanding as to the nature of deterrence, or simply the absence of any serious intention to implement his own set of *casus belli*. Clearly, a formulation of *casus belli* has two objectives: to deter a potential challenger by threat of military action, and to signal an intention not to act militarily if the challenger does not infringe the set guidelines. Clearly, the war undermined the new attempt to introduce a system of *casus belli*.

Other aspects of Israeli deterrence were also adversely affected by the war. Sharon and the then Foreign Minister, Shamir, declared several times that Jordan would have to become the Palestinian state. These declarations caused alarm in Jordan. The Hashemite regime may have concluded (against the background of the Israeli invasion of Lebanon) that Israel was searching for an opportunity to topple the regime in Amman. Israel was increasingly seen as operating against the regional status quo. This had the effect, at the deepest level, of undercutting Israel's deterrence strategy.

The coming to power of the "national unity" government in Israel in 1984 may have reassured the Hashemite regime of Israel's intentions. As such, the Israeli deterrence posture vis-à-vis Jordan was again strengthened.

As detailed before the strategic stability created in Lebanon in 1976 on the basis of the quiet understandings between Israel and Syria, probably convinced Syria that Israel was not seeking an offensive operation against her. The Israeli caution was evident in the Litani operation in 1978, and on other occasions. But in 1982, Israel deliberately sought a direct military confrontation with Syria, and attacked the Syrian forces there.

This change in Israeli strategy probably convinced Damascus that Israel might try to attack Syria again, were the opportunity to arise. Moreover, the 1982 War painfully demonstrated to Damascus that she is totally isolated in the Arab world. Consequently, Syria decided to rapidly increase her armed forces, and to invite greater Soviet military presence on her soil, as a deterrent against Israel. The USSR obliged by sending a large Soviet contingent of military advisers and SAM technicians. The latter eventually withdrew from Syria.

The Israeli perception has always (with variations) emphasized the need to enhance the credibility of deterrence through continued manifestations of resolve. Resolve could be best demonstrated (according to a prevailing view) through tough military reactions to provocations. Whereas some political and military leaders recommended only limited operations as signals of resolve, Sharon apparently perceived recurrent wars launched by Israel as a valuable instrument in demonstrating resolve. In that sense, he probably saw the 1982 War as enhancing Israel's deterrence. Needless to say, this approach runs basically counter to deterrence in the deepest sense. In the first place, the main aim of deterrence is to avoid war and not to cause it. In the second place, as mentioned before, deterrence is basically a strategy of the status quo. Recurrent wars destabilize strategic relations, and also stimulate the other side to launch wars in a preventive or preemptive mode. Finally, as mentioned before, there is no need to continuously demonstrate the Israeli resolve in order to enhance general deterrence.

In addition to these general considerations, the very course of the war in Lebanon may have affected Syrian perceptions of Israeli military capabilities. On the one hand, the tremendous superiority of the Israeli air force was again demonstrated. On the other hand, the Syrians were probably somewhat encouraged by the course of the ground battles.

However, beyond all these complex considerations, it appears that Damascus still perceived the balance of military power with Israel as tilted strongly against her. This is indeed the only conclusion that they could reach on an objective analysis of the balance of conventional forces. The Assad regime is highly rational and most probably recognizes the wide discrepancy in military capabilities, which would obtain even were other Arab countries to join forces with Syria in a war coalition against Israel. But the formation of a coalition seemed a remote possibility, and the position of the superpowers far from encourages Syrian military adventurism. In the second part of this chapter we shall assess the effects of the nuclear factor on the dynamics of the Israeli–Arab conflict. We shall return there to a discussion of its possible past effect on the deterrence equation between Israel and Syria.

To sum up, it seems that the Israeli general conventional deterrence has been highly successful for long periods of time. It failed only in 1969–1970 and again in 1973. These failures resulted from critical changes in the levels of Egyptian and Syrian motivation, caused by a raised intensity of political grievance (even then, the failure was only partial, since the attackers opted for limited campaign only). This historical experience demonstrates that had Israel been conscious of the delicate interactions between the balance of military power and the balance of political interests, she might have saved herself these two wars. Moreover, such Israeli understandings of the nuances of deterrence, coupled with a moderate political approach, could further enhance Israel's conventional deterrence. One of the important instruments for this would be the formulation of a system of *casus belli*, defined in a rational and sophisticated way, and which would be designed to protect only vital security interests.

PAST EFFECTS OF THE NUCLEAR FACTOR ON THE DYNAMICS OF THE ARAB–ISRAELI CONFLICT

In the first chapter we noted that Israel's strategy of nuclear ambiguity emerged gradually, rather than as the result of a deliberate conscious decision. But once it emerged, Israeli decision-makers were able to grasp the utility of such a posture.

The literature on nuclear proliferation has primarily focused on three major topics: the possible implications of future worldwide proliferation for world and regional stability,[41] nuclear developments in various countries; and the efforts to curb proliferation and the emergence of the non-proliferation regime. With the occasional exception, the literature has not focused on how or to what extent actual proliferation, or the emergence of threshold countries, has already affected various regional conflicts. In this chapter we shall consider the role that the nuclear dimension has played in the dynamics of the Arab–Israel conflict.

On the one hand, we shall discuss to what extent the nuclear factor has deterred war or limited it, while on the other hand, whether it has led to peace. These are two of the most important assumed uses of Israel's nuclear posture. In Chapter 7, we shall return to this issue in a discussion of the current "uses" of the Israeli threshold posture.

The ambiguous posture: did it deter conventional attacks? An historical analysis

In this chapter we discussed the evolvement of Israel's conventional deterrence posture. Here we shall discuss the historical role, if any, of the nuclear issue in Israel's overall deterrence. Has it deterred Arab war initiatives or limited them? Ironically, it should be remembered that some Egyptian observers argued in the mid-1960s, that an Israeli nuclear development would lead to an Egyptian preemptive strike. This stands in stark contrast to the presumed objective of Israel's policy of ambiguity, viz. precisely to deter Arab attacks. Indeed, it has even been claimed that the nuclear factor played a critical role in the 1967 crisis. According to this argument, Egypt initiated the crisis in order to strike militarily at the Dimona reactor, thus preempting Israeli attempts to go nuclear.[42]

The 1967 War

A close examination of the historical events will indicate that the nuclear issue was simply irrelevant to the 1967 crisis and the later outbreak of war. As described in this chapter, the crisis arose due to the convergence of two processes: fierce inter-Arab competition, and the escalation along the Israeli–Syrian border. Within the first process there were several conflicts between "conservative" and "radical" states, and also between the radical states themselves, specifically among Egypt, Syria and Iraq. As a result, Egypt's position in the Arab world declined sharply towards 1967. Egypt was also caught up in the difficult dilemmas caused by her defense treaty with Syria signed in November 1966. As noted earlier, Egypt intended that the treaty would control Syrian military activity and deter Israel. However, the treaty failed in both respects: Syria was not constrained and Israel was not deterred.

Another factor in the outbreak of the crisis was the escalating violence on the Israeli–Syrian border, and Soviet (and Egyptian) concern that Israel was about to attack Syria. An additional explanation has been that Nasser sought to reassert his claim for leadership in the Arab world. He suffered from declining influence in the face of Syrian, Iraqi, Jordanian and Saudi opposition, and from continued Egyptian involvement in the civil war in Yemen.[43] These contexts are sufficient to provide a full explanation of the crisis. Concern about possible Israeli nuclear developments was not a factor. By the same token, Egyptian moves were not constrained by possible suspicions about presumed Israeli nuclear capability. All this seemed to be completely lacking in Egyptian calculations.

The Road to the 1973 War

It has also been argued that Egypt and Syria limited their objectives in the 1973 War because of the Israeli nuclear posture.[44] However, this argument can also be dismissed.

In the first part of this chapter we discussed the three sets of considerations affecting cost/gain calculations in the calculus of deterrence: the military balance, the balance of interests, and the balance of resolve. We pointed out that the first two were the most relevant to a dyadic conflict, when the challenger intends to attack the deterrer directly.

While the 1967 Israeli victory considerably enhanced Egyptian perceptions of Israeli military superiority, the balance of interests changed in a radical way. Prior to 1967, Egyptian animosity towards Israel resulted partly from identification with the Palestinians, and partly from Egyptian Pan-Arab ambitions. In addition, the dynamics of the conflict itself also became an independent factor. Egyptian frustration at two defeats, in 1948 and 1956; encroachment on Egyptian sovereignty following the deployment of UN observers subsequent to the 1956 War; and mutual anxieties resulting from the arms race and suspicions about the intentions of the opponent. But following 1967, the loss of Sinai and the continued presence of Israeli troops in the Sinai and along the Suez Canal, became the overriding factor. This development shocked Egypt to its core. The political grievance was such that its redress became the most important national objective. The conflict became a "traditional" national one, about national territory and prestige. The same applied to Syrian grievance over the loss of the Golan. These are well known causes for interstate conflict, yet they are more amenable to rational solutions than when the conflict is ideological.

Egypt chose a dual track strategy—diplomatic and military. Diplomatic efforts to bring about a superpower resolution of the ongoing crisis through a framework acceptable to the Arabs were undertaken by the Soviet Union with the full endorsement of Egypt. Simultaneously, a decision was made to initiate a limited military campaign designed to hurt Israel and make her presence along the Canal difficult and costly. Thus the War of Attrition was launched, in September–October 1968. A tough Israeli reaction led to its postponement, until it was renewed in March 1969.[45]

The War of Attrition of 1969–1970 was a limited war, which aimed to change the political status quo. The politico-strategic objectives of the war were limited and sophisticated. There was no plan to reconquer the Sinai, let alone to destroy Israel. One aim was to impress upon the United States the dangers involved in the continuation of the status quo. It was hoped that the United States then would force Israel to change her political position. Militarily, the objective was to harass Israel and to undermine Israeli security doctrine. That latter objective was repeatedly mentioned in Egyptian definitions of the war's objectives.[46] We shall return to this point when analyzing Egypt's objectives in the 1973 War.

The War of Attrition was tailored to Egypt's conventional capabilities and designed to utilize those features of the strategic-military situation in which the Egyptians had an advantage over Israel. It should be stressed that these plans took into consideration only the sides' conventional capabilities, and can be explained fully and exclusively in those terms. Egypt recognized Israel's superiority in mobile and armored battles, and was fully aware of Israeli air superiority. On the other hand, the Egyptians could count on a tremendous advantage in terms of stationary firepower concentrated along the Canal. They were able to deploy all their standing army along the Canal, whereas Israel—dependent on a reserve army—was able to deploy on a tiny force there. Israel's capability in the Sinai consisted of little more than one armored division. But that division was, by its very nature, unsuitable for stationary deployment along the Canal.

The War of Attrition ended without any clear military advantage to either side. However, the calm that subsequently obtained along the ceasefire line served the Israeli purpose of maintaining the status quo. Egypt had to try and change that.

The death of President Nasser in autumn 1970 and the election of President Sadat created a new context for flexibility. Sadat was not bound, as was Nasser, by a particular political position in the Arab world. This freed him to initiate new ventures. Thus, the diplomatic effort was pursued with greater vigor than before. Indeed, a major formal concession was incorporated into Sadat's response to the UN appointed mediator Ambassador Gunar Jarring's letter of February 1971. In his response to Jarring, Sadat, for the first time in the history of the Israeli–Egyptian conflict, stated publicly that Egypt was ready to sign a peace agreement with Israel, provided that several conditions were met. Moreover, Sadat involved himself in a dialogue with the United States—and indirectly with Israel—concerning the possibility of an intermediate agreement for a partial Israeli withdrawal from the Canal (an initiative that in fact originated with one of Israel's decision-makers—Moshe Dayan). In brief then, it was clear that Sadat appeared ready and even eager to undertake further steps towards a diplomatic resolution of the impasse between Israel and Egypt. His moves in 1971 were unsuccessful, however, due to the gap between his demands and the conditions that Israel was ready to offer. Nevertheless, it should have been clear to any objective observer that Sadat had presented the most flexible Egyptian position to date. Indeed, in retrospect, and in the light of Sadat's peace initiative of the latter half of the 1970s, his feelers in the period 1971–1973 appear to outline a definite policy of placing Egyptian interests before those of the Arab front. Moreover, his interpretation of Egyptian interests appeared to require a lowered profile of the conflict with Israel and possibly even its resolution. The foundations for Sadat's visit to Jerusalem had already been laid in 1971.

The change in policy direction towards Israel was correlated with Sadat's desire to create ties with the United States. His expulsion of the Russian military presence from Egypt in 1972, and the activity of his national security adviser Hafez Ismail in the United States in 1972 and 1973, both underlined that readiness for change of policy, both toward Israel and the United States.[47] Kissinger, who was in fact already in charge of U.S. Middle East policy before 1973, and with whom Sadat sought to form the new policy before the war, completely misunderstood that tentative new opening in Egyptian policy. He realized it only during the 1973 War itself.[48]

Sadat's flexible position in 1971 demonstrated his assessment of the heavy costs involved for Egypt in the continuation of the conflict. It also showed that he realized the liberation of the Sinai could not be secured through the use of military force, and that diplomacy was the only feasible means. This was a result of the Israeli deterrence posture based on Egyptian perceptions of the balance of conventional military power.[49] In summary then, Sadat's policy in 1971–1973 was the basis on which his later policy was established. Indeed, a direct and logical line leads from 1971 to the Sinai I agreement in 1974, through to the 1975 Sinai II agreement, and finally culminating in Sadat's visit to Jerusalem in 1977.

However, the diplomatic initiative of 1971–1973 failed and Egypt gradually realized that the use of force was required in order to facilitate a diplomatic resolution of the Sinai issue. Military power could not secure the liberation of the Sinai; it was needed, however, to set diplomacy in motion. Such an attempt had been made during the War of Attrition, but had failed. Indeed, the politico-strategic objectives of the second attempt, the 1973 War, were precisely the same as those of the War of Attrition: a change in the political status quo, and the shattering of the Israeli strategic doctrine.[50]

Of course there were differences as well: at the political level Egypt was ready in 1973 for a new international orientation. During the War of Attrition, Nasser was still intent on continuing his close relationship with the Soviet Union. In 1973 Sadat was clearly trying to transform his posture, and to turn to the United States, provided the latter would accept certain Egyptian conditions. Second, and most importantly, Nasser would probably have maintained an "Arab" orientation, which would have made it difficult for him to reach a resolution of the conflict with Israel. He probably aimed at a system of "no war" rather than formal peace. Sadat was apparently more ready to adopt novel approaches to end the conflict.

When the Egyptian decision-makers planned their war, they were cognizant of Israel's military superiority, and of the high risks they were taking, based on their experiences of 1967. But they came to the conclusion that even a military failure would contribute to a change in the international political climate, and that in any case the war would be only one phase in the Egyptian people's long campaign. "It is essential that this frozen situation [no peace and no war] from which we suffered will be broken and if we shall fail in war, there will come another stage and the people will continue in the campaign. Whatever the results [the military results of the war], we shall have the benefit."[51]

It should be noted that the writings of the Egyptian leaders contain no references to an Israeli nuclear option or actual capability.[52] As was pointed out in Chapter 1, some Egyptian leaders and observers did refer to the nuclear issue after 1973, but most of them emphasized the elements of uncertainty and ambiguity. This was Sadat's approach as well. Even when Sadat said (after 1973) that he did believe that Israel possessed a nuclear capability,[53] he referred to the post-1973 situation and not to the Egyptian planning leading to that war. But the best way to judge whether the nuclear issue played any role in the Egyptian war preparations, is to analyze the war plan itself and its execution.

The objectives of the war were—as in the War of Attrition—limited and primarily political. Even securing the very limited military objectives was uncertain. Two variants of war were considered: a general repeat of the War of Attrition, roughly similar to the one conducted in 1969–1970; and the one which was actually executed in 1973. In discussions of the two possibilities, President Sadat ultimately supported the second model. In explaining that choice, the Egyptian leadership argued that it expected that the Israeli reaction to both modes of war would be a major military effort involving all of Israel's military capabilities. If that was the expectation, then Egypt should also bring to bear, from the very start of the war, all her military capabilities. Hence the decision to apply the second mode of operation.[54] Ahmed Ismail Ali also argued: "We have to think about a bigger effort, which would be similar in scope at least to the [predicted] enemy's reaction".[55]

Here it is clear that the Egyptian leadership referred to all the military capabilities which, she assumed, were at Israel's disposal. But an analysis of those perceived (by Egypt) capabilities again demonstrates that they were only conventional. Indeed, Ismail Ali referred to "similar Egyptian capabilities," which surely did not include nuclear capabilities.

When the Egyptian leaders did refer to a possible failure in the planned campaign, it was again clear that they referred to a military failure by conventional means. After all, if the failure resulted from the use of nuclear weapons, then the whole situation in the Middle East would be totally transformed. The appearance of nuclear weapons in the strategic theater of the Middle East would be of such profound consequence that any political elite that considered such a possibility, even if they were unaware of the subtleties and complexities of nuclear weaponry, would have at least made some reference to it in war planning. It is significant therefore that the Egyptian perception of a possible defeat did not include even an indirect hint of the consequences of a nuclear strike or a nuclear threat by Israel.

An additional objective of the war was to undermine the Israeli security doctrine. Indeed, Sadat referred to the coming war as "struggling with Israel's security doctrine and its complete destruction."[56] References to this purpose were also apparent during the War of Attrition. It seems that this was an element to which the Egyptian leadership attached great importance. Sadat referred to it in the following way:

> The mission which I ordered the armed forces to fulfill was clearly defined: to destroy as many as possible of the Israeli armed forces. That because Israel believed—rightly or wrongly—that her security depends on her deterrence capability, and that armed power is the means for her objective. . . . Our forces had to secure an important political objective through a military action. That is, to defeat the Israeli security doctrine by military means.[57]

This reference to Israel's security doctrine also demonstrates that Egyptian concern related to Israel's conventional capability and not the nuclear dimension. After all, if Israel's security doctrine was based at least partly on nuclear weapons, then the "destruction of as many as possible of the Israeli forces" could not have shattered that doctrine. A nuclear capability is not dependent on the size of conventional forces. Then again, Sadat referred to Israel's deterrence posture and argued that the coming operation would shatter it. Similarly, if Israeli deterrence was based on a nuclear capability, then the planned Egyptian operation could not affect her deterrence posture.

Egyptian references to Israeli "security doctrine" are worth elaborating on. According to Egypt, the main elements of Israeli doctrine were:[58]

1 military and technological superiority;
2 military moves designed to split the Arab military effort, to be achieved by a quick switch of the main military effort from one front to the other;
3 a quick transfer of the war to territory outside Israel;
4 the war must be *blitzkrieg* and should last no more than a week; and
5 the number of casualties should be minimized.

At the operation level, the Egyptians referred to the following elements favoring the Israeli forces:

1 air superiority;
2 superior capability to conduct mobile armored battles in open territory;
3 superior technical capability of the forces;
4 rigorous training; and
5 reliance on American support which promised sustained logistical support in arms and ammunition.

The weaknesses of the Israeli forces, on the other hand, were enumerated as follows:[59]

1 long lines of logistical support;
2 limited resources for manpower;
3 difficulties in sustaining the economic burdens of a long war; and
4 exaggerated self-confidence and arrogance.

It is clear that all these elements of the Israeli security doctrine and the strength and limitations of the Israeli forces, as they were perceived by Egypt, refer entirely to a conventional-arms environment. Indeed, Egyptian military planning was tailored precisely to counter these strengths and to utilize these limitations.[60] Thus, the Egyptian plan called first for the achievement of strategic surprise. The emphasis on surprise is again related solely to the conventional level and has no relevance to the nuclear dimension. In a nuclear environment, the initial purpose of a surprise attack should be to neutralize the enemy's nuclear capacity. The Egyptian plan also sought to split Israel's military forces. At the strategic level, this had to be secured through a simultaneous attack on two fronts (Egypt and Syria), which would force Israel to divide her forces and render her unable to concentrate on one front. At the operational level, the plan outlined an attack along the entire length of the Suez Canal, involving five Egyptian infantry divisions reinforced by armor and mechanized units. Thus, there would not be one *schwerpunkt*, and the small

Israeli defending forces would be divided and unable to counter the wide Egyptian thrust. Moreover, the fighting would inflict high casualty rates on the Israeli units. Once again, this operational strategem has no relevance to the nuclear dimension.

The plan set forth countermeasures to Israel's superior operational capabilities. An extensive belt of air defense systems would constrain the Israeli Air Force and cause it high rates of losses. On the ground, the proliferation of anti-tank weapons at all levels of the infantry units would blunt the superior Israeli armor.

For the execution of this plan the Egyptians had at their disposal the following ground forces: five infantry divisions (with tank units attached to each of the infantry brigades with the divisions); two armored divisions and two mechanized divisions. These were the main battleground formations. In addition, there were several independent armored and infantry brigades and several formations of paratroopers and commandos.[61]

Bearing in mind the need to achieve these objectives, and fearful of Israeli conventional military superiority, Egypt planned a three-phased operation: first, crossing the Canal and conquering a ten-kilometer-wide strip on the Israeli side of the Canal; second, absorbing—with the aid of static air defense systems and abundant anti-tank weaponry—the expected Israeli counterattack; finally, and only after completion of the second phase, a push toward the Sinai passes. The last phase, if successful, would have left Egypt in control of about a third of the Sinai.

The truth of the matter was that the Egyptian high command very much doubted the possibility of success in even the first phase of the operation, let alone of the latter ones. Thus, for example, one Egyptian source mentioned that the high command expected 10,000 casualties in the course of the first phase,[62] while another source quotes an unexpected 20,000 casualties.[63] Consequently, the first phase was prepared and planned with great detail, whereas the second, and especially the third phases were planned only in very general outlines. This lack of detail is particularly noteworthy in the Egyptian army, which as generally known had lacked the ability to execute operations if thorough and extremely detailed plans for them are not drawn up beforehand. Indeed, the success of the first phase was due to the great detail in planning, and to the repeated exercises in its implementation by the Egyptian forces.

But why were the Egyptians so worried about the success of their operation, especially in regard to the third phase?

It has been argued that Egypt planned a limited operation because of concern about an assumed Israeli nuclear capability. In other words, according to this view, the Egyptians felt confident about their ability to win the war by conventional means, but were forced to define limited objectives because of fear of the nuclear factor. The lack of planning for the third phase of the operation testifies to the falsity of this argument, and for the following reasons: if the nuclear argument had any validity, the Egyptians would have had to define a threshold that they would not violate for fear that it may lead to explicit nuclear threats or the actual use of nuclear weapons. Moreover, Egyptian behavior would have signalled their awareness of such a threshold. Let us accept, for argument's sake, the nuclear argument. Since Egypt implemented phase A and eventually tried to implement phase C, it follows that both these phases were perceived by the Egyptian leadership as not infringing on the nuclear threshold. They were both (as the Egyptians perceived them) "acceptable" to Israel, and did not justify the resort to nuclear threats or the use of nuclear weapons. If that is so, the clear distinction drawn by the Egyptian leadership between the planning of the two phases—a distinction which is very meaningful within the context of the Egyptian military tradition—must be explained by another variable, and *not* by the assumed Israeli nuclear capability. In other words, the Egyptian assumption that the probability of implementing the third phase was very low, (and this is the meaning of lack of detailed planning of that phase), must be explained by another factor and *not* Israel's assumed nuclear capability. This factor was clearly the Egyptian perception of Israel's conventional superiority. Indeed, one might add that had the Egyptians been concerned about a possible Israeli nuclear response if they reached the Passes, they would never have planned this third phase. The conventional factor determined the self-imposed limitations of the Egyptian war plan.

The entire plan is characterized by the preparation of countermeasures and responses to what the Egyptians rightly considered were Israel's superior qualities in *conventional* warfare, while exploiting her weaknesses. The focus of the plan was strictly conventional rather than nuclear.

The attack[64]

Thanks to the element of surprise, the consequent postponement in the mobilization of the Israeli reserves, and the attack on a very wide front, the first phase of the Egyptian offensive on October 6 and 7 proved successful. On October 8, the Israelis counterattacked, but the counterattack was premature and was conducted with insufficient preparation. One division counterattacked again on October 9, but this was without authorization. The counterattacks were repulsed. In the next few days the Egyptian forces concentrated on consolidating their hold east of the Suez Canal, by linking the positions of their five divisions to the extent that their two armies—the Second and the Third—each controlled a solid front manned by infantry with tanks in support. These maneuvers were conducted under the umbrella of the thick air defense system deployed on the Egyptian side of the Canal. However, Egyptian efforts to conquer several important positions which were essential for consolidation of the areas under their control failed due to increased Israeli resistance.

Although the Israeli counterattack was repulsed on October 8, and while the Egyptians secured most of their frontline within a few days, they still hesitated to execute the third phase. Only after long and tortuous deliberations and soul-searching did the Egyptians decide, with a marked lack of enthusiasm, to execute the third phase—that is, a push toward the Sinai Passes.[65] This decision was taken against the best military judgment. The attacking Egyptian armored formations would not enjoy the critical air defense umbrella nor the anti tank support of the infantry. Moreover, Egyptian armored units would be exposed to precisely the kind of battle in which Israel excelled—mobile armored battles in open territory. But the decision was motivated by political factors; Israel began a counteroffensive in the Golan Heights on October 10, and, on the following day, began a slow advance toward Damascus. The Syrian regime panicked and demanded a major Egyptian action so that Israeli attention would be redirected toward her southern front. Under that pressure, two Egyptian armored divisions crossed the Canal on October 12–13 and joined the five infantry divisions already there. On October 14, these armored divisions, backed by elements from the five infantry divisions, attacked. The attack failed completely due to Israel superiority in tank warfare.

In this context it is interesting to refer to yet another argument raised in relation to the nuclear issue. Seymour Hersh has argued that on the night of October 8, 1973, the Israeli "Kitchen Cabinet" held a special meeting. The participants were: Prime Minister Golda Meir, Deputy Prime Minister Yigal Allon, Defense Minister Moshe Dayan, Minister without portfolio Yisrael Gallili, Chief of Staff General David Elazar, and the Prime Minister's military aide, Yisrael Leor. All of them are now dead. Hersh argues that the Cabinet took a major step toward nuclearizing the war by deciding to arm and make operational Israel's nuclear arsenal and the missiles and aircraft which were earmarked for their delivery. The Cabinet also decided on targets for these weapons and on their activation if the Israeli forces were to collapse.[66]

According to Hersh, the Israelis suspected that Soviet spies had successfully penetrated the Israeli security establishment and would learn about the steps taken. The Israeli assumption was that the information sent to Moscow would be immediately transmitted to Egypt and Syria, thus forcing them to limit their operations. Indeed, Hersh continues—basing his account on an interview with Heikal—the Soviets did warn Egypt early in the war that Israel has assembled three nuclear warheads.[67]

It appears however, that the Israeli "Kitchen Cabinet" did not take the "nuclear" decision described by Hersh. Needless to say there had been no official Israeli version on that meeting. But reliable accounts circulating suggest that Moshe Dayan, who was deeply disturbed by the failure of the Israeli counteroffensive on the Egyptian front on October 8, did indeed raise in a rather tentative manner some ideas connected with Israel's nuclear capability. However, both Yisrael Galili and Yigal Allon strongly and vehemently opposed Dayan's idea. They insisted that the war should be fought completely by conventional means. Indeed, this version is consistent with the known antinuclear views Galili and Allon had (see Chapter 1). Golda Meir, who usually relied heavily on Galili's views, accepted their advice and ruled against Dayan's tentative proposals.[68] It should be added in parenthesis that already before the meeting Golda Meir began to doubt Dayan's grasp of the war developments. On October 7, following a very pessimistic account about military conditions on the Golan Heights delivered to her by Dayan, she sent the highly trusted retired Israeli Chief of Staff, Haim Bar-Lev, to the Golan in order to assess conditions there. The next morning, he came back and reassured her that the situation was difficult but by no means desperate. This report deeply shook Golda Meir's confidence in Dayan.[69]

In summary, the plan for the war and its execution by Egypt are completely explicable in terms of the conventional arms environment perceived by Egypt. That they planned only a limited operation in terms of the military objectives they sought to accomplish is explained by their perception of the balance of military forces and their detailed assessment of the strengths and weaknesses of Israel's conventional military power and her security doctrine. In their detailed analysis of that security doctrine, they referred exclusively to elements which are relevant only within the terms of a conventional strategic doctrine. The 1973 War was planned and executed in a purely conventional arms mode. It was limited because Arab goals were limited. In any case, they assumed that even a military failure (which seemed a likely scenario) would result in a political success.

Egyptian fear of Israeli conventional superiority, or put differently, the credibility of the general Israeli deterrence posture, was high, as demonstrated by the repeated references to the "fear block" of the Egyptians. Thus, for example, President Sadat, referring to the outcome of the war, stressed that: "Today we are in a much better position than we were in before October 6, 1973. We have regained our self-confidence and our trust in our armed forces. We destroyed the fear block and changed in the eyes of the world from a dormant people incapable of fighting, to a people which rediscovered itself and its power."[70]

Respect for Israel's military capability was also evident in Syrian behavior. Her military plan aimed only at the liberation of the Golan Heights.[71] It is likely that President Assad was relying on the element of surprise and was hoping his forces would be able to accomplish their objective within the first two days, or at least cause the change in the political status quo which was the joint objective of Egypt and Syria. But the Syrians were probably even more pessimistic about the military aspects of the intended war than were the Egyptians. They expected an immediate Israeli counterattack which they feared may be disastrous for them. Hence, Assad planned the following strategem: he invited the Soviet Ambassador to Damascus on October 4, 1973, and informed him of the coming war, which would start on October 6. Simultaneously, he requested that the Soviet Union ask for a cease-fire on October 8, only 48 hours after the beginning of the war.[72]

As emphasized in this chapter, the Egyptian war plan completely ignored the nuclear dimension. It is instructive, however, to analyze the logic of the "nuclear explanation." As mentioned, this explanation attributes Egypt's limited war objectives to an implied Israeli nuclear threat. Such an explanation assumes very sophisticated nuclear reasoning on the part of the Egyptian planners. To begin with, it presupposes that the Egyptians knew or suspected what was the Israeli tolerance threshold for the use of nuclear weapons (presumably only a threat to the very existence of Israel). But Israel's threshold for the use of nuclear weapons (a capability which Israel has persistently denied) has never been voiced formally. For instance, no important Israeli decision-maker has ever, let alone before 1973, made a statement such as: "Israel does not have nuclear bombs. But if she did have them, she would use them only if— say—Arab armies were to reach the outskirts of Tel-Aviv," or "only if Arab armies were to penetrate Israel (within the pre-1967 borders) and Israeli forces were badly licked in the process," and so forth. Nor is there any indication that such threats have ever been communicated to the Arabs through third parties. In view of the lack of sophisticated political strategic debate within Israel about a nuclear policy, it is improbable that any such threats have been channelled to the Arabs. Moreover, prior to the 1973 War, Israel was so confident of her conventional superiority that it is very unlikely that she would have resorted to such threats.

Furthermore, the Egyptians would have had to assume that their intention to launch only a limited attack would be communicated to the Israeli side. There is no evidence whatsoever of any attempt by the Egyptians to communicate such an intention to Israel. Indeed, the only way the Egyptians could have hoped to communicate their limited war objectives to Israel was through the developments in the field, i.e., through the actual execution of the war. While possible, this method is prone to dangerous potential eventualities. The theory of limited war assumes that the sides reach a tacit understanding to limit the war, based on actual military actions and their perceptions of the other side. However, in most cases, the evolution and success of such tacit understandings is realized only after the event. Both sides undertake actions, are affected by the actions of the other side and the final outcome indicates that a tacit understanding has been created. There are fewer cases where strategic planners

73

assume beforehand that their action will trigger or not trigger a certain type of response from the other side. Moreover, for such preplanning to obtain, an accumulation of experience and precedents is required. Limited wars were indeed the rule in the Middle East, but they had been conducted completely within a conventional context. It would have required much subtlety and knowledge of nuclear affairs on the part of the Egyptians for them to assume the emergence of an understanding in Israel of Egypt's limited war objectives. For example, the Egyptians would have had to assume that because they left two armored and two mechanized divisions on the western side of the Canal during the first phase, Israel would realize that the war was limited and did not justify a nuclear threat. The above analysis seems further to invalidate the "nuclear explanation."

It appears clear, therefore, that Egyptian war planning with its limited objectives and manner of execution was conducted within a purely conventional approach. One may, of course, raise the following argument: strategic planners tend to consider the worst case analysis (even if they do not always behave according to it). Is it not surprising that the Egyptian planners did not refer at all to the probability that Israel may have had the possibility (albeit ambiguous) of an Israeli nuclear capability and its possible use during the war? The main reason for this was—as argued earlier in this chapter—the complete Egyptian focus on the conventional balance.

An additional explanation may be that the Egyptians did not consider a total war whose objective was the destruction of Israel. Had they considered such a war, they may have been compelled—on the basis of a worst case analysis—to consider the possible existence of an Israeli nuclear capability. But as they did not at all think in terms of a general war, they did not even begin to consider the nuclear factor, even tentatively. This, of course, is very different from the explanation which suggests that it was the nuclear threat itself which forced the Egyptians to design a limited war. My explanation posits that all the Egyptian plans of the war had to do exclusively with a conventional battlefield, and the nuclear issue did not enter their calculations at all.

Beyond that, one is tempted to argue that the complete Egyptian disregard of the nuclear issue is not entirely surprising. After all, even if the Egyptians did assume that Israel may have had an actual nuclear capability (and it is not clear whether they did fully accept that possibility) their planning and action fits a well-known pattern of behavior of conventional powers facing nuclear opponents, even when the opponent's nuclear capability is certain. Thus, the Soviet Union (until its first nuclear test in 1949 and a for a while after that), and China (before acquiring a nuclear capability and to a certain extent up to the present), tended to belittle the centrality of nuclear weapons in the strategic relations between themselves and their nuclear opponents. Both powers were anxious to achieve a nuclear capability themselves, but even after they secured it, they maintained a posture which was less nuclear-oriented than that of the United States. Appreciation of the centrality of nuclear weapons in the international system forced itself upon Soviet leaders only in the second half of the 1950s. These approaches appear to be the natural reaction when in a position of nuclear inferiority: they could be explained as a propaganda ploy, i.e., the non- or weaker nuclear power's desire to maintain a deterrent posture against the nuclear power by demonstrating resolve and fearlessness in the face of the ultimate weapon. But they could also be explained by a genuine belief that nuclear weapons are less important in the strategic balance.

Sadat's peace initiative

When Sadat went to Jerusalem in 1977 and made it clear that he was seeking an end to the Israeli–Egyptian conflict, explanations for his move abounded. Among others it has also been suggested that Egypt believed that Israel had nuclear weapons, that therefore no hope remained of defeating Israel, and hence the time had come to reach a peace agreement. A variant of this explanation is that the Egyptian leaders reached the conclusion that, because of Israel's nuclear capability, the Sinai, Egypt's prized objective since 1967, could not be liberated by military means. Consequently, they made the peace initiative.[73]

As has been suggested before, no Egyptian source made that assertion publicly. All of Sadat's references to his motivation for the peace initiative mentioned primarily the positive fruits of peace for both sides, and as a secondary reason, the costs involved in the conflict until then. Therefore, the burden of proof lies with those who contend that Israel's nuclear capability played a crucial role in Egypt's calculations. Admittedly, the absence of such public references is not conclusive evidence, because open public references by Arab decision-makers do not necessarily present an accurate picture of the real intentions behind their policy. They might, however, be more relevant when a public assertion could serve the policy, and primarily so within the context of inter-Arab rivalry. Thus, for example, extreme anti-Israeli rhetoric, especially when directed to Arab audiences, should usually be taken with a grain of salt. On the other hand, moderate policy statements are usually more meaningful. With that background, the complete lack of reference to the nuclear issue in Egypt's public justification of the peace initiative appears to present the real picture for the following reasons: Egypt came under tremendous criticism in the Arab world following every step she took towards peace, from November 1977 onwards. Giving the assumed Israeli nuclear capability as one of the reasons for Egyptian moderation could have helped Egypt in presenting her rationale for the peace effort. Even if she hesitated to do so until the peace treaty was signed in 1979, for fear that raising that argument would ostensibly weaken her position, vis-à-vis Israel, that particular reason faded away after the peace treaty was signed. From then on, Egypt's most difficult test lay in her relations with the Arab world.

Sadat referred to the experience of the wars with Israel and their heavy costs to Egypt as one of the reasons for his initiative. But their previous wars were all conventional wars and had nothing to do with the nuclear issue. It should be added that Sadat was careful not to admit Egyptian military inferiority after 1973, but he did stress the high costs involved for both sides resulting from continuation of the conflict.

Thus, for example, Fahmy states concerning Sadat's mood after the end of the 1973 War:

> However, in the end the concessions [in the negotiations on the first disengagement agreement of 1974] reflected not our military capability but Sadat's aversion to any further fighting. He was not prepared to reopen the military confrontation with Israel. His repeated statements to the contrary were pretence.[74]

It is interesting that even Fahmy—a hardliner and Nasserist, who opposed Sadat's peace initiative—also summed up the situation in a way which justified and explained a peace initiative: "militarily, it could be argued, Israel had proved once again [in 1973] its superiority and Egypt has been defeated," but "the Egyptian assault had demonstrated to Israel and to the United States that Egypt was now in a position to inflict heavy damage on Israel,[75] making it pay very highly for the continued occupation of the Sinai." A similar assessment was voiced by a leading Egyptian political scientist and strategist who emphasized that Egypt realized both in 1967 and in 1973, Israeli conventional superiority and saw no reason to continue an extremely high-cost conflict.[76]

But before all that, it appears that Sadat's policy on the conflict developed quite consistently since 1971. He introduced a major change in the Egyptian position vis-à-vis Israel in his response to the initiative of early 1971 and in his approach to the various ideas about a partial settlement around the Canal. By his expulsion of the Soviet advisors and his feelers toward the United States during the period 1971–1973, he signalled a readiness for a major change of policy vis-à-vis the United States as well. The 1974 War was not a reversal of the policy. Quite the contrary, it was the same policy pursued by other means. Witness for instance his message to Kissinger on the second day of the 1973 War, in which he outlined his conditions for a peaceful solution and described his approach to the war as having primarily political objectives.[77] The same approach is clear from the haste with which he was ready to reach the partial agreements of 1974 and 1975. All these can now be seen as the evolution of the same policy. Thus, the foundation for the new policy lay in Sadat's perceptions of Egyptian interests in 1971, although at those early stages the full scope of the new policy had probably not yet been formulated by Sadat. At that early stage in 1971, the nuclear issue was certainly not prominent in Egypt's considerations. What was salient was the grievance resulting from the occupation of the Sinai, the fear of the conventional Israeli military might demonstrated so forcefully in 1967, and a general reevaluation of Egypt's role in the Arab world.

Politically, the new approach emphasized more an "Egypt first" posture (as distinct from a Pan-Arab posture) and an overwhelming desire to better the miserable economic conditions in Egypt. Finally, it was probably connected with the realization that only the West could provide Egypt with the necessary economic support needed for recovery. But, in turn, such a connection with the West, and in particular the United States, required an end to the conflict with Israel.

Thus, both the reassessment of Egypt's position in the Arab world, as well as the pragmatic strategic, political and economic considerations, led to the same policy choices: regaining the Sinai was a crucial *Egyptian* national objective and thus had to be secured. Other general Arab objectives were important, but not so urgent and crucial and did not dictate the continuation of the conflict. Once the Sinai was secured, either by war or by peace, the conflict with Israel could be abandoned, and other policy objectives attain priority. But following 1973, it became clear that the Egyptians were incapable of conquering Sinai, even when only conventional arms were used.

Israel's nuclear posture and its effect on deterrence after 1973

In Chapter 1, I pointed out the gradual increased Arab awareness of Israel's nuclear capability during the 1980s. But it is not at all clear what role this played in deterrence. After all, as argued in the first part of this chapter, the conventional balance coupled with political developments made the initiation of general Arab hostilities unlikely. Egypt opted for a political settlement probably already in 1970–1971, and certainly following the 1973 War. The only other "confrontation state" which theoretically was capable of mounting a military operation was Syria. But the latter, quite prudently, has always realized that she was incapable of doing so— in view of the conventional balance of power—unless she first formed a war coalition with another Arab state. In this she repeatedly failed.

Syria's quest for "strategic parity"[78] was designed to overcome her conventional inferiority vis-à-vis Israel, and was supposed to serve two objectives: a deterrent against Israel, and the creation of an option for a limited military operation. The second objective had as its goal either the capability of an actual attack, or the creation of a strong position for political negotiations with Israel.

Indeed, two speeches delivered by President Assad in early 1986 about "strategic parity" with Israel, following a marked increase in Syrian military capabilities since 1983, caused concern in Israel. Although the conventional balance certainly favored Israel by a wide margin, there was nevertheless the perceived possibility that Syria might launch a surprise *limited* attack in the Golan in order to try and grab part of this territory and then seek a cease-fire. The Syrian objective would be to create an option for political negotiations from a position of strength.

Whether Syria in fact contemplated such an operation at any time since the mid-1980s is not clear. What could be speculated, however, is that Assad did not consider the nuclear factor as relevant to such an operation. This is the possible conclusion from the following analysis. Although Syrian leaders probably suspected that Israel had a nuclear weapons capability for quite some time, the Vanunu story which appeared in November 1986, probably strengthened that suspicion. However, the Syrian quest for "strategic parity" and the possibility even of a limited military operation do not seem to have disappeared following the Vanunu story. In April 1987 Assad went to Moscow[79] and raised with Soviet leaders the question of "strategic parity". The Soviet leadership came out clearly against both the idea of "strategic parity" and the notion of a "military solution" to the Arab–Israeli conflict. The Soviet position probably had a greater effect on Syria's military calculations than did the Vanunu revelations.

Assad, himself, did refer to the Vanunu affair in a programmatic long interview given in January 1987.[80] While accepting that Israel has the capacity to produce nuclear weapons (for one reason or another, even then he did not refer to an actual Israeli arsenal of nuclear weapons), this did not change, so he emphasized, Syria's overall position and did not negate the possibility of a military option to resolve the conflict.

The nuclear issue did possibly affect Syria's military planning in a different way. Since 1987–1988 Syria began the deployment of surface-to-surface missiles, some armed with chemical warheads. These were designed—according to the Syrians (see below in Chapters 6 and 7)—as a deterrent against the overwhelming Israeli air force superiority, as well as against the Israeli "unconventional capabilities."

Nuclear postures and political influence

While Israeli nuclear developments were—as analyzed in this chapter—largely irrelevant to Sadat's decision to seek accommodation with Israel, the question could be raised whether they had any impact on Arab political attitudes toward Israel. The two most important states in this context are Jordan and Syria.

On the basis of available knowledge, King Hussein of Jordan has been ready since 1967 to sign a full peace treaty with Israel, provided Israel returned the entire West Bank to Jordan. Clearly Hussein's motives were independent of the nuclear dimension; instead, they derived from a desire to regain lost territory, coupled with a justified assessment of Jordan's profound conventional inferiority. Moreover, King Hussein has always been aware (as was his grandfather King Abdallah) of the geo-strategic important interests that Jordan has shared with Israel. This interest in accommodation with Israel has therefore also been based on positive goals. Because of the *Intifada*, the King at present prefers a political solution which may include the creation of a Jordanian–Palestinian confederation, but this does not change his constant readiness for full peace with Israel, which has again been demonstrated by his readiness, in 1987 (the "London Protocol") to enter negotiations with Israel and his immediate acceptance of the new peace process which has begun in Madrid.

Two of Israel's four Arab neighbors—Egypt and Jordan—had acquiesced to the legitimacy of Israel's political existence in the Middle East long before the nuclear issue gained much salience. Currently, the overall Arab approach is based on a mix of political, strategic, and attitudinal considerations, all of which point toward an effort to manage and limit the overall Arab–Israeli conflict. The roots of this approach can be traced back to the early 1970s. Since that time they have gradually gained strength. It obviously had to do with the changed Egyptian position, the fragmentation in the Arab world, and the decline of Pan-Arab ideology. In addition, the Iran–Iraq War diverted Arab attention to the Iranian and Shiite fundamentalist threats and the Gulf Crisis and War further deepened mutual Arab suspicions and strengthened the central Egyptian position. All this served to moderate Arab policies toward Israel. Israel's presumed nuclear capability does not appear to have played a significant role in these processes.

With respect to Syria, Assad's programmatic interview of January 1987, mentioned above, clearly demonstrates that he was not ready to change Syria's political and strategic postures because of the nuclear factor. What has changed and did affect Syria's position in the past few years, are the relationships within the Arab world, the changed attitude toward Israel mentioned before, and most importantly, the change in the Soviet Union and the ascendance to dominant power of the United States.

Indeed, at present Syria is ready to move toward a position where she is ready to accept a peaceful system of relations with Israel, provided Israel relinquishes the Golan Heights. Coupled with the desire to regain lost territory, this posture is consistent with Syria's assessment of Israeli conventional superiority and with her political objectives. The nuclear dimension did not change that basic posture. For example, even under nuclear threat, Syria would not have acceded to signing a peace treaty that did not involve the return of the Golan Heights. Similarly, there was no need for a nuclear threat to bring Syria to the negotiating table, as she did in 1991 once Assad's regime became convinced that there was a good chance that Syria's sovereignty over the Golan Heights could be restored through diplomatic means.

If Syria really was still adhering to general Arab interests, as expressed in her public rhetoric, such as in her unyielding commitment to the Palestinian cause and the denial of legitimacy to Israel, no nuclear threat could have changed Syria's position. If this were a true representation of Syria's objectives, then the country could have resigned itself to a long wait and refuse to enter into any negotiations with Israel while, at the same time, designing a military campaign in which the Israeli capability would not be effective in denying an Arab attack. Syria could also just wait and hope for the development in the long run of an Arab nuclear capability to counterbalance the presumed Israeli one.

3

NUCLEAR WEAPONS IN THE MIDDLE EAST
The Consequences for Strategy and Policy[1]

This chapter focuses on the possible results of the influx of nuclear weapons into the Middle East and, most critically, the likely impact of nuclear armaments on regional stability.[2] To pose the question in its starkest form: are nuclear weapons likely to prevent the outbreak of regional wars in general, and wars between Israel and Arab states, in particular?

The basic working assumption for our analysis will be that if one state explicitly introduces nuclear weapons into the region, several states will eventually follow suit. That is, according to this assumption, the Middle East would become a multipolar nuclear region. It also assumes that the regional powers and the international community do not yet consider Israeli threshold strategy to constitute a full-fledged nuclear power.

Nuclear weapons have had a major impact on the structure of the global international system, and their proliferation will most probably have a profound influence on affected regional subsystems. But their influence will be conditioned by the character of interstate relations within the regional subsystem, and by the sociopolitical fabric of the individual states. It is then obligatory that the main topic of our discussion be preceded by a survey of the Middle East subsystem. On the basis of this analysis, and in the light of the conceptual framework that has been developed for nuclear relationships between the superpowers, an attempt will be made to examine the possible consequences of regional nuclear proliferation.

It must of course be emphasized that the interstate system in the Middle East differs markedly from the system of relations between the two superpowers. Analogies cannot be drawn directly from one system to the other. In the present discussion, the borrowing of global nuclear terms and concepts serves only as a starting point for understanding the specifics of the regional situation. Moreover, we will have cause to point to structural and behavioral differences between the two systems. The impact of these differences on regional nuclearization will also be examined.

The eight main characteristics of the Middle East subsystem are as follows:[3]

81

1 Multipolar, in Terms of the Number of Actors

For our purposes the following states can be regarded as comprising the "heart" of the Middle East—Egypt, Israel, Jordan, Lebanon, Syria, Iraq and Saudi Arabia. Of this group, Israel, Jordan, Syria, Lebanon and Iraq can be identified as the inner unit. These states are included in the "Fertile Crescent," and have also been included in various definitions of "Greater Syria." Iraq, we might note, has only at times been included in the map of Greater Syria. Egypt, and to a lesser extent Saudi Arabia, have been directly and deeply involved in the events of the "heart." In an important sense then, our definition of the "heart" of the Middle East corresponds with the arena of the Arab–Israeli conflict.

In addition to these states, it is possible to conceive of more distant Arab states as also belonging to the region. These states would include North and South Yemen, Sudan, Libya, Kuwait, and the Persian Gulf kingdoms. Finally, it is necessary to add a number of states at the periphery of the region, of which the most important is Iran.

In defining the "central actors" in terms of foreign and strategic policy issues, the list would comprise the following states: Egypt, Iran, Iraq, Israel, Syria, and Saudi Arabia. These actors give the region its multipolar character.

2 Power is Distributed Asymmetrically Among the Central Actors

Egypt is the leading Arab state both demographically and culturally. Until recent years, she was also the leading military power in the Arab world. (Iraq now has more troops than Egypt, Syria has fewer troops, but more tanks and combat aircraft.) However, Egypt has redefined her national priorities, and is no longer seeking military dominance. She is confronted by apparently more pressing problems in the socioeconomic realm. Indeed, were military power to be elevated in the order of national political priorities, Egypt, due to the size of her population, could regain her position of military dominance in the Arab world.

Iran is also possessed of a large population (second after Egypt) and she maintains a regionally significant military force. By virtue of her oil reserves, Iran is also capable of expanding her economic strength. Nevertheless, the Iran–Iraq war has also exposed her limitations as a regional military power when faced by another strong regional power. Furthermore, the fact that Iran is a non-Arab state imposes a barrier to any attempt to play a leading political role in the Middle East.

Iraq trails both Egypt and Iran in population size, and also suffers from ethnic and religious divisions. Numerically, she used to have—until the Gulf War—the largest standing army in the Middle East, but that war revealed her military limitations. At the time of writing the future of

Iraq's military capability is still unclear. Like Iran, Iraq has great economic potential due to her oil reserves, but the future of her economy depends to a large extent on political developments. In any case it is likely that for the short and medium range, the Iraqi economy will suffer tremendous difficulties.

Syrian military power is relatively large given the size of her population and available resources. However, her economic resources are limited and she also suffers from sharp ethnic and religious divisions.

Finally, Saudi Arabia is a major financial power, due to oil, but her demographic base is narrow, her military power is limited, and she is socially backward.

Israel holds a substantial lead—in political, social, industrial, techno-logical and scientific terms—over all other states in the Middle East. However, Israel suffers from a relatively small population in comparison to other states in the region, and also from economic problems caused in no small measure by massive military expenditures.

Thus, asymmetries in types of power are a major feature of relations between critical central actors in the Middle East. In the past these factors have been critical in defining mutual strategic concerns.

3 The Centrality and Persistence of Interstate Competition and Conflict

The regional subsystem is replete with conflicts, derivative of a number of different causes. First, the central Arab states compete for positions of power and influence in the Arab world, and in so doing, become engaged in serious conflicts. The pattern of this competition has changed to a certain extent in the last decade. Previously the competition was charac-terized by the attempts of a small number of central actors—Syria, Iraq and especially Egypt—to attain hegemony in the Arab world. Around this central group of actors, various competing coalitions would form. The areas of these inter-Arab conflicts reflect the classic causes of interstate conflicts: the contest for power and territorial disputes. The modern history of the Middle East is testimony to the persistence of those factors. Paradoxically, the decline of Pan-Arab sentiment has contributed to the easing of competition among the main Arab actors, by reducing the stakes of Arab leadership. In any case, during the 1970s, the Arab world became so totally and deeply divided that no state could aspire to effective hegemony. Although contention over positions of influence continued, its salience declined.

Among the Arab states, some conflicts also did arise from ideological differences. An outstanding example of this phenomenon was the dispute between "radical" and "conservative" states in the 1960s. At the present time it appears that ideology has diminished as a cause of conflict, and the current disputes cut across ideological grounds. However, it is a factor that ought not to be completely discounted.

The emergence in 1988–1989, of a central bloc comprising Egypt, Iraq, Jordan, and Yemen, with the backing of several other Arab states, appeared at the time to signify a new pattern of relations: the diminution of competition for leadership, and increased readiness for economic and political cooperation. The invasion of Kuwait in 1990 and Iraqi hegemonic ambitions revealed just before and during the crisis, demonstrated all too clearly the persistence of traditional patterns of inter-Arab competition.

Beyond the inter-Arab level, the region is, of course, also marked by conflicts between Israel and the Arab states, and between Iran and Iraq. Significantly, the end of the Gulf War does not necessarily signify the end of the latter conflict. There seems no need to detain the reader with an analysis of the persistence and centrality of these conflicts.

4 States in the Region are Engaged in a Series of Arms Races

The arms races are fueled and complicated by the large number of regional conflicts, and by the financial reserves at the disposal of the oil states. The quantity of conventional arms in the Middle East (including the Persian Gulf and Libya) is astonishing. The number of tanks in the region (just before the Gulf War), for instance, apparently totals between 18,000 to 19,000, while attack and intercept aircraft total approximately 2,500. Taking into account the underdevelopment and relatively small size of states in the region, the concentration of force in the Middle East is proportionally greater than in any other region in the world.

Furthermore, since the 1960s and more particularly since 1973, there has been a change in the nature of weapon systems in the region. Highly advanced systems, frequently representing state-of-the-art technology, have appeared in the region. Thus, arms races are both quantitative and qualitative.

5 The Prominence of Military Regimes

Many states in the region are ruled by military regimes, and lack established procedures for the change of government. This makes military coups a possible route for leadership change.[4] Furthermore, in some states there exists widespread political instability, quite apart from the military nature of the regimes. The instability derives from the ethnic and religious divisions within some of the states, and from the persistent threat of Islamic fundamentalism. The latter factor may, however, recede in importance in the future. In Iraq and Syria,[5] the current military leaderships have succeeded, through a combination of repression and the wide distribution of economic resources, to achieve a remarkable level of stability. Thus, we have a paradoxical situation. On the one hand, the governing regimes in these states appear to be solid and capable of enduring. On the other hand, with the exception of Egypt, all these states contain domestic sources of potential instability. Furthermore, in Syria and Iraq, changes in regime and government are possible only through the military.

6 The High Level of Superpower Involvement

The superpowers have clear economic and strategic interests in the Middle East, and obligations to regional allies. Until the late 1980s, they were also involved in intense competition among themselves. Within the scope of their activity, the superpowers have had some ability to control escalations and to manage extreme crisis situations. However, their ability to prevent wars and politico-strategic initiatives by regional states has been, until recently, limited and problematic. They have been more effective in putting an end to regional wars, once they have begun. Thus, until the Gulf Crisis, it used to be the case that in the absence of their reaching broad consensus on a common regional policy, the superpowers cannot serve as a focus of power capable of imposing their will on the region. The United States has always held an advantage over the Soviet Union in terms of the extent of its influence over events in the "heart" of the Middle East. Both superpowers fear the development of unstable situations in the region that might involve them in undesired superpower confrontations and crises. However, there have been cases when the behavior of the superpowers has exacerbated regional instabilities, even if this had not been their intention.

Finally, the dramatic changes in the superpower global relations introduced fluidity and uncertainty to their relations inside the Middle East. The Soviet Union, for one, began to lower the profile of its activity in the region. Against that background it was unclear what the American posture would be. However, as detailed in Chapter 6, U.S. behavior during the Gulf Crisis and War, partly made possible precisely because of Soviet retreat, led to a new pattern of superpower relations in the Middle East. The United States emerged as the dominant external actor in the region, capable of affecting, in a meaningful way, at least part of the "rules of the game" there. The Soviet Union accepted the new U.S. position and appeared ready to cooperate diplomatically with the United States as an important, yet secondary actor. Russia has applied the same posture.

7 The High Level of Interstate Violence

Since the creation of the Middle East subsystem late in World War II, there have been six wars between Israel and Arab states; a civil war in Yemen which involved a number of Arab states; a limited war between North and South Yemen; the Iran–Iraq war; the Syrian involvement in Lebanon against the background of the civil war there, the invasion of Kuwait and the Gulf War. In addition, the region has been characterized by widespread nonwar violence between Israel and Arab states, and among the Arab states themselves. Finally, the threat to use military power has often functioned as a vehicle for obtaining political and strategic ends.

The widespread use of military force, both in its application and in its threat, is indicative of the regional view of the relation between military violence and the attainment of political ends. Military force is perceived as a legitimate political tool. This conception was obvious to the Arab states in connection to causes considered legitimate and just, such as the battle against Israel. However, it is of interest that military means are also widely used in inter-Arab conflicts, despite the constant reiteration of the deep solidarity linking the Arab world. This pattern of behavior reflects a certain set of attitudes to international order.

8 Factors Moderating Interstate Violence

A number of regional "rules of the game" have developed that moderate the tendency to resort to organized violence in interstate relations. These rules are the function of various causes: stable balances of conventional deterrence (in particular, between Israel and the Arab states); the evolving Arab–Israeli peace process; the assessment of a number of political elites as to the high cost of war; the preference of some political elites for economic development and modernization; the configuration of certain Arab coalitions that have moderated the preparedness to use military force; the Egyptian preference not to use military force against Israel or other Arab states; and finally, the restraining influence of the super-powers. While all these factors have had a moderating effect, as yet they have not been sufficient to prevent the frequent occurrence of wars in the region. The threat and actual use of military force remains a basic feature of interstate behavior in the Middle East. For the political elites of the region, the development of these rules of the game has not encompassed any fundamental change in their attitude to military force as an instrument of policy. However, the miserable experience of the two Gulf wars has probably had a moderating effect on this attitude.

Summary

The behavior and rules of the game characterizing international systems are not easily malleable. Rather they reflect basic structural attributes of the respective systems. This is true of the Middle East system which, as we have seen, has the following main characteristics: various levels of social divisiveness in some of the states; numerous political actors; the centrality of the military establishments, and their involvement at all levels of society and politics; societal retardation alongside the advanced state of military technology; foreign policy activism leading to involvement in interstate conflicts and competition; and finally, ideological and religious tensions. All this leads to the tentative conclusion that radical changes in military technology, such as the introduction of nuclear weapons, will not affect fundamental changes in sociopolitical structure. To complete the picture, reference should also be made to moderating factors: the "rules of the game" which constrain the proneness of the region to war; the apparently growing realization among some political elites of the high costs of war and their ineffectiveness as instruments of policy; the stability of some of the military regimes; the possible decline of Islamic fundamentalism; the commitment of most of the regimes to economic development, and finally, the moderating impact of the United States. The unfolding peace process surely strengthens these tendencies.

Preconditions for a Stable Balance of Deterrence between the Superpowers

The nature of political and strategic relations between the superpowers in the post-Cold War era is still uncertain, as will be the role of their nuclear weapons. However, for the purpose of our study, the model of the superpowers' nuclear relations obtaining until the recent transformation of global politics, still provides a useful starting point for an analysis of the possible effects of proliferation in the Middle East. Therefore, throughout this chapter, there will be only brief mention of the recent change in the superpower political relationship; the model of their nuclear relationship will be discussed as it obtained until the late 1980s. Although it has by now become an historical model, it is still the only model we have for a nuclear conflict relationship.

The long period of stability in the balance of nuclear deterrence between the superpowers is the result of a number of factors, some historical in nature, some related to the structure of the international system, some deriving from the political and social makeup of the superpowers, and some ensuing from technological developments.

In the course of the following analysis of these factors, comparisons will be drawn with the Middle East, with the purpose of locating similarities and differences. In this connection, the following theses will be presented:

1 The system of strategic relationships between the superpowers differs from the Middle East in several fundamental respects.
2 The introduction of nuclear weapons created a marked discontinuity in the history of global international relations. Nevertheless, in the nuclear period, many features of the prenuclear period remained intact. Thus, the present international system is characterized by elements of both continuity and discontinuity. Similarly, in the Middle East, the introduction of nuclear weapons will cause significant change, but the elements of continuity will be more salient than in the case of the global system.
3 The differences between the global system and the Middle East regional subsystem will also be reflected in the impact of nuclear weapons on system stability. This point is related to the hypothesized persistence of prenuclear behavior patterns.

Historical Factors

The historical background to the emergence of the nuclear relationship between the superpowers is well known, and there is no intention to present here a full recounting. However, a number of critical points are worthy of our attention. When nuclear weapons were first introduced to the global system toward the end of World War II, the two superpowers-to-be were allies. The tension which at that time developed between them, and which by 1948–1949 had attained the dimensions of an emergent Cold War, took root against the background of the previously existent alliance. More importantly, the Cold War developed only a few years after the end of World War II. Neither side, and particularly the Soviet Union, was ready to become entangled in another general war. Russia lost approximately 20 million people in the war, and this human loss, which was accompanied by the destruction of her economy, was a critical factor in her determination to refrain from any continued military engagement. As George Kennan has pointed out,[6] the Russians emerged totally exhausted from the war and were not ready for another such experience. According to Kennan, there was no danger of a Soviet military attack on Western Europe. Furthermore, in the final stages of the war, and immediately following it, Russia established an empire in Eastern Europe, and she was absorbed in efforts to strengthen her hold on the fledgling communist bloc. Indeed, as a result of the war, both superpowers had undergone a dramatic change in status, and this reduced their willingness to become involved in a mutual confrontation. Neither side had territorial claims against the other; the conflict between them revolved on issues of influence and control in other regions, which in the case of the United States were distanced from her by thousands of kilometers. The direct friction between the two superpowers bore no serious threat to their own national territories. The frictions that emerged in 1947–1948 were related to spheres of influence, particularly in Europe. These disputes worsened the relationship, but implied no risk to national territorial integrity.

Thus, the gross destruction resulting from World War II, the political and strategic gains that the war accrued to the superpowers, and the absence of direct conflict and mutual territorial claims, acted to prevent the outbreak of another world war, and allowed both sides to develop their nuclear arsenals, unimpeded by the other. It is possible that in the absence of this historical background, nuclear weapons may not have prevented the outbreak of a large-scale war in the late 1940s or early 1950s.

Widespread recognition of the radical significance of nuclear weapons was not immediate.[7] It was only gradually that the strategic and political leadership of the West came to recognize that the main function of nuclear weapons was deterrence. The notion of nuclear deterrence, originally alluded to by Bernard Brodie in 1946,[8] obtained its initial official recognition in the 1952 British "White Paper" on defense.[9] In the United States, the notion was first officially adopted in a document NSC–162/2, which was presented on October 30, 1953. This document formed the basis of John Foster Dulles's doctrine of "massive retaliation," which based American global strategy on deterrence.[10] The widespread criticism of the doctrine and its simplistic assumptions was in the main justified. However, it must be borne in mind that the notion of massive retaliation marked a watershed in American strategic thinking, denoting realization of the radical impact of nuclear weapons. This realization came only a decade after the introduction of the weapons themselves. Indeed, as will be enlarged upon later, to this day there exists conceptual confusion in both East and West regarding the significance of nuclear weapons, and as to whether their function is purely deterrent.

Structural Factors

During the Cold War, the global strategic (rather than political) system had three main characteristics: first, it was bipolar, that is, only two powers had the assured capability of inflicting a second strike (and, apparently, the capability for additional rounds of strikes) against the other, or against any possible nuclear coalition. Second, both superpowers stood at the head of a military alliance. Finally, there existed no direct point of territorial friction between the two superpowers. It was only their spheres of influence that were geographically contingent, and these points of contact were generally located at a great distance from the

89

superpowers themselves.[11] The ground forces of the two superpowers also had little contact, and the army of neither side posed a direct land threat to the territory of the other. Thus, the points of direct friction were very limited.

It was only in Germany that the ground forces of the superpowers were directly adjacent. And, indeed, the Berlin crises of 1948, 1958, and 1960–1961 aroused deep concern throughout the world. The situation in Germany eventually stabilized, and since the mid-1960s, Europe has been in the midst of a process of detente. The European detente preceded the general Soviet–American detente that developed in the 1970s. The partial reintroduction of cold relations during the first half of the 1980s has since given place to the more far-reaching detente of the late 1980s.

The decline of the global detente has not been accompanied by the deterioration *of the European detente,* even though the latter has undergone certain difficulties. Thus, the political environment of strategic relations in Europe has been more relaxed since the mid-1960s, than in preceding years. Nevertheless, from the military point of view, in both the conventional and nuclear domains, there existed difficult problems that were liable to have an adverse impact on the political context. The INF agreement, and the changes in East–West relations that occurred during 1988, have led to a radically improved political and strategic relationship globally and in Europe.

The Character of Societies and Regimes

Both the United States and the Soviet Union had been characterized by high levels of social and political stability. There is no need to enlarge upon the nature of American society in these pages. In the Soviet Union, until the late 1980s, individual freedoms had been repressed, but the regime nevertheless enjoyed the broad support of the population. This support, and the strength of the central regime, ensured political stability. Furthermore, the major institutions of the state: the party, the army, the bureaucracy, and the secret services, worked together toward maintaining and preserving the society. A serious future threat to the stability of the regime has been posed by the tension between nations and religious groups, in particular among the Eurasian population. The realization of that threat indeed led to the disintegration of the Soviet Union, accompanied by dangers in the nuclear domain. The stagnation of the Soviet economy, which dovetailed with her difficulties in conducting the arms race, was also problematic, but the destabilizing impact of this factor became apparent only by the late 1980s.

The stability of the regime ensured an established procedure for the transfer of power, and avoided the dangers of military revolutions and political turmoil. These factors ensured, to a *certain extent*, the avoidance of mistakes and risks in the management of nuclear strategy.

Technological Factors

Both superpowers developed second-strike capacities, with the United States holding the lead in this area. This is one of the most important components of the stability of nuclear deterrence. In the absence of an assured second-strike capacity, a state tends to fear that the opposite side might deliver an initial knockout blow, destroying all one's warhead delivery systems. This fear is liable to provide motivation for both sides to be the nuclear aggressor. This issue will be taken up at length later.

Another area that has been highly developed by the superpowers is the field of Command, Control, and Communication (C^3) systems. Early warning, command and control systems are critical elements in any military system, and particularly in the modern nuclear context. Toward the end of this chapter reference will be made to the dangers which threatened Soviet–U.S. relations in this area. Meanwhile, suffice it to say that the existence of sophisticated C^3 systems is crucial to the maintained stability of the nuclear balance.

It emerges from the foregoing then, that the stability of the nuclear balance of deterrence between the two superpowers was not *deus ex machina*, but rather the outcome of a multiplicity of factors. A stable balance is dependent on the historical circumstances of its development: the political context, the extent of friction between the sides, the motivation to undermine the balance as a solution to internal political difficulties, the character and structure of the societies and regimes of the participant states and, finally, on a number of critical technological factors. These factors also served as the framework within which decisionmakers and political elites underwent a process of "socialization" with respect to international relations in the nuclear context. This process has been active in the global context for many years, and yet remains far from complete. It is a dynamic process influenced by the configuration of the abovementioned factors, and also by perceptual elements.

Finally, despite the contribution of nuclear weapons to the prevention of global war, the relations between the two superpowers were under constant threat. International stability can only be preserved by continuous attention to various stabilizing vectors in the complex of their political and strategic relations. The task of stability maintenance is a dynamic one, requiring a high level of intellectual sensitivity. Thus, Hedley Bull[12] pointed out that while peace between the superpowers depended on mutual deterrence, it was even more dependent on their capacity to prevent crises or manage them. Bruce Russett has argued, referring to the fact that no war broke out between the superpowers even at the height of the Cold War, that "such a non-event may be the result of successful deterrence. It might also, however, be the result of two states that were not expansionist but simply trying to protect existing spheres of influence."[13]

The dread of nuclear escalation motivated the development of the study of "crisis management," and later of a theory of "crisis prevention," and other measures to limit the risks of nuclear war.[14] The attention being devoted to this issue by decision-makers and scholars alike, bears witness to the widespread concern that nuclear deterrence of itself was insufficient to ensure the stability of relations between the two super-powers. Rather, nuclear deterrence was only one among the many elements that might have contributed to more stable relations and the prevention of war.

In summary, the nuclear balance of deterrence between the super-powers, otherwise termed "strategic stability," was the outcome of political, strategic, and technological factors. These factors must also function to preserve "crisis stability."[15]

The main factors that have served to prevent the outbreak of a third world war can be summarized as follows:

1 The shape of developments in the first stage of the conflict was determined by the peculiar historical circumstances of the two sides and their previous alliance.

2 Decision-makers on both sides remained rational[16] and cautious.

3 Over the years, the two sides underwent a process of "socialization" regarding the significance of nuclear weaponry. This process took place in a political and structural context that enabled the nuclearization of the conflict without nuclear confrontation. Furthermore, both sides generally perceived the other as rational and cautious. The rationality and cautiousness characterized both states even prior to the introduction of nuclear weapons.

4 U.S. and Soviet decision-makers have amassed considerable experience in the political dynamics of a nuclear environment, in particular in crisis situations.

5 Nuclear weapons were generally perceived by both sides as weapons of deterrence rather than of war fighting. However, there were marked distortions on this point, and these bore the potential for creating serious risks.

6 The sides did not adopt a doctrine of coercion (compellence), in which nuclear threats were used to obtain political ends that alter the status quo (although there have been exceptions to this rule too).

7 To a growing extent, efforts were invested in preventing the outbreak of serious international crises (of course, despite these efforts, a number of major crises have nevertheless occurred).

8 There existed no point of territorial contact between the two states.

9 It was only in one area, on the central front in Europe, that the ground forces of the two superpowers faced each other. But even in this case, the forces were deployed on foreign territory, and not on the homeland of either superpower.

10 Both sides possessed an assured second strike capacity, despite the persistence of irrational fears to the contrary.

11 Notwithstanding the U.S. advantage in this respect, both sides possessed highly advanced and sophisticated systems of command and control.

ANARCHY AND THE SECURITY DILEMMA IN SUPERPOWER RELATIONS

Beyond playing a central role in avoiding world war, have nuclear weapons affected other dimensions of international conflict and security? Two issues seem to be relevant here: first, the effect on the dimension of anarchy in global international relations; that is, the impact of nuclear weapons on the use of military force and its centrality. Second, the question of the contribution of nuclear weapons to the resolution of international conflicts.

The superpower conflict developed out of an entangled cluster of ideology and realpolitik. The situation of conflict was relieved at a certain point by detente, but, at the global level, détente has been far from uninterrupted, and, indeed, has suffered serious regressions. These regressions have occurred despite the large buildup of nuclear arms. Despite the massive accumulation of knowledge concerning the nature of nuclear weaponry, the weaponry itself does not appear to neutralize international conflict. There was no guarantee that following a certain dissolution of intensity, the conflict would not reemerge with renewed vigor. Its complete resolution appears to have been dependent more on political factors and basic changes in threat perceptions rather than on the existence of nuclear weapons.

In the foregoing survey of the historical background to Soviet–American relations in the period after World War II, a central focus of discussion was the role of nuclear weapons in preventing the outbreak of a third world war. Indeed, the conventional academic wisdom has been that nuclear weapons have forced the superpowers to behave with moderation and restraint, consequently reducing the element of anarchy in the international system.[17] However, it has also been argued, and recently more forcefully, that the order of things may have been precisely the opposite: it was the inherent cautious behavior of the superpowers that enabled nuclear deterrence to function effectively.[18] Moreover, there was an urgent need to work out additional rules of political behavior in order to forestall possible future crises.

The starting point of the latter argument is to view the behavior patterns of American and Soviet decision-makers as the independent variable, and the success of nuclear deterrence as a function of those behavior patterns. The conclusion is that the foundation of international stability was not the nuclear weapons system, but either the caution and moderation of the respective national leaderships, or their lack of motivation to further expand their spheres of influence.

In any case, and no matter what the relations of dependence between the two variables be, neither the restraint of the superpowers, nor nuclear weaponry have reduced the ubiquity of international anarchy. First, the superpowers' conflict persisted for more than forty years. Second, international disorder shows no sign of decline, in the sense that military force remains the final refuge of all states involved in conflict, whether the force be exerted by threat or by war. Third, military force remains a factor in many international situations short of war. Military threats used to be exchanged between the superpowers in crisis situations in which they were involved in direct conflict (as instanced in the Berlin, Cuba, and 1973 crises), and, more frequently, the superpowers threatened to intervene militarily in regional crises. Moreover, both superpowers have actually applied military force in various situations: the United States, in Korea and Vietnam, and the Soviet Union, against her satellites in 1953, 1956, and 1968, and more recently in Afghanistan. The superpowers also made widespread use of more limited force in a variety of situations. In short, military force has always been the ultimate tool of superpower influence in conflict and crisis. It should be added that 1988 witnessed the end of the actual use of force in several regional conflicts. This may have indicated the beginning of a certain change in international behavior, viz. the declining utility of the application of actual military force. However, the later eruption of widespread violence in Yugoslavia and Central Asia demonstrates the persistent salience of military force.

Similarly, the realization that nuclear weapons cannot realistically be used as a means for achieving political objectives had been shared by the Soviet political leadership (though possibly not by all the military leadership) since the late 1950s and early 1960s. Yet, the "new thinking" in Soviet foreign policy apparently derived not from that realization but from immense economic difficulties, coupled with the understanding that the perceived threat from the West was unfounded.

Finally, the well-known notion of the "security dilemma," and the further interesting addition of the "power dilemma"[19] gives succinct expression to a central feature of anarchy in international society. It is not only that no state can enjoy complete security. But a state's attempt to improve its security by strengthening its military power (either by engaging in an arms race or by forming a military alliance) inevitably draws counter reactions, with the final result being that that state's relative security is not improved, and may even be worsened. Underlying the security dilemma is the essential uncertainty characterizing the international system: states can never be sure of others' intentions. Under conditions of uncertainty, states aspire, albeit in vain, to improve their relative security.

It has been argued that nuclear weapons have solved the security dilemma. The argument runs as follows: first, nuclear weaponry is nonadditive, that is, beyond a certain point, an increase in the quantity and power of nuclear weapons does not increase their effectiveness. After all, if a state can destroy all an enemy's major social targets with a number of nuclear warheads, additional weaponry becomes strategically irrelevant and obtains decreasing marginal utility. Thus, such an arsenal would be an effective deterrent against an opponent's undertaking any military action endangering the deterrer. Second, the argument goes, in nuclear strategy, offense is decisively superior to defense. This is stated on the assumption that a certain percentage of an attacker's warheads will always penetrate the opponent's defense screens, even if the latter are very elaborate and advanced. The attacker therefore, always has an absolute advantage over the defender. The conclusion is then, that in order to attain an effective deterrent capability, it is unnecessary to accumulate offensive nuclear weapons beyond a certain minimum level. This approach is close to the strategy of "minimal deterrence." McGeorge Bundy has given expression to an extreme version of this school of thought:[20]

> In the real world of real political leaders—whether here or in the Soviet Union—a decision that would bring even one hydrogen bomb on one city of one's own country, would be recognized in advance as a catastrophic blunder. Ten bombs on ten cities would be a disaster beyond history; and a hundred bombs on a hundred cities are unthinkable.

Indeed, the pure logic of nuclear deterrence would suggest that "minimal deterrence," which is based on the assumed nonadditivity of nuclear weapons, should have been accepted by both superpowers as their preference strategy. This would presumably have resolved the security dilemma.

Let us now turn again to the relations between the superpowers, and examine the extent to which nuclear weapons in fact solved their security dilemma. In the context of their relations, it is patently obvious that the security dilemma has not been solved. Indeed, the paradox is that in the 1980s—up to the overall relaxation of relations between East and West which began in 1987–1988—it even intensified.

First, both superpowers had continued to develop their strategic nuclear capability. Due to the limitations imposed by SALT-II (which obtained even though the agreement had never been ratified) strategic developments have been qualitative. It would appear, however, that the superpowers could have attained stable mutual deterrence at far lower levels of armament. While the various proposals within the START framework, especially the 50 percent reduction plan (which in fact amounts to a smaller reduction), indicated a basic change in attitude, it is nevertheless instructive to consider the approach to nuclear weapons which had characterized perceptions about nuclear strategy until the late 1980s, and which had persisted for some time.

Two basic strategies characterized nuclear buildup and targeting in the United States in the 1970s and 1980s: Mutual Assured Destruction (MAD) and Flexible Response, which—according to one of its variants, the countervailing strategy—also comprises a substantial counter-force doctrine.[21] Neither represented a nonadditivity approach. A third approach—Strategic Defense—which is even more distant from nonadditivity, gained influence during the Reagan administration.

On the face of it, MAD could have been based on assumptions of nonadditivity, but, in fact, it goes far beyond it. According to this doctrine, in order to secure an optimal deterrence effect, the United States had to be capable—after absorbing a nuclear first strike—of destroying 20–25 percent of the Soviet population and approximately half of her industry. This destructive capacity required 200–300 EMT (Equivalent Megatonnage).[22] Such destruction, especially when concluded within a short time frame (within days, or even hours or minutes), was far beyond the level required to deter a rational Soviet leadership, and this held even without resort to Bundy's extremely limiting definition. In fact, however, by 1982 the United States already possessed 3,752 EMT,[23] while the Soviet Union had 6,100 EMT,[24] and it can be assumed that the quantities she required for the assured destruction of the United States parallel American requirements for the destruction of Soviet society.[25]

The continued accumulation of nuclear weapons by both sides had been repeatedly rationalized, not by disputing the logic of nonadditivity, but rather by the claimed need to maintain survivable offensive systems. This logic led to extremely conservative estimates of nuclear force size requirements. Critics of this approach pointed out that even if account is taken of the other side launching a disarming strike, both sides' arsenals exceeded MAD requirements several times over. For example, in 1982, on their submarine-launched systems (SLBM) alone, which is virtually invulnerable against a Soviet first strike, the Americans had 785 EMT. The remainder of her nuclear power is divided among intercontinental missiles and strategic bombers. The latter two categories are more vulnerable to a first strike, but it can be assumed that a significant proportion of them would have survived and been functional in the delivery of counterattacks. Various theses have been proposed to explain the exceptional quantities of nuclear arms possessed by the superpowers, and I dwell on certain of these arguments elsewhere in this book. But despite these explanations, the essential point remains that at least until START, the superpowers did not consider nuclear weapons to be nonadditive. On the contrary, they generally attached the utmost importance to the unabated expansion and improvement of their respective nuclear arsenals, in order to overcome the basic sense of mutual insecurity. Indeed, they have applied the logic of conventional arms to nuclear weapons.[26]

The signing of the START agreement suggests that this approach may have begun to change. However, it does not necessarily indicate a principle change in attitudes regarding the nonadditivity of nuclear weapons. It probably represents more a growing feeling that cuts in nuclear weapons would further improve the political climate. Needless to say, the process leading to START was affected by changes in the political context of the superpowers' relationship. In any case, the two sides insisted that the cuts must be symmetrical. This is a further indication that they continue to perceive of nuclear weapons as additive.

Another instance of continued insecurity, even under nuclear conditions, is the famous argument about the "window of vulnerability." With the passing of time, and the agreement to reduce offensive systems by 70 percent, this issue appears irrelevant. However, it is nevertheless worth recounting. Briefly, it was argued that the capability of the Soviet ICBM force far exceeded that of their U.S. counterparts, because a significant proportion of the Soviet ICBMs were equipped with multiple warheads. Even if only some of the Soviet missiles were launched, it was argued, they would be sufficient to destroy most or all of the American ICBMs. This relative vulnerability undermined the credibility of the overall American deterrence posture.

A more sophisticated argument was that were American deterrence based on a pure countervalue strategy, it would indeed remain credible. However, the United States also had to have a credible capability to launch a retaliatory strike against military nuclear targets in the Soviet Union. For this she had to depend primarily on the more accurate ICBM component of her force. Finally, the concern demonstrated in the "window of vulnerability" argument related to the urge to win in crisis situations. Hence, the well-known call for "escalation dominance."

However, counterarguments forwarded by various writers, invalidated the logic behind the "window of vulnerability" claim: at the outset, the "window of vulnerability" argument referred primarily to ICBMs, and only to a limited extent to submarines in port, and to bombers that might be caught in a surprise attack on the ground. Since the vast majority of American warheads are sea-launched, or carried by bombers, by the end of a first strike, the United States would be left with a massive number of warheads.

Second, due to the asymmetry between the deployment modes of the United States and the Soviet Union (the majority of the latter's warheads installed on ICBMs), following a Soviet first strike that used most of the ICBMs, the United States would have retained an even higher quantitative preponderance.

In addition, it is extremely doubtful whether a Soviet first strike could indeed have destroyed all American ICBMs. Problems of accuracy, weapon reliability, and the fracticide effect would in all likelihood have significantly reduced the impact of a Soviet first strike. Thus it was argued in 1976 by Steinbruner and Garwin (and this argument has not been effectively contradicted since then), that following a Soviet first strike of even optimal effectivity, a certain percentage of American ICBMs would have survived to participate in a counterstrike.[27] Finally, with the increase in the accuracy of the SLBM and airborne cruise missiles, the United States had built a credible second-strike capability against military targets throughout the USSR. This deals with the more sophisticated arguments of the "window of vulnerability."[28]

These are criticisms under which the "window of vulnerability" argument collapses. It can be stated with considerable certainty that both superpowers had, and would continue to have, a viable second-strike capacity, the destructive potential of which exceeds by far the more than ample requirements defined by the MAD doctrine. Nevertheless, and in this is lodged the paradox, the assumption of the nonadditivity of nuclear weapons was not accepted by the makers of strategic policy in the United States nor in the Soviet Union, and both superpowers were constantly engaged in activities intended to solve problems that would vanish were nuclear weapons perceived as nonadditive.[29]

Finally, the SDI program suggests that a policy of deterrence based on the superiority of offense over defense did not meet American security requirements as seen by American decision-makers, or at least some of them. SDI appears to have had two underlying aims: to achieve strategic superiority over the Soviet Union, and to preclude any chance of a Soviet first strike. These two aims are rooted in a conception of nuclear arms as both additive and usable.[30]

Moreover, it is not only that both the Soviet Union and the United States had serious doubts as to whether nuclear weapons have solved the security dilemma in the nuclear context itself, but in the conventional context these doubts were critical. Until the late 1980s, both superpowers were active in the expansion and improvement of their conventional forces. Conventional power was important to them in two related respects. First, both sides had to confront the direct threat of the opponent's conventional forces. This aspect was most clearly manifest in Europe.

Here, especially on the Central Front, both the Warsaw Pact and NATO indexed the increase of their own power against power increases introduced by the other.

The second reason for the strengthening of conventional forces related to the possibility of confrontation in the Third World, in which the superpowers might be directly opposed, or pitted against regional forces of various types. The two superpowers placed great emphasis on the maintenance of large and effective conventional forces as the means to the attainment of political, strategic, and military goals across the globe. In addition to being superpowers, they were also "global powers," able to deliver conventional forces throughout the world or to large portions of it (in that role the United States always had a marked advantage over the USSR).

Thus, the demands of global power—requiring military presence and mobility throughout the world—have a logic independent of nuclear weapons. Global power requires conventional force, and involves those engaged in its pursuit in the security dilemma. The increase of the opponent's conventional forces, and particularly of its capacity to intervene, cannot be left unmatched. And because the bipolar system comprised both nuclear and conventional aspects, security problems and fears in the conventional realm could have overflowed to the nuclear realm, and intensified the security dilemma that is in any case at work there.

In their unsuccessful struggles to overcome the security dilemma, the superpowers sought to increase their military power, by means of arms racing and military coalitions. The resort to alliance—NATO and the Warsaw Pact—was another manifestation of the persistence of prenuclear patterns of behavior.

Indeed, as Kenneth Waltz among others, has pointed out, the major function of these alliances was the provision of a nuclear deterrence umbrella by the nuclear patron. Nevertheless, the superpower also depended to an extent on the resources of its alliance partners, and would surely have viewed their loss with the utmost gravity. Moreover, the foundations of these alliances were rooted not in the logic of nuclear strategy, but in the dynamics of the prenuclear era. NATO was established out of fear of Soviet aggression, and the need for American support in the defense of Western Europe. Significantly, in 1949, that support was perceived as essentially conventional in nature. In the case of the Warsaw Pact, its founding relates more to traditional Russian imperial ambitions (together with the desire of the Communist elites in the satellite states to remain in power) than to the logic of nuclear strategy. Thus it is that traditional and prenuclear elements played a significant role in the foundation, and even in the continued existence of the alliances. In terms of nuclear strategy per se, both the Soviets and Americans could have forgone the alliances, and concentrated their efforts in the defense of "Fortress America" and "Fortress Russia." Nevertheless, such isolationist tendencies, which were reinforced by the logic of nuclear deterrence, were singularly rejected by both powers.

Beyond the political reasons outlined above, it has been argued that military alliances contributed to the security of the superpowers. In other words, even in the nuclear era, security was enhanced by the aggregation of military capabilities of various forms. The continued existence of military alliances during the Cold War, and the persistent attempts of both superpowers to act throughout the global international system, and to prevent the expansion of the other's influence, indicate that in this aspect of international behavior nuclear arms have not provided a solution to the security dilemma.

THE ANARCHICAL DIMENSION IN A NUCLEAR MIDDLE EAST[31]

One of the main conclusions emerging from the foregoing discussion is the persistence of a dimension of anarchy and of the security dilemma in the postwar gobal international system. (Even though these features of the superpowers' relationship have almost disappeared since the end of the Cold War, the reasons for this decline are political and perceptual, and in the case of the USSR economic as well, and are not the function of the continued existence of nuclear weapons.) It will be argued in the following that the same phenomena would probably recur in a nuclear Middle East. The starting point for the argument will be to note certain peculiarities of the Middle East regional subsystem, referred to at the beginning of the chapter, and which will have the effect (even more strongly than in the bipolar system) of preventing the erosion of anarchy and the security dilemma in a nuclearized Middle East.

In this respect, the four relevant characteristics are as follows: the persistence of interstate conflicts along several axes; the domestic instability of several states in the region; the social tension deriving from fundamentalist opposition to processes of modernization; and, finally, the multipolar structure of the system.

While these phenomena are widely known and recognized, an elaboration on certain aspects is nevertheless in place. First, however, it should be added that in the past few years, the intensity of some of these characteristics has been constrained by various developments and new perceptions. I shall note these changes throughout the discussion. It remains to be seen whether these constraints will bring about entirely new patterns of behavior.

The persistence of interstate conflict in the Middle East results from the existence of a multitude of states in the region, and from the pursuit by some of an activist foreign policy aspiring to the expansion of political and military influence. Later in this chapter we will return to the issue of coalitions in the Arab world, and to the theme of "continuity" in international systems. For the moment suffice it to note that interstate conflicts are a fundamental characteristic of the modern Middle East system. It is difficult to conceive of the decline, let alone the dissolution, of such conflicts in a nuclear environment. These conflicts are rooted in the sharp division of political interests. They are sometimes exacerbated by ideological differences (though the importance of the latter is generally subordinate to the competition for positions of influence).

As mentioned above, of late there has been readiness on the part of certain actors in the Middle East to moderate their conflicts. Egypt and Israel signed a peace treaty, and for quite some time Jordan has been ready to reach a peaceful understanding with Israel. Syria has also moved twoard a moderate posture. Moreover, Egypt is less affirmative in her search for influence in the Arab world. Indeed, the decline of Pan-Arabism has somewhat blunted the competition for influence by all the main Arab actors. The emergence of a new moderate Arab bloc may also signify a change in traditional patterns of conflict.

Another source of conflict and instability in the Middle East are the deep-seated tensions opposing the idea of the "nation-state" or the "territorial-state." These tensions pull in two opposing directions: on the one hand, the continued prominence of ethnic and religious conflicts within the territorial-state, while on the other, trends toward Pan-Islamic and Pan-Arabic unity. In the long view, it would seem that the territorial-state, as a pattern of political relations between the individual and the collective in which he lives, has the upper hand over these negating tendencies. However, in some states, such as Lebanon (which disintegrated due to internal divisions), Syria, and Iraq, the territorial-state is prone to such pressures, especially to internal ethnic and religious divisions. An important caveat is in place here. In both Syria and Iraq, the regimes succeeded in overcoming all opposition and in mobilizing a degree of support. Indeed, as the Iran–Iraq war has demonstrated, the division between Sunni and Shiite in Iraq was maintained at a low level, and the Shiites were ready to participate in a war against the Shiite Iranians. Loyalty to Iraq was clearly more important than adherence to their particular religious orientation. The situation was different in the case of a large part of the Kurdish community, which continued to oppose the Baghdad regime. (The situation in Iraq in the aftermath of the Gulf War is still unclear, but it appears that the opposition to the Baghdad regime is much stronger in the Kurdish area than it is among the Shiites.)

Internal divisions are at play in Jordan too, namely between "Jordanian" and "Palestinian" elements, although the intensity of this conflict has faded considerably over the years, and the Hashemite regime succeeded in achieving wide support. Under such conditions, enemy states might well be tempted to exploit these internal conflicts, for political gain. In other words, these internal conflicts have their negative upshot on the arena of interstate conflict. It can be assumed that until the eventual installment of the nation-state as the dominant pattern of internal political relations throughout the Middle East (and the present writer tends to the view that there is an accelerated trend in this direction) internal societal divisions may continue to exacerbate the level of interstate conflict in the region.

The internal division afflicting various Middle Eastern societies is a prime cause of the instability in those states, and demands that the ruling establishments raise the profile of their military power, as a tool for the maintenance of internal order. These internal divisions also heighten the fears of the ruling elites against the possibility of attempts to undermine the regime by a combination of internal and external pressures. At this point the salience of military regimes in the region enters the picture. Such regimes tend, unless severely constrained, to continually strengthen the military, which comprises their political constituency. The constant inflow of funds to the military, some of which are used for the purchase of modern weapon systems, accelerates the regional arms race. The security dilemma for all states in the region is thereby intensified.

The internal social pressures, and the fundamentalist reaction to processes of modernization, are social forces that are insensitive to the effects of nuclear weapons. First, the extreme reaction toward modernization apparent in various states in the Third World and the Middle East, is a force with a domestic social dynamic. As such, the logic of nuclear strategy, and the recognition of the costs deriving from interstate anarchy under nuclear conditions, are singularly irrelevant. The Khomeini revolution, for example, would have erupted even had Iran, or its regional opponents, possessed nuclear weapons. The prevention of such revolutions may result from the implementation of certain social policies and/or the effective management of internal security. Nuclear weaponry is in this respect irrelevant. Thus, to the extent that there develops a violent fundamentalist reaction to processes of modernization, the entire nuclear issue will probably disappear from the domestic political agenda.

But if the revolution does take place, and succeeds, the new regimes such as those of Khomeini and Ghaddafi tend, at least in their initial stages, to export the revolution. The inevitable result is interstate conflict and violence. An instructive example is Ghaddafi's activities against Chad, Sudan, and Egypt, and his support for various terrorist organizations. An even more extreme case was Khomeini's insistence on continuing the Iran–Iraq war, while imposing impossible conditions for its conclusion.

As a qualification to the above, it should be noted that extreme Muslim fundamentalism has nowhere become the decisive determinant of foreign policy when it stands in direct opposition to the state's essential interests.

102

The primary thrust of Libyan and Iranian foreign policies continues to be the extension of political influence. In the case of Iran, for instance, the Gulf War was initiated by Iraq. Furthermore, the regime of the Shah was itself consistent in the pursuit of political influence, and a clash with Iraq had been a possibility for many years.

However, religious fundamentalism does have various detrimental effects on regional stability: first, during the revolutionary period itself and in the first stage of the new regime, there is a tendency for revolutionary fever to spread to neighboring states, and thereby constituting the basis for international conflict; second, fundamentalism infuses a state's political interests with a dimension of messianic righteousness, and provides impetus to the pursuit of an activist and sometimes even aggressive foreign policy; and third, extremist revolutionary regimes representing messianic ideologies tend to act in accordance with their ideals, while remaining largely inert to the cost of their implementation. These regimes are ready to bear the burden of costly actions that further the interests of the revolution and the state. Thus, even if the revolutionary regime essentially continues the aggressive and the ambitious foreign policy of its non-revolutionary predecessor, it will do so with a readiness to pay a far higher price for the attainment of policy goals.

It would seem, then, that fundamentalist trends contribute to the *degree* of anarchy characterizing the system of interstate relations in the Middle East. Due to their readiness to pay high costs for the attainment of their objectives, at least in the initial stages of the regime, it would appear that their sensitivity to nuclear threats would be relatively low.

If we turn to the two main characteristics of international anarchy, viz. the continuation of interstate conflicts and the centrality of the military dimension, and drawing on the superpowers' experience, it appears unlikely that nuclear weapons could moderate interstate anarchy in the Middle East. They will probably be inconsequential in terms of the resolution of conflicts and the advancement of processes of political compromise: the various political conflicts will remain rooted in the dynamics of activist foreign policies and internal tensions so salient in the region. Second, military force – both its threat and its use – will probably continue to play a central role in the regional system. Basic changes in this pattern of behavior will arise, not from nuclearization, but from other developments in the political and strategic realms (for a detailed account see Chapter 7). Indeed, as mentioned, we may be on the verge of certain such developments, but it is as yet unclear to what extent they may succeed.

A claim stronger than the one outlined above has also been forwarded, namely, that the influence of nuclear weapons, rather than moderating conflicts, is liable to *exacerbate* regional political relations.[32] For the most part, there would appear to be no logical substance to this argument, with but one exception: namely, there would be destabilizing effects were decision-makers to become convinced that nuclear weapons constitute a viable alternative to efforts to obtain political compromises intended to lower the profile of interstate conflict.

In any case, there are additional reasons supporting the view that anarchy and the derivative security dilemma will persist even in a nuclearized Middle East. Once again, the basis for the argument is a comparison with the system of relations between the superpowers. First, nuclear weapons were introduced to the global system toward the end of World War II against the historical background of an alliance between the would-be nuclear opponents. This would be far from the case if and when nuclear weapons were to proliferate in the Middle East. Similarly, the proliferation of nuclear weapons in the Middle East would not be juxtaposed with any war as awesomely destructive as World War II, a war that substantially reduced the readiness to activate military force in another large-scale war. Finally, in the wake of World War II, the United States and the Soviet Union obtained major political gains, and became the two leading powers in the world. These gains also reduced their readiness to become involved in another war. It is unlikely that such an historical constellation will exist in a nuclear Middle East.

Similarly, most of the Middle Eastern states that are presently engaged in conflict, are territorially contiguous and are thereby prone to direct friction. This is the case for the Arab–Israeli conflict, for Iraqi relations with Syria and Iran, and for Libyan relations with Egypt and the Sudan. The geographical disposition of these conflicts underpins anarchy, typically manifest in sub-war violence. The latter carries with it the constant potential for escalation.

Finally, the conflicts are marked by mutual claims on the national territory of the opponent, as for example between Israel and Syria and between Iran and Iraq, and not just on the territory of an alliance partner. All these factors are in direct contrast to the U.S. Soviet relationship.

A NUCLEAR MIDDLE EAST: DETERRENCE, WARFIGHTING, AND POLITICAL COERCION

A major issue attending the nature of nuclear weaponry is its role either as a tool of deterrence, or as an effective military instrument in the actual waging of war. Part of the analysis of this issue is integrally related to the problem of interstate anarchy in a nuclear Middle East, which was the focus of the preceding discussion.

We have noted previously that the perception of nuclear weapons as an instrument of deterrence developed only gradually, and also, that it is this notion that underpined the stability of the central nuclear balance. There are those that dispute this perception, and their arguments will serve as the starting point for our discussion. Nuclear strategies emphasizing deterrence are opposed by "warfighting" approaches, according to which nuclear weapons are useful instruments of war, for securing political, strategic and military objectives apart from deterrence.

In addition there is the approach which holds that nuclear weapons can serve as a tool for the implementation of political goals by means of coercive threat (compellence) or as an effective instrument of political pressure (apart from deterrence) in international crises. The warfighting approach has three variants: first the use of tactical nuclear weapons on the battlefield of the future; second, the initiation of counterforce strikes against the enemy's nuclear weapons systems, in order to neutralize its nuclear power; finally, the most extreme possibility, their use for the destruction of the enemy's society in a first strike, or alternatively, to impose immense damage in the hope of obtaining a surrender. Needless to say, both the use of battlefield weapons and of counterforce strategies are also justified as building blocks in a comprehensive deterrence strategy. This is the origin of the concept of "warfighting-deterrence." Be that as it may, both approaches nevertheless involve pure warfighting elements.

This warfare orientation to nuclear weapons might derive from a number of different sources: the influence of a prenuclear politico-strategic tradition; misunderstanding of the nature of nuclear weapons; structural features of the interstate system; and strategic, ideological-cultural or technological factors.

We will examine here the factors behind the adoption of concepts of political compellence and some aspects of warfighting approaches in a nuclear Middle East, and this in the light shed by the U.S.–Soviet experience. The questions of tactical nuclear weapons and doctrines of a counterforce first strike are addressed in Chapter 5.

Political Coercion using Nuclear Weapons in Relations between the Superpowers: A Brief Introductory Comment

At the outset it must be recalled that in the U.S.–Soviet context, the relationship between nuclear weapons and political coercion was complex and has not received conclusive exposition. The issue can be divided into two separate questions. First, to what extent did nuclear weapons serve as an effective instrument for the expansion of political influence, by means of direct threats? Second, what did the nuclear weapons contribute to the management of crises? Did nuclear threats affect the outcome of crises? And a closely related question: Can nuclear superiority decide the way in which crises are settled?

It is interesting to note that during the period in which the United States held a monopoly on nuclear power (in the latter half of the 1940s), no use was made of nuclear weapons for purposes of political coercion.

The reasons for this are specific to that period, and it is not clear whether, in the same circumstances today, the United States would behave with the same restraint. The Cold War began to unfold only in 1947–1948, just prior to the first Soviet nuclear test in 1949. Moreover, and this would seem to be the main reason, a nuclear "consciousness" was as yet underdeveloped. Nuclear weapons were not perceived as effecting a critical qualitative change in the balance of military power. Against the American nuclear monopoly loomed the imposing Soviet advantage in conventional force in Europe. These two factors were seen as balancing each other out.

Furthermore, had a world war broken out as a result of American nuclear coercive threats, Europe would have been exposed to the immediate threat of a Soviet invasion. This danger acted as a constraint on the American readiness to make political use of nuclear threats. In parenthesis note Michael Mandelbaum's[33] argument that had such a war broken out, it would most likely have resulted in a victory for the West. Even without nuclear weapons, the overall military, economic, and technological power of the West, since 1945 exceeded that of the Soviet Union. He argues that it is this *overall* power that would have determined the result of the war.

Since the attainment by both sides of a nuclear capacity, there were a number of attempts to apply political coercion (in contrast to deterrence) by means of nuclear threats, but the precise characteristics of the circumstances and results of these incidents are yet to be fully clarified.[34] Altogether it appears that nuclear weapons are poor instruments for securing success in exercises of political compellence. In the first place, because in any case it is much more difficult to succeed in compellence (as against deterrence),[35] and with nuclear weapons in particular compellence successes are very difficult to attain.

In the mid-1980s, the question was framed with greater clarity: in an international crisis situation, can a nuclear threat render political dividends? This gives rise to an important sub-question, which is framed within the debate on the doctrine of "escalation dominance," can a side possessing a nuclear advantage earn political benefits from this advantage in a crisis? Opinion on these questions is divided, but recent historical experience seems to indicate that nuclear asymmetry does not translate into political rewards.[36] However, this is rarely the view of national decision-makers. Because they tend to apply the logic of conventional arms to nuclear weapons, they generally consider nuclear asymmetry, a factor in determining the political outcome of a crisis. Using the same logic, decision-makers also tend to see nuclear weapons as effective instruments of political influence or blackmail. A clear expression of such patterns of strategic thinking was the reaction of the political establishments in Europe following the deployment of the Soviet SS–20 missiles in the 1970s. Fears reverberated throughout Europe that the change in the regional strategic balance would lead to the imposition of Soviet political pressure on Western Europe.

Let us now summarize the arguments offered so far. After more than 40 years of "living with the bomb," and despite the accumulation of knowledge as to its political and strategic characteristics, there still exists wide differences of opinion regarding its possible use. The "pure" theory of deterrence (based on the absolute advantage of offense over defense) emphasizes that in the case of two nuclear powers, the existence of a second strike capacity, able to destroy the infrastructure and population of the opponent (or even most of it – and there are those that talk in terms of relatively small percentages), is sufficient to deter a national leader from creating a war situation, or from using nuclear weapons for purposes other than deterrence.

One would have expected the superpowers to behave in accordance with such patent logic. And, indeed, the history of the nuclear era demonstrates that this was the objective outcome of superpower interactions. But this was not necessarily how events and potential possibilities were perceived by leaders and strategists. The two superpowers pursued nuclear acquisition programs far beyond the levels required for deterrence. Furthermore, there were schools of thought in both states that viewed a quantative and qualitative strategic advantage as an effective instrument in obtaining the favorable resolution of political crises. That is, the defenders of such a line would have been ready to exploit their nuclear strategic advantage, to the extent that it exists, in order to compel the resolution of international crises in accordance with that state's particular interests. It would seem that until the period of the Reagan administration, such a school of thought was stronger in the Soviet Union than in the United States. In the Soviet Union—that is, among certain elements within the political-military establishment—nuclear weapons were conceived of as an integral part of overall military power, and it is the latter, as an entirety, that was regarded as a usable threat for the achievement of political goals. This position probably lost much of its influence in the last years of the USSR.[37]

By way of digression, it might be added that the echo of such thinking (albeit from a diametrically opposite point of view) was audible in the opposing school, that can be referred to as "liberal," and which has embraced the fundamental assumptions of a deterrence orientation. Among the liberals, there has been a certain parallelism between hawkish views and the arguments of those that support the adoption of a strategy that gave greater emphasis to conventional NATO forces in Europe. The basis of this view is that the situation in which military force is founded on nuclear weapons is inherently dangerous, and is an ineffective guarantee of Western security. Furthermore, the danger of nuclear war is only

107

exacerbated by the acceleration of the nuclear arms race. There were even references to the possibility that European security could not depend on the American nuclear umbrella (that is, on the effective stability of nuclear deterrence) and thus, new ways needed to be found to defend the West.[38] It goes hardly without saying that the demise of the Soviet Union and changes in Eastern Europe have made this debate quite obsolete.

This conclusion is in direct contradiction to the "hawks." However, the underlying assumption—the instability of nuclear deterrence in a crisis— is similar to the hawkish assumptions mentioned above. The two schools share the claim that in a crisis situation, nuclear weapons do not constitute an effective or sufficient deterrent. It follows from this that in times of crisis, it would, in principle, be possible to use an advantage in nuclear power in order to obtain political ends. The "hawks" favored this idea because they called for nuclear supremacy. The "liberals" feared that this was actually the case and that one of the sides might actually use nuclear weapons.

Political Coercion in a Nuclear Middle East

In the modern Middle East system, there have been six major wars between Israel and the Arab states in a period of 44 years, and continual violence at the sub-war level. The Arab states have also engaged in a number of interstate wars, and some have been active in supporting violence in other states.

It seems reasonable to assume that this long tradition of war and violence has created certain patterns of thought and behavior among the political and military leaderships of both sides, and has influenced the psychological environment of their decision-makers. Let us begin with the Israeli side. As we noted in a preceding chapter, deterrence was at various times an important dimension of Israeli political and strategic doctrine. However, the deterrence component of conventional strategy rested on notions of denial capability, which was linked to the capacity to defeat challengers. The latter, in fact, has dominated Israeli thinking at the operational level. The deterrence-based approach has been more clearly manifest at the political-strategic, rather than the operational level. However, even at the political-strategic level, a warfare orientation has at times been dominant, such as in the years 1953–1956, in 1970 (at the time of the deep penetration bombing of Egypt), and never more clearly than in 1981–1982. There exists then, a reasonable chance that under some circumstances the conception in Israel of nuclear arms as essentially weapons of deterrence, might be distorted. The danger is that nuclear weapons will be considered effective not only for deterrence, but also in other contexts. For example, they might be viewed as effective in the enforcement of political goals.

In this respect, it should be added that among the arguments raised by Israeli commentators and observers during the mid-1960s, was the view that nuclear weapons might be effective tools of political coercion.[39] It was argued, for example, that nuclear arms could galvanize Israeli demands that the Arabs agree to accept the current status quo, that is, to accept the current borders and to sign a peace treaty. Related ideas, in a different form, appeared in commentary on Sadat's peace initiative (see Chapter 2).

The idea that nuclear weapons are an effective instrument of political coercion, and not just of deterrence, appeared in Israel in two forms. As noted above, its initial appearance was as a prescription for foreign policy. Later it appeared as a retrospective explanation of Egyptian and general Arab behavior. Such thinking is not foreign to part of the Israeli political elite. And it is possible that this view would be influential were Israel to adopt an open nuclear doctrine. Decision-makers whose notions on the use of military force are free of any sophisticated constraints, are likely to project such views onto nuclear weapons.

We will turn our attention now to the political and strategic behavior of the Arab states. It has already been noted that in their pursuit of political influence, the central Arab states used to demonstrate little hesitation in applying military force, either by threat or by its actual use. In both cases, the intention is the coercive procurement of political goals. And of this there are numerous examples. In the last decade, we can count the use of Libyan forces against Chad and Sudan, and the maneuvers of Libyan and Egyptian forces, and the clashes between them. Similarly, there has been a series of military threats and clashes between North and South Yemen, and between South Yemen and Saudi Arabia. The Iran–Iraq war was a destabilizing factor in the Persian Gulf region for almost a decade. Syrian activity in Lebanon, the Syrian threats against Jordan (for example, toward the end of 1980), and the mutual exchange of threats between Iraq and Syria, characterize political relations in the "fertile crescent." Finally, and most glaringly, the invasion of Kuwait again demonstrated the same pattern. And all this violent activity follows in the wake of the difficult and erosive war in 1973 between the Arab states and Israel. Thus it seems that the Middle East system operates according to principles, among which the use of military force ranks highly. To the extent that a more constrained approach toward force might emerge, it is likely that the *actual* use of force would diminish while the *threat* to use force would probably persist as an important instrument of policy.

The system of relations among Arab states has been characterized by a pattern of internal competition, in which each of the central states has sought the expansion of its relative political influence, and up to the 1970s even to the point of obtaining regional hegemony. While Egypt withdrew from this competition in the late 1970s, Syria and Iraq have persisted in their competitive efforts. It is likely (though admittedly not certain) that a similar trend will continue in the future. If this happens in a nuclear environment, the Arab states will be confronted by a serious dilemma. The nuclear force that some of them will possess will be perceived by them, for at least some substantial period, as an instrument of traditional power, and as such, of utility in the attainment of political ends. Furthermore, the development (or purchase) of nuclear weapons and delivery systems, together with their supervision and control (even of a primitive and limited nature), will require the investment of considerable financial and non-financial resources. It is difficult to believe that in the wake of such an enormous outlay, the political leaderships will refrain from reaping the political harvest made available by the newly acquired military force. The political activism in which they excel, furnishes the assumption that these investments will be able to obtain political returns. For example, Iraqi statements concerning her early and late nuclear projects, are indicative of the apparent link between these projects and her view of her central role in the Arab world and in the Middle East, and of the importance of the projects in extending Iraqi political influence.

Generally speaking there are a number of different, conflicting norms, that exist in the Middle East in parallel. There are "anarchical" approaches which emphasize that military force is a legitimate instrument in interstate relations. Alongside this attitude account must also be given of various behavior patterns imposing constraints on the preparedness to use military power. However, the preparedness to accept restraints on the *actual* use of military force, does not necessarily lower the preparedness to apply military *threats* for political ends. This tendency may well spill over into the nuclear arena.

As we stated earlier, the patterns of thought and behavior in the Middle East are rooted in the conception of military power as a legitimate instrument in the attainment of political ends. To the extent that the political elites undergo a process of "nuclear socialization" (assuming the best case) they will almost certainly learn from the Soviet–American situation. In this respect, they will discover that one of the prevalent views is that nuclear weapons are an instrument with which political gains can be made. This conception will certainly be more easily learnt than notions involving limitations on the utility of nuclear weapons beyond deterrence.

On this point two additional issues need to be addressed. The first relates to the extent of the centrality of nuclear weapons in the makeup of the state's overall military forces. In a nuclear Middle East there will be an extended period in which the nuclear states will possess only a limited quantity of nuclear warheads. Their main power will continue to be comprised of conventional forces. Beyond sheer inertia (which counts), this will most probably be the case also because many of the threats these states face could be deterred credibly or defeated primarily by conventional arms. Indeed, this has been the experience of the super-powers when faced with the spectrum of real threat. Those responsible for the conventional forces can be expected to have considerable influence on the handling of political and strategic issues. They will probably tend to act in accordance with traditional patterns of military thought, with the result that they will either diminish the importance of nuclear weapons or, alternatively, attribute them the politico-strategic characteristics of conventional weaponry. In other words, they are unlikely to recognize the radical change in the relationship between military power and the attainment of political ends.

Another problem relates to the heterogeneity of the Middle East. As we have noted, were nuclear weapons to proliferate in the region, it is likely that only a few states would obtain them, and at different times. It seems probable that for a lengthy period, nuclear states will exist alongside nonnuclear states. What would be the impact of such a regional configuration on the relationship between military power and political goals? It seems improbable that the logic of pure nuclear deterrence would dominate. That is, the thought and behavior patterns of decision-makers would be far more complex than those typical of relations between the superpowers. This has two aspects. First, in failing to grasp the realities of nuclear logic, states with only conventional forces will consider themselves free to behave in accordance with traditional patterns. Second, the nuclear states will be highly motivated to prove that nuclear weapons impose no constraints on their political and strategic behavior: one, because they are operating in a region which is not purely nuclear, and two, because they will be subject to the strong temptation to use nuclear threats against nonnuclear states. In both these respects, their behavior would probably differ from that of the superpowers. The latter are constrained by the logic of bipolar nuclear deterrence. Their political gains and losses usually affect faraway regions. They also fear that nuclear threats for political gains may set dangerous precedents for the adversary and also for potential nuclear powers. All these factors would be far less salient when a nuclear Middle Eastern power tries to rectify a political grievance against a nonnuclear regional opponent.

Furthermore, as was stated earlier, great effort and cost will be involved in obtaining nuclear weapons. Once obtained, those decision-makers that had supported the project, are likely to consider the investment wasted if conventional use cannot be made of the weapons acquired at such expense. The learning of restraint in this respect threatens to be a long and exhausting process. The conceptual gap that must be bridged is broad: what must be unlearnt is not only the traditional idea of fighting war to obtain political goals, but even to the very *threat* to do so.

To all this must be added the suspicions of the other side's intentions. Even were the political leadership of one of the nuclear states convinced that nuclear weapons are unusable as tools of political coercion or in political crises, there would remain an underlying fear that the other side thinks differently.

What are the risks involved in issuing coercive nuclear threats? Let us first consider the case of threats against a state possessing only conventional weapons. If the threatened state were to concede, a dangerous precedent would be created that may have global systemic implications. Nuclear weapons would be perceived of as effective instruments of political coercion, and their use in this respect would become much more acceptable. However, at some point, the demands made of a state will be considered excessive, and it will refuse to concede. In such circumstances, the motivation to deliver a nuclear strike will be heightened, as the state issuing the threat seeks to prove its credibility. The nuclear threshold would be dangerously lowered.

We might contemplate an alternative scenario, more complex, but perhaps more realistic. It seems unlikely that a crisis involving nuclear threats against a conventionally armed state would remain isolated from the regional environment, but would probably soon involve other states, among them regional nuclear states. The state issuing the threat would then confront a difficult dilemma: to refrain from the use of nuclear weapons would not only undermine her credibility, but would also represent a failure to obtain the object of her political desire. But to implement the threat would require a dangerous escalation (this issue will also be analyzed further in the discussion of coalitions in the Middle East).

To state it differently: the very communication of a coercive nuclear threat creates the risk that in certain circumstances the state issuing the threat might be willing to exercise it. If this is the case, the nuclear "taboo" (to use the concept coined by Raymond Aron), would be infringed and the nuclear threshold significantly lowered. In this context, mention should be made of the psychological impact of infringing this taboo. Its first effects will be felt in the Middle East, but it will also undoubtedly be of influence throughout the international system. But whatever the validity of this scenario, the main point of the argument remains: in a heterogeneous system (involving both nuclear ad conventional powers) the preparedness to use nuclear weapons as an instrument of political enforcement will be relatively high. Such preparedness for nuclear action is liable to create dangerous risks.

Another aspect that must be added at this point relates to the tendency of the political-military establishments to consider military force in terms of waging war, rather than in terms of deterrence. As was described in Chapter 2, despite the dominance of a deterrence orientation, that was prominent in military policy in 1957–1967, and to varying degrees both before and after this period, Israel tended to view war fighting as the primary function of military power. It would seen that this concept is at least as salient among some, though not all, the Arab military establishments. Add to this the longstanding tradition of war in the Middle East, and especially in the last 40 years, and the clear impression is the emphasis on warfighting. The tentative conclusion is then that nuclear weapons may come to be perceived as an integral part of conventional inventories.

Feldman[40] has argued that the superpowers became nuclear after participation in two world wars, but nevertheless adopted deterrence strategies. From this he concludes that a similar development is possible in the Middle East. However, as we have noted previously, the introduction of nuclear weapons to the global system occurred in an historical context vastly different from the context that will characterize a parallel event in the Middle East.

The historical context for the superpowers comprised a recent alliance (during World War II); the awesome destruction of the war; major political dividends accruing to both powers as a result of the war; and finally, the absence of shared borders and the consequent reduction in felt threat. Another point important to mention in this respect is that from the outset the conflict was perceived as political rather than military, and the claims of both sides against the other related to third parties, such as the pursuit of influence in Europe, or the prevention of the other's obtaining influence.

Furthermore, references to various aspects of warfighting occur frequently in various schools of thought on nuclear strategy, and this despite years of "nuclear socialization" among the political elites and governmental establishment in both the West and East, during which period one might have expected all references to non-deterrence functions of nuclear weapons to disappear. Similarly, as was mentioned earlier, both sides suspect the other of holding notions of the warfighting functions of nuclear weapons.

Finally, it is possible that over the years there will develop in some of the states in the Middle East, a more sophisticated understanding of the role of nuclear weapons, and that their overriding aim will become strictly deterrent. However, in a confrontation between two nuclear states, it takes only one of the sides to adopt a warfighting-oriented nuclear strategy, for the rules of the game between the two sides to undergo a radical change. A stable nuclear deterrence between two sides is possible only when both sides are ready to play according to the rules of deterrence.

A SECOND-STRIKE CAPABILITY

The existence of a second-strike capability had long been recognized as essential to the maintenance of a stable balance of deterrence. We have noted in the foregoing that a stable nuclear balance is dependent, according to one mainstream approach to nuclear strategy, on the absolute

113

superiority of offense over defense, and on a "countervalue" targeting strategy. Even other contending schools of thought, viz. those that recommend the adoption of various "counterforce" strategies, nonetheless accept the centrality of these two notions.

This approach requires constant attention to the survivability of launch facilities. The success of an attack against the opponent's nuclear forces, is liable to result in the inability of the attacked side to launch a counterattack. The attacked side will be left vulnerable and indefensible against any additional nuclear or conventional attack and, at the least, will be exposed to nuclear threats.

When side A develops the capability of destroying, in a first strike, side B's nuclear systems, there arise two sets of dangers. First, side A will be strongly motivated to undertake such an attack, since it would earn thereby a decisive advantage. Second, side B is liable to estimate that side A will indeed launch that first strike. Thus side B will urgently seek to launch the first strike in order to neutralize the potential damage to the extent possible.

Shai Feldman[41] has listed the factors contributing to the establishment of a second-strike capability: variety of delivery systems; hardened launching facilities; mobility of launching systems; diffusion of launching systems; camouflage and secrecy of launching installations. Indeed, the superpowers have resorted to all above techniques in order to ensure the protection of their second-strike capability.

In the literature on nuclear proliferation in the Middle East, two different positions have been expounded on the issue of the second-strike capacity. According to the first of these views, the development of an advanced and sophisticated second-strike capacity is essential to the maintenance of a stable regional balance. In the absence of such a capacity, there emerges the danger that out of fear of an enemy's first strike, the sides might be tempted to strike first themselves. It is highly unlikely, or perhaps even impossible, that the states of the region could attain second strike forces.

According to the second view, in the Middle East, in contrast to the superpower context, it is unnecessary for states to develop a second-strike capacity in order that the deterrence balance be stable. At the most, a primitive second-strike force is all that is required, and the establishment of such a force ought not to represent any major barrier. I would, however, argue for a third view, which stakes out a middle path. Thus, while a second strike capacity is essential for the region, it need not be very elaborate and sophisticated. Nevertheless, certain critical points— especially relating to problems of command and control—may demand considerable effort in order to be met.

It is reasonable to assume that several Middle East countries possess the potential for the development of differentiated launching systems, and for their diffused deployment. These factors limit the certainty that an enemy's first strike will be decisive. There are, however, three principal difficulties here. First, the effort requires expenditures on a large scale, and is liable to adversely affect other aspects of the defense budget. It is possible that due to budget and technological constraints, an asymmetry might develop in the Middle East in terms of second-strike capacities. Second, there will likely be serious difficulties in maintaining adequate command and control over the decision-making process. These latter problems derive not from lack of nuclear hardware, but from problems inherent in command and control systems in the Middle East. And third, it is also possible that among some of the states likely to be nuclear, it may take some time before the significance and implications of a second-strike capacity are fully grasped. A situation in which several states in the region are without a second-strike capacity, is likely to encourage fear and provoke instability. Similar effects are likely to emerge from the hardware asymmetries mentioned above. We will expand on this cluster of issues in the paragraphs to follow.

The first focus of the discussion will be the delivery systems currently existent in the Middle East. All the central states are already equipped with systems that are potentially capable of delivering nuclear weapons. The main delivery system currently available to them is combat airplanes suitable for the carrying of nuclear weapons (in certain cases, changes would be required in the configuration of the external loading mechanisms on the aircraft). Among the planes included in this category are the F–15, F–16, Phantoms, Mirage F–1, SU–20, SU–24, Mig 23, and, according to non-Israeli sources, also the Israeli Kfir.[42]

The main problem with these delivery systems is that all the aircraft are located in the vicinity of airfields that may be fully or partly vulnerable to air strikes, or to nuclear and even conventional missiles. Therefore, they cannot constitute a reliable second strike capability.

The proliferation of surface-to-surface missiles in the Middle East in the past few years creates several options for improvement in terms of second-strike capabilities. Missile proliferation also complicates calculations concerning the possibilities of successful first strikes. Israel is reported internationally to be testing a version of surface-to-surface missiles with ultimate range of up to 1,500 km. According to international reports, this missile may be capable of carrying a nuclear warhead. Syria has two categories of missiles which are capable of carrying nuclear warheads (although of course they are at present armed with conventional warheads): SS–21 and *Scud* B. Only the first has a range covering most of Israel. Egypt has the *Scud* B (again only with conventional warheads) but, because of the demilitarization of the Sinai, its range covers only about half of Israel. Iraq has equipped herself with the *Scud* B, and doubled its range. With the extended range it could cover all of

115

Israel. Whether the new configuration of the Iraqi *Scud* B enables a nuclear warhead to be fitted is not clear. Iraq has had (until the Gulf War) a relatively large stockpile of missiles with ranges of up to 600 kms. Saudi Arabia has purchased from China the CSSS–2 missiles (again without nuclear warheads) with a range of 3,000 km. Finally, Iran is negotiating with North Korea the purchase of long range missiles.

It can be assumed that those states that "go nuclear," will attempt to expand and improve their second-strike forces. Taking account of the conditions affecting the use of weapons systems in the Middle East, there are a number of options that might be pursued. First, further expansion of the inventories of surface-to-surface missiles and a hardening of the missile silos. This task, however, requires enormous financial resources. Another possibility is the use of Vertical Take Off aircraft (VTOL) that do not require airfields, and which can be deployed at various points within the nuclear states.

This issue involves a number of associated problems relevant to technological developments and their introduction to the Middle East. Shai Feldman has argued that Israel, for example, can adopt Bernard Brodie's blueprint list for the ordering of priorities for the hardening of launch facilities. The blueprint requires, for instance, that a small number of launch facilities be hardened at any cost. It is intended that those facilities would survive any attack. The reasonable chance of their survival would have a deterrent effect on any party considering a first strike. This idea is indeed worth consideration.[43]

Clearly, the most effective means of ensuing a second-strike capacity is the deployment of submarines carrying nuclear missiles. This would of course involve a massive investment of financial and technological resources (unless the submarines were supplied directly by the nuclear powers, in which case the outlay would become either political or financial). Finally, there is the possibility of basing short-range missiles with nuclear warheads on missile boats operating in the Mediterranean Sea.

A consideration of these alternatives suggests that the last-mentioned is the most acceptable in terms of price. All states in the region are already equipped with missile boats deploying conventional missiles. These boats exhibit a varying degree of sophistication. The adoption of a missile boat configuration will require of the various states that they obtain small nuclear warheads, and this is a problem that cannot easily be dismissed. A second difficulty is that the sea-to-sea missiles fired from missile boats are of short-range. Thus, they will be effective mainly against coastal targets. To illustrate the point, note that the Harpoon missile, which has the longest range of any missile available for deployment on the light missile boats, has a range of approximately 100 km. The advantage of the missile boats is of course their high degree of mobility, although it is possible to track them from the sea or air.

Thus it seems that Israel and some of the Arab states have the capability of developing a viable second-strike capacity. However, the principle of conservative planning is liable to play a role here, and will catalyze a race for the development of means for striking at a rival's second-strike capacity. Such means could be either nuclear or conventional. Thus, in the course of such a race, situations might develop in which it would be unclear whether a side's second-strike capacity was intact.

Feldman, in assessing the possible means for ensuring an Israeli second-strike capacity, concludes that despite the multifarious alternatives available, Israel could not achieve a second-strike capacity as reliable as that of the superpowers.[44] For example, concealment, secrecy and dispersion are limited because of Israel's small territory. Aerial preparedness is complicated by the short flight times of enemy delivery systems, while hardening and mobility will suffer from budgetary difficulties. Nevertheless, he argues, prior to the Arabs becoming armed with nuclear weapons, Israel will have sufficient time to develop her second-strike capacity to the extent that a certain quantity of Israeli nuclear weapons will survive an Arab first strike. He writes:[45]

> Israel could create in the minds of Arab leaders sufficient uncertainty that their disarming first strike would succeed in destroying absolutely all Israeli delivery vehicles. . . . Israeli activity [in developing a second-strike capacity] . . . may not guarantee that the majority of Israeli weapons would survive an Arab counterforce strike; but the probability that a minority would survive would prevent Arab leaders from ordering the attack.

This statement of the case is correct at the level of considerations concerning a first strike intended to destroy a rival's nuclear power. But the situation is more complicated than that. First—and here it is possible to draw a direct parallel with the relations of the superpowers—fears of the possible survival of nuclear weapons systems will instigate an arms race in two directions: the deployment of additional systems that are perceived as survivable, and continued quantitative extension of nuclear power. In other words, the nuclear arms race will be accelerated. At no time will any nuclear state perceive her strategic situation as meeting the criteria of a second-strike capacity. It can be expected that during a lengthy arms race, there might be certain points in which there develops a salient asymmetry of power to the advantage of one of the sides. Would such an asymmetry tempt that side's strategic leadership to consider the possible effectiveness of a first strike? There is no clear-cut answer to this question, but it can be assumed that the uncertainty surrounding the ability of such a strike to completely destroy a rival's forces would persist.

A hypothetical case has also been argued, according to which the small size of Israel prevents her from matching the combined nuclear power of the Arab states. The latter can inflict on Israel a strike of such immensity that it would ensure the complete destruction of her nuclear capacity. According to Feldman, who mentions this argument and later criticizes it,[46] a strike designed to totally destroy Israel, would require 600 warheads, each of 40 kilotons. Such a strike would be sufficient to absolutely destroy all land-based launching facilities, including all means of camouflage concealment, and secret location, weapon delivery aircraft of all types (including the V/STOL) regardless of the dispersion configuration, and land-based continental missiles.

Feldman argues quite rightly that the prospect of a concentration of Arab nuclear force of this magnitude suggests the ponderings of a wild imagination. Furthermore, the attack would have to be coordinated with immense precision, in terms of accuracy and timing. Even after the Arab states have equipped themselves with nuclear weapons, such a possibility could be dismissed out of hand.

In terms of second-strike capabilities, there is another crucial difference between the Middle East system and the relations of the superpowers. In respect to the superpowers, it is possible to conceive of a theoretical distinction between "counterforce" and "countervalue" strikes. The distinction revolves on the variant results of such strikes. Thus, for example, it is possible to dismiss the theoretical (and perhaps even practical—but the point is in fervent dispute) scenario of a limited reciprocal strike against some or all of the ICBM bases of both superpowers. The collateral civilian damage would be heavy, but acceptable. This scenario is less applicable to the Middle East, and absolutely impossible with respect to Israel. A nuclear attack against Israeli missile sites and military airbases would perpetrate such collateral damage that it is doubtful whether the state could ever recover. In other words, were Israel the target of a counterforce strike, there would be no difference between such a strike, and a strategic strike intended to destroy Israeli society.

This point deserves brief elaboration: despite Israel's military power and impressive technological and scientific infrastructure, her society is characterized by a number of weak points. Her foremost weakness is the concentration of population and economic activity in a radius of 40–50 kilometers around the Tel Aviv metropolis. A major blow struck in this area would involve tens of thousands killed, and double or higher that number of injured. It would be difficult for Israeli society to recover from such a strike.

This has two consequences: in one respect, it strengthens the nuclear deterrent effect, and raises the threshold of the activation of military violence. In contrast, however, it creates deep concern that in the event of an escalation bordering on the use of nuclear weapons, there will be no intermediate stages between conventional level and a full nuclear strike.

A no less complex issue relates to the command and control systems for second-strike forces. To what extent would the rationality of the decision-making process be maintained in a country just hit by a first strike? Without the existence of a second-strike command and control system, the second-strike capacity loses much of its effectiveness and reliability. This discussion should be placed within the broader analysis of command and control systems of nuclear states in the Middle East. It is to this discussion that we now turn.

COMMAND AND CONTROL SYSTEMS (C³)

This topic comprises two main dimensions: the technical systems for early detection, warning, command and control; and the decision-making process in the authorities responsible for the activation of nuclear weapons.

Our analysis of these issues will be as follows: first, we will examine the relevant differences between the Middle East and the superpowers. This will be followed by a brief survey of superpower command and control systems, and finally we will consider the applicability of these systems to the Middle East.

The main differences between the Middle Eastern system and the superpowers system that are relevant to the command and control issue are as follows: the relatively short distances in the Middle East in comparison to the strategic distances between the superpowers; the multipolar structure of the Middle East; the high level of friction between states with long histories of mutual antagonism; the generally low level of sophistication in mechanisms for the determination of public policy in general, and, in some states, of strategic policy in particular.

Let us now consider briefly the situation of the superpowers.[47] Since the 1950s, both superpowers have been engaged in constant efforts in the development of early detection, warning, command, and control systems. These are extremely large and complex systems.

In overview, the early detection and warning systems are vertically integrated with the command and control systems of the defense system and nuclear launch facilities. In other words, aside from the transfer of information upwards to the different command levels, the warnings are also delivered immediately, at the various levels of the system, to command and control focii for aerial defense and nuclear level facilities. The upshot is that these systems might be activated immediately in a reactive mode. In parallel, there has been horizontal integration of the various geographically dispersed command focuses. The following survey of the systems will concentrate on the American systems, and particularly on

119

the vertical integration systems, which are of most relevance to the Middle East.

The American (and, it might be assumed, the former Soviet) warning and control systems have been characterized by a number of traits:

1 There is an enormous problem of information pressure. This creates needs, on the one hand, for selective data processing and sorting, with the associated risks of error and even disaster, and, on the other hand, for the development of standing orders for handling the stream of information.

2 Information collection is often determined not by a rational ordering of priorities, but rather by the technical intelligence-collecting capability of the system on the one hand, and by organizational constraints on the other. Thus, for example, the introduction of satellites increased manyfold the volume of information about certain objectives and turned attention to these targets.

3 In any case, it is possible to process only a portion of the information.

4 There is a necessity for secrecy and compartmentalization of information. However, these factors are themselves problematic, in that they prevent the coordination of pieces of information, and even distort the data's correct interpretation.

Thus, warning and control systems, and the nature of the organizational structures that were developed to deal with them, themselves hinder correct understanding of the information, the adequate response to possible stimuli acting on the warning system, and finally, the process of rational decision-making at the politico-strategic level.

These systems, then, reflect a fundamental dilemma: on the one hand, if the systems lacked sophistication, critical information might not be collected or processed. On the other hand, in sophisticated systems, the stream of data is enormous, and its processing and understanding are the source of intractable difficulties. In this way, the dangers of the incorrect processing of information are multiplied.

Another danger derives from the vertical integration of the warning systems with the nuclear command systems. As a result of this integration, a false alarm might cause a chain of activities connected with offensive systems, that would otherwise not have occurred. Another paradox: the warning systems of the two superpowers are comprehensive and highly sophisticated systems (the American system is more advanced than the former Soviet system), and have developed their own set of mutual interrelations. Hence, the very detection and identification of some entity by one side, is immediately detected by the other side. When one side issues a warning, as a result of which it is undertaking a series of actions, the event is detected by the other side, who also issues a warning. The result is a quite astonishing vertical linkage of four systems: the detection and warning systems of the United States with the detection and warning systems of the Soviet Union, and both of these with each other's mechanisms for the command of aerial interception and nuclear launch facilities. A false alarm on either side would have echoed immediately through all four systems.

The problems faced by the principal decision-makers are without precedent, and indeed seem insurmountable. Within 20–30 minutes they are required to reach decisions that are liable to determine the fate of the world. Moreover, various automatic processes will by this time have been set in motion, in response to the received warning, and independently of the political decision-making. The dangers of erroneous decisions or misconceptions, and of an unwarranted escalation, are ever-present.

In command and control systems there are two categories of events and processes that might lead to the launching of a nuclear weapon without the prior intention of the decision-makers:

1 errors and technical failures within the command and control systems; and

2 unauthorized decisions by local commanders.

It is hardly necessary to add that these categories are interrelated, and exhibit mutual influences.

Would it be possible for a false alarm deriving from some technical error, to set off an accelerated process that runs out of control? The danger of war by mistake, that so occupied scholars in previous decades, seems to have lessened somewhat as a result of the increased sophistication of warning and control systems, and from the comprehensive deployment of listening and jamming devices built into the detection and warning systems. It would seen that there has been a reduction in the danger of mistaken decisions and escalation caused by technical failure, such as for example, a malfunction in the radar or computer information-processing systems.

This improvement is largely the result of the deployment of multiple parallel systems, and a large measure of positive redundancy. Thus, if there is a false alarm deriving from some technical error in one system, the situation can be balanced by the parallel systems. By 1962, Herman Khan had concluded that the probability of war by mistake is low. In saying so, Kahn was referring both to purely technical failures and to decisions by local commanders deriving from faulty judgment or unauthorized independent decision.[48] It seems that this is a reliable assessment as far as it goes. However, it takes account of the possibility of one or a small number of technical errors.

But, as has been argued by Paul Bracken, there does exist a danger in principle, that a critical error will occur nevertheless. It seems that this danger is a function not of one isolated technical failure, but of a series of technical failures, and involving elements of human error. Cases in point are the Three Mile Island accident in 1979, and the failure of the electricity system in the northeast of the United States in 1965, and again in New York in 1977. These were highly sophisticated systems, which according to all probability estimates were safe from any chance of accident or technical failure. Indeed these systems had proven themselves effective over many years. The risk is, however, resident in some enigmatic "development"—even though it be of very low probability—involving technical errors that inhere with certain human errors and organizational limitations.[49]

There have been two published reports of famous false alarms issued by the American NORAD system. The incidents, which occurred in 1979 and 1980, led to major steps being taken by defensive and offensive systems. In both these instances, the system of internal checks and balances managed to correct the erroneous information in time. However, these incidents occurred in periods of relative calm in U.S.–Soviet relations, and in the absence of any notion of crisis whatsoever. More uncertainty would attend the behavior of decision-makers operating in an international crisis situation, or even in a period of tense relations. One is tempted to consider the prospect of severe warnings (based on technical or human errors) being issued in the middle of a serious crisis, for example, during the superpower crisis at the tailend of the 1973 War. In such a situation, the elements of which are not inconceivable, there would be an increased danger of erroneous, irreversible decisions.

Unintentional escalation may also result from the transfer of control over the activation of nuclear weapons from the highest political level to some lower level. This question has a number of aspects. First, de facto control of nuclear weapons by ranking military officers: in this case, the formal authority remains in the hands of the political leadership, but the technical control of launching resides among the ranks. This is the effective situation in the submarines bearing nuclear weapons (SSBN),[50] and apparently also in the case of tactical weapons. In these cases, the local commanders can physically activate the nuclear weapons, because the "electric lock" can be opened by them.

A second possibility is the prior transfer of authority for decisions on the use of nuclear weapons from the political leadership to some lower level. In some cases, the prior transfer of authority is mandatory because of three possible eventualities: in the case of a failed communications link between the political leadership and the operators of the nuclear weapons; if the political leadership is wiped out by an enemy nuclear strike, and finally, the possible necessity to respond with immediacy to a nuclear attack when there is no time or it is impossible to wait for instructions from the political leadership. It can be assumed that at various stages the high command of the U.S. Strategic Air Command has been vested with authority of this nature, and perhaps this authority remains intact today. Furthermore, there are certain difficulties in maintaining stable communication with the SSBN. It would then seem likely that the submarine commanders are authorized to act in certain predefined circumstances.

A third possibility is the "automatic" activation of nuclear weapons at the various levels. Two doctrines are relevant here: Launch On Warning (LOW) and Launch on Impact (LOI). Both doctrines dictate a series of actions and behavior that are independent of decision-making by the political leadership. The operators of the weapons themselves, at certain predefined ranking levels, have clear guidelines on how to proceed in such circumstances.

It hardly need to be added that these three alternatives—control, but not authority, at lower levels; predefined authority for device activation (accompanied, of course, by technical control) at lower levels; and doctrines for a reactive counterstrike, are liable to generate dangerous situations. The lower levels might act due, for example, to reasons relating to local, concrete conditions, from a lack of knowledge of the overall situation, or from experience. In such circumstances, the dangers associated with false alarms are accentuated.

Notwithstanding the increased reliability of the various warning, command and control systems, the concern about inadvertent nuclear wars continued. Indeed, it motivated two leading politicians who are also concerned as astute strategic experts, Sam Nunn and John Warner, to launch a major initiative in 1984 designed to reduce such threats. Their report and the studies connected with it, indicate that the scope for accidents, errors, and inadvertent steps in the superpowers' nuclear relationship remained considerable until the end of the Cold War.[51]

Command and Control Systems in a Nuclear Middle East

The potential risks involved in the functioning of the superpowers' C^3 systems may recur in the Middle East, and, in some cases, with apparently greater intensity. The probability of erroneous decisions is therefore higher.

These factors center on technical failures of warning systems, or the combination of technical failure and human error, deriving from misperception of the enemy's behavior. There also exist processes of escalation that are totally distinct from technical failure, and which derive exclusively from human error. The latter case is most often a function of the erroneous interpretation of various enemy actions. These factors are liable to yield disastrous outcomes. The outcomes can be divided into two major categories of events: misperception of an enemy action that is mistakenly understood as a conventional or nuclear attack on the state's nuclear

123

bases or on the state in its entirety. Such a misperception could cause a rapid escalation. The second category comprises the escalation from a conventional war to the use of nuclear weapons.

The persistence of interstate conflicts in a nuclear Middle East will of course contribute to the potential danger of misperceptions. Hence, for example, if the Arab–Israeli peace process fails to advance, and in particular were the situation to return to the level of conflict that preceded the Egyptian–Israeli peace agreement, the intensity of the conflict would reinforce the potential for errors of perception among decision-makers. A high level of conflict tends to promote the tendency of decision-makers to view the other side's actions with great concern.

The generic problem of misperception in conflict situations may be accentuated in the Arab–Israeli conflict by the prevalence of extremist assumptions, some of which are patently irrational, concerning the intentions of the enemy. Thus, for example, the image of Israel as a satanic force is still accepted in various Arab circles. It is true that many groups among the Arab elite have adopted a more sober view, and are ready to pursue a political accommodation. This is not the case among the extreme Arab and Islamic ideological movements. In Israel, for her part, belief in the genocidal intentions of the enemy is widespread. While such a view may be an accurate reflection of ideas held by certain Arab groups, it is irrational as a representation of the general Arab position, and is certainly not the first priority of the Arab states. Another view current among some Israelis is that the Arab position takes no account of the costs to them involved in perpetrating a genocide against Israel. Menachem Begin once provided a classic example of such a viewpoint, in his warning that when Iraq acquired its first nuclear bomb, it would immediately use it against Israel.

The intensity of the conflict, and the background images of the enemy influence the interpretation and evaluation of the enemy's actions, whether the source data be a false alarm or an accurate intelligence report. Thus, for example, an impending conventional attack might be interpreted as preparations for a nuclear attack. A false alarm concerning the enemy's actions might also gain momentum and be the source for a perception of the enemy's intention to launch a nuclear offensive.

The high level of friction between Middle Eastern states, and the intense concentration of conventional air forces capable of flying nuclear missions, form a backdrop against which warning systems errors can easily occur. We will now examine this problem from the Israeli point of view.

Israel possesses an advanced and sophisticated early warning system.[52] However, even a system as advanced as this, is not immune to false alarms. Indeed, a case could be made for the opposite. As detection and identification capabilities increase, so too does the volume of data that must be interpreted. The intensity of air traffic in the region increases the chances of error. The upshot is that commanders at the operational level tend to opt for the worst case alternative, and prefer to respond rapidly. This tendency would be reinforced in view of the continued possibility of air penetration by single aircraft. The successful penetration of a Syrian Mig 23 into Israeli airspace serves as an example of that possibility. In conventional conditions, such penetration is not that dangerous. However, in nuclear conditions, even a single strike aircraft may be perceived as a highly dangerous object. Hence the problem is likely to worsen.

The superpowers are also free of another problem attending the situation in the Middle East: there is no possibility that either superpower will launch a strategic *conventional* attack by means of aircraft. In other words, the only threat posed against the metropolitan states is an attack by ground or sea launched nuclear missiles, or aircraft borne cruise missiles. In contrast, in the Middle East, there will remain a major difficulty in distinguishing between a conventional and a nuclear attack. In this environment, the early warning system may be unable to clearly identify the nature of the threat, and the occurrence of situations of uncertainty will multiply.

Uncertainty will also be fed by the multipolar structure of the Middle East. In terms of command and control systems, this factor will cause three major difficulties for decision-makers. First, false alarms that derive from tension or even war between two other states. Thus, for example, if there is extreme tension or even limited war between Syria and Jordan (as was the case in 1970, and again—although only at the level of threats and troop movements—in 1980) there is likely to be a massive increase in aerial activity on both sides. The Israeli warning system is liable to incorrectly interpret some of these movements, and could initiate a process of conventional or even nuclear escalation.

Second, there is the possibility of a catalytic war instigated by a third party. The probability of a catalytic war between the superpowers had been reduced due to the development of early warning systems, and also because the rationale of an indeterminate, highly limited attack by one superpower against its rival seemed of the most doubtful validity. Since a catalytic attack would almost certainly have been indeterminate, it would have been relatively easy to ascertain that the source of the attack was not the rival superpower. However, notwithstanding these conditions, fears persisted about the possibility of an inadvertent war between the superpowers resulting from actions taken by third parties.[53] In the Middle East, the probability of some actor instigating catalytic actions is relatively high. Obviously, such an action would only be undertaken if the initiating party believed that his plot would not be uncovered. This is not an inconceivable scenario. The catalytic action need not necessarily be nuclear. It could be conventional, but to such an extent that the nuclear tolerance threshold of the attacked state be significantly lowered. It should be added that the catalytic action need not consist of an actual attack. The action might be indirect, such as the electronic deception of the warning system, to create the impression of an impending attack.

The third problem derives from the possibility that the nuclear launching systems of several different states will be located in the same zone. A relevant scenario would be the dispersion of small missile boats bearing short-range nuclear missiles throughout the Eastern Mediterranean. It would be difficult to identify with absolute certainty the national identity of each of these boats. Thus, there will be a degree of uncertainty as to the source of an attack launched from one of these boats. Moreover, it might also be possible that agents of some state or underground organization will gain control of a boat belonging to a certain state, and then activate the nuclear launch systems. Apart from the obvious inherent dangers, situations of this sort could also serve as the basis for catalytic activity.

As an illustration of the extreme problems involved in decision-making under conditions of uncertainty and time pressure, we will examine the 1973 case involving the Israeli downing of a Libyan jet. In this incident, the Libyan passenger jet had lost its way, and had penetrated the airspace over Sinai, which was then under Israeli military control. The place was detected, and Israeli aircraft were dispatched to intercept it. They ordered it to follow them, but the Libyan jet had turned around, and was on its way out of Israeli airspace. Nevertheless, the interceptors received an order to destroy it, and they did so. The Israeli action was not undertaken out of imprudence, but because of the nature of standing orders, because of the immense difficulty in identifying the plane's destination, and because of the extremely short time that was available to the decision-makers. The incident did demonstrate Israel's ability to respond rapidly. Nevertheless, because of the standing orders and time pressure, the wrong decision was eventually taken. In a mixed environment—involving both conventional and nuclear elements—decision-makers will be under pressure several times greater. A fundamental dilemma will haunt them incessantly: on the one hand, a rapid response to a warning is liable to instigate a dangerous process of escalation, ending in possible catastrophe. On the other hand, because of the short distances, and the more reasonable possibility that the warnings have been set off by a conventional attack, rather than by a sudden nuclear attack, a failure to respond is also liable to give rise to critical and terminal results.

Let us consider this final issue from the Israeli viewpoint. Due to the state's limited territory, a strike involving the explosion of even one nuclear device in the heart of the metropolitan urban center on the coastal plain would have a disastrous impact on the state. It would not necessarily mean the destruction of the state, but the direct damage inflicted and the resultant psychological impact would be immense. It is obviously of the utmost importance that any penetration of Israeli airspace be dealt with by an immediate response (that might take on a variety of forms). Israel is operating in this matter within the very narrowest of security margins. In this respect, there is an enormous difference between the superpower context and the situation in which Israel finds itself. Both the United States and the Soviet Union I could have absorbed a limited nuclear strike. That is, if there is a false (or true) alarm as to a *limited* attack, the decision-makers are likely to respond slowly to the warning, without risking intolerable damage to the state. The decision-making process, though under enormous pressure, would nevertheless be conducted in a procedurally rational manner. The situation is vastly different in Israel. Indeed Israel's situation is even more difficult than that of other states in the region.

Delegation of authority

In a nuclear Middle East, would the authority to activate nuclear weapons be transferred to lower echelons? No clearcut delineation of this issue is possible; rather the discussion will dwell on certain aspects of the situation that will enable the framing of a tentative answer. We will begin with Israel. From the historical point of view, the issue of nuclear developments has been handled by a civilian committee—the Atomic Energy Committee—that was originally under the auspices of the Defense Department, and later transferred to the Prime Minister's Office. This structure suggests the tentative conclusion that were Israel to acquire a nuclear-weapons capability, the politico-strategic authority for its use would rest with the Prime Minister. In this context, one may refer to the story that appeared in *Time* on April 12, 1976, according to which, in the 1973 War, the then Minister of Defense, Moshe Dayan, issued an instruction to prepare nuclear weapons. Dayan referred the issue to Prime Minister Golda Meir, and she referred it to the unofficial "War Cabinet" (comprising of Meir, Dayan, Allon, and Galili), where it was decided to discontinue the order. From this story it might be concluded that the authority to decide on the use of nuclear weapons rests with the government or war cabinet, while the physical control is in the hands of the Defense Minister, or more accurately, with military technical personnel. If this is the case, then it would appear that Israel does not use the complex mechanisms of "electronic locks" and "double keys," that are used in the United States and apparently in Moscow, and which allow only the political leadership to activate nuclear weapons (with the exceptions mentioned earlier of SLBM systems, and, apparently, tactical weapons deployed in Europe).

Since no reliable information is available concerning Israel's nuclear situation, or concerning the command and control of nuclear weapons (if the latter indeed exist), the above speculations can serve only as a tentative indicator. However, it will be instructive to consider certain structural aspects characterizing the relations between the defense and military establishments, on the one hand, and the civilian establishment on the other. The analysis of these relations suggests a correspondence with the speculative description of nuclear weapons control that was suggested above.

The description in *Time* suggests that the final decision on the use of nuclear weapons rests with the government or war cabinet. This indeed assures that such momentous decisions will rest only with the highest political authority. Indeed, in the history of military-civilian relations in Israel, all major strategic decisions have been taken by the government or by a limited group within it. Nevertheless, the defense or defense-military establishment has always had a considerable influence on these decisions. Decisions on the use of nuclear weapons, it can be assumed, will be the product of similar channels of decision-making. We might also assume that the degree of influence of the defense-military establishment in question of nuclear weaponry will be relatively greater than, for example, the influence of parallel agencies in the United States.

It is, of course, difficult to predict the response of this establishment to the use of nuclear weapons. Intuitively, however, it is conceivable that were Israel to adopt a nuclear doctrine, there would be a tendency for the defense-military establishment to extend its influence and authority to this area. It is also conceivable that its approach on the nuclear question will be rather warfighting-oriented, and that this will be the nature of its advice to the government. This of course might change if the defense-military leadership were to undergo a thorough process of socialization concerning the nature of nuclear weaponry.

This hypothetical analysis is not intended to provide any indication of the current position of the military establishment on the nuclear issue. It is quite possible that *prior* to the adoption of a nuclear doctrine, the majority of the military establishment will be quite reserved in their support for the endorsement of a nuclear doctrine. This is also the natural tendency of a conventional army. The critical issue is rather the attitude of the military after the introduction of a nuclear doctrine, especially if it also comprises battlefield uses.

The relationship between the political leadership and the military-defense establishment will be largely dependent on the personalities and attitudes of the Prime Minister, the Defense Minister and the Chief of Staff. A weak Prime Minister, or one whose understanding of strategic matters is limited, is likely to allow a pattern of behavior and spheres of authority, in which the hands of the Defense Minister and the military are strengthened.

128

Further, the set of relations between the government, the Defense Minister and the army has never been satisfactorily formalized by legislation. This issue achieved prominence during the hearings of the Agranat Commission, inquiring into the 1973 War. Despite the commission's recommendations, and the legal amendment that was later proposed in its wake, the system of relations remains ill-defined. It is still unclear who is the Commander-in-Chief—that is, the person responsible for making the major political and strategic decisions—is it the Prime Minister? Or is it the government as a whole? If so, what is the relationship between the Prime Minister (or the government) and the Defense Minister? These issues have, of course, a decisive role to play in the context of nuclear weapons.

The fact of the matter is that the Israeli political leadership has never been able to define these limits and borders of responsibility with any clarity. This ambiguity and inability to effectively solve the problem of legislation, originated in the 1948 War.[54] It would appear that the Israeli political system is unable to deal with this issue structurally.[55]

Apart from these difficulties, will objective circumstances induce the Israeli system to transfer the authority for nuclear weapons to lower echelons? The answer to this question is complex, and not definitive. On the one hand, Israel is small, and the quantities of nuclear weapons and launch facilities she may possess are limited. These factors tend to ease the retention of nuclear authority by the political leadership. On the other hand, the scenario of the activation of nuclear weapons as a last resort requires a control system according to which, under certain predefined circumstances, a delegation of authority would indeed occur. The use of nuclear weapons as a last resort will occur following at least a partial military collapse, and the advance of enemy forces into areas crucial to the state. In such circumstances, the nuclear bases might be under the direct threat of enemy takeover, or the centers of political and strategic leadership may be exposed. The use of nuclear weapons as a means of last resort tends, by definition, to require the predefined transfer of authority. This also involves serious risks. First, it should also be noted that the predefined transfer of authority would be liable to become an accepted channel of control were a doctrine for the use of tactical weapons to be developed.

It is difficult to estimate the likely form of systems for the authority over and control of nuclear weapons in the various Arab states. It can only be noted that the patterns of decision-making are likely to vary from state to state. This heterogeneity of forms is likely to create perceptual problems for decision-makers in other states. Another related issue is that the army is the direct political ruler, or the principal constituency of the regime in many Arab states. This has a number of different and to a certain extent contradictory consequences. On the one hand, since the ruler of the state is also the head of the army, the decision-making process is highly centralized, enabling the head of state to exercise his control and authority over nuclear weapons. Its activation will be controlled by a clearly defined hierarchy. This configuration of government–army relations creates the potential for a rational decision-making process concerning the use of nuclear weaponry. The centralization of the decision-making process also enables a clearer view of the intentions of that state, and thus facilitates the task of decision-makers in other states, and enables them in principle to enforce a relatively more rational process of decision-making.

On the other hand, if the military ruler does not directly command the army, but is forced to rely on it as the main foundation of his political power, there is the potential danger that the army will demand that it be delegated the authority for controlling the use of nuclear weapons. This is a situation riddled with dangers, foremost of which is that the military leadership is likely to be lacking any political or strategic background at a level that would allow it to come to terms with the complexities associated with the use of nuclear weapons. Similarly, this situation would be the source for major concern in other states: it will not be clear who is in control of the nuclear weapons, nor under what conditions they are likely to be used.

In military regimes, or in regimes that rely on the military as their prime source of power, there is the persistent threat of a military coup or revolution. This also has dangerous consequences for the command and central systems, and decision-making processes. Thus we have two types of dangers: (a) ill-considered decisions by those responsible for the coup or its opponents; and (b) deep anxiety during the coup among decision-makers in rival nuclear states, that might lead to the activation of force, and even of nuclear force.

The dangers relating to the first of the above two categories, that is, the use of nuclear weapons by the opposing sides in order to further their cause in the internal conflict, have been described by Lewis Dunn.[56] Feldman, in contrast, argues that these dangers are not realistic.[57] In his view, a group of military conspirators has no need of nuclear weapons in order to realize their revolutionary plan. Moreover, the use of nuclear weapons within the state will wreak havoc among the citizen population, and the potential casualties will almost certainly include relatives of the revolutionaries themselves. This factor will act as a deterrent against such an action. Finally, the internal use of nuclear weapons will totally destroy the revolutionary group's popularity and support, and indeed would constitute an unscrupulous and mindless act. Feldman does accept Schelling's argument[58] that in a military revolution or civil war situation, both sides will seek to gain control of the nation's nuclear arms, in order to prevent its falling into the other's hands. However, in Feldman's view, capturing the nuclear arms will be of no strategic consequence; neither side would use it in any case.

Feldman's arguments, while logical, seem to be of doubtful practical validity. First, the competitive struggle to gain control of the nation's nuclear arms, were it to occur under conditions of a military coup or civil war, would itself be evidence of both sides' fears that its opponent might use them. However, does not this mutual fear seem to offer some implicit indication of the sides' own readiness to use nuclear weapons? It is important to differentiate here between two situations: first, let us consider the case of a military coup or an attempt at same. In this situation, Feldman's argument that both the conspirators and the incumbent rulers will be reluctant to use nuclear weapons against the other, seems generally to hold. However, even here, the case is not clearcut. It should be borne in mind that both conspirators and rulers are aware that they are fighting for their own lives, for the lives of their families, and for their comrades. Indeed, the long history of military coups or revolutions in the Middle East suggests that the "losers" and their supporters generally lose their lives too. This phenomena is exacerbated when the revolutionaries and rulers are divided by ethnic or religious differences. This is, for example, the situation in Syria today, in which a successful Sunni uprising against the ruling Alawite military rulers may bring about not only a change of regime, but also a quite general slaughter of Alawites. In such conditions, the use of nuclear weapons as a last desperate move is not entirely impossible. Moreover, a nuclear device need not necessarily be used against the capital city, but, for example, it could be activated against an armored division of the rebels that is moving towards the city.

The second situation is an ethnic civil war. In this case, the readiness to adopt a strategy involving genocidal intentions will be relatively high. The experience of the Iraqi operations against the Kurds, which included the use of chemical warfare, is evidence of this. The recent, extremely brutal and bloody repression of the Shiite and Kurdish uprisings against Saddam Hussein's regime, serves as another demonstration of the extremes to which a beleaguered regime, which is also identified primarily with one community, is ready to resort. Under such conditions, one can conceive of nuclear weapons being used against population centers of the enemy community.

Furthermore, in both a civil war or military coup, the entire system of authority and control of nuclear weapons might collapse completely. In such conditions, situations could occur in which minor officers, totally ignorant of the significance of nuclear weapons, might gain control of a nuclear base, and, under stress, activate the weapons.

The fear that the nuclear weapons might fall into enemy hands is also a motivation to use them. Here we return to the starting point of our discussion of this issue: the attempt to prevent the enemy gaining control of the nation's arsenal of nuclear weapons, in a situation in which one of the sides is losing the conflict, but still retains control over the nuclear installations. There may be a temptation to fire it off anywhere, just that the enemy not gain control of it. The choice of targets will depend on the situation of the particular state, but the mere launching of a nuclear weapon is liable to have severe repercussions throughout the regional system.

However, more serious than the risk that rebels or rulers might use nuclear weapons, are the possible reactions of the other states in the region. In a situation in which government and authority in a nuclear state are in a process of dissolution, states in the region that are within range of the delivery systems of the state undergoing the revolution, will find themselves confronting a major dilemma. They are liable to fear that the nuclear weapons will fall into the hands of irresponsible elements, who will activate the weapons against targets as they see fit, without rational consideration of the consequences. Alternatively, the adjacent states may fear the development of a situation, as we described above, in which one side attempts to rid the state of its stock of nuclear weapons before the enemy takes control. The nuclear weapons might be targeted on any one of the adjacent states. Under circumstances of this nature, there will be a very strong temptation to launch a preemptive strike against the nuclear weapons bases. This strike could be either conventional or nuclear. However, a preemptive conventional strike might set off a process of nuclear escalation.

THE INFLUENCE OF NUCLEAR WEAPONS ON THE STRUCTURE OF THE MIDDLE EAST STATE SYSTEM

The multipolar character of the Middle East, and of the system of Arab states within it, allows for a number of possible different developments under nuclear conditions. Our categorization of the various alternative developments turns on the distinction between a fragmented system involving multiple, small coalitions, or no coalitions at all, and a system in which coalitions continue to play the decisive role. The formation and dissolution of coalitions in the Arab world is one of the most important features of interstate relations in the Middle East. The configuration of a coalition also has a substantial bearing on the dynamics of the Arab–Israeli conflict. Analysis of Arab coalitions has revealed certain patterns of behavior and "rules or the game":[59]

1 Coalitions are most often established or made to balance another Arab coalition, and as such play a role in the continual process of equalizing aggregations of power in the Arab world.

2 Despite the balancing function, during 1967–1974, Israel has become a relatively more important factor in determining groupings.
3 While ideology (radical vs. conservative, or fundamentalist vs. modernist, etc.) is not devoid of significance, it remains secondary to power and balancing factors.
4 The main function of establishing a coalition is the accumulation of power, and not the restraint of minor coalition partners.
5 Generally, informal groupings are of more significance than formal groupings.
6 The lifespan of these coalitions is relatively short.
7 Until the 1970s, most of the coalitions were led by one state. However, since then, following the development of asymmetries in the attributes of power in the Arab world, coalitions have been led by either one or a partnership of two states of approximately equal power, or alternatively, coalitions have lacked any clear leadership.
8 Since the 1970s, there has been a certain process of fragmentation within the Arab world. This had the affect of making coalition membership even less binding than it was previously. Nevertheless, the tendency to coalesce, even though it be in very loose groupings, remains.
9 As mentioned earlier in this chapter, there has emerged of late a new central bloc led by Egypt (already before the Gulf Crisis, and even more so following it), which may replace both the traditional tendency to form competing coalitions and the more recent partial fragmentation of the system. It remains to be seen, however, whether this association will change the previous "rules of the game" of coalition formation.

The Gulf Crisis served to demonstrate yet again the persistence of these "rules of the game". Iraq's increase of power caused concern among its neighbors and led—even before the invasion of Kuwait—to the creation of a new association between Egypt and Syria. Iraq's invasion of Kuwait resulted in the immediate creation of a balancing coalition of all the Gulf states with Egypt and Syria. Thus, the balance of power mechanism, motivated by real power interests, was the most important.

We will now turn to an examination of the possible influence of nuclearization on coalition formation, and of the impact of different models of coalitions on Arab–Israeli strategic relations. It hardly needs mentioning that this discussion is tentative, and is intended to provide only a schematic outline of different possible developments in terms of the various models. Moreover, it should be stressed that several variables—political, strategic, and economic—affect relations among Arab states. In the present analysis, only the nuclear variable is taken into account.

Model 1: Several Arab States become Nuclear, but do not form a Coalition

This model assumes that a number of Arab states obtain a nuclear capacity, and that the current pattern of behavior in the system—encompassing the Arab–Israeli conflict, and the competition, and, at times conflict between the Arab states—remains unchanged. The acquisition of nuclear weapons will serve a number of different purposes, in approximately the following order of importance: deterrence of the Israeli nuclear capability; a warfighting role against Israel (for example, a destructive first blow); deterrence of other Arab nuclear states; political coercion of Israel and other Arab states; considerations of prestige and status within the Middle East; and if Iran were to become nuclear, the priorities of a nuclear Iraq would also include strategies of deterrence, coercion and warfighting against Iran.

There may be at least three reasons for inter-Arab competition connected with nuclear weapons; first, conflict between two Arab states; or second, general competition, in which considerations of prestige and status provoke two or more contenders for leadership of the Arab world or central positions in it, to match the other's nuclear capacity. The third reason links the Israeli nuclear capacity with intra-Arab competition. In order to deter different possible nuclear or conventional challenges, Israel will have to adopt a strategy of "*tout azimut*," that is, the nuclear targeting of every Arab state, nuclear and nonnuclear. We will also assume that Israel publicizes her decision to adopt this strategy, but that there is no clear indication of the size of the Israeli nuclear force, nor of the quantities of weapons directed against each of the Arab states. In this case, each of the threatened Arab states will have to develop its own individual capacity for the deterrence of a possible Israeli attack. Israel, for her part, will try to match the combined power of all these states, in preparation for the contingency among them. She will probably consider this important for at least three reasons: first, perceiving nuclear weapons through a conventional prism and consequently adopting a philosophy demanding quantitative nuclear increases to match adversaries' quantitive increasing capabilities; second, to ensure second-strike capabilities in the face of adversaries' growing capabilities; and finally to have a potential of first strike against all adversaries' nuclear facilities. An intensive nuclear arms race would result.

Another issue has to do with the probability of catalytic wars. If within the region there are several nuclear states, then there may be motivation on the part of some Arab states to initiate a military confrontation between Israel and another Arab state that had been hoping to remain uninvolved.

In summary then, in this model there is a high probability of an escalating nuclear arms race, and some possibility of catalytic wars. Also, processes of decision-making in times of crises will be extremely complex and difficult.

Model 2: A Coalition of some Arab Nuclear States (Separately from or together with Nonnuclear States

A coalition of this form could arise from the simultaneous nuclearization of several Arab states (of equal of variant nuclear capacities). The main motivation behind the formation of the coalition would be the aggregation of the nuclear power of its members. The need for aggregation would most likely derive from an advantage obtained by Israel in terms of nuclear warheads and command, control and communication systems. An additional condition for the formation of such of coalition would be the continuation of the Arab–Israeli conflict.

The organization of such coalition would be a task of the greatest difficulty. The absence of a clearly hegemonic power will require the establishment of an egalitarian structure. Decision-making bodies will have to include representatives of all the nuclear members of the coalition. In time of crisis, such organizations might be totally paralyzed: no state would have final authority, and the member states may become entangled in conflicts of interest among themselves. For example, it will be difficult to restrain a state that errs in her strategic calculations and that behaves irresponsibly. The channels of command and control will of necessity be highly complex, and fraught with difficulties. The setting up of efficient command, control and communication systems is a challenging task under the best conditions; in the Arab world, in a situation in which there are a number of Arab states of roughly equal nuclear capacity, and which are possessed of a relatively low level of strategic sophistication, the task would be well nigh impossible.

Difference of opinion between the different members of the coalition, that originate in disparities of economic and political power, and of scientific and technological development, will endure. Nevertheless, it is not inconceivable that the weaker and smaller states will achieve a nuclear capacity that is the equal of otherwise stronger states. Nuclear arms may be the "Great Equalizer" within the coalition, but the achieved equality may not simplify the functioning of the coalition. First, the coalition will be able to exist and operate only if the member states abide by the coalition's political objectives and agenda, and agree to integrate their control, command and communication systems, as required. In the light of the considerable differences of political orientation current in the Arab world, it is reasonable to expect that the coalition will suffer from substantive structural tensions. These might intensify as a result of the various states' diverse sources of supply for nuclear weapons and technology—the different members of the coalition will probably adopt different routes in order to attain nuclear status. Some states will acquire nuclear weapons directly from an external nuclear power, while others will develop an independent infrastructure with the assistance of external nuclear powers. It is likely that each member of the coalition will seek to further its own security needs; some will emphasize the nuclear aspect of the coalition, while the "confrontation states," that must take account of the possibility of a conventional war, are likely to lay stress on the coalition's conventional power, and even to demand that the combined conventional forces of the coalition, or a good part of it, be set aside for their use. Some members may demand that the coalition focuses on tactical nuclear weapons (once again, the chief candidates to lay such a claim would be the "confrontation states"), while others, less fearful of an Israeli conventional attack, might urge that the thrust of the coalition's efforts be "strategic" nuclear. Members that are less developed technologically, such as Saudi Arabia and Lybia, might oppose the tight integration of command, control, and communication systems, out of fear (apparently justified) that it would favor the more developed states, particularly Egypt, and, to a certain extent, Iraq and Syria. Another source of differences will undoubtedly be the selection of nuclear strike targets and the policy for the deployment of nuclear weapons.

In a crisis situation, it is possible that some of these differences and conflicts will be sharpened, and might even occasion the dissolution of the coalition.

Model 3: Two Arab Nuclear Coalitions

Until the 1970s, the Arab "mashrek" states tended to form two competitive coalitions, the membership of which fluctuated. This pattern is rooted in underlying political and structural parameters, and it is possible that the pattern will persist, although in a nonnuclear environment there may be reason to expect more fluid configurations. The need for the aggregation of nuclear power fits neatly into this pattern. The competition over hegemony between the two coalitions will continue, with nuclear weapons simply being entered into the calculus of power. The primary difference will be manifest in the necessity for other coalitions to be more permanent and stable than traditional Arab coalitions. The requirement for coalition stability is derivative of nuclear strategic environments—the need for certainty, the necessity of stable command, control and communication systems and the physical exigencies of weapon deployment and warning systems.

In terms of arms races, each of the Arab blocs is forced to assume that in a nuclear crisis with Israel, it will have to stand alone. As such, each bloc will have to develop a nuclear capacity equivalent to that of Israel.

Israel, for her part, will apply a worst case analysis, and assume that the two blocs combine forces at the beginning of a crisis with her. The practical upshot of this assumption is that Israel must seek to match this combined power: the way is opened for the escalation of the regional arms race.

This system of coalition will also be affected by instability. First, the arms race is likely to create crisis points, characterized by uncertainty as to the second-strike capactiy of one of the states. Second, since it is likely that members of some Arab coalitions will share borders with Israel, there will be a certain difficulty in locating the origin of missiles and bombers that attack Israel. The outcome is a triangle of fear, in which each coalition suspects the other of trying to engage in catalytic activity. And both coalitions will fear Israel, and vice-versa. The mutual fears might promote military restraint, but if political issues remain unresolved the probability of crisis will increase, heightening mutual fears and enhancing the danger of war.

In summary, were nuclear weaponry the *singular* determinant of inter-state policy in the Arab world, its influx to the region might lead to one of two extreme situations. On the one hand, it might accelerate the process of division, in the system of Arab states. The stability of such a situation would be highly suspect. The arms race would accelerate, there would be frequent possibilities for catalytic activity, and the problem of command and control would be greatly exacerbated. An alternative extreme scenario is the formation of an inclusive Arab coalition under the firm leadership of one nuclear power. This situation would be more stable, but differences between the Middle Eastern system and superpower bipolar system would still be manifest, and may result in instability. More-over, an inclusive Arab coalition would be of uncertain durability: it would be undermined by the pattern in which the components of power are distributed throughout the Arab world, and by the traditionally conflict-oriented behavior of its members.

It is perhaps more plausible to assume that the tendency to form coalitions in multipolar interstate systems will persist in a nuclear Arab system. Nuclear weaponry will not alter the tendency of Arab states to form loose coalitions or associations, in the framework of which they retain their separate sovereignty. The two extreme alternatives described above seem less credible, and if they were to occur, they would almost certainly be transient. Instead, we ought to expect the constitution of various coalitions, whose structure enables a certain aggregation of nuclear power, with the aim of matching the nuclear capacity of Israel (and of other Arab coalitions), and which at the same time imitate the more traditional pattern of coalitions in the Arab world. All these coalitions will be hard-pressed to establish effective, unified and sophisti-cated systems for command, control and communication. The political, strategic, and technical problems involved in establishing such systems under conditions of complexity will generate serious tensions in the Middle East. The way would be littered with danger points, that may be the cause of crises, nuclear confrontations and even nuclear exchanges. These tensions will be the source of incessant changes in the makeup of the coalitions, and of movement back and forth from the traditional bi-coalition structure to alternative frameworks—divided coalitions, an inclusive coalition or a coalition of "equals."

4

INTERNATIONAL REACTIONS TO NUCLEAR PROLIFERATION IN THE MIDDLE EAST

With the end of bipolarity and the emergence of a new international system in which the United States plays the predominant role, proliferation in the Middle East depends on the interplay between regional states' urge to proliferate and American efforts, backed by the other big nuclear powers, to stem it. This chapter will focus mainly on American policy on proliferation in the Middle East, but will address briefly also other nuclear suppliers' likely reactions to regional proliferation. Among the latter, Russian policy will be discussed in greater detail.

Although possible Russian policy on that issue is far less important than American policy, its discussion is relevant because of the following reasons: Russia[1] is still the second largest nuclear power in the world and is likely to remain so for a long time. Nuclear developments anywhere are therefore of concern to Russia. In that sense, Russia is the inheritor of the Soviet Union. By the same token, were the nonproliferation regime to collapse and many states to "go nuclear" there may be pressures on Russia to transfer nuclear weapons or technology to allies and friends. Moreover, although Russia does not border on the Middle East (as the USSR did), she is still geographically close to the region and important strategic developments there may affect Russian interests. No less importantly, some of the Central Asian and Caucasian ex-Soviet republics (mostly Muslim) are even more closely connected to Middle Eastern events and their interactions with the Middle East can, in turn, affect Russian strategic interests. Finally, the unauthorized leakage of fissionable materials and nuclear technology from Russia (and some of the republics formerly in the Soviet Union) to the Middle East is also a possibility.

Although this chapter's main focus is on current and likely future processes and policies, it will benefit from an historical discussion of American and Soviet policies regarding proliferation in the Middle East. This will help us recognize the roots of policies being enacted at present. Thus, the first part of this chapter will give a brief historical account of American and Soviet policies. (Though as mentioned Russia, the inheritor of the Soviet Union in nuclear-related affairs, has become less central in the current nonproliferation effort.)

Will the new emerging structure of world politics enhance tendencies toward global proliferation, or will it foster an environment in which the dispersion of nuclear weapons can be checked and possibly reversed? How will this new structure affect proliferation tendencies in the Middle East? These questions will be addressed in the second part of this chapter. This analysis also provides the background for an account of the new ideas about arms control in the Middle East initiated by the United States following the Gulf War.

The U.S. and the Soviet Positions on Proliferation: An Historical Account

Shared and coincidental interests in preventing proliferation

Aside from the imperative to prevent global nuclear war, there was no area in international relations in which the interests of the two superpowers overlapped to such an extent as in the need to prevent nuclear proliferation. Although these overlapping interests developed and obtained during the bipolar period, many of them persist in the new international system that is emerging in the post-bipolar era. Nuclear proliferation constituted a threat not only to the stability of the international system as a whole, even under conditions of competitive bipolarity but also to the immediate security of the two superpowers themselves. The threats encompassed a broad spectrum; the present discussion focuses on those that were of most pressing concern. The emergence of a new international system does not diminish American and Russian interest in nonproliferation. The opposite is actually true—new concerns have been added to the old ones.

First, the structure of the bipolar international system assigned a unique and central status to the two superpowers. This status derived from a number of factors, of which one of the most important and, for the Soviet Union, *the* most important, was military nuclear force. Widespread nuclear proliferation was liable to threaten this unique status. Limited proliferation has already occurred—to Britain, France, and China. However, Britain and France have been integrated within the framework of NATO, while China has maintained a special status in international relations that existed even prior to her acquisition of nuclear weapons. On the other hand, the proliferation of nuclear weapons to various other states, among them small states in regions of intensive conflict did pose a potential threat to the superpowers' exclusive status.

Second, nuclear proliferation could have altered the character of regional crises and wars by its addition to them of the nuclear dimension.

This could have led to a number of serious consequences for the super-powers:

(1) Given their commitments to regional states, they could have found themselves involved in a nuclear crisis or even a regional nuclear war over which they would have had no control;

(2) As a result they could have found themselves involved as opponents in a serious nuclear crisis;

(3) Given these dangers, they would have faced a dilemma: should they remain involved in the region because of their own particular interests and thus endanger themselves as described above, or should they rid themselves of their regional commitments and thereby adversely affect other sets of regional interests?

The disintegration of the Soviet Union and the total change in U.S.–Russian relations have, of course, eliminated this particular threat.

Third, nuclear proliferation tends to increase the threat of regional nuclear wars, thereby removing the taboo on the use of nuclear weaponry. Apart from the catastrophic outcomes for the affected regions, the removal of the taboo during the bipolar era would have had a damaging effect on the central balance of nuclear deterrence.

Fourth, extensive nuclear proliferation could have complicated, and perhaps even impeded the two superpowers' systems for strategic decision-making. This could have been particularly serious during a period of regional or global international crisis.

Finally, proliferation could have restricted the ability of the superpowers to undertake arms reduction agreements requiring very substantial cuts in their nuclear arsenals.

U.S. Policy on Nuclear Proliferation—Introductory Notes[2]

Shortly after the end of World War II, the United States, the world's first nuclear power, began to take steps to prevent nuclear proliferation. The famous Baruch Plan, the central effort of this strategy, failed due to Soviet opposition. The United States later adopted a strategy of secrecy concerning nuclear technology to prevent proliferation. However, with the first Soviet explosion of an atomic device in 1949, followed by the British test of 1952, it became clear that a strategy of secrecy was inadequate. Subsequently, the United States initiated the Atoms for Peace Plan but stipulated that recipients of U.S. nuclear technology not use it for weapon development, and that they accept American monitoring of the nuclear installations.

In 1957, the United States was the prime mover in founding the International Atomic Energy Agency (IAEA) whose dual function was to encourage the development of nuclear energy for peaceful purposes and to organize a monitoring system for nuclear installations. However, the American efforts were not infused with any sense of urgency.

The Kennedy administration was the first to adopt nuclear nonproliferation as a priority foreign policy objective. Indeed, during this period, in the early 1960s, there was a new awareness among scholars of strategic studies in the United States and Britain concerning the underlying dangers of proliferation.[3]

Serious diplomatic endeavor regarding nuclear nonproliferation began in 1963–1964. Discussions on the signing of a treaty to prevent the proliferation of nuclear weapons began in the ENDC (Eighteen Nations Disarmament Committee) in Geneva, and concluded with the signing of the Non-Proliferation Treaty (NPT) in 1968. The United States was a major force behind the treaty, and her efforts in the ENDC were supported by the Soviet Union. The NPT was adopted by the United Nations in 1970 and became the principal tool for what was termed the nonproliferation regime. The United States, the Soviet Union and Britain signed it as nuclear powers. By mid-1992, 144 nonnuclear weapon states acceded to the NPT. But the leading threshold countries—Israel, India, and Pakistan—have refrained from signing the NPT. Two other threshold countries, Brazil and Argentina, though not yet joining it, have nevertheless stopped their nuclear programs, and another threshold country, South Africa, joined the NPT in 1991. All the former Soviet republics had joined or agreed to join the NPT as nonnuclear parties (and Russia inherited the status of the Soviet Union as a nuclear power-party of the NPT). Finally, France and China acceded to it in 1992 as nuclear-weapon states.

The Johnson administration actively pursued the Kennedy administration's nonproliferation policy. However, with the attainment of a treaty on nonproliferation on the one hand, and the installment of the Nixon administration in January 1969, on the other, interest in this question appeared to dull. It seemed that the treaty by itself could prevent nuclear proliferation, and, as such, the administration should concentrate its efforts on persuading those states on the "nuclear threshold" to sign the NPT; thus could a stable international regime[4] be achieved in the area of nuclear nonproliferation. Furthermore, Secretary of State Kissinger viewed the prevention of nuclear proliferation as a relatively low-priority foreign policy issue. Indeed, a memorandum issued by the NSC (National Security Council) on February 6, 1969, recommended that American officials not pressure the various states to endorse the NPT.[5] It is possible that one of the reasons for the low profile which Kissinger adopted on this issue derived from his pessimistic view as to the possibility of preventing the development by other states of a nuclear capability. Thus he argued[6] that "The causes of proliferation are so embedded that no superpower could influence them in any significant manner."

There were certain developments, however, that caused a change in the administration's attitude toward nonproliferation. Most critical in this respect was the nuclear test conducted by India in 1974. Also important was the impact of the initial reports regarding Pakistani attempts to develop a nuclear capability. It seems that these two factors changed Kissinger's stance, and indicated that a low American profile would not strengthen the nonproliferation system. Furthermore, concern arose that even within the framework of the NPT, the continued transfer of nuclear technology by nuclear suppliers to nonnuclear states might eventually lead to nuclear proliferation. In 1974 the United States initiated a meeting of all the states exporting nuclear technology which were members of the NPT, with the purpose of establishing a set of norms regarding self-restraint in the supply of sensitive nuclear technology. This became known as the NPT Exporters Committee (or the Zangger Committee). At this meeting it was agreed that the export of nuclear items would be placed under the supervision of the IAEA; this would serve as an export stipulation. Another suppliers group (the London Suppliers Group) comprising, apart from the former states, also France (at the time not yet a member of the NPT) agreed that the suppliers would abide by the same rules and, in addition, accept self-imposed restrictions in the export of installations or equipment for uranium enrichment and plutonium separation. In 1976 and 1977 Congress adopted amendments to the legislation on foreign aid. According to these amendments, the United States would not grant economic or military aid to states importing or building nuclear technology for uranium enrichment or plutonium separation, unless they accepted IAEA monitoring of all their nuclear installations. These were indicative of the change in Kissinger's policy on nuclear technology, as well as Congress' increased sensitivity to the proliferation issue. Kissinger's revised policy resembled, to a certain extent, the position held by previous administrations, which had seen nuclear nonproliferation as a foreign policy goal of central priority. Furthermore, Kissinger initiated various diplomatic measures to impede the transfer of sensitive nuclear technology to states which seemed interested in military nuclear development. In this effort the government won Congressional support; indeed the Congress pressed for even more aggressive action.

The activities of the administration were concentrated in a number of areas. One of the administration's major efforts was the attempt to persuade Pakistan to abandon its plans to acquire technology and equipment for plutonium separation. This policy was conducted with the carrot and the stick: the United States promised to supply Pakistan with conventional weapons should she decline the acquisition and establishment of plutonium-separation installations in Chasma, while threatening to withhold the weapons should Pakistan pursue the acquisition program. When these efforts failed, Kissinger tried to exert American influence on France. At first, this attempt met with Chirac's refusal to cooperate. Later in 1976, however, Giscard changed French policy and bowed to American pressure. While France continued to extend limited support to Pakistan, the extent of this assistance gradually declined.

On another front, the U.S. government attempted to cancel the clause in the Brazilian–German nuclear aid agreement concerning the transfer of sensitive nuclear technology (enrichment and separation installations). Similarly, an effort was made to limit the transfer of sensitive nuclear technology to South Korea and Taiwan. With respect to India, the government prevented the export of enriched (low grade) uranium to the nuclear reactor in Tarapur in 1976; the United States demanded, among other things, that India accept IAEA monitoring of all her nuclear installations[7] as the condition for the American granting of export licenses.

The Carter administration focused on nuclear proliferation to a much greater extent than had been the case in the Kissinger era, making nonproliferation an issue of top priority. Indeed, it hardly seems an exaggeration to suggest that the interest of the Carter administration in the problems of proliferation exceeded that of any previous administration. Vigorous efforts to advance the cause of nonproliferation were initiated, although from the start they generated considerable internal debate in American circles,[8] and between the United States and nuclear technology exporters regarding the preferable nonproliferation strategy. As Lawrence Scheinmann points out, the debate dealt with four issues: capability, motivation, denial, and control.[9] In the final analysis, all four of these issues turned on the question of whether to concentrate on preventing or limiting the transfer of nuclear technology, or whether to focus on the motivation of those states on the nuclear threshold (and also of those other states that had begun to investigate military nuclear options). Another issue considered was the "universality" of the restrictions that were to be imposed on nuclear development; was the approach to be comprehensive or differential, in that it would focus primarily on certain specific states?

In the event, the Carter administration pursued a variety of activities, most of which were related to limitations on the transfer of sensitive nuclear technology. While the suppliers of nuclear technology were not always willing to agree to American demands (for example, West Germany refused to refrain from transferring sensitive technology as part of her comprehensive agreement with Brazil), the combined efforts of the suppliers and consumers of nuclear technology did reap certain dividends. Brazil, for example, eventually decided not to insist on the supply of sensitive technology from Germany as part of the said agreement. Similarly, the United States applied intense pressure on Pakistan, particularly in 1979, to terminate its nuclear development program. On the legislative side, the Glenn Amendment to the foreign aid bill, adopted in 1977, provided for terminating American economic and military aid to states that had acquired uranium enrichment or separation facilities or that had carried out nuclear testing. In 1978 Congress passed the Nuclear Non-Proliferation Act, which determined that the United States would not sell nuclear reactors or nuclear fuel to states unwilling to adopt NPT or equivalent undertaking for bringing their installations and other activities under IAEA monitoring. Another effort initiated by the Carter administration on the international front was the convening in October 1977 of the International Nuclear Fuel Cycle Evaluation (INFCE) Conference. Over a period of over two and a half years, the INFCE, which included representatives of the nuclear technology suppliers, conducted research into the development of alternatives to the nuclear fuel cycle that would not lead to the production of nuclear weapons.

Even the Carter administration, however, which placed such great emphasis on nuclear nonproliferation, confronted dilemmas which characterized the entire nonproliferation effort. These dilemmas have related first, to the structure of the bipolar international system, and second, to contradictions which existed between a vigorous antiproliferation policy and other requirements of American policy. During the Cold War this was reflected in four major areas (the first two persisting into post-bipolarity):

First, the United States found it difficult to impose her will on allies, whether they be suppliers or consumers of nuclear technology, and aside from a few exceptional instances, the United States did not apply uncompromising and decisive pressure on her allies. The success of a policy of nonproliferation has depended on the existence of a consensus both within the United States and between the United States and her allies. Furthermore, the effectiveness of the policy is also dependent on the United States occupying a position of international hegemony in both the Western world, and in most parts of the third world, a situation which existed only until the middle or end of the 1950s (and even then, American hegemony was relevant only to some dimensions of the international system).

Second, a number of American allies that are on the threshold of developing a nuclear capability, suffer from serious regional security problems. Since the United States is unable to fully satisfy these states' demands for security, it is difficult for her to require that they refrain from nuclear development.

Third, the American–Soviet nuclear arms race made it difficult for the superpowers to demand that nonnuclear states refrain from equipping themselves with nuclear weapons.

Finally, and most importantly, Soviet–American competition, which, had been perceived as the central foreign policy issue by every American administration, constrained the nonproliferation effort, inasmuch as policies of nonproliferation were considered to hamper the competitive effort. This issue was, of course, highly complex, and involved many factors. On the one hand, nuclear nonproliferation was one of the only areas in which the two superpowers have reached agreement. Despite this agreement, competition between the superpowers forced the United States to practice occasional restraint in her nonproliferation efforts. An outstanding example of this phenomenon was the case of Pakistan. As mentioned previously, through the end of 1979 the United States intensified its pressure on Pakistan to refrain from any advances in the area of nuclear development. On the one hand, there had been talk of possible rewards (for example, the supply of F–16 planes) in return for Pakistani restraint. On the other hand, American aid was cut off, and there were even hints in the media (which, while denied officially, seemed to reflect a certain atmosphere in the administration) that secret American military action might be taken in order to eliminate the Pakistani enrichment installations.[10]

Following the Soviet invasion into Afghanistan, however, American policy changed. The Carter administration made every effort to strengthen relations with Pakistan as quickly as possible. This policy was seen as the administration's first priority, and it was also seen as a constraint on the prior effort to prevent nuclear proliferation. Given the changed circumstances, the United States adopted additional objectives as fallback positions for her nonproliferation policy. She continued to pursue the previous policy that had sought to totally prevent the Pakistani development of nuclear weapons. However, she adopted a more graduated policy including the following fallback positions:

1 a prohibition on nuclear testing;
2 the slowing of Pakistani development of nuclear weapons;
3 demanding a commitment from Pakistan not to transfer nuclear technology or nuclear-weapon components to nonnuclear states.

As a result of the new leniency in American policy, the door was opened for Pakistan to develop—if she so desired—nuclear weapons in secret, and, if successful, to enter the category of states which may have a "bomb in the basement" without fear of American sanctions. Nevertheless, Pakistan had been able to achieve this status only by her own efforts, as the United States continued strongly to urge the nuclear suppliers to refrain from transferring sensitive nuclear technology to Pakistan. It can also be assumed that any Pakistani statement to the effect of the actual existence of nuclear weapons (albeit without any testing) would have met a very stern American reaction.

The Reagan administration lowered even further the profile of American nonproliferation policy in relation to other foreign policy goals. This partial change may be understood against the background of the Reagan administration's special emphasis on the Soviet–American conflict, which became the focal point of American foreign policy. This change in the American position regarding nonproliferation had three outcomes: first, the United States did not exercise excessive pressure on states which were allies in the struggle against the Soviet Union. Second, the readiness to cooperate with the Soviet Union in global efforts diminished. Finally, the intensification of the nuclear arms race between the two superpowers again aroused concern that nonnuclear states were being required to refrain completely from equipping themselves with nuclear arms. Moreover, as contended in earlier chapters, the administration's perception of nuclear weapons as warfighting instruments narrowed the qualitative gap between nuclear weapons and conventional weapons, and raised doubts regarding the importance of a nonproliferation regime.

Nevertheless, the Reagan administration also continued in its efforts to prevent proliferation. It seems that its efforts intensified somewhat after the Israeli attack on the Iraqi reactor. In July 1981, following the attack, President Reagan reemphasized American foreign policy objectives regarding nonproliferation. Nonetheless, the profile remained lower than that of the Carter administration. Underlying Reagan's approach was an attempt to communicate with American allies, including those supplying and those receiving nuclear technology, rather than to pressure them in the area of nonproliferation. Moreover, this new approach opposed the universal application of nonproliferation policies, and emphasized rather the need to prevent "irresponsible" states from acquiring nuclear technology.[11] The approach was flexible rather than doctrinaire so that each case was to be dealt with on its own merits.[12]

American nonproliferation policy has been the outcome of the ongoing tension between the American will to prevent proliferation on the one hand, and political pressures and other political priorities on the other. In order to deal with these conflicting pressures, the United States has, over the years, adopted a number of ground rules to guide her behavior regarding nonproliferation. First, the United States limits the export of sensitive nuclear technology to nonnuclear states. In addition, she requires that the states to whom she does export nuclear technology or materials sign the Non-Proliferation Treaty and/or equivalent nonproliferation undertaking and accept full scope American or IAEA safeguard systems. Furthermore, she applies heavy pressure on other suppliers of nuclear technology that they refrain from transferring sensitive nuclear technology. She also demands as a condition for the transfer of nuclear technology or materials that they require IAEA safeguards on such transfers. As for the nuclear consumers—and this, in the final analysis, is the critical test of the nonproliferation policy—the United States pursues an integrated strategy of material assistance and pressure:

the material assistance comprises economic and political aid, with special emphasis on assistance in the acquisition of conventional weapons, while the pressure is manifest in her repeated demands to refrain from nuclear development and most certainly from the manufacture of nuclear weapons.

Nevertheless, at various junctures, in response to changing political circumstances and regional conditions, the United States has resigned itself to steps taken by regional states toward development of a nuclear capacity. It seems, for example, that for friendly states the United States has been willing to accept a strategy of ambiguity, even though such a strategy is probably indicative of an undeclared weapon-capability. It is important to distinguish in this regard between a number of issues. First, American resignation to the situation does not suggest that she has been pleased with it; rather, this resignation is the result of an awareness that her ability to impose her will on allies is limited, and that heavy pressure can often lead to results opposite to those desired, both from a general political perspective and in terms of halting proliferation. Second, in the absence of her ability to completely prevent the secret production of nuclear weapons (or the wherewithal for such production), the United States has focused her efforts on restraining those states already suspected of manufacturing nuclear weapons or weapon components. In this respect, the American objective is twofold: to prevent nuclear testing and to prevent the adoption of an openly nuclear strategic doctrine. Third, with one exception to be discussed below, the United States prevents the export of sensitive nuclear technology and materials to states suspected of having attained, or nearly attained, a nuclear capability. These states are confronted with the requirement that they place all their nuclear installations under the IAEA system of safeguards. The one exception to this policy rule was the American delivery in 1980 of nuclear materials to India. As of 1976, the United States had refused to supply nuclear fuel to India's nuclear reactors in Tarapor, unless India agreed to accept supervision over all her nuclear installations. India refused. In 1980, however, the Carter administration agreed to send two containers of low-grade enriched uranium to India despite the Indian refusal, but she did it only because of prior commitments made before the Act came into power. There were no further deliveries. (It must be stated that the reactors in Tarapur are safeguarded by the IAEA and the American demand concerned the application of American safeguard systems to *all* the Indian nuclear installations, including her reprocessing facilities. Eventually a political compromise was achieved by which France under-took to supply the nuclear fuel to Tarapoor.) Finally, the United States has applied pressure on the threshold states that have, or are close to having, a nuclear capability, in order that they refrain from the transfer of nuclear technology or materials to third parties.

Altogether, then, the United States over the years has adopted several methods and measures in pursuit of its nonproliferation policy. These included, in the first place diplomatic interactions with potential proliferators and technology suppliers. In these interactions the United States tried to discourage proliferation tendencies by suggesting positive incentives and pointing out potential costs involved in decisions to proliferate. Among the latter were not only threats of adverse American and international reactions, but also references to security, political and economic costs attendant on the acquisition of nuclear weapons. Second the United States enacted national legislation designed to restrict transfers of sensitive technology and to apply pressure on potential proliferators to desist from their efforts. A third avenue was bilateral contacts with the Soviet Union to coordinate antiproliferation measures. Significantly, even the strongly anti-Soviet Reagan administration renewed these bilateral meetings in 1982, and therefrom these were held at half-year intervals.[13] Fourth, the United States worked out multilateral arrangements and measures designed to impose technical constraints on transfers of sensitive materials to potential proliferators.

The United States and Proliferation in the Middle East

Most American decision-makers as well as most students of proliferation belonging to the security studies community have long been aware of the uniquely dangerous implications of proliferation in the Middle East. Proliferation in this region would be likely to generate major threats to world stability as well as to vital American interests. The Israeli nuclear effort has, therefore received much attention in Washington and caused deep concern. Washington became aware of this effort, of course, sometime before it became public in December 1960 (see Chapter 1). The Kennedy administration in particular was sensitive about proliferation and consequently applied diplomatic pressure on Israel in connection with it.[14] Indeed, President Kennedy and Prime Minister Ben-Gurion exchanged letters concerning this issue, and the Israeli nuclear project became a major bone of contention between the two leaders. It has even been speculated that among the reasons for Ben-Gurion's decision to resign in 1963 was the continued American pressure on the nuclear issue.

An illustration of the saliency of the proliferation issue among American objectives at the time was Dean Rusk's memorandum to President Kennedy of May 16, 1963. In it Rusk listed six American fundamental interests in the Middle East, among which was ... "E. Preventing proliferation of nuclear weapons."[15]

Throughout the Israeli–American discussions regarding Israel's security in general and the nuclear issue, Israel demanded American formal assurances to Israel's security, in the form of a defense treaty between the two countries. This would also comprise the transfer of needed American conventional arms.[16] It remains an open question whether if the United States did agree to sign a full-scale defense treaty with Israel (similar to the NATO treaty) she would have given up the nuclear program.

Under American pressure, as mentioned in Chapter 1, Israel agreed to accept biannual supervisory visits to the Dimona reactor. These, however, were stopped in 1969 because of American concern lest she be internationally implicated in the Israeli efforts, which apparently continued unimpeded.

American pressure on Israel did not subside during the Johnson administration. However, the American visits to Dimona, coupled with the more congenial relationship between President Johnson and Prime Minister Eshkol (compared to that obtaining between Kennedy and Ben-Gurion), apparently made the issue somewhat less salient. Moreover, the 1967 War and its various outcomes gained priority over all other American–Israeli issues. Nevertheless, from 1968 onward, Washington persisted in demands that Israel sign the NPT. One example out of many, reflecting continued American concern about the Israeli nuclear effort, was the discussion held between Deputy Prime Minister Yigal Allon and Secretary of State Dean Rusk on September 10, 1968, in the presence of Ambassador Yitzhak Rabin. In this discussion, Rusk stressed the American concern regarding nuclear developments in Israel; he also demanded once again that Israel sign the NPT.[17]

Indeed, the United States increasingly preferred to avoid the difficult dilemmas of how to react to Israel's ongoing nuclear development. This was made somewhat less problematic by Israel's caution and its keeping to an ambiguous posture. The American–Israeli "special relationship" also contributed to America's refraining from pursuing a vigorous diplomatic campaign to pressurize Israel into signing the NPT and giving up her nuclear development. Altogether, then, as we shall soon see, the United States' approach to nuclear development in Israel was in some respects similar to its policy toward other threshold countries. At the same time, the special relationship, and Washington's recognition that Israel indeed continuously faces existential threats added to the former's reluctance to apply major pressures on Israel in this respect.

The suspicions and concerns of the United States justified the claim of those in Israel opposed to full nuclear development that the Americans might respond sharply to any major steps taken by Israel in this direction. On the other hand, the United States in fact "accepted"—though with great reluctance—Israel's overall activity in the nuclear field.[18] At the same time, however, the United States adopted another rule in regard to Israel (already mentioned in this chapter), which she similarly endorsed in her relationship with other threshold states: the United States will punish states that adopt an open nuclear doctrine. In a policy statement

150

on this issue, it was stated that their non-adoption of a nuclear doctrine is, in fact, Washington's objective regarding the existing "threshold states." In the same statement, Washington made it clear that it would continue in its efforts to prevent additional states joining the category of "threshold states."[19]

Until the late 1980s, the Israeli effort appeared to be the only immediate proliferation issue in the Middle East. The Iraqi effort revealed during the late 1980s and much more so following the Gulf War, led to a refocusing of American concern about the dangers of proliferation in the area. This will be discussed later in this chapter.

Soviet Policy on Proliferation—Introductory Notes

Soviet policy on nuclear proliferation was characterized by three distinct periods.[20] During the first period, until 1954, the proliferation problem was considered by the Soviet leadership to be an issue of secondary importance. The Soviet leadership's primary interest was in contending with the United States and in building her nuclear power. However, it should be noted that throughout this period, the Soviet Union strictly prevented the circulation of nuclear technology, a policy that was complete in symmetry with that of the United States. The second period began in the mid-1950s. Whether for its own reasons, or as a reaction to the new American "Atoms for Peace" policy, announced by Eisenhower in 1953, the Soviet Union decided to begin exporting nuclear technology to its allies. Nuclear cooperation agreements were signed with China, East Germany, Czechoslovakia, and Hungary. Nonetheless, nuclear technology of any significance was transferred only to China. Critically, this transfer also included, as is known, a uranium-enrichment facility. In 1958, however, the Soviet–Chinese crisis began to unfold and this led to the Soviet strategic decision to terminate all nuclear aid to China; the transfer of nuclear technology and equipment to China was halted completely, and by 1960 all Soviet nuclear experts had been removed from China.

It seems that during this second period, the Soviet willingness to transfer nuclear technology to states in the Soviet bloc was based on the assumption that she would be able to monitor the installations and to prevent her clients from developing independent nuclear capacities.[21]

In contrast to the second period, the third period, which began in the wake of the crisis with China, was marked by the Soviet adoption of an energetic nonproliferation policy. This policy had a double-edge: the Soviets joined the American initiative to create an international regime for the prevention of proliferation, and also consistently refrained from the large-scale export of nuclear technology, and especially of sensitive technologies such as plutonium-separation and uranium-enrichment

151

facilities. To the extent that the Soviet Union was willing to export nuclear technology, she demanded that the recipient state join the IAEA and that safeguards be applied to all of the client's nuclear installations.

During the Geneva talks on the NPT, the Soviet Union focused on a traditional Soviet posture on the danger of the acquisition of nuclear arms by West Germany. It seems, however, that the Soviet Union had reached the same conclusion as the United States: viz. that nuclear proliferation in general threatened her hegemonical status in the international system, and that it bore within it direct and indirect threats to Soviet security. This was the basis of the Soviet interest in cooperation with the United States in establishing the NPT regime, and in the setting up of other international forums such as the Zannger Committee and the INFCE. When participating in these organizations, the Soviet Union generally took an aggressive stand against proliferation. Finally, as mentioned previously, she was also willing to institutionalize bilateral meetings with the United States to deal with problems related to the proliferation issue.

It has been claimed that during the 1970s the Soviet nuclear reactor industry developed at a rapid pace, forming the basis of a Soviet economic interest in the commercial export of reactors. Among other things, it has been claimed that this interest explains the actual Soviet export of reactors, and her proposals to export nuclear power reactors to a number of states.[22] Three states may be noted in this context: India, Libya, and Cuba. A careful examination of this claim suggests that despite the existence of such an economic-based interest, the Soviet Union continued to proceed with great caution. The Libyan example will be discussed later at greater length. Regarding the other two states, it seems that the Soviet Union made various demands regarding the application of international safeguard systems as the condition for transferring nuclear technology or materials. She demanded that Cuba accept the supervision of the IAEA; there is also circumstantial evidence that she pressured Cuba to sign the Non-Proliferation Treaty and the Tlatelolco Treaty. Cuba refused these conditions, although eventually she did accept IAEA supervision. In any case, Soviet nuclear export to Cuba has been particularly slow and has not included sensitive technology.

The Soviet Union did sell heavy water to India, and also offered to sell her a power reactor. In both these cases, India was not asked to sign the NPT, but was requested to adopt a strict monitoring system for the reactor and for the use of the heavy water. In the end, and after extended negotiations, the reactor deal fell through. Heavy water was supplied to the Tarapoor reactor, which was already under IAEA supervision, but the Soviets demanded that the monitoring procedures be made more stringent. From the perspective of nonproliferation, the criticism of the Soviet decision to supply heavy water to India does not seem unjustified.

It must be stressed that a marked symmetry exists between the political-strategic considerations of the two superpowers regarding proliferation. An examination of Soviet behavior in general, however, reveals a much greater readiness than that of the United States to limit the export of nuclear technology and knowledge. Indeed, Soviet behavior proved far more responsible than that of the prominent Western suppliers of nuclear technology, such as France, West Germany, and Italy.

In summary, the Soviet Union adopted a consistent policy against nuclear proliferation, and applied the policy beyond the boundaries of its traditional opposition to the arming of West Germany with nuclear weaponry. Unlike the United States, the Soviet Union did not make many public statements on the dangers of nuclear proliferation, and did not even pressure the suppliers and consumers of nuclear materials. Nevertheless, she was extremely cautious in any matter related to the export of nuclear technology, and was willing to cooperate with the United States in different international forums set up to control proliferation.

From a different perspective, there existed an additional asymmetry between the two superpowers. Almost all the states on the "nuclear threshold" (those suspected of actually possessing undeclared nuclear weapons and those with the potential for their production) are states in the western bloc or politically close to it. India had been the only state with a neutral status. Moreover, some of these states—particularly Israel, Pakistan, Taiwan, and South Korea—were situated in close proximity to the Soviet Union; arming them with nuclear weapons was likely to constitute a direct danger to the Soviet Union, in addition to the danger that regional nuclear crises might deteriorate into nuclear crises between the superpowers.

The Soviet Union and Processes of Nuclearization in the Middle East

Soviet nuclear policy in the Middle East had two facets: first, Soviet policy on the export of nuclear technology to Arab states, and, second, the Soviet reactions to nuclear developments in Israel, both in general and as related to its readiness to grant nuclear guarantees to the Arab states. The Soviet Union had behaved stringently regarding the first facet; she did not transfer nuclear technology of any significance to the Arab states. In fact, excluding small research reactors set up in Egypt in the 1960s, in Libya and in Iraq (see below)—all reactors of no military significance whatsoever—no components of Soviet nuclear technology had been transferred to any Middle East state. The issue of the supply of nuclear power reactors to various states had been the subject of widespread debate in the Soviet Union, and these debates had received extensive coverage in the international media, but, as yet, none of these agreements had been realized.

153

Due to the irresponsible nature of the Libyan leadership, the connections between the Soviet Union and Libya in the area of nuclear technology had been the focus of special interest. Libya signed the NPT in 1968, but endorsed it only in 1975. The Soviet Union stipulated that Libya endorse the treaty as the condition for the transfer of nuclear technology.

In any case, despite the fact that Libya fulfilled the stipulation of becoming a party to the NPT and accepting the IAEA monitoring system, nuclear negotiations were conducted very slowly. In the event, a small research reactor with no military significance was set up and seems to have begun operation in 1981.[23] Moreover, the fact that the reactor had been operating with enriched uranium made Libya completely dependent on external sources for this material, thus minimizing her ability to operate the reactor independently. At a certain point, negotiations began on the supply of a large nuclear power plant, reports of which appeared frequently in the international press; it was soon ascertained, however, that no action had been taken to effect a deal. In addition, Libya decided at a certain stage to seek nuclear aid in the West, and reached an agreement with the Belgian company Belgonucleaire. The United States, however, began to exert its influence by pressuring Belgium to stop the supply of nuclear technology to Libya. It seems that this pressure caused the suspension of at least a certain portion of the Libyan–Belgian deal. These developments regarding the nuclear power plant testified to the Soviet Union's hesitations and caution in exporting nuclear technology. This caution in the context of the Middle East was also expressed, for example, by the Soviet rejection of Iraq's request to purchase a reactor to produce plutonium.

Significantly, the Soviet Union, while calling upon Israel to sign the NPT, also refused to treat Israel as if it violated the nonproliferation regime. The Israeli ambiguous posture was accepted by Soviet spokesmen who rejected the notion that Israel indeed had produced a nuclear weapons capability.

Another aspect of Soviet policy concerned the extent to which Moscow was ready to grant nuclear guarantees to friendly Arab states. Despite the many reports in both the Arab and the international press of agreements between the Soviet Union and various Arab states (in the last decade, particularly with Syria), there was never any public or official indication of such a Soviet commitment, and there may be good reason to doubt the accuracy of those reports.[24]

In any event, with the major change in Soviet policy vis-à-vis the West during the late 1980s, Moscow had retreated from military commitments to Middle Eastern allies. Simultaneously, Soviet spokesmen emphasized the need for various measures of arms control in the Middle East. Thus, in addition to the longstanding Soviet caution on nuclear issues, the

Soviet Union began searching for wider cooperation with the United States and regional powers designed to bring about extensive arms control agreements comprising also a ban on all weapons of mass destruction.

The Dissolution of the Soviet Union and its Potential Impact on Proliferation in the Middle East

The disintegration of the Soviet Union created a unique and dialectical situation in regard to proliferation. First, the end of the Cold War and the far-reaching agreements on major cuts in the nuclear arsenals of the United States and the Soviet Union (and, since the latter's disappearance, of its successors) mark the beginning of a major process of deemphasizing nuclear weapons in the international system. Against that background, the nonproliferation regime would appear initially to be greatly strengthened.

But, on the other hand, this disintegration creates several new proliferation threats. First, instead of one nuclear power—the Soviet Union—there are at present four such powers in the old territory of the Soviet Union: Russia, Ukraine, Kazakhstan, and Belarus. Furthermore, the level of control over and safeguarding of nuclear weapons in all these four states may be lower than it was in the Soviet Union. Similarly, the level of control over nuclear technology, nuclear materials and nuclear scientists may be much lower than in the former Soviet Union.

Finally, the new structure of the international system resulting from the disappearance of bipolarity will probably have profound effects on proliferation. We shall discuss this question in greater detail later in this chapter. Such discussion will also deal with the tendencies toward global denuclearization mentioned earlier. In the meantime we shall turn to the immediate potential of the disintegration of the Soviet Union on proliferation in the Middle East.

Problems of Control

A series of agreements between the United States and the Soviet Union (and later its inheritors in nuclear matters) is already having far-reaching effects on nuclear arsenals. First, the INF treaty has already resulted in the final dismantling of all the intermediate systems in the Soviet arsenal. Second, START, together with the subsequent Bush initiative of September 27, 1991, Gorbachev's response of October 5, 1991, the Lisbon agreement of May 23, 1992, and the agreement reached in the Bush–Yeltsin summit of June 1992, promise to reduce strategic nuclear arsenals by the year 2000 or 2003, to about a third of their current size. Moreover, according to the Lisbon agreement (and several previous undertakings), Ukraine, Kazakhstan, and Belarus have committed themselves to denuclearize completely by the year 1997.[25]

But in terms of horizontal proliferation, the real problem has not been the strategic systems deployed in Russia, Ukraine, Kazakhstan, and Belarus, but the tactical nuclear systems, primarily those deployed outside Russia. Controlling and safeguarding these weapons is much more difficult than with strategic systems, and all the more so in the republics outside of Russia. However, this problem was resolved to a large extent by the quick removal, between January and May of 1992, of all these weapons, some 6,500 in all, from all the eleven republics to Russia. Furthermore, according to the abovementioned Gorbachev undertaking of October 5, 1991 (which came as a response to the Bush initiative of September 27), all former Soviet tactical weapons will eventually be dismantled.[26]

There are, however, still several major unresolved proliferation threats resulting from the disintegration of the Soviet Union. First, notwithstanding the undertakings by the three republics, Ukraine, Kazakhstan, and Belarus, they might eventually refuse to dismantle the strategic nuclear forces still deployed on their grounds. At least the Ukraine appears to have adopted delaying tactics regarding the signing of the NPT as well as other measures toward its eventual denuclearization. The impact of such behavior on other potential proliferators could be primarily psychological and highly significant: hence, a refusal by Ukraine to abide by her official undertakings could adversely affect the nonproliferation regime.

Another uncertainty concerns the exact size of the inventories of tactical weapons. In the confusion following the disintegration of the Soviet Union, suspicions linger that some tactical weapons may have been left behind and unaccounted for. Have some of the republics, or groups within them, got hold of a few tactical warheads? Although the likelihood is low, there is no certain answer to this. If indeed some tactical weapons have been left behind, some of them may find their way into the hands of eager buyers.[27] The most common fear is that Iran would be such a buyer. One of the more reassuring counterarguments is that in the absence of launching systems, such as appropriate artillery or missiles, these nuclear arms may in fact be useless.

Another uncertainty has to do with fissionable material that may have been left behind in the republics without appropriate controls and may fall into the hands of local mafias who would smuggle it to potential proliferators. Alternatively, or in addition, governments in one or more of the republics may also be tempted to sell fissionable materials to proliferators. The tremendous financial problems of all the republics, together with the lack of internal order in some of them, all combined, as it were, with the absence of socialization of the decision-makers in the enormous dangers involved in nuclear weapons, creates a conducive context for irresponsible behavior with nuclear materials. Indeed, this situation may be dangerous also in regard to the enormous quantities of fissionable materials that are located in Russia itself.[28] These would increase in size with the process of dismantling of tactical and strategic weapons under the various arms control agreements. Part of this problem has been resolved with the American–Russian agreement for the purchase of U–235 taken out from dismantled nuclear weapons.[29] But uncertainties about control may increase if the internal situation in Russia were to deteriorate.

Post-Bipolarity and Proliferation

The Cold War and the competitive bipolar relationship which character- ized the international system until the late 1980s had contradictory effects on the probability of proliferation. On the one hand, the creation of the two big military alliances, NATO and the Warsaw Pact, as well as other military alliances, led by the two superpowers respectively, served as a major antiproliferation measure. Member countries of the alliances felt secure under the nuclear umbrellas extended by the superpowers. More- over, the structure of the alliances allowed the United States, and especially the Soviet Union, a considerable degree of control over their allies, a control designed to discourage them from becoming nuclear- weapons states. It is reasonable to assume that had it not been for these alliances and for bipolarity, several European powers (in addition to Britain and France), Japan, and possibly Canada would long ago have become nuclear-weapons states, and that some of the near-nuclear powers in Asia, such as Taiwan and South Korea, would by now have acquired a nuclear weapons capability. The chances are that, left unchecked, with no other collective security systems created, this would have led to universal proliferation.[30] On the other hand, as elaborated upon in this chapter, it was precisely competitive bipolarity which constrained the emergence of a more stringent nonproliferation regime.

That the disappearance of bipolarity, the end of the Cold War and the dissolution of the Soviet Union are already leading to the emergence of a new structure in the international system is almost too trivial to note. But what will be its nature and, more relevant to our discussion, what could be its effects on proliferation, is more difficult to assess. Many observers raise the possibility of a total change in the "rules of the game" organizing the future behavior of states, with economic competition and cooperation rather than traditional "high politics" becoming the compel- ling factors in international politics. This change, coupled with the con- tinued democratization of states, will resolve outstanding interstate and interethnic conflicts, and the world will gradually move toward inter- national regimes that guarantee peace and stability.[31]

While these trends do appear to have much influence on some dimen- sions of international politics, it appears more likely that, for the foreseeable future, traditional "high politics" interests and instruments will prevail in interstate relations in large parts of the international system. The process toward greater stability in the international system depends, therefore, not on complete transformation of the international "rules of the game," which is unrealistic, but rather on the emergence of a new *order* based on a coalition of great powers led by the United States. This new order will substitute for the bipolar system which, in some ways, served for forty-odd years as the guarantor of global stability. The influence of some of the new trends placing greater emphasis on economic competition and cooperation, mentioned above, together with the disappearance of the competitiveness that characterized the bipolar system, may provide greater stability in the international system than that which prevailed during bipolarity. Greater fragmentation of the international system resulting from multipolarity or, even more, from the difficulties in introducing order into regions characterized by high interstate and interethnic conflicts, may militate against such stabilizing developments. Another important factor militating against stabilizing developments may be the reluctance of the United States to play the difficult role of hegemonist, a role that might prove even more taxing than the role of leader of the West during the bipolar period. Bearing in mind these very general possibilities, I would like to pose two alternative configurations of the international system that might result from the termination of bipolarity. Although both configurations are extremely schematic, they nevertheless present a reference framework for the discussion of possible American and other big powers' policies toward proliferation and nuclear arms control in the Middle East. Both configurations are based on assumptions borrowed from a "realist" model of international politics, but recognize different variations of realism.

The first configuration sees the further strengthening of the U.S. position as world leader, backed by a coalition of the big economic powers and of Russia. The West European powers and Japan support overall American leadership because it can ensure their security and the stability of the international system. Russia is ready to accept the role of a secondary power and to cooperate with the United States both because it will, in the near and mid-term future, have no active and competitive foreign policy objectives, and because of its virtual dependency on Western economic support. This model does not suggest that the basic "rules of the game" governing interstate relations changed, so that eternal peace dominates, but rather that a new system of order replace the bipolar one, as the guarantor of international strategic stability. Moreover, the big powers are ready to cooperate strategically on most issues and confine their competitiveness to the economic sphere.

The second configuration is much more pessimistic. It assumes that the end of competitive bipolarity will lead to the disintegration of the military alliances led by the United States (the Warsaw Pact having already been dissolved), the withdrawal of the United States from the European scene and possibly from other parts of the world, and the resurgence of many centrifugal tendencies in the international system. The disintegration of Yugoslavia and the civil wars in Croatia and Bosnia, as well as the disintegration of the Soviet Union and the various ethnic conflicts and wars that have broken out in some of the new republics, are only the first signs of what lies ahead. And if these processes of disintegration, accompanied as they are by violence or potential violence, transpire in what until a few years ago was the most stable continent—Europe—it is likely that the situation would be more extreme on continents that are more turbulent. Under such circumstances, it is improbable that antiproliferation strategies would be enhanced. In fact, as John Mearsheimer has been arguing,[32] it is likely that more and more European states will choose to defend their security by arming themselves with nuclear weapons. One must assume that threshold countries in other parts of the world would do the same. Consequently, not only is control of proliferation unlikely, but it is probable that proliferation would become much more prevalent worldwide.

While it is difficult to predict future trends, it does appear that at least in the short- and mid-terms, the first model is more likely to materialize. Clearly the Gulf Crisis and War demonstrated that the United States is ready to impose order and use its force in the process. Moreover, it demonstrated America's ability to mobilize the backing of an impressive international coalition. In this case, obviously, all circumstances favored American policy and there were no strong contradictory interests that might have pushed coalition members in a direction different from that of America. But even with this reservation in mind, it appears likely that the system of interdependencies between the United States and the leading West European countries and Japan is so solid and robust that in most future eventualities their coalition would withstand pressures and even conflicts of interests if they occurred. At the very least, though they might not necessarily act in unison with the United States, they would avoid resisting American desires. The same obtains in the present American–Russian relationship. Russian foreign policy is already very supportive of Western, and especially American, aspirations and objectives, and because of economic needs which are becoming the dominant factor influencing policy, is likely to continue in its present course.

Beyond these general and partly theoretical considerations, it appears that a coalition of great powers committed to nonproliferation appears easier to maintain than coalitions designed for other purposes. This is so for two reasons. First, the nonproliferation regime is already in place and enjoys general support among all the big powers. The accession of France and China to the NPT during 1992 is a clear affirmation of this situation.

This in itself serves as a strong constraint on counter-tendencies. Second, the respective national interests of the nuclear powers (the case of China may be more ambiguous) in preventing proliferation is clear and strong. Assuming that no other priorities (such as those resulting from the bipolar competition) intervene, it is likely that the big powers would be eager to cooperate even more vigorously in the future to strengthen the nonproliferation regime.[33] Indeed, in the Russian case, the fear that some ex-Soviet Central Asian Muslim republics have somehow got control over some Soviet tactical nuclear weapons, is an additional major reason for deepening the overall nonproliferation policy.

In addition to the shared anti-proliferation interests discussed above, the United States and Russia have entered an era of major cuts in their own nuclear arsenals. This tends to further strengthen their interest in controlling and preventing proliferation, and if possible, also in reversing the state of current nuclear capabilities held by threshold countries.

Reductions in the nuclear arsenals of the United States and Russia are also likely to have a psychological effect on the leaderships of potential or threshold nuclear powers. They are likely to increase the hesitation of these leaderships concerning further nuclear weapons developments. But this psychological effect should not be overstated. States primarily motivated by security concerns would not be overwhelmingly sensitive to major arms control and arms reduction agreements between the two big nuclear powers. They would rather determine their nuclear policies by what they perceive as security threats on the one hand, and international pressures and real security assurances, on the other.

While reductions in the nuclear arsenals of the United States and Russia are likely to strengthen their commitment to nonproliferation and simultaneously to have a sobering effect on threshold countries, a caveat should be added. As argued previously, the success of the nonproliferation regime depends on an hierarchical structure of the international system in which the United States maintains her predominant position and in which Russia acts cooperatively and accepts the role of a secondary power. In order to play these roles, the United States must maintain its major means of military power, including nuclear capability. It follows, then, that *complete* nuclear disarmament of the US would not necessarily contribute to stability or, more specifically, to nonproliferation.

Developments during the 1980s and even before the end of bipolarity have suggested that nuclear development has indeed been maintained in the threshold states. However, due to a peculiar constellation of political, economic, strategic, and military conditions, they have decided to refrain from reliance on an open nuclear strategic doctrine because this is of suspect political and military benefit. Among these conditions was the high sensitivity to the possible reactions of the superpowers, and especially of the United States.

The recent changes in the international system appear already to have further strengthened decisions in some threshold states to reverse proliferation policies. Although in most of these cases the main causes for this reversal were regional considerations, nevertheless the new international realities appear to have influenced these decisions. Thus, Brazil and Argentina have agreed among themselves to control and halt their respective nuclear weapons programs. They have also opened their facilities to mutual inspection. India and Pakistan appear to be sufficiently concerned about their mutual nuclear relationship, that they are trying to work out rules of behavior concerning it. Pakistan has also declared that she is ready to turn the Indian subcontinent into a nuclear-free zone provided India agrees to this plan. India, however, because of concern about the Chinese threat, has rejected the idea. South Africa has acceded to the NPT and has opened her nuclear facilities to the AEA inspection teams.

On the other hand, there are other instances which indicate the desire of states to attain the threshold posture. To this list belong the recent revelations about the clandestine Iraqi program (described in Chapter 6) and information about the Iranian program. The North Korean nuclear-weapons effort also constitutes a threat to the nonproliferation regime. However, increased international pressure appears likely to result in this country halting its military nuclear program. More ominously, the Iraqi effort underlines the possibility that developing countries blessed with extensive economic resources, could establish a clandestine program for uranium enrichment based on a relatively low technology, without being detected by the IAEA system. Such an effort could be replicated by other countries with similar characteristics.

The preceding discussion suggests that the most likely situation in the coming years is the continuation of the nonproliferation regime, at least at today's level and, more probably, greater international effort to reverse proliferation tendencies. This would suggest, on the one hand, that threshold states aware of these new conditions, would be ready to accept two "red lines"—refraining from producing nuclear weapons, or in the case of states suspected of possessing undisclosed nuclear arsenals, refraining from nuclear testing and from declaring a strategic nuclear doctrine—and on the other hand, commitment on the part of the big powers to support the nonproliferation regime at least at its existing level. Such a commitment would require the application of strict sanctions against threshold states that infringe the said red lines.

Several international measures designed to strengthen the nonproliferation regime have already been taken. First, the IAEA inspection and safeguarding system has been expanded. This was done by activating the IAEA authority to conduct "special inspections," viz. inspections of undeclared (by the state members of the NPT) nuclear sites. Moreover, a special unit was established to receive intelligence regarding construction of undeclared sites. Complementing these measures was the growing involvement of the Security Council in stemming the proliferation of weapons of mass destruction. In addition, the London Suppliers Group in April 1992, significantly expanded the coverage of its export controls.[34] Finally, in July 1992, the United States initiated a new global initiative designed to halt completely all the production of PU–239 and U–235. The same initiative also provides for tightened controls on nuclear exports.[35] Whether the latter measure could fully be applied remains to be seen; probably it would at least become a focusing issue for international activity.

Post-bipolarity and Proliferation in the Middle East

Will the structural changes in the international system, arising from the end of bipolarity, have any specific implications for proliferation in the Middle East? As argued in this chapter, on the global level it is likely that the big powers, led by the United States, will be if anything, more active against proliferation than during bipolarity. It is likely, therefore, that this activity will be projected into the Middle East as well.

Indeed, in view of the important role that the threat of Iraq shortly becoming a nuclear power played in the public justification for the American decision to fight against Iraq, and the American fear that another regional war might lead to escalation to the nuclear threshold, the United States initiated, already in May 1991, an arms control plan for the Middle East.

The new initiative[36] placed the nonproliferation element within a broad arms control plan that comprised such elements as the elimination of nonnuclear weapons of mass destruction as well, along with the control of conventional weapons. This broad approach indicated that the U.S. administration realized that nonproliferation cannot be treated independently of other factors, such as security and arms control factors. The plan calls for a freeze on the production of weapon-grade plutonium and uranium as an initial step toward denuclearization. It also invites all regional powers to join the NPT and defines a NWFZ in the Middle East as the final objective. All these elements—treating nonproliferation as part of a more comprehensive arms control policy, perceiving it as part of broader issues of security, the call for a freeze on nuclear activity as the initial phase toward a gradual process of regional denuclearization— were already formulated in an earlier document that was the result of a UN study group.[37]

On the other hand, the motivations of some regional powers to proliferate may increase. In the Middle East, it appears that four proliferation issues are presently of concern: first, the need to complete the destruction of the Iraqi nuclear facilities and maintain a vigilant guard against renewed nuclear activity; second, the possibility that Iran may move toward the production of fissionable material and create the infrastructure for an eventual nuclear-weapons capability; third, Israel's threshold posture and the possibility, at this point rather hypothetical, that she will decide to adopt an explicit nuclear strategy; and finally, the concern that other regional states may decide to begin a nuclear-weapons program.

We shall address here primarily the Israeli issue, since it is relevant to the main theme of the book, namely, the costs–benefits calculus involved in alternative Israeli strategies. In Chapter 7 we shall discuss the different military, strategic, and political implications of this calculus. Here we shall address only international reactions to one possibility: an explicit Israeli adoption of a nuclear strategy.

Currently, with the peace process unfolding, the peace with Egypt stable, and Israel's main decision-maker, Prime Minister Rabin, significantly concerned about the dangers involved in proliferation (also see on this matter, Chapter 7), the likelihood of the adoption of such a strategy appears low. However, a speculative discussion of such a possibility is instructive, as events may change Israeli perceptions of her security environment, and as strategists may argue that in view of possible future proliferation in the Middle East and also of the ongoing threat of chemical weapons, Israel should move toward an explicit nuclear strategy.

Likely American Reactions

Even before the Gulf Crisis and War, following which the United States re-emphasized its antiproliferation policy, the likelihood of a strongly adverse American reaction to an Israeli move toward an explicit nuclear strategy would most probably have been very high. With the new emphasis on nonproliferation, the probability of such a reaction has only increased.

There would be several reasons for such a strong reaction. First, in view of the several successes of proliferation reversals—Brazil, Argentina, and South Africa—any major move toward explicit proliferation would signal a major defeat for the new trend. Second, and linked to the first reason, the American efforts to halt proliferation beyond the states mentioned above, would become very problematic if a close ally of the United States such as Israel, were to adopt an explicit nuclear posture. Three instances of these efforts clearly stand out. The United States is in the midst of intensive activity, apparently in varying degrees of coordination with Russia, China, and Japan, to halt the nuclearization of North Korea. In the Middle East itself, American antiproliferation efforts toward Iraq and Iran may become increasingly more problematic if Israel not only refrains from adopting some measures to lower the saliency of her nuclear posture but, on the contrary, moves in the opposite direction of greater explicitness.

In all the abovementioned antiproliferation cases, the United States may face two difficulties: in maintaining the pressure on the potential proliferators; and, as important, in mobilizing international effort to back this pressure. At present, all this is more relevant to Iran and North Korea. As far as Iraq is concerned, its regime is so revolting in the eyes of international public opinion that the United States has, and will have, sufficient international backing to maintain its antiproliferation activity.[38] But even there things may change. A new regime that is more acceptable to the international community may emerge, and then eventually decide to continue a search for a nuclear-weapons infrastructure. Similar considerations may then apply to it as well.

A counter argument is that all these countries—North Korea, Iraq, and Iran—are extremely hostile to the United States and the West and hence are the *par excellence* current anti-status quo powers. Consequently, antiproliferation activity can and should be directed at them without any reference to the status of proliferation in other states, especially those that are closely allied with the United States, such as Israel. Although there is some credence in this argument, it nevertheless appears difficult to expect that the United States could maintain a totally different nonproliferation policy regarding Israel on the one hand, and the anti-status quo countries on the other. The difficulties would multiply if Israel went beyond her current policy of ambiguity toward greater explicitness.

One reason for these difficulties has to do with the universalistic dimension of the nonproliferation regime. Although there are clear differences in proliferation status among states, and this should dictate different policies within the overall nonproliferation regime, nevertheless it is difficult for the United States to apply totally variant and contradictory policies vis-à-vis threshold countries. The difficulties multiply precisely with the increased emphasis put on nonproliferation. This issue may become a major problem when the United States searches for cooperation with the nuclear suppliers, aimed at curbing transfers of sensitive technology and materials to the anti-status quo powers. It appears likely that nuclear suppliers such as China, and possibly Russia (though she has strong strategic and political reasons not to do that), which have strong commercial incentives to sell such technology, may utilize the nonuniversal application of antiproliferation tactics as a good reason to justify transfers of technology to countries such as Iraq (if the embargo is removed), Iran, and eventually other proliferators.

Another relevant instance is that of Pakistan. Whereas Iran, Iraq, and North Korea are hostile countries to the United States, Pakistan has been an ally and has enjoyed considerable American financial and military support over the years. In 1990, however, in accordance with the

Glenn–Symington Amendment to the International Security Aid Law as well as the Pressler Amendment, the United States stopped her financial support to Pakistan because of the latter's nuclear program. This pressure has already resulted in two limited successes: first, Pakistan's apparent readiness to accept the idea of a nuclear weapons free zone in South Asia (a proposal that India rejects); and second, a partial capping of her nuclear activity. In February 1992, Pakistan's foreign minister declared that his country had frozen production of elements that, if put together, could become nuclear devices. He also declared that his country would not test a nuclear device and would not export nuclear technology to other countries.[39] However, continued American pressure on Pakistan in the field of nonproliferation may ultimately also be affected by American policy toward Israel and the Middle East.

In sum, then, it is likely that an Israeli move toward greater explicitness in the nuclear field would ultimately constrain overall American efforts in the area of nonproliferation both in terms of direct interactions with the threshold states and, even more so, in her interactions with the nuclear suppliers.

In addition to these difficulties, the explicit nuclearization of Israel might pose difficulties for the United States in her relations with Arab allies, and primarily Egypt. Egyptian pressure to secure a nuclear weapons free zone in the Middle East (see the discussion in Chapter 7) might be dealt a major blow by such an Israeli step, and this might complicate American–Egyptian relations.

Then again, the American legislative system is such that an explicit nuclearization of Israel would force it to react sharply. The Glenn and Symmington Amendments of 1977 prohibit the granting of economic or military aid to a nonnuclear state (according to the definition of the NPT) that carries out nuclear testing or that imports or exports nuclear explosives or devices or facilities for plutonium extraction or uranium enrichment. Although a hair-splitting argument may point out that Israel's nuclear activity no longer relies on imports of nuclear explosives or facilities, it stands to reason that these amendments could be applied against Israel as well.

In addition, explicit nuclearization of Israel may also result in strong pressures in the United States against sales of conventional arms to her. The argument would probably be that once Israel had based her defense on nuclear arms, the need to maintain her conventional superiority against hostile Arab states would disappear.

Furthermore, against the background of the general trend toward the dismantling of large parts of the American and Russian nuclear arsenals as demonstrated by the START 2 agreement, a countermove by Israel may result in an overall, adverse American political reaction to her.

Finally, explicit nuclearization by Israel might have two implications:

on the one hand, it might strengthen deterrence and thus reduce the probability of war; on the other hand, however, it might encourage regional proliferation and also lower the threshold for the use of nuclear weapons. This might bring about the actual use of these weapons. The effects on the international system as well as on the nonproliferation regime, then, might be catastrophic (and see a further discussion of this point in Chapter 7).

Feldman listed (in the early 1980s)[40] a number of factors likely to moderate the American reaction. Some of them have gained in strength since then; others have lost their relevance. It is worthwhile, in any case, to recount and discuss them. First, in the wake of the Israeli declaration (which might include testing), a sharp American reaction would in any case be ineffective. The Israeli action, once taken, could not be retracted. The United States would do better focusing on ways to minimize the possible damage, an end that could not be achieved by punishing Israel. Second, were American military aid to be cut off, Israel's conventional weapon capability would be weakened, paradoxically increasing her reliance on a nuclear deterrent; the danger of nuclear war would similarly intensify. In contrast, the continuation of military aid would enable Israel to rely on conventional weapons in response to threats which do not endanger the very existence of the state. Third, an Israeli declaration of this nature would not constitute a major surprise to most members of the "strategic community" in the United States, among whom Israel is already suspected of possessing nuclear weapons; the psychological impact would thus be relatively mild. Fourth, in order to protect the nonproliferation regime, the United States might seek to convince Israel to sign the NPT as a *nuclear* state. To accomplish this, the United States must refrain from punishing her. Fifth, and most importantly, the strength of the American commitment to Israel is sufficient to overcome any damage due to Israel's nuclearization. Israel is perceived, in any case, as an "exceptional case" in terms of America's nonproliferation policy. For example, no explicit American action was taken against Israel when reports appeared in the mass media (reports that often had their origins with American official sources such as the CIA) that Israel was secretly arming with nuclear weapons. Similarly, the United States at one time expressed a readiness to transfer a nuclear power plant to Israel (on condition that it would be placed under a safeguard system), at the same time that the CIA was leaking information regarding the existence of an Israeli nuclear weapons arsenal. Feldman takes this argument one step further, in his claim that in direct clashes of the American interest in nonproliferation with her other vital interests, nonproliferation emerges the loser. Indeed, the American commitment to Israel is perceived in Washington as having priority over the interest in nonproliferation. This consideration, Feldman argues, prevented the Reagan administration from initiating a legislative process in the Senate to pass another amendment which would have demanded that the United States terminate aid to any state "which produces nuclear weapons" (the Glenn Amendment deals rather with nuclear testing, or with the import or export of plutonium-separation and uranium-enrichment facilities).

While there is a significant degree of realism to some of Feldman's arguments, in other respects the opposite case, it would seem, could be argued at present with greater force. Regarding his first claim that the punishment of Israel would be ineffective, account must also be taken of the potential damage to American credibility in her role in the international nonproliferation regime, that might result from her failure to impose sanctions. For this and other reasons, there is a high probability that the United States would be forced to carry out a substantial, painful cut in aid to Israel. Turning now to the claim that the "strategic community" in the United States would not be surprised by Israel's adoption of an unambiguous nuclear strategy, here too the issue is by no means clear-cut. Indeed, on the one hand, by the early 1990s this argument was strengthened because of the partial erosion of the ambiguity surrounding Israel's nuclear capability. On the other hand, however, the nonproliferation regime is based on the inviolability of the "red lines" mentioned earlier, prohibiting threshold countries suspected of having an actual nuclear capability from testing or declaring a nuclear doctrine. Israel's crossing a red line would constitute a pronounced blow, both symbolic and real, to the nonproliferation regime. American strategists are well aware of this, and therefore it is difficult to imagine that the United States and certainly the other nuclear powers would encourage Israel to join the NPT as a nuclear member. Such a move would lead to very strong pressures to allow Arab states to become nuclear as well and accept a similar status under the NPT regime. Furthermore, it would undercut the pressure on these countries to join the treaty prohibiting the production of chemical weapons. The Arab countries consider chemical weapons as a counterweight to Israel's nuclear capability (see, in Chapter 7, a discussion of this issue).

Israeli membership under these conditions would also be infused with legal complications. The NPT explicitly delineates the criteria for nuclear and nonnuclear status; on these definitions, it is not at all clear whether an openly nuclear Israel could gain entry *with nuclear status*. Moreover, Israel's joining the NPT as a "nuclear state" would constitute a major blow to the nonproliferation regime. Since its creation in 1968, when the NPT was accepted by the ENDC, this regime has held to the principle that new nuclear states would not be permitted to emerge, and that states that nuclearize do so in absolute opposition to the spirit of the treaty. If the United States is interested in the continued existence of the NPT, it is likely that she would also be interested in preventing Israel from joining the treaty as a "nuclear state." In passing it should be noted that according to a very limiting interpretation of the wording of the NPT, Israel might be able to join the NPT as a "non-nuclear" state. According to NPT definitions, a "nuclear state" is one which conducted a test prior to January 1, 1968. Theoretically, therefore, Israel could join irrespective of her past actions, and her joining would not affect whatever capability she had previously achieved. The only limitation would be on the future activity of her nuclear installations which would have to be safeguarded by the IAEA inspection mechanism. It is, of course, not clear at all whether this peculiar status would be acceptable by the NPT and the IAEA. Indeed, in the case of South Africa's accession to the NPT, the agreement with the IAEA appears to cover all the stockpile of fissionable material already accumulated until the accession to the NPT.

Another argument raised by Feldman is the depth of American commitment to Israel, and the relatively low priority assigned to nonproliferation in comparison to her other policy objectives. The commitment to Israel is certainly very strong. But, as discussed earlier in this chapter, nonproliferation has gained considerably in significance in American priorities since the end of the Cold War and since the Gulf War. It is highly likely that under the Clinton administration it will become—if need be—even more central and important. Moreover, the commitment to Israel itself is not absolute; in the past it has withstood difficult tests, but this is perhaps no sure indication of its strength in the future. Israeli decision-makers must bear in mind that certain courses of action are liable to have a wearing effect on this commitment, and that —whether the results be immediate or long term—could be critical for Israel.

Feldman points to two possible contexts in which, he argues, the severity of the American response would be softened:[41] were the nonproliferation system to show signs of weakening, that is, were a number of threshold states to nuclearize; and were Israel to be forthcoming within the framework of a generous peace plan. A few comments are appropriate in this regard. First, were the nonproliferation system to crumble and even limited worldwide nuclear proliferation to become a fact of life, then, indeed, American reactions to an Israeli move in this direction would be constrained. However, such a development is likely to change overall American activity in different regions of the world. It is probable that the United States would gradually lessen her international involvement in dangerous, conflict-ridden regions such as the Middle East. Over the long, or perhaps even short term, the weakening of American regional involvement would be accompanied in any case by less American aid to Israel. However, in any case—as indeed is argued in this chapter—there is at present a higher likelihood of movement in the opposite direction, viz. considerable strengthening of the nonproliferation regime. Second, regarding Israel's nuclearization in the framework of a peace plan in which she was required to make generous concessions, the following comments may be made: a comprehensive Arab–Israeli peace, although it would not suspend the need for an effective Israeli deterrence force, would significantly weaken Arab motivation for initiating war. It would almost certainly prevent the creation of a grand Arab war coalition. In such circumstances, the need for explicit nuclear deterrence would be doubtful, even in the eyes of those who fear a general Arab attack which would endanger Israel's very existence. Similarly, Israel has many needs, particularly in the economic realm and in the realm of conventional weapons. A peace agreement with Jordan and with Syria would certainly include significant Israeli territorial concessions; in exchange for these concessions Israel could demand, and receive considerations not only from the Arab side but also from the United States. This is a scenario for which there already exist precedents. For example, in the framework of the peace agreement with Egypt, the United States granted Israel three billion dollars in credit to build alternative air bases in the Negev. Were it not for the peculiar sense of pride of then Prime Minister Menachem Begin, Israel might have received this sum as a grant. In addition, the United States made a far-reaching commitment to supply fuel should Israel suffer energy problems as a result of the transfer of the Gulf of Suez oil wells to Egypt. It seems reasonable to assume that similar, if not greater, compensation might be forthcoming following any future peace agreement. Israel's announcement, in the context of a peace agreement, that she possesses nuclear weapons, may sap most American willingness to compensate Israel. The upshot will be a trade-off between two possible types of compensation: American willingness to refrain from punishing Israel for nuclearizing (the punishment, if carried out, would probably be by means of a large cut in the usual aid package), versus the presumably extensive special compensation, financial, strategic, or diplomatic, that might be expected following Israel's signing of a peace settlement. The proponents of an open nuclear doctrine as the solution to Israel's security problems, would, we can presume, be willing to bear the costs of the American reaction. However, those skeptical of the potential efficacy of a nuclear doctrine, must consider the loss of the expected American compensation for Israeli concessions for peace. The opportunity cost would comprise the loss of possible large-scale economic compensation, continued transfers of state of the art conventional weapons, American military guarantees for the peace agreement, and possibly an American–Israeli defense treaty (and see, on the latter point, the brief discussion in Chapter 7).

It seems fair to speculate that American considerations would be completely different were Israel to declare a nuclear doctrine in the context of one or more of the Arab states arming themselves with nuclear weapons. A number of scenarios are possible in this regard, of which perhaps the most relevant is the transfer of ready nuclear weapons from a nuclear power to an Arab state. In such a situation it is likely that the United States would try first (in coordination with the other big powers) to denuclearize this country, in which context it would also perforce have to pressurize Israel to lower her nuclear profile. Failing that, the United States would be likely to accept Israel's explicit nuclearization, and American–Israeli relations would remain undamaged, at least in the first stage. Nonetheless, as mentioned earlier, it is possible that the United States' relations with Israel might weaken over time, as part of a general strategic decision to lessen her involvement in a nuclearized Middle East. A partial American diplomatic withdrawal may arise from an assessment of the dangers to American security deriving from continued intervention in an unstable and nuclear Middle East.

How Would Russia and Other Nuclear Powers React to Israeli Explicit Nuclearization?

Although the reactions of the United States to Israeli explicit nuclearization are the most critical, the policies other nuclear powers may adopt also have considerable significance. First, the United States requires these countries' support in the application of diplomatic and economic pressures on other threshold states aimed at preempting violations by these states of the various nuclear thresholds mentioned in this chapter. Indeed, the recent experience of the international effort against the nuclearization of North Korea demonstrates the importance of cooperative activity by the United States, Russia, China, and Japan in halting that country's nuclear program. Similarly, American attempts to halt proliferation to other Middle Eastern countries such as Iraq and Iran may prove to be dependent to a large extent on cooperation with the leading nuclear suppliers and other big powers. But such future support would probably depend, in turn, on the firmness with which the United States would react to Israel's explicit nuclearization. Such a move by Israel may threaten to disrupt the whole nonproliferation regime. Therefore, lack of a firm American reaction may lead to weakening of other nuclear powers' commitments against global proliferation, and to their hesitancy in supporting American-led efforts vis-à-vis other threshold countries. This, overall, would again be liable to weaken the nonproliferation regime.

Second, the acknowledged nuclear powers are currently bound by their commitments to the NPT not to transfer weapons-related nuclear materials and technology to nonnuclear states. Israeli explicit nuclearization, if it is not reversed under American and international pressure, may signal to these suppliers that they can relax their own constraints on the transfers of sensitive technology and materials to other Middle Eastern countries, especially those with which they have close diplomatic and economic ties. These Middle Eastern countries would in any case probably apply much pressure on the nuclear suppliers to help them balance the Israeli capability.

Among the nuclear powers, the case of Russia is special in several respects. First, she still harbors a nuclear capability roughly similar to that of the United States. Second, while the Soviet Union existed it was the second most important external actor in the Middle East, having special strategic relationships with some of the leading regional powers. Although Russian involvement in the Middle East has markedly declined compared to that of the Soviet Union, she still, as a big power, maintains keen interest in the region. In this context it should be noted, however, that Russia at present is cultivating good and close relations with Israel and has certainly abandoned her significant bias in favor of the Arab states. Third, Russia has a strong interest in nonproliferation and in that respect is continuing the policy of the Soviet Union described in this chapter. Fourth, at present Russia is generally supportive of American policy and, both because of her own interest in nonproliferation, as well as her economic dependence on the United States and the West, is likely to follow the American lead on nonproliferation policy. On the other hand, because of her major economic problems, Russia has a strong commercial motive to export whatever she can, including nuclear technology. Paradoxically, this motive may at present be less constrained by political and strategic considerations than was the case while the Soviet Union existed.

So long as the Soviet Union was actively involved in the Middle East and pursuing a competitive policy against the United States, it was likely that Israeli explicit nuclearization would have resulted in a meaningful, independent Soviet reaction. The Soviet Union, bound by strategic commitments to several Arab countries involved in deep conflict with Israel, would have had to demonstrate its credibility as an ally and strategic patron. Some observers, in the past, went so far as to suggest that Israeli explicit nuclearization would have resulted in a Soviet preemptive strike against Israel.[42] Such assessments already appeared at the time to be completely imaginary and devoid of any realistic understanding of the great caution the Soviet Union displayed in all nuclear-related issues and toward the possibility of escalation to a Soviet–American crisis (which might have followed such a strike). Another possibility discussed in the literature was that of the Soviet Union transferring nuclear weapons to Arab allies. Bearing in mind the great caution which the Soviet Union displayed concerning nuclear proliferation, this also appeared to have been of extremely low probability. A more realistic proposition would have been the extension of military (nuclear or nonnuclear) guarantees to Arab allies designed to counter Israeli nuclear threats of actual nuclear strikes. The Soviet Union might have also sought to cooperate with the

United States in applying direct pressure on Israel to reverse her policy. But all this belongs to the past.

Turning to possible Russian reactions to Israeli explicit nuclearization, it should be noted that Russia does not at present have political and strategic commitments that would compel her to demonstrate credibility as a patron and ally in the Middle East, nor is she involved in competition with the United States. Therefore, it is unlikely that she would undertake steps involving her in unilateral military guarantees in the region.

Since Russia continues Soviet antiproliferation policy and has a strong commitment to the far-reaching nuclear arms reductions agreements with the United States, it appears unlikely that she would transfer ready-made nuclear weapons to regional countries. The most probable scenario is that Russia would back the United States in its diplomatic efforts to reverse an Israeli move. Only if such an effort were to fail and the United States—contrary to my previous analysis—accepted the Israeli move without sanctions or other focused activity, might Russia then resort to independent measures. With the decline of foreign policy and global strategic considerations in her overall calculations, Russia may feel less responsible for international security and stability globally as well as in the Middle East. She might, therefore, allow commercial and economic considerations rather than political and strategic factors gain priority in influencing her decisions. She might, hence, become readier to sell sensitive technology and materials to Arab countries.

It is also likely that under conditions of explicit Israeli nuclearization, the reactions of most of the other nuclear suppliers such as Britain, France, Japan, and Germany, as well as other large industrialized countries would be likely to follow the American lead. It is also likely that if American efforts were to fail, the inhibitions on transfers by these suppliers of sensitive technology to Arab countries would diminish. The situation may be even more critical for other nuclear suppliers who at present appear to be suspicious, in any case, of the dominant American global posture. China, India, and Pakistan may find it in their political and strategic interests, in addition to their commercial considerations that exist in any case, to make liberal sales of sensitive technology and materials to other Middle Eastern countries. In any case, Israeli explicit nuclearization is liable to seriously disrupt the global nonproliferation regime. Under these circumstances it is possible that these countries might also be tempted to sell readymade nuclear weapons as well.

In sum then, it appears likely that an Israeli decision to explicitly base her defense on a nuclear-weapons capability would result in far-reaching, international, political and strategic consequences. Apart from direct political costs to Israel, a likely development would be the removal of many of the constraints on wider nuclearization of the Middle East.

5

MANAGEMENT OF A NUCLEAR MIDDLE EAST

Chapter 3 focused on the possible dangers inherent in nuclear prolifer-ation in the Middle East. This chapter will deal with the difficult problem of moderating and delimiting these dangers, should proliferation indeed occur in the region. Of course, this is not to say that the author views nuclear proliferation in the region as either desirable or unavoidable—precisely the opposite. It should also be noted that the measures outlined in this chapter, aside from the complexity of the political arrangements, are in themselves problematic and replete with contradictions. Clearly then, the discussion is hypothetical in that it proposes measures for the management of a situation that has not yet arisen. An important upshot of the analysis is the apparent difficulty in managing a nuclear Middle East. The basic assumption underlying the discussion is that a nuclear Middle East will include a number of nuclear states and a number of states with conventional weapons.

There are four domains in which activity might moderate the dangers of the nuclearization of the region. The objective of this activity is, on the one hand, to prevent political and military crises from deteriorating into situations of nuclear confrontation, and on the other hand, to influ-ence nuclear development, weapons deployment, and strategic doctrines so as to lessen the dangers that might undermine regional stability. The four domains are as follows:

1 Political arrangements between regional countries, particularly between Israel and her Arab neighbors, across the spectrum—from management of the conflict through conflict reduction, to conflict resolution incor-porating a political solution of the conflict;
2 The external powers' political and military influence on processes of escalation;
3 The role of conventional military power in the framework of interstate relations;
4 The deployment of nuclear forces and the doctrines for their use.

Activity in the first domain (this matter will be developed further in

Chapter 7) is important whatever the military circumstances, even if nuclear weapons are not introduced into the region. Only moderation of the political environment, and ideally a peace settlement, can obtain relative stability for the region. As such, the first domain is the most important of the four. Similarly, the control and regulation of certain aspects of conventional military forces is desirable even in a nonnuclear Middle East.

In Chapter 3 we surveyed the structure of the Middle East system and the prominence and persistence of conflict and competition in that region. At first glance, this structure and these behavioral patterns would seem to impede the development of a stable strategic system. Nevertheless, we can assume that such patterns of behavior are subject to moderation, and indeed, we noted the beginnings of initial developments in that direction. In the paragraphs that follow, we will attempt to draw attention to those aspects of regional politics that may act as the generators of stabilizing developments. The main focus of discussion will be relations between Israel and the Arab world, and in particular, Israeli policy.

Restraining Political Conflicts

The starting point of this discussion assumes that the level of friction between Israel and her neighbors is relatively high, and liable to result in periodic political-military crises. As was argued in Chapter 3, if such crises were to develop, the nuclear threat would not always suffice in preventing the deterioration of a crisis situation into war. Moreover, there is an attendant risk that an intense political-strategic crisis would bring about limited military operations with catastrophic results. Another situation in this category is one in which a high level of political conflict could serve as the background for intensified terrorist and guerrilla activities carried out by one or more Arab states against Israel. If such activities were to become intolerable, Israel might respond with a limited military operation, resulting in a severe strategic crisis and ensuing escalation of dangerous proportions.

Nuclear weapons do not delete the balance of political interests from the overall equation of deterrence. Thus, an intolerable level of political grievance felt by one state, caused by a rival state, disturbs the balance of political interests, with a consequent impact on the stability of the overall deterrence equation. The side which suffers the political grievance is liable to initiate a military operation.[1] In this context, it is interesting to note that even Shai Feldman, who gives extreme expression to the view that nuclear weapons create a decided discontinuity with the preceding conventional environment, and that they radically improve the effectiveness of deterrence, vigorously supports the pursuit of political solutions

174

to ease the imbalance of interests.[2] In other words, even the proponents of the notion that nuclear proliferation stabilizes the Middle East system, recognize that the balance of political interests is a significant component in the equation of nuclear deterrence. Note that the political balance affects not only the motivation of the challenger, but also the credibility of nuclear threats issued by a defender, and which are intended to deter attacks on its less-than-vital interests.

The territories occupied by Israel in 1967 present, without doubt, the most difficult political problem to have confronted Israel in the wake of that impressive military victory. The question of Sinai was resolved with the signing of a peace agreement with Egypt. However, the entire question of the West Bank remains open. The Palestinian issue, charged by partial Arab identification and solidarity, further complicates the situation. Let us analyze this question in greater detail.

There is no doubt that from a chronological point of view, the Palestinian problem constitutes the source of the Arab–Israeli conflict. In other places in this book we have pointed out that from the time the Arab–Israeli issue became an interstate conflict, that is from 1948 on, the conflict was enacted on a series of independent levels, each with a dynamic of its own, between Israel and a number of Arab states: Israel and Egypt; Israel and Jordan; Israel and Syria. Iraq was also involved in the Arab–Israeli wars, as were other Arab states, but all to a lesser extent.

However, the formation of a specific interstate dynamic in these independent conflicts did not dispel the Palestinian motif. The latter retains a high profile and partially shapes, in various ways, the positions of the different Arab states toward Israel. As long as the potence of this factor is not significantly reduced, it will continue to be a catalyst of conflict in the region.

This point must be clarified further. On the one hand, every Arab state looks to its own special interests. From this perspective, a solution to the problem of the Sinai and the Golan constitutes a significant easing of the diadic conflicts with Egypt and Syria respectively. On the other hand, despite the current fragmentation in the Arab world, the dimension of Arab identity remains centrally important, creating sensitivities and political commitments on a number of shared Arab interests, the foremost among them being the Palestinian issue. It is true that when the national political interests thus dictate (for example, Jordan in 1970, Syria in 1976 and again in 1983, and Kuwait in 1991), the various Arab states do not hesitate to harm the Palestinians, to attempt the destruction of their independent organizations and even to kill them *en masse*. Nevertheless, these states consistently identify with the national plight of the Palestinians. Their readiness to go to war for only the Palestinian issue was always questionable, but it has a cumulative effect; when other reasons are added, their threshold to initiate military action against Israel is lowered.

The resolution of the Palestinian issue would remove one irritating factor. In addition it would strengthen the particularistic tendencies of the various Arab states precisely because it would diminish one of the main factors generating Arab solidarity.

The absence of a partial solution to the Palestinian issue (or rather, lowering the prominence of the national plight of the Palestinians) may also harm, during the course of time, the basis of the 1979 Israel–Egypt peace agreement. As a result, during severe strategic-political crises between Israel and other Arab states, there would be a greater probability that the peace agreement would be undermined and that a process of escalation would develop, with the participation of Egypt (this was not the case in the Gulf Crisis and War, because these were primarily inter-Arab events which involved Israel only marginally).

It seems then that a political agreement regarding the West Bank, that included a partial solution to the Palestinian problem (a comprehensive solution does not seem possible), would remove a powerful cause of political friction from Israeli–Arab relations. The balance of interests would be affected, and the danger of Arab–Israeli crises would be reduced.

More specifically, it seems that the return of Arab sovereignty to most or part of the West Bank would constitute, to a large extent, a satisfactory solution to Arab aspirations. In the view of the present writer, the most desirable settlement would be a Palestinian–Jordanian solution; that is to say, Israel would eventually withdraw from the West Bank, where a confederation arrangement, to be agreed upon between Jordan and representative Palestinians, would be formed.[3] (See below a further discussion in Chapter 7.)

A solution to the problem of the West Bank would weaken the ideological dimension of the Arab–Israeli conflict, strengthen the peace agreement between Egypt and Israel, make possible a peace agreement with Jordan and with a significant part of the Palestinian people, and quite possibly lead to explicit or implicit peace agreements with other Arab states such as Morocco, Tunisia, Saudi Arabia, the Gulf countries, and perhaps even Iraq.

In contrast, it must not be assumed that such an arrangement would reduce the level of conflict with Syria. Syria is highly perturbed by Israeli control of the Golan Heights. The fact that Syria has reemerged as the most decisive, influential external factor in Lebanon may have reduced the level of political grievance resulting from Israeli control of the Golan Heights; her role in Lebanon obtained political gains, while keeping her intensely occupied.[4] Yet, until the question of the Golan Heights is settled, the Israel–Syrian conflict will persist. Consequently, a Jordanian–Palestinian solution to the West Bank, which is not accompanied by a solution of the Golan issue, would constitute a strategic-political blow to Syria and would intensify her motivation to subvert the system of political arrangements.

At the same time, it may be assumed that Syria, should she be isolated (following a Jordanian–Israeli agreement and the strengthening of the Egyptian–Israeli peace), would find it very difficult to invoke military options against Israel, even without the nuclear deterrence factor.

In any case, a solution to the problem of the Golan Heights would further diminish the risks of a military confrontation. This is not the place to enter into a detailed discussion of the parameters of such an agreement. However, suffice it to say that a Syrian–Israeli agreement would further reduce the dangers inherent in political crises and military escalation in the Israeli–Arab sector. It seems clear that such an agreement would have a positive influence in either a nuclear or conventional weapons environment. In the aftermath of the Gulf War, and with Syria opting to side with the United States and Egypt, the likelihood of a political settlement on the Golan Heights has increased.

Peace agreement in a nuclear context might also have a paradoxical effect. The "deepening" of peace agreements by means of explicit or implicit arrangements with neighboring countries could lead to the intensification of Israeli political activity in the Middle East. Thus, for example, dispensing with the West Bank and the tribulations associated with its occupation, and enacting a peace arrangement with Jordan, would have the effect of tightening Israel's political relations with Egypt, perhaps even to the extent of strategic cooperation. The same, perhaps more so, might hold for Israeli relations with Jordan. Indeed, something of the sort arose in Israel's involvement in 1970 in defense of the Jordanian regime against Syrian intervention.

In this respect Israel is confronted by a complex dilemma. It can be assumed that following an Israeli–Arab peace agreement, political conflicts between the Arab countries in the region may continue. It must also be assumed that Egypt and Jordan will occasionally become involved in these conflicts. Israel must recognize the dangers that might arise from the deterioration of these conflicts into crises or even military confrontations, when involved in an alliance-type relationship with one of the conflict protagonists. In such circumstances, Israel is liable to be drawn into a crisis unrelated to her vital interests, and involving a military escalation that might end in a nuclear exchange. Thus, while explicit alliance relations are desirable for Israel from a number of perspectives, both political and strategic, they also involve a degree of risk. In a nuclear context, the intensity of the problem is manifoldly increased.

Another variant of this paradox should also be noted: will the alliance members themselves be nuclear? If not (as would probably be the case for Jordan), the security arrangements made with these countries might lead to an explicit or implicit nuclear guarantee from Israel. Were Jordan under threat from other Arab states, Israel would need to consider whether to intervene on Jordan's behalf. The danger of nuclear crisis (that is, in which the countries threatening Jordan are nuclear, such as Iraq) would be even greater. In contrast, should Israel refrain from extending her security perimeter to include Jordan following an agreement on the West Bank, the Jordanians might face difficulties in the conventional military sphere. It is difficult to find an adequate solution to this dilemma.

This contradiction between nuclear and political logic may arise in every complex of close relations between Israel and other Middle Eastern countries or parties. Ties that are too tight are liable to result in dangerous strategic involvements. Ties too loose are liable to harm Israel's political interests.

One of the possible conclusions to be drawn from this analysis is that aside from critical strategic-political interests, as for example, relations with Jordan, it is desirable that in the context of a nuclear Middle East, Israel pursue a policy of strategic nonintervention. Not only must she refrain, to the extent possible, from any active military initiative, she must also avoid deepening political and strategic ties that might involve her in nuclear complications.

In summary, then, the continuation of the current conflicts is liable to undermine the stability of a nuclear Middle East. Generally speaking, the most that can be stated with confidence is that the ideal model for political relations in a nuclear Middle East would require the significant reduction of interstate conflicts. Since cooperative relations among certain countries in the region might be a source of concern to other countries (as a function of the logic of establishing competitive regional coalitions), it is desirable that strategic cooperation in the Middle East be relatively limited. In other words, so long as the interaction between countries is reduced, the danger of conflict is reduced. The preferable alternative model is one that Stanley Hoffman has termed "polycentrism," that is, figuratively speaking, each country's withdrawal behind high strategic and political walls.[5] It should be obvious that this is only an "ideal type" (in the Weberian sense), which could not be fully realized. The proposition of this model is intended only to modify political reality in this direction. However, it is likely that the presence of various political and economic variables would make such a configuration difficult to secure.

The Task of the Big Powers

Chapter 4 dealt with the policies the superpowers applied in the past against nuclear proliferation in the Middle East. It further discussed likely international reactions to an Israeli endorsement of an explicit nuclear posture. We will now deal with the question of possible big powers' policies assuming the general failure of nonproliferation in the Middle

178

East. The question thus becomes: barring the possibility of withdrawal from active political role in the Middle East, how should the United States in the first place and Russia and possibly other nuclear powers in the second place behave in order to reduce the dangers inherent in the nuclearization of the Middle East? As argued in Chapter 4, with the changes in the relative power of the United States and the Soviet Union, followed as it was by the dissolution of the Soviet Union, it is clear that the main actor would be the United States. However, as Russia remains the second nuclear power in the world, and because—in the long run— the Middle East will most probably remain an area of great interest for her, she may also play a role in policies aimed at reducing the risks involved in proliferation.

The end of the Cold War has sharply reduced the danger that a regional nuclear crisis or the actual use of nuclear weapons in a regional conflict might escalate into a global nuclear crisis. Consequently, one of the main concerns about proliferation in general and in the Middle East in particular, has been removed. Nevertheless, regional proliferation would continue to pose risks to the United States, Russia, and the global security. One way to deal with the dangers would be to impose an hierarchical structure on the Middle East under the leadership of the United States playing the primary role and Russia a secondary and supportive role.[6] In such a system these powers may extend military guarantees to all the regional states and commit themselves to come to their aid in case of attack. Thus, for example, they could reach an understanding regarding the management of regional conventional and nuclear crises, by which they would jointly compel the parties involved in the crisis to reach a settlement.

Russian cooperation is needed by the United States for three reasons: first, continued Russian influence with some of the regional states; second, the continued Russian role as a major arms supplier to the region, and finally, to provide international legitimacy to the American role.

One variation of this model is the creation of a permanent management mechanism for Middle Eastern crises to be administered jointly by the United States and Russia,[7] which would be activated immediately upon the development of any crisis. It should be mentioned that several mechanisms for inspection of arms control agreements and for crisis management are already in place, managed jointly by the United States and Russia (and before 1992 the Soviet Union). These include *inter alia* the mechanisms agreed upon to supervise the SALT–1 agreement and later on the START and CFE agreements. A crisis prevention mechanism had been established within the framework of the CSCE.

The crisis management mechanism described here is different from the CSCE one, in that it represents the power of the "managers" of the hierarchical system, which are external actors in the Middle East. (It is possible to establish a mechanism for crisis management with the participation of the regional states within a non hierarchical regional system. But this is not discussed here.) It could also comprise capabilities for political and technical advanced warning. The latter would allow for diplomatic preemption of crises. To be sure, the effectiveness of such a mechanism is a correlate of American–Russian relations; given better relations, they can more effectively anticipate crises and plan strategies for their resolution—rather than simply dealing with crises as they arise.

In the model presented as well as in its variation there exists a fundamental paradox. Since the United States and Russia rightfully view nuclear proliferation as a potential threat to their essential interests, they will invest considerable efforts to limit proliferation or to prevent it altogether. Their ability to do so, in the past however, was limited by three constraints: the opposition of regional countries to superpower coercion, the readiness of nuclear suppliers to provide regional powers with sensitive technology, and competition between the superpowers themselves. At present the third constraint has become irrelevant; similarly, since the United States and Russia have at present cooperative relations, they may be in a stronger position to overcome regional states' opposition together. Thus, given the premises of the model, the probability is higher than in the past that proliferation would be prevented from the outset, or to the extent that proliferation has occurred, regional countries would be required to dismantle their nuclear weapons. A tentative conclusion is that situations of hierarchical management (by external big powers) in a nuclear Middle East, will be fleeting. Either the "managers" succeed in dismantling the regional powers' nuclear weapons, or they withdraw from the region as a result of their inability to manage it.

Another area in which the external nuclear powers (primarily the United States and Russia, but in addition the other formal nuclear powers), could contribute is related to the transfer of nuclear "hardware," auxiliary systems, and doctrines. John Weltman and, in a more extended way, Lewis Dunn[8] have suggested, for example, that were nuclear proliferation to take root in any region, the external nuclear powers could help stabilize that region by transferring, jointly or separately, different nuclear components that might help stabilize regional nuclear relations. In other words, once proliferation begins, the United States and Russia are to reverse the strategies they had followed prior to proliferation. Instead of preventing the transfer of nuclear knowhow and technology, they are now to transfer select elements of nuclear technology and auxiliary systems in order to intensify regional stability. Such transfers would include:

1 different components for improving the effectiveness of regional states' second strike capacity;

2 components for command and control systems.

Measures of this nature would be, of course, highly problematic.[9] First, nuclear powers have in the past refrained from transferring actual nuclear weapons to other countries, and even to their allies. The only exception has been the occasional American transfers of delivery systems to Britain. In addition, there have been transfers of sensitive nuclear technology, such as the Soviet supply of nuclear aid to China in the second half of the 1950s, but similar instances have also been limited. (Private Western companies did transfer at times sensitive technology, but usually against the policies of their respective states.) A conceptual revolution would have to occur before decision-makers might consider such actions. Second, were widespread distribution of certain types of nuclear weapons to occur, the United States (and perhaps Russia and other nuclear countries as well) would likely demand political or financial payments in exchange for those transfers. The outcome would be the possible asymmetrical transfer of retaliatory systems, and command and control systems, to different countries according to commercial or political considerations. Moreover, the nuclear suppliers might fear that the strengthened nuclear power of the regional countries is liable to be turned against them. Russia is particularly sensitive on this issue, given that the distance between her (and especially her southern regions) and the Middle East is not all that great. Russia is liable to be concerned that the development of retaliatory power by Middle Eastern countries with relatively well-developed nuclear forces, might contribute to the creation of "minimal deterrence" against her. Moreover, with the uncertain situation in some of the Central Asian ex-Soviet republics, Russia might fear a possible coalition between a nuclear Middle Eastern country and one or more of these republics. This coalition might very well have an anti-Russian objective.

Similarly, will the transfer of the required nuclear technology be coordinated among the nuclear countries? Past experience does not guarantee that this would be the case. Medium nuclear powers, such as France, have been willing in the past—in exchange for economic and commercial considerations—to take only partial account of the limitations on transfer of nuclear knowhow and technology. Later on China was ready to transfer sensitive technology for a mix of political and commercial reasons. But both countries have since become parties to the NPT and become much more restrictive in their nuclear technology exports. But in a world of widespread nuclear proliferation, all the limitations of the past would rapidly disappear. Consequently the transfer of technology would most likely include dangerous components from the point of view of strategic stability.

The actual transfer of nuclear weapons to nonnuclear countries would precede the transfer of components for second-strike systems, and command and control systems. The question that would arise is whether it is desirable from the point of view of stability to promptly supply nuclear weapons to nonnuclear countries whose neighbors possess any sort of nuclear capability. It seems that this issue will occupy the formal nuclear powers even before any question arises regarding the transfer of stabilizing nuclear technology. It may be assumed that the various supplier countries' political, strategic and commercial considerations will influence these decisions more than considerations regarding the strengthening of regional stability. The inevitable conclusion that emerges from this analysis is that the adoption of a strategy such as that proposed by Weltman, and in a more critical way by Dunn, would require stringent preparations and, it may be assumed, even intensive coordination between the nuclear suppliers. Three sets of considerations are at play in this matter: first, the different interests of the nuclear countries; second, these countries' concern at the possibility of an undesirable extension of the military power and sophistication of the regional nuclear powers; and third, the improvement of regional stability. It is possible that these three sets of considerations will be in conflict. As stated previously, only the highest level of preliminary coordination, requiring a congenial atmosphere of cooperation, will allow the application of such means to achieve nuclear stability in the area. Such an atmosphere would likely lead to preliminary attempts by the external powers to preempt proliferation. Finally, in a period in which the United States and the Soviet Union (and later Russia) have reached agreements on extensive cuts in their own nuclear forces, it is unlikely that they would transfer nuclear weapons to third parties. The overall conclusion then, is that the strategy proposed by Weltman (and those elements of which that Dunn develops) does not seem realistic or practical. On the other hand Dunn's ideas concerning advice on doctrinal formulation appear more practical.

Conventional Military Behavior

In Chapter 3 we noted that in today's Middle East system there is a relatively high state of readiness to use military force to achieve political objectives. This readiness is reinforced by the system's multipolar structure and the persistence of inter- and intrastate conflicts; these factors intensify the anarchic character of international relations in the area and render the possibility of nuclear proliferation in the area a dangerous prospect. Thus, a critical prerequisite to the reduction of regional anarchy is a qualitative change in the perception of the role of military power in relation to the achievement of ideological and political objectives. This point relates to three levels of conflict.

First, eliminating the initiation of large-scale conventional wars such as

Israel–Arab wars, or the Iraq–Iran war, or the Iraqi invasion of Kuwait, and even of limited military confrontations such as the South Yemen–North Yemen confrontation. Second, the management of limited military campaigns which break out occasionally within or between regional countries. Thus, for example, regional countries ought to avoid military intervention on behalf of an ethnic or religious minority in a neighboring country, something which could quickly lead to a comprehensive, even nuclear interstate confrontation. A third level relates to the support of large-scale terrorist activity. It seems that such activity is far from harming the nuclear tolerance threshold. Wide range terrorist activity, however, could lead to a limited conventional military retaliation by the victim, which in turn, could lead to a dangerous process of escalation.

Exercises and Maneuvers: The Application of Confidence-Building Measures (CBM)

Another area in which the countries must proceed cautiously is that of military maneuvers and troop deployment in conditions of peace (or nonwar).[10] The enormous conventional military power that exists in the region, and the short distances between protagonists, constitute an unusually fertile background for errors in perceiving the intentions governing an opponent's military activities and maneuvers. This effect will be exacerbated by the possible future use of delivery systems with a "dual capability;" that is, that can carry either conventional or nuclear warheads. This is the case, first and foremost, regarding the large number of attack planes presently in the region, many of which could serve as suitable platforms for the delivery of nuclear warheads. Many of the short and medium range surface-to-surface missiles deployed in the region also possess a "dual capability." Their deployment in forward positions in an exercise may create anxieties.

In any case, military exercises and the deployment of conventional forces in sensitive areas are liable to provoke immediate concern in neighboring countries, particularly during times of political conflict. Such activities might be perceived as an indication of possible imminent attack. An outstanding example of an escalation of this sort occurred on the eve of World War I. This escalation process was the result of decisions on the part of various countries regarding the mobilization of reserves and troop deployment. Each of these decisions was a central input in the other countries' decision-making processes. Thus, for example, the Russian decision to mobilize was among the major inputs in Germany's decision-making process. Permanent instructions were issued regarding behavior during mobilization; this framework of instructions dictated the initial behavioral pattern in each country, to which was added input regarding mobilization in other countries. The result was a process of recurrent and reflective inputs involving multiple actors.

Precedents can also be found in the Middle East. The most prominent example is the deployment of Egyptian forces to Sinai in 1967. These forces were activated as a measure intended initially to deter Israel. In the event, their deployment initiated a process of escalation, the result of which was the 1967 War.

In an Arab–Israeli nuclear environment, the movement of conventional forces would be many times more serious, in particular given the two sides' tendency to view surprise attacks and preemptive retaliatory attacks as the preferred strategy. The dilemmas facing Israel would be, in such circumstance, acute. Israel depends on the mobilization of her reserve troops in times of emergency. The mobilization of reserves both places a heavy burden on the state and might indicate to hostile countries that Israel is planning a preemptive military attack against her neighbors. It appears that then it would be essential to obtain far-reaching agreements limiting military maneuvers and exercises. In addition, it will be necessary to determine arrangements for the mutual supervision of military exercises, that is, the validation of the two sides' intentions by means of verification and control. Such arrangements would have to include a number of elements: first, open communication lines via third-party states to enable the smooth flow of information regarding planned maneuvers and exercises; second, the positioning of observers from neighboring countries to participate in and to closely observe military exercises; third, the possible transfer of information regarding the character and objective of these drills. It is, of course, obvious that monitoring situations of this kind provoke a difficult dilemma: verification techniques are effective only if the nature of the exercises is not kept secret. But secrecy is part of the arsenal of conventional power. The cited dilemma would almost certainly be the background to the opposition to such methods on the part of the domestic military establishments. However, in the absence of these controls, every exercise or mobilization of reserves could, theoretically, lead to a chain reaction involving escalation unintended by the rival parties. In short, given the permanent nature of the "security dilemma" in environments in which the profile of conventional weaponry is high, as is the case of the Middle East, the spiral of escalation is an ever-present possibility. In this respect, it is unlikely that the introduction of nuclear weaponry would have any positive effect. It should be noted that notwithstanding the intensity of conflicts in the Middle East, *de facto* CBMs have already been applied in the Middle East and have provided some important constraints on potential escalations.[11]

More problematic are air force operations. The states of the region would have to reach agreements regarding the scope of air activity. In the absence of agreement, the merely routine training activities of fighter squadrons is liable to register on rival countries' warning systems. There would be a tendency for states to overreact to any movement in their territorial air space. This problem seems to have no apparent resolution, and only the institution of detailed, credible control arrangements might somewhat reduce its acuteness. Paul Bracken has noted[12] that as the sophistication of the control and warning systems of two rival sides increases, so too does the intensity of their mutual interaction. One side's irregular activity can cause the other's immediate reaction. To the extent that early warning systems are linked directly to the country's aerial interception forces, the danger of rapid escalation increases. The inherent logic is as follows: When an early warning system is directly linked to all levels of defense and interception systems, the issuing of warnings will activate the interception system without the involvement of the strategic-political level.

However, given the small warning distances in the Middle East, anything but an integrated direct link between the warning and interception systems is, from the point of view of air defense, not feasible. The corollary risks of politically or strategically undesirable escalation are the outcome of geographical-military necessity.[13]

The participation of the nuclear factor would dramatically exacerbate the dangers stemming from problems of command and control. In a nuclear environment there will be an urgent need to attain explicit agreements regarding the activation of aerial systems, and on opening channels of communication between the political and strategic command hierarchies of the different countries in the area. Ideally, neighboring countries would arrive at agreements strictly delimiting air exercises. In addition, it would be necessary to transmit regular messages regarding planned air movements. Even under these conditions, the mutual interconnection between the command and control systems of different states would remain a highly problematic issue. It is possible, however, that interstate agreements can reduce the attendant dangers. Here again, the fear of unintended escalation has already in the past, forced Israel and some Arab states to reach *de facto* understandings about aerial "rules of engagement."[14] However, because of the risks involved, "rules of engagement" under nuclear conditions must be more strict and demanding than before and should be formalized.

The Deployment of Nuclear Forces and Operational Doctrine

At one time there was a consensus among most nuclear strategists that a stable balance of nuclear deterrence was a function of three conditions: the absolute superiority of offensive systems over defensive systems; the existence of a reliable second-strike capacity; and a targeting doctrine emphasizing a countervalue rather than counterforce targets (that is, a targeting doctrine with a deterrence rather than a defense orientation). The development of systems that might undermine one of these three conditions was perceived as a threat to the stability of the nuclear balance. It should be noted, however, that this view of things is not held to unanimously: powerful schools of thought have argued against the relevance of the first and third of these assumptions, and the practice of the superpowers also deviated from the norms that adherence to these assumptions would oblige (see Chapter 3).

One of the major reasons for American hesitation about a "pure" countervalue deterrence strategy was the problem of credibility, given the requirements of extended deterrence. This would probably be of less relevance in the Middle East, and thus, in the regional context, the logic of the third assumption seems to hold.

According to the logic of the above three assumptions, it would be desirable that nuclear powers in the Middle East develop an exclusively "countervalue" (or countercity) posture while refraining from "counterforce" deployments.

As for the development of a second-strike capacity, it would be clearly possible to influence the balance of nuclear deterrence by encouraging the transfer of certain kinds of systems and discouraging the transfer of others. For example, V/STOL aircraft could act as a relatively efficient second-strike system. Their dispersal among a number of states would raise the profile of the second strike in regional strategic perceptions. Moreover, this issue could be linked with the issue of early warning systems. Since the V/STOL system is suitable as a second-strike force, it is even more important that understandings or special arrangements regarding its use for reconnaissance or exercises during peace time be obtained (see the discussion in Chapter 3).

A countervalue doctrine would also dictate the number of nuclear weapons that ought to be possessed by nations in the region. In fact, for the purposes of deterrence in its most limited sense, that is to say, the ability to inflict an intolerable punishment on main population centers in each one of the states of the area, the number of nuclear weapons need not be very great. If we consider this from the Israeli point of view, then the Israeli arsenal would need to be sufficient to deter each of the possible nuclear powers in the area, of which there may be no more than four or five. Assuming that five or six nuclear bombs hitting their target would be sufficient for the relatively efficient destruction of primary population centers in each one of these states, a total of only 25 to 30 warheads would be required. Adding a margin of security in the event that some portion of this arsenal be destroyed by a nuclear preemptive strike, and another part would perhaps fail to reach its target, possession of about 50 nuclear bombs would seem reasonable from the Israeli point of view.

As the ceiling for all other nuclear powers in the region as well, it would seem to guarantee that no state's arsenal could constitute a first-strike counterforce threat against any other. Moreover, it would be sufficient to comprise a rudimentary second-strike force. Any extension of a state's nuclear forces beyond this point may generate immediate concern among the other nuclear states; fear would be aroused as to its possible intentions of developing a reliable counterforce first-strike capability.

Needless to say, the achievement of regional agreements guaranteeing limitations on the number of nuclear weapons would be difficult and extremely complicated. For example, we can assume that nuclear development in the area will be asymmetric. It is also reasonable to assume that Israel will precede the Arab nations in this field by a large gap. Within the framework of negotiations on such agreements, Israel could claim, fairly justifiably, that since her population is concentrated in a very limited territory, she is more sensitive to nuclear war than the Arab nations. She could also claim that even though the Arab world is split on many issues, it is highly unlikely that there would be any nuclear coalition between Israel and an Arab nuclear power. An Arab coalition against Israel is a more probable scenario. On this basis, Israel's possession of a nuclear arsenal exceeding that of all the Arab states would appear justified. Beyond the question of arsenal asymmetries, there is also the actual problem of supervising the arsenal ceiling. If the principal nuclear strength were to be land-based missiles, and to a lesser degree missile boats, then it would be possible to supervise the quantitative ceiling by means of aerial observation. The problem becomes much more complex if a significant component of a nuclear force were to be delivered via ground attack aircraft, something that is well within the realm of possibility. There are a considerable number of ground attack aircraft in the region, and no way of supervising the number of nuclear bombs in storage. Supervision can be conducted only by intensive on-site inspection. Such a mechanism would meet extreme opposition on the part of some or all regional states.

Nevertheless, it would be highly desirable to reach agreement on effective mechanisms for supervising stocks of nuclear weapons. Only in this way can it be possible to guarantee that the various states pursue a "countervalue" strategy, which, as such, is of purely deterrent intent. This would diminish fear of counterforce attacks and first strikes.

The regional states might be reticent in reaching agreements for mutual on-site inspection. The solution to this problem would seem to be that the task of inspection be performed primarily by the superpowers, jointly or separately, but more likely by the United States by itself, depending on its credibility with different states. In the event that the local states suspect one superpower of unfriendly intent, it would be possible to arrive at an agreement whereby each superpower inspect its allies. In this

187

regard, the superpowers would need to reach an understanding that, in turn, would be dependent on a measure of cooperation between them.

Abstention from the development of a "counterforce" potential would also be conditional on the development of defensive measures guaranteeing the effectiveness of a second strike. However, the case of the superpowers has shown that despite the development of a highly dependable second-strike capability (and a third, and a fourth, and beyond), both powers continued to emphasize the development of "counterforce" power. There is at work here an internal dynamic in the development of nuclear weapons. In order to avoid the repetition of this phenomenon in the Middle East, it is important that, under the supervision of the superpowers, arrangements be concluded for the imposition of quantitative limitations. This should be done before the quantity of nuclear weapons attains the level of a rudimentary "counterforce" capability, or even the very appearance of such.

Tactical Nuclear Weapons

First, let us begin by reviewing the various distinctions between strategic, theater, and tactical weapons as they apply to the regional context. In the Middle East these distinctions are blurred, because of the short range in comparison with intercontinental and even intra-European distances. The existence of relatively few population centers, and the relatively small size of the cities in the region, also contribute to the blurring of these distinctions.

The principal nuclear warheads to be deployed in the region, at least in the first stage, will comprise fission rather than fusion bombs (while not ruling out the possible eventual introduction of fusion technology). The destructive effect of these bombs is relatively small (in nuclear terms). In the superpower and European contexts, these bombs are classed, in most cases, as tactical nuclear weapons, and sometimes as theater weapons. However, the distinctions between strategic and tactical weapons becomes blurred by the special conditions obtaining in the Middle East. Here, even what may be considered in other contexts as tactical weapons, may have strategic implications. Nevertheless, the deployment of nuclear weapons intended primarily for battlefield uses, such as some short-range artillery shells, is not a possibility that should necessarily be dismissed.

Is it desirable that the states of the Middle East arm themselves with battlefield weapons and develop doctrines for battlefield uses? We begin with Israel. Let us examine the possible implications. First of all, tactical nuclear weapons in the superpower context have two related functions, but which are in partial mutual contradiction. On the one hand, they form an additional layer in the fabric of nuclear deterrence, in that they bridge the gap between the use of conventional and nuclear force.

The use of tactical weapons has less destructive results than the use of strategic weapons, and therefore from a psychological point of view are "easier" to use. The use of a tactical nuclear weapon creates a new psychological climate, in which the use of strategic weapons becomes more feasible. The upshot is that the deterrence posture of states possessing tactical weapons is strengthened because their threat to use strategic weapons becomes more credible. On the other hand, tactical weapons have a combat function. That is, beyond the sense in which they shorten the route to the use of strategic weaponry, tactical weapons can have a significant impact on the battlefield, especially in a situation in which conventional forces have been routed. The contradiction is in this: while the first function underpins deterrence and lends credibility to deterrence threats, the second function relates to an actual battlefield role. The first function assumes the affectivity of deterrence in preventing war; the second function assumes its failure.

It was noted in the foregoing that in the Arab–Israeli region, and indeed throughout the Middle East, the distinction between tactical and strategic weapons is much less sharp than in the super power system. Since the use of tactical weapons can have strategic outcomes, the psychological difficulties inherent in the decision to use such weapons in the Middle East are greater than in the framework of superpower relations. A decision regarding the use of tactical weapons will be more difficult to make and would have to take full account of the likely strategic outcomes.

Consequently, in the absence of gradation—which is the cornerstone of the "bridging" effect—deterrence will not be strengthened. The decision to use tactical weapons will be problematic and dangerous to the same extent as the use of strategic weapons. The irrationality of such a decision will be greater than that of a decision in Washington or Moscow to shoot a few tactical nuclear shells in Europe or Southeast Asia. As a result, the credibility of a threat to use tactical nuclear weapons in the first stage of a war, while refraining from the use of strategic weapons, will be low.

The blurring of the distinction between the use of battlefield and strategic weapons may, in fact, weaken the deterrence effect. Moreover, in a war situation the blurredness of the distinction is a potential source of danger in terms of the deterioration from the use of conventional to nuclear weaponry. These conditions are unlike the situation which used to exist between the superpowers. For example, in the European theater, until the major political changes of the late 1980s which transformed all the strategic environment, the doctrine of "graduated response," left open the possibility (albeit problematic) that following the use of battlefield nuclear weapons, military action will be terminated. Tactical weapons had a bridging effect, but could also halt the process of deterioration prior to the use of strategic weapons. The military action would all along be accompanied by intense diplomatic efforts to achieve an end to hostilities. The use of tactical nuclear weapons acts as an indicator of a willingness to escalate, as well as an intermediate stepping-off point, that might prevent further deterioration.

In the Israeli–Arab sector battlefield weapons will have no "firebreak" effect, because of the blurring between the different stages of nuclear escalation. Thus, the danger of losing control of the process of escalation will be greater than in the European arena. From this perspective, it appears that tactical nuclear weapons impose serious additional dangers, and hence, their deployment in the region must be considered strategically unwise.

In this respect, there is another point to be made. As has been detailed in other parts of this book, in the Middle East there has been a considerable emphasis on the preemptive strike. Moreover, from the Israeli perspective, having defined for herself a system of "casus belli," a preemptive strike might be a necessary strategy in the event that she is faced with a war coalition of Arab states.[15] Consider the following possible scenario: The political situation in the area worsens, and an Israel–Arab crisis develops in which there is a war coalition comprising a number of Arab states. Concentrations of Syrian, Jordanian, and Iraqi armor are moved near the Eastern border of Israel. In terms of existing forces, this might involve 3,000–4,000 tanks deployed along a number of axes directed at Israel. Simultaneously, additional armored forces are being concentrated in the Sinai and the Golan. These have the task of pinning down Israeli forces and of preventing a full alignment against the major concentrations of Arab armor. The Arab forces are not necessarily intending to attack, but concentrate, for purposes of deterrence, against a supposed Israeli attack, or for purposes of political coercion. Under the conditions of a conventional environment, Israel would likely launch a limited preemptive strike on one front, along with a deployment for blocking the main Arab force, first in a defensive battle, to be followed by a counterstrike. Alternatively or simultaneously, Israel must launch a preemptive air attack on the main Arab concentrations.

Were Israel to have tactical nuclear weapons, she would be strongly tempted to use these arms against heavy concentrations of Arab armor. Given the blurring between tactical and strategic nuclear weapons, the Arab armies would have to consider the possibility that tactical nuclear weapons will be used. The Arabs will, in turn, be tempted to invoke the preemptive use of nuclear weapons in an attempt to destroy Israel before she has the chance to use any tactical weapons.

It can, of course, be argued that the existence of tactical nuclear weapons will cause the Arabs to refrain from concentrating armor in such a way that it would be a convenient target for such weapons. However, it is possible to conceive of extenuating politico-strategic circumstances in which a large concentration of armor would indeed be necessary. Consider the case of Arab anxiety over Israeli intentions to deliver a conventional strike against Jordan or Syria. In the presence of an effective Arab coalition, the other states might decide to provide major reinforcements. These reinforcements would generate major anxiety on the Israeli side and might lead to a response of full mobilization followed by a decision to use tactical nuclear weapons. Alternatively, it might arouse Arab suspicions that Israel intended to inflict such a strike in any case.

In the present scenario we have been dealing with a massive concentration of Arab armor. In this context, it should be added that the emphasis on the concentration of armor in "iron fists" is one of the major themes in the operational thought of the Israeli Defense Forces (10F). Therefore, the existence of tactical nuclear weapons able to destroy substantial concentrations of armor, is first of all an operational threat to the IDF. As a result, Israel should have a major interest in preventing the deployment of tactical nuclear weapons in the Middle East.

It is therefore important that both sides refrain from adopting doctrines for the use of tactical nuclear weapons, and that they make every effort to clarify their decision in this respect to the other side. Similarly, the suppliers of nuclear weapons should refrain from providing nuclear artillery shells, or miniature nuclear warheads, which can be mounted on short-range missiles.

The supervision and control of strategic doctrines is an extremely problematic issue. The same is true for the supervision of nuclear warheads. It may be argued that it is possible to perceive the development of a doctrine for the use of tactical nuclear weapons by observing conventional preparations during peacetime. Throughout the Cold War, NATO and Warsaw Pact forces in Europe trained for two types of battle—purely conventional battles and battles with tactical nuclear weapons. Warsaw Pact preparations for the conventional battlefield included exercises in which extremely large concentrations of armor were directed against a specific relatively narrow pressure point in an attempt to break through for the deep penetration of enemy lines. In exercises for tactical nuclear battlefield, the emphasis was rather on the dispersal of forces and on avoiding the dense concentration of large quantities of weapon systems and personnel. In short, it is possible to trace doctrines for the use of tactical nuclear weapons through the prism of military maneuvers. In principle, therefore, it should be possible to arrive at reasonably dependable agreements to refrain from such exercises. It is much more difficult to attempt to supervise the arms themselves.

The possibility of coming to an agreement to refrain from arming with tactical weapons or to refrain from their use in the battlefield is at best fairly remote. In this respect, there is singular importance to the "socialization" of the strategic behavior of the nuclear states in the region, in particular in their coming to understand the dangers involved in the development of a tactical nuclear doctrine.

Related to this is the problem of the organizational dispersal of command and control over nuclear weapons. Battlefield weapons in the armies of the superpowers were dispersed at different levels of command. This created a serious problem of losing centralized control over the weapons. Interestingly, it is in this area that a nuclear Middle East may be less problematic. Since it is probable that each country will possess only a small number of nuclear weapons, it can be assumed that the central authorities will be able to maintain effective control over the use of tactical weaponry.

6

THE NUCLEAR DIMENSION OF
THE GULF CRISIS AND WAR

There were a number of nuclear-related issues that emerged as a result of the Gulf Crisis and War. The first and major focus of this chapter deals with these issues, particularly with the Israeli–Iraqi strategic relationship between 1989 and 1991 (especially since April 1990), when the nuclear factor attained considerable saliency. Iraqi nuclear developments, Baghdad's suspicions about assumed Israeli and Western plans to destroy its nuclear facilities, the perceptual linkages between chemical and nuclear weapons, the "deterrence dialogue" between the two countries concerning these issues starting in April 1990, further articulation of this dialogue during the crisis, and finally the missile attacks on Israel and implied Israeli nuclear deterrent threats, all together form an intricate body of conflict behavior which requires analysis as one integrated topic. The possible linkages between these issues and the overall Iraqi regional policy will also be discussed.

The prospect of a nuclear Iraq has only added to the general international assessment that nuclear proliferation in the Middle East is a major threat to regional and world stability. No wonder then, that following the end of the war, there is an evolving international consensus that a new nuclear arms control regime should be worked out for the Middle East. Recent ideas about regional nuclear arms control, therefore, are included in Chapters 5 and 7.

The nuclear dimension of the crisis manifested itself against the backdrop of a renewed Iraqi effort to manufacture a nuclear-weapons capability. We will, therefore, first describe that effort and only later turn to an analysis of the Israeli–Iraqi strategic dialogue.

The Renewed Iraqi Nuclear Effort—The Enriched Uranium Path[1]

Apparently, sometime in the early 1980s, probably after they realized that France would not be forthcoming with another reactor, the Iraqis renewed their effort to produce a nuclear-weapons capability—only this time they focused on the enriched-uranium route. If France had supplied them with another reactor, it is possible that they might have persisted with the plutonium route. But, France was not forthcoming, and the Iraqis intensified their enrichment operation. The full extent of the program became known only after the war, through intelligence collection, defections of Iraqi scientists, the inspections of the IAEA teams, and by Iraq's own admissions. Until then, especially during the crisis and war, the general assumption of the nuclear-proliferation community was that Iraq used only the centrifuge method for enrichment.[2]

Demonstrating great ingenuity, the Iraqis approached the enrichment operation on a very wide front, developing three alternative technologies simultaneously. Their guiding principles were to adopt those technologies that could be developed secretly and for which knowhow could be bought. The element of secrecy was apparently needed in order to pre-empt the possibility of external intervention, either diplomatic or possibly even by violent means. Clearly, in light of the 1981 attack on Osiraq, this consideration was a very high Iraqi priority. In addition, the failure of one or even two of the alternatives would still leave a third operative. Similarly, in the event that one was discovered (as indeed happened), the assumption internationally would be that this had been the only technology used, thus allowing Baghdad to continue with its other efforts. Clearly, such a strategy required readiness to invest enormous financial resources.[3] It can be assumed that this huge diversion of resources was among the main causes of Iraq's great financial difficulties in 1990.

The three technologies were:

1 the centrifuge method (the details of which were described in Chapter 1);
2 the electromagnetic isotope separation technique (EMIS, also called the "calutron" approach); and
3 the chemical separation method.

An initial step for all these routes is the conversion of natural uranium ("yellow cake") into other forms of uranium. In the case of centrifuge technology, conversion is into uranium hexafluoride. While the experts have always generally assumed that Iraq did not have a plant for the production of this material,[4] Iraqi disclosures in July 1991, included the surprising reference to its existence and to its production in significant quantities.[5]

The Centrifuge Route

The main challenge of this route is to produce the appropriate centrifuges and to assemble them in an integrated form. The required centrifuges are precisely machined cylinders made from special materials which can withstand the stress of spinning at high speeds, viz. 400 meters per second, over a long period of time. Several other sophisticated components of equipment are also required. A rule of thumb is that about 1,000 centrifuges, each 1.5 meters long, operating continuously in an integrated fashion (in a "cascade" form) for a year, would be needed in order to accumulate the minimum amount of U–235 required for one weapon of the "implosion" type—about 20–25 kilograms (for details of the two categories of bombs, see below).

Apparently, Iraq chose to rely heavily on outside expertise for the production of the centrifuges as well as for other aspects of her nuclear weapons research, development, and production. There is extensive evidence that many West European companies, especially German, were involved in this effort. They used the knowhow accumulated by the URENCO consortium, of which Britain, the Netherlands, and Germany are members.[6]

The Pakistani enrichment program took about ten to twelve years from its inception in 1974–1975 until the beginning of production of weapongrade material in sufficient quantity for the assembly of bombs in 1986. Similarly, Brazil which has benefited from a more sophisticated industrial and nuclear infrastructure than Iraq's, began her enrichment program in the late 1970s and by 1990 was still at least two-three years away from enriching sufficient material to make bombs. All this may lead to the conclusion that (before the war) Iraq was at least five to ten years away from an ability to extract the material needed for nuclear weapons through centrifuge technology. If, however, Iraq obtained very extensive European and Pakistani expertise, it can be reasonably assumed that she would have needed a shorter lead time in order to reach the stage at which the actual enrichment operation could have begun. Several accounts have suggested that by late 1990, Iraq had already succeeded in constructing a pilot plant with several centrifuges in place. She had also succeeded in purchasing many, if not all, the materials needed for independent production of the centrifuges.[7] When the war ended, however, Iraq let it be known that she was only in the preparatory stages of constructing a plant for the manufacture of 100 centrifuges. The IAEA inspection teams were unable to reach a conclusion as to the status of the centrifuge effort.[8]

The Chemical Separation Route

This is a new technology developed during the last decade in Japan and France. Not much is known about the extent to which Iraq applied this technology or the progress made there as a result of it. It appears, however, that this was a secondary effort to the centrifuge and calutron routes.

The EMIS Route

This method turned out to be the main Iraqi effort. It had been used during the Manhattan Project and was abandoned because of its inefficiency and its very high demands on electricity (even higher than the classical gaseous diffusion method—an enormous energy-consumer itself). Surprisingly, the United States allowed its declassification and many of its details were freely available. Interestingly, details of this technology received attention in Chinese professional literature, which inevitably leads to the speculation that Chinese experts were involved in the Iraqi effort. Apparently, the Iraqis concentrated primarily on this approach because it is a low technology method and is well known. The high electricity demand was not a handicap for a country blessed with extensive natural energy resources—oil and hydroelectricity. Precisely because the technology had been abandoned years before, no one suspected that it would be utilized for a clandestine effort. Consequently, the Iraqis were able to purchase many of the needed components—primarily huge electromagnets—on the open, international market. In addition they had the ability to produce some of the needed magnets themselves (and they probably did). It is assumed, however, that foreign expertise was critically needed for the entire project.[9]

By late 1990, the Iraqis had already succeeded in building one plant with 70 large EMIS machines and 20 smaller ones at Tarmiya, while the R&D effort was conducted at the main nuclear center in al-Tuwaitha. The IAEA inspection teams reached the conclusion that this plant could have commenced operation within 12–18 months, and once in operation, could have produced up to 15 kilograms of weapons-grade uranium per year.[10]

Applying the same method of positive redundancy, the Iraqis began building an additional EMIS plant, a replica of the one in Tarmiya, in al-Sharqat, in the northern part of the country. When the war started, that facility was already about 85 percent complete.[11]

With the onset of the Gulf Crisis, the Iraqis launched a crash program aimed at extracting the required material. By their own admission, by January, 1991, they had succeeded in producing about half a kilogram of low enriched uranium.

Another source of concern has been the 12.3 kilograms of 93 percent enriched uranium Iraq received from France for use in the Oziraq reactor. This remained after the reactor was destroyed. In addition, Iraq is in possession of 30 kilograms of 80 percent enriched uranium supplied by the Soviet Union for the small research reactor, IRT–2000. If these masses are combined, then theoretically, a nuclear weapon of the Nagasaki type could be assembled.[12]

All the known enriched uranium in Iraq is safeguarded by the IAEA.

196

An IAEA inspection team visited Iraq in November 1990 and found all the material in place. The material could, of course, have been removed from these sites after the IAEA visit. Concern about a short-term assembly of some kind of a primitive nuclear device persisted until the outbreak of war, but it is unlikely that Iraq had indeed assembled such a device prior to the war.

The degree of expertise in bomb development that the Iraqis have achieved—either through independent research and/or through external advice—is still not clear. This, and the lack of clear evidence regarding their successes in enriching uranium through either of the technologies, makes assessments of lead time to weapons production entirely open. Nevertheless, in view of the extensive effort that Iraq had invested in the various nuclear programs, and their intensified effort during the crisis period, it can be assumed that the lead time was most probably shorter than the 5–10 years suggested before the war by various experts, and may have been closer to 2–3 years. However, at the time of this writing, the answers to these questions remain unclear.

The Israeli–Iraqi Strategic Dialogue

Israeli–Iraqi strategic dialogue existed on three different levels: the Iraqi public stance regarding Israel's nuclear capability and Iraq's reactions to it; dialogue concerning Iraq's nuclear developments and potential Israeli reactions to it and Iraq's deterrent threats against an Iraqi-perceived Israeli intention to attack Iraqi facilities; and Israel's deterrent threats against attack by conventional or chemical surface-to-surface missiles. All these dialogues involved both the exchange of verbal signals as well as the deployment of capabilities which could have backed these signals.

Throughout this book, an attempt has been made to place the nuclear issue within a broader politico-strategic context. In accordance with this approach, the various linkages between this strategic dialogue and the broader politico-strategic context will be explored. This pertains primarily to the possible connections (or the absence thereof) between the Iraqi policy vis-à-vis Israel, the Arab world, and the invasion of Kuwait.

While these subjects—both the "dialogue" and its wider linkages—lend themselves to an analytical discussion, nevertheless some chronological order can be introduced. Thus, the first "layer" of the dialogue, viz. Iraqi perceptions of Israel's capability and its reactions to it, will be discussed at the outset, since it refers primarily to the period extending up to April 1990. We shall then turn to Israeli perceptions of Iraqi intentions and to the Iraqi deterrence threats against Israel during the spring and summer of 1990.

The Iraqi policy vis-à-vis Israel on the one hand, and vis-à-vis Kuwait on the other, will lead us to the third layer, namely, the strategic dialogue during the crisis and war. Needless to say, in some places the discussion of the different "layers" will overlap.

Iraqi Perceptions of Israeli Capability

During the 1970s, there were few Iraqi public references to the nuclear issue. One exception was a detailed memorandum presented in 1977 by Iraq to the Arab League, which stated that Israel had the capacity to produce nuclear weapons, as well as the means to deliver them once they had been produced.[13] It is interesting to note that at that stage the Iraqis did not state that Israel had already actually produced nuclear weapons.

During 1980 and until the bombing of Oziraq in June 1981, the Iraqis, primarily President Saddam Hussein and his foreign minister, Tariq Aziz, increased the scope of their discussions of Israel's nuclear developments. As with the memorandum, their main objective was most probably to justify the nuclear effort in Osiraq by pointing out the Israeli capability. Shortly after the attack, Saddam Hussein referred extensively to the nuclear issue and for the first time expounded on the possibility of introducing a "balance of nuclear terror" into the Middle East.[14]

Since that speech and up to 1988, Iraq's public references to Israeli nuclear development appeared to have been put on the back burner. This was probably due to the all absorbing war with Iran.

However, once the war was over in 1988 Iraq's public references to Israel's nuclear efforts resurfaced. Thus, for example, the launching of Israel's communication satellite, OFEK 1, was presented by Baghdad as a major challenge to the security of all the Arabs. Indeed, such a challenge necessitates, according to Baghdad, a coordinated Arab effort for "techno-logical advancement," probably a euphemistic reference to a nuclear effort.

During 1989–1990, Iraq continued to emphasize the Israeli nuclear threat to all Arabs and to Iraq in particular. Simultaneously, the Iraqi media, admittedly in a rather sporadic way, argued that Israel was planning to attack Iraq's nuclear installations.[15] Several articles argued that Israel was trying to base her security on an exclusive nuclear capability and would try to destroy any Arab effort to adopt advanced technology.[16]

Under these circumstances, what was the Iraqi reaction? On the public, declaratory level, Iraqi spokesmen suggested two strategies: first, an appeal to the international community to obligate Israel to put her nuclear facilities under international control, or—a more ambitious objective—the removal of all nuclear weapons from the Middle East. The other strategy was to develop a visible and declared counter threat to Israel. Surface-to-surface missiles were one response, and here Iraq, so her spokesman suggested, was in the forefront. Furthermore, Iraq repeatedly perceived herself as having a key role in the development of military technology which could counteract Israel's capabilities. The Iraqis were careful, however, not to discuss Iraq's independent nuclear development and played it down. They rather suggested that the effort should be a general Arab one. There were probably several reasons for this caution: first, there was the possibility that Israel might utilize Iraqi references to an independent Iraqi nuclear effort and create a political background for a preemptive strike against the Iraqi facilities. Second, there was a general concern that international attention might be focused on the renewed Iraqi nuclear effort, which might lead to international intervention designed to prevent external aid to the Iraqi effort. Third, it is also possible that the Iraqis were concerned lest other Arab states become suspicious of their nuclear development.

Public references aside, the Iraqis, as mentioned, concentrated on a military-technological effort. For the short and medium run, they relied on the acquisition of chemical weapons, some deployed on the short-range *Scud* missiles, while others were in the phase of indigenous development in order to be fitted on the longer-range *al-Hussein*[17] missiles. For the long run, they intensified and enlarged their nuclear weapons program.

Iraq's nuclear effort was probably motivated by several considerations. The Iranian threat was probably paramount. Next came the Israeli nuclear capability. Third, Saddam Hussein and his aides believed that nuclear weapons would strengthen the claim for leadership in the Gulf area and possibly throughout the Arab world. Finally, Iraqi Ba'ath ideology called for scientific and technological development as a precondition for social and political advancement.

Because Iraqi–Western relations gradually began to improve in the mid-1980s, Iraq's chemical and nuclear activity was not a focus of Western attention. However, by the end of the Iran–Iraq war and as a result of increasing information leaks about Iraq's nuclear effort, official agencies became more interested in it. By late 1989–early 1990, several Western governments had become sufficiently alarmed to take actual steps to block transfers of sensitive technology to Iraq. (For example, British officials caught Iraqi agents attempting to smuggle special capacitors that can be used for the detonation of nuclear weapons.)[18] These efforts were paralleled by a wave of press reports in the international media focussing on the Iraqi effort.

The Israel–Iraq "Chemical-Nuclear Dialogue"

Israeli concern about nonconventional developments in Iraq has become much more salient following the end of the Iraq–Iran War in July 1988. Although it was presumed that Iraq was exhausted by the long war, and although—as will be detailed below—Iraq at first chose to join the

Egyptian-led bloc of countries that was more moderate in its attitude toward Israel, Israel nevertheless still considered Iraq a potentially danger- ous opponent. Indeed, the "War of the Cities"[19] underlined the potential threat of Iraqi surface to surface missile to Israel's civilian population. This concern, however, was not critical. After all, Syrian missiles, tipped with chemical warheads and which could reach any target inside Israel, had been deployed in reinforced silos since 1987–1988. In contrast, the renewed nuclear effort appeared to be potentially much more threatening.

While Israeli concern gradually increased, Iraq's chemical-weapons' capability also came increasingly under international scrutiny. The inter- national effort to reach a treaty banning the production and stocking of chemical weapons would have been of little import if Middle Eastern countries had not accepted it. Iraq's extensive use of chemical munitions was a major reminder that it was ready to employ these agents indiscrimi- nately against both troops and civilians in total violation of the longstand- ing treaty banning their use. Under these circumstances, no international treaty would have succeeded unless Iraq and other Middle Eastern coun- tries had been ready to join the new proposed regime.

In January 1989, in an international conference on chemical weapons convened in Paris, Iraq stated that she would accept restrictions on her chemical weapons only if similar restrictions were imposed on Israel's nuclear weapons.[20] This statement signaled the beginning of a new Iraqi position linking chemical with nuclear weapons. As we shall see, that became both a public stance as well as the basis for a real strategy. Israel, for her part, reacted by emphasizing Iraq's renewed nuclear effort.[21]

To Iraq, the steps taken by Western authorities in early 1990—steps designed to halt the Iraqi nuclear effort—combined with the repeated references in the international media and in the Israeli press to Iraq's nuclear program, appeared to be a calculated plan to create an inter- national backing for a repeat of the Osiraq attack of 1981. For sure, Iraq's new nuclear effort was executed in a way that would have made an Israeli strike much more difficult to carry out. Facilities were dispersed in a variety of locations, some of them in northern Iraq, farther away from Israel than the Osiraq reactor (which had been located near Baghdad). Moreover, it was safe to assume that these locations were heavily guarded by surface-to-air assets. Nevertheless, Iraqi concern about a possible Israeli strike was demonstrated as early as June, 1989, by a series of public deterrent messages in which three Iraqi newspapers made the point that "Iraq today is not the Iraq of 1981, and enemies would pay dearly for an act of aggression now."[22] A further warning was delivered by Saddam Hussein himself in a speech delivered on January 5, 1990, in which he said that an Israeli attack on Iraq's scientific and military installations would lead to an Iraqi reaction.[23] However, as we shall see below, the main step in the dialogue was taken in April 1990, again by Saddam Hussein.

Concern about an Israeli preemptive strike against Iraq, coupled with an ambition to develop a credible military option against Israel for political or military objectives, prompted Iraq to deploy part of her long-range capability against Israel. This was done by completing the construction of fixed launchers for the *al-Hussein* missiles in western Iraq.[24] By doing that, Iraqi leadership was aiming at convincing Israel that Iraq had, for the first time, established a credible strategic balance with the Israeli air force's conventional superiority as well as with the assumed Israeli nuclear capability.

Once that capability had been deployed, Iraq escalated her deterrent threats against a presumed Israeli intention to attack Iraq's nuclear facilities. On April 1, Saddam Hussein came out with a public speech in which he threatened to "make fire burn half of Israel" [alluding to Iraq's chemical binary weapons] if Israel should strike "at some [Iraqi] industrial metalwork."[25] The extreme phrase used led to a shift in Israeli and international perceptions of Iraq's intentions and capabilities.

The Iraqi threats caused concern in Israel. At the time, Israeli assessment of the Iraqi leadership tended to be cautious and tentative. On the one hand, Iraq's military buildup was seen as a potential threat to Israel. Moreover, Israel was aware of the deepening military relations between Iraq and Jordan. On the other hand, the Iraqi leadership was perceived as rational and not necessarily having military plans against Israel. Since Israel, for her part, was not planning a strike on the Iraqi nuclear infrastructure, it was feared that Iraqi misperceptions about Israel's intentions might lead to escalation. Consequently, during the spring and early summer of 1990, Israel sent messages to Baghdad through Washington and Cairo, in which she sought to reassure the Iraqis that she was not planning to attack them.[26]

Similarly, Washington became openly concerned about the Iraqi threats, which received very wide coverage in the international media. Apparently worried about the international political implications of his threats, Saddam Hussein sought to reassure Washington of his nonescalatory intentions. He did it by emphasizing that his intentions were only to deter Israel and not to launch a first strike.[27] Moreover, probably under Egyptian and American pressure, he clarified that Iraq would respond with chemical weapons only if Israel attacked first with nuclear weapons.[28]

In any case, the Iraqis sought to equate chemical with nuclear weapons. Hussein emphasized that relationship in another interview in late June 1990, when he invoked the case of the superpowers and the balance of deterrence created between them by communicating to the other their deterrent threats. He concluded by saying that Iraqi chemical weapons should be seen as a deterrent to Israel's nuclear capability.[29] Equating

201

chemical and nuclear weapons became standard Iraqi policy, a policy that would be adhered to during the coming crisis and war, as well.

The equation served Iraq in her strategic and deterrence dialogue with Israel as well as in her international political communications. As mentioned, by January 1989, the Iraqis had already justified their chemical capability by referring to Israel's nuclear capability. Thus, the question of international legitimization of weapons systems became important in Iraq's overall strategy.

While Saddam Hussein had personally referred to Israel's nuclear capability once before—in 1981, after the strike at Osiraq[30]—he never mentioned it again until 1990. As early as 1981, then, he spoke of Israel's assumed capability within the context of justifying Iraq's nuclear developments. The same approach was noticeable in 1990. Israeli capability was referred to only within the context of justifications for the Iraqi development and for the maintenance of an Iraqi chemical-weapons capability.

While the nuclear issue was certainly a very important one for Iraq, other political and strategic developments tended to capture the attention of her leadership. In different ways these became either directly intertwined with the nuclear issue, or the nuclear issue was perceived by all actors as being part of them.

Iraq's Overall Strategy and the Kuwait Crisis—Interaction with the Nuclear Issue

Iraq emerged from the war with Iran quite exhausted. It seemed likely that she would turn to economic and social reconstruction. Indeed, she began demobilizing part of her very extensive army. Apparently, between the war's end in July 1988, and the summer of 1990, about 250,000 soldiers were sent home.[31] All of these released soldiers, however, were from the second-rate infantry divisions. The eight high-quality and loyal Republican Guard divisions remained intact, as did the seven armor and mechanized divisions. What is most significant, however, is that Iraq intensified her efforts to develop an extensive military industry. After the war the nuclear program in particular was not only maintained, but apparently received a new impetus.[32]

Consequently, and notwithstanding the enormous infusions of money from Saudi Arabia, Kuwait, and other Persian Gulf Emirates, as well as the extensive revenues received from the exports of Iraqi oil, Iraq's financial situation kept worsening. By 1990, Iraq owed her various creditors close to 80 billion dollars, of which about half was due to her rich Arab neighbors. The Iraqi financial situation became the main constraint on Baghdad's ambitions.[33]

What were these ambitions? Public declarations are not necessarily the best test of the real objectives of any leadership, least of all a Middle Eastern one. It is, however, safe to assume that Saddam Hussein was searching for a greater role than sitting at the helm of a single Arab state. As pointed out in Chapter 3, competition for leadership in the Arab world has always been one of the main factors in Arab interstate politics. Indeed, Iraq had already sought such a position in the past. At varying intervals, Iraqi leaders of different political shades have competed with Egypt for hegemony over the Middle East.

At the end of World War I, Prince Faisal, son of the Sheriff of Mecca, arrived in Damascus, expecting, on the strength of British promises to his father, to become king of a large, new Arab state that encompassed the whole of the Fertile Crescent. He was pushed out of Damascus by the French and eventually became king of Iraq. But he did not abandon the hope of reuniting the new Arab states of Syria, Lebanon, Iraq, and Transjordan (where his brother Emir Abdallah became the ruler) into one princedom. The notion of Hashemite rule over the whole of the Fertile Crescent preoccupied the minds of Hashemite princes both in Iraq or in Transjordan. These hopes clashed with Egyptian claims for Arab hegemony which began to surface in the second half of the 1930s, as well as with Saudi concern about Hashemite ambitions. The "struggle" for Syria, which characterized much of inter-Arab state politics during the 1940s and the 1950s, was yet another demonstration of that historical competition. The different Iraqi regimes which succeeded the monarchy in Iraq carried on the tradition of these ambitions.

In terms of distribution of power, clearly, Iraq stands out as the second pole in the Arab eastern Middle East. Although her oil reserves are estimated to be much smaller than those of Saudi Arabia, she is blessed with fertile lands and has a population twice the size of her much larger neighbor to the west. She is second to Egypt in population in the area, and far richer than her. Thus, if different attributes of power are combined, Iraq is well posed to compete with Egypt for a position of hegemony in the eastern Middle East, and certainly for a position of great influence in the Gulf area. One of her main weaknesses compared to Egypt is her lack of societal cohesion.[34] The Iraqi claim for hegemony is thus not only the result of history and dynastic aspirations but also grounded in the logic of power and resources.

Iraq's hegemonic ambitions in the Arab world probably reawakened when Saddam Hussein rose to ultimate power in 1979. However, Hussein first had to deal with the Iranian threat and its projected revolutionary zeal. He utilized the opportunity of a perceived weakness in Iranian power and lack of internal stability and attacked in 1980, hoping to finish the war quickly, and then, on the wave of that success, to turn Iraqi ambitions due west and south.[35] Some observers even suggested that he had intended in fact to first turn south and absorb Kuwait, but the Iranian threat forced him to tackle that country first. In any case, once the war ended he began his search for a new Arab role, cashing in on his assumed success in the war. The difference in that respect between Saddam Hussein and previous Iraqi leaders, however, is that Hussein created a frightening, repressive police state apparatus[36] driven by the proto-fascist Ba'ath ideology, and that the military machine he has built is more extensive than that of any other regime in the Middle East.

During the war with Iran, and until early 1990, Baghdad chose to be part of the broad moderate Arab coalition in which Egypt played a central role. The ACC, in which both Egypt and Jordan have participated, has been primarily concerned with economic problems and with improving the economic conditions of the Arab states. In addition, the ACC has chosen a moderate policy vis-à-vis Israel, searching for a peaceful solution to the ongoing Arab–Israeli conflict.[37]

By early 1990, Iraq began to develop another strategy, apparently aimed at defining for herself a special leading role in the Arab world. She became critical of the Egyptian-designed and backed American–PLO dialogue. She apparently stood behind the Abul-Abbas naval raid on Israel conducted in the spring of 1990, and once the United States terminated dialogue with the PLO following that raid, encouraged the PLO to move its bases and headquarters to Baghdad. At the ACC meeting in February 1990 and again more forcefully in the Arab Summit held in Baghdad in May 1990, Iraq placed herself at the head of the anti-Egyptian coalition, calling for the termination of the peaceful process in the Arab–Israeli relationship and for a show of force as the only way to pressure Israel and the United States into making political concessions to the Palestinians.[38]

There have been other pronouncements by Saddam Hussein concerning Israel during that period which were designed to place him as the leader of an Arab coalition against Israel.[39] But the speech which received most international attention was delivered on April 1, 1990, when he threatened massive retaliation should Israel attempt to destroy Iraqi facilities. While that speech could have been interpreted as a deterrent signal (see above), it was followed by other Iraqi pronouncements in which deterrence became an instrument of wider threats. Thus, on June 18, Saddam Hussein, in a speech before the Islamic Conference convening in Baghdad, threatened retaliation against Israel if she attacked Iraq, but also if she attacked any other Arab territory "from Mauritania to Syria."[40] This, of course, was a much wider threat, which could cover many contingencies, even, for example, Israeli countermeasures to the Palestinian *intifada*. Thus, in one stroke, Saddam Hussein took up the mantle of general Arab leader. It was a mantle that extended his responsibility to all of Israel's Arab neighbors. This obviously was the political objective of the speech.

The new posture may have been genuinely intended by Iraq as purely deterrent within the context of "extended deterrence," in the case of Jordan. Since 1981, when some leading Israeli decision-makers from the

Likud Party began referring to Jordan as the "Palestinian State," meaning in fact that Jordan should be the place where Palestinian national aspirations should be fulfilled, King Hussein became very suspicious of Israel. He realized that such talk meant, in fact, the removal of his regime, and the annexation of the West Bank by Israel. For forty-odd years his grandfather, the Emir (and later King) Abdallah, and then he himself on the one side, and the Zionist and then successive Israeli governments, on the other side, had created and maintained a system of tacit strategic cooperation. In the early 1980s, for the first time, it appeared that Israel ceased to see the advantages encapsulated in that cooperation. These suspicions deepened when Prime Minister Shamir sabotaged the "London Plan" of April 1987 which Shimon Peres, then Israel's Foreign Minister, and King Hussein had agreed upon. The king's anxiety further deepened with the outbreak of the *Intifada*, and reached an even higher level as mass Soviet Jewish immigration to Israel began in 1990. By that time, Hussein had probably reached the conclusion that his tacit cooperation with Israel had come to an end and that either because of deliberate Israeli intention or because of escalation beyond Israel's control triggered by the *Intifada* or an Israeli–Syrian confrontation, Israel would turn against Jordan. Moreover, the United States appeared to him to be less and less concerned about the welfare and security of Jordan. In his plight, the king probably perceived of Iraq as a credible guarantor. Saddam Hussein was only too happy to extend that guarantee.

However, beyond the case of Jordan, the adoption of a policy of extended deterrence might have immediately set Iraq on a collision course with Israel, which not only continued acting violently against the *Intifada*, but more importantly, routinely used her air force (and sometimes ground forces) to strike at South Lebanese military targets from which terrorist and guerrilla operations were conducted against Israel.

An even more ominous interpretation might be that Saddam Hussein was already then thinking in terms of a military strike against Israel once Iraq's military preparations had been completed, perhaps after the final assembly of nuclear weapons in the mid- or late 1990s. The new posture could have provided him with the appropriate pretext for such an operation.

Thus, Iraq has defined an alternative approach to solving the Arab–Israeli conflict, has mobilized the PLO to her side, and by developing and deploying a significant military capability, has also projected to the Arab world her assumed capacity as well as willingness to challenge Israel. While the Israelis did indeed become suspicious of Iraqi intentions and capabilities—the real challenge was directed not at them but at other Arab leaders. And these Arab leaders, sophisticated statesmen well versed in the dynamics of inter-Arab state maneuvering, were quick to react. Egypt and Syria were the first to feel threatened by the new Iraqi challenge. In Syria, the traditional rivalry between the Ba'ath regimes in Baghdad and Damascus was reinforced as a result of the personal rivalry between Saddam Hussein and Hafez al-Assad, and the countries' clash over geopolitical interests. Egypt, for her part, was motivated by concern that Iraq was challenging her newly emerging leadership in the Arab world. Moreover, Iraq renewed a pan-Arab approach which contrasted with Egypt's more moderate and restrained posture concerning both inter-Arab politics and the Arab–Israeli conflict. Not surprisingly, within a very brief span of time, Egypt and Syria forged an unexpected association.

While the Israeli–Arab issue became more salient, more pressing to Saddam Hussein were his worsening financial difficulties. A claim to Arab leadership demanded continued military buildup. This was also necessitated by the unresolved conflict with Iran. Control of Kuwait's riches would satisfy his appetite. He also argued that Kuwait and the other Gulf Emirates were conducting an "economic war" against Iraq.[41]

The decision to invade Kuwait could be seen, therefore, as part of a well-calculated design to increase Iraq's overall capabilities and to secure a dominant position in the Gulf as well as in the whole Middle East. To that extent, the new policy toward Israel and the Kuwait operation were two sides of the same coin. Motivated by the same general urge, Iraq conducted a two-pronged operation. There was, therefore, a link between the two moves, yet it was a very different link from the one suggested by Iraq herself or, for that matter, by the Palestinians and other observers sympathetic to their cause. It was not the Israeli position which caused the seizure of Kuwait. It was rather Saddam Hussein's hegemonic ambitions which pushed him in both directions.

Another interpretation linking the posture Iraq adopted against Israel with the invasion of Kuwait, assesses that Iraq's main objective was the annexation of Kuwait. The extreme anti-Israeli posture was used primarily as a ruse to mobilize Arab support. Receiving PLO backing was important to this strategy, since it would confer on the invasion a symbolic legitimization.

Finally, there may be an altogether different interpretation. According to it, the Kuwait operation was not in any way linked to Baghdad's policy vis-à-vis Israel. Moreover, even if Saddam Hussein did (and still does) entertain wider ambitions in the Arab world, his deterrent threats against Israel on the one hand and his move against Kuwait on the other, were not interconnected, nor were they integral elements in his general Arab ambitions. Each was motivated by different external threats and dilemmas. His Israel policy was connected with what he perceived as Israeli threats, whereas the attack on Kuwait was motivated by historical Iraqi annexation claims which had never been abandoned by any Iraqi regime, the strategic need to secure at least the islands at the entrance to the Shatt al-Arab, and finally and probably most important, Iraq's 1990 financial situation.

According to this view, the nuclear "dialogue" between Iraq and Israel should be discussed without necessary adherence to wider politico-strategic contexts, but according to the logic of nuclear relations between two rivals.

It is difficult to assess which of the explanations that link overall Iraqi policy to Israel and the invasion of Kuwait is the correct one. Saddam Hussein is the main and, at times, the exclusive decision-maker in Iraq and he is not necessarily inclined to publicly reveal his designs and calculations. But it appears clearly, that his ambitions for hegemony in the Arab world have played an important role in his overall policy since 1988–1989. His decision to invade Kuwait in 1990, however, was prompted only partly by these ambitions and, to a larger extent, by direct financial needs and specific historical claims Iraq has had on Kuwait.[42]

The Crisis

Iraqi threats to strike at Israel continued throughout the crisis.[43] They were partly phrased as deterrent signals but increasingly became intertwined with the overall Iraqi attempt to link Israel with the crisis, thus serving a totally different strategic purpose.

The deterrent communications were colored by a measure of ambiguity on two issues. Some of the references did not specify the nature of retaliation should Israel strike at Iraq whereas others specifically mentioned the use of chemical weapons. Chemical weapons were invoked either as a deterrent to possible Israeli use of nonconventional weapons, or as a response to *any* Israeli attack on Iraq.

As the crisis unfolded, Iraqi strategy changed and moved from deterrence to coercive threats. Thus, for example, Iraq warned that if the economic embargo continued,[44] or if the United States initiated war, she would attack Israel. This threat may have had two dimensions: First, it may have been used as a deterrent against the United States, the assumption being that Israel would apply pressure on the United States not to attack for fear of Iraqi retaliation. Second, and probably more important, was the general intention to link the Kuwait crisis to the Israeli–Palestinian conflict. A well-known Iraqi posture throughout the crisis was the emphasis on the linkage between the two issues. The Iraqis, for propaganda and diplomatic purposes, tried their best to evade international pressure by presenting themselves as the defenders of the Palestinians. Threatening Israel, in their view, served that purpose.

As outbreak of war drew closer, Iraqi threats intensified. Thus, for example, after the failure of the Geneva meeting between James Baker and Tariq Aziz on January 7, the Iraqi said explicitly, in response to a question, that if war broke out Iraq would certainly strike at Israel.[45]

The Iraqi threats were credible precisely because they reflected a wider political strategy. An essential component of Saddam Hussein's *war* strategy was to create a general movement in the Arab world directed against both the U.S. and the Arab regimes participating in the international coalition in order to break the coalition. His intention, therefore, was to try and provoke Israel to the point where it would retaliate. That retaliation, presumably, would violate Jordanian territory or airspace, following which there would be a general escalation, involving Israel, Jordan, and probably Syria, which would have to back Jordan. The international coalition would then disintegrate.[46]

In addition, successful missile attacks on Israel would bolster Saddam Hussein's prestige in the Arab world and inflame popular feelings. The Iraqi signals, therefore, ceased to serve a deterrence strategy and became a valid indication of Iraqi intentions.

Throughout that period, Israeli spokesmen insisted that Israel was not involved in the Gulf Crisis and that she would not intervene in it. At the same time, they adopted a strong deterrence posture against Iraqi attacks on Israel. Iraq was warned that Israeli retaliation would be extreme. Two main ambiguities were maintained: the nature of the provocation and of the possible reaction. Three different contingencies were mentioned in regard to the nature of the provocation: conventional air and missile strikes; the use of chemical weapons; the introduction of Iraqi forces into Jordan. The nature of the possible reaction—whether air strikes or ground operations—remained unclear. The volume and intensity of retaliation was also left open-ended.

This response was partly intentional but also partly due to the nature of the Israeli political system. Israel is a democracy with its share of politicians who compete for popularity by taking a tough and firm stance. The number of public references comprising deterring signals, therefore, was extensive and varied.

While Israeli politicians and official spokesmen continued to refrain from mentioning nuclear retaliation, many international and some Israeli observers did interpret the Israeli utterances as referring to nuclear retaliation. According to leading strategic commentator, Ze'ev Schiff,[47] for example, two contingencies might lead to "unconventional" Israeli response—an extended surface-to-surface conventional missile campaign against Israel, and the use of chemical warheads. Respected international sources were even more forthcoming in suggesting that Israel might retaliate against Iraqi anti population attacks with nuclear weapons.[48] Indeed, such interpretations appeared rational in view of phrases such as "Elements contemplating an attack on Israel know very well they will pay a terrible price should they attempt such an attack."[49] Thus, although the term "nuclear weapons" was never mentioned by Israeli decision-makers or politicians, it was used liberally by respected and serious international sources.

Prewar Israeli strategy reflected several inconsistencies regarding deterrence and its effectiveness. By and large, it appears that the defense establishment assumed that deterrence would succeed and hence there would be no Iraqi missile strikes. In addition to credible deterrence, it could also have been argued that once war erupted, the Iraqi strategic and military leadership would be so preoccupied with military moves in Kuwait that little attention and time would be devoted to less important fronts. Then again, in view of Israel's total air superiority, Iraqi aircraft were not likely to engage in air strikes since all of them would undoubtedly be shot down by Israeli interceptors. In any case, the only Iraqi aircraft capable of reaching Israel was the Suhoi 24, of which only 25 had been counted. Finally, the effectiveness of the only Iraqi SS missiles capable of reaching Israel—the *al-Hussein*—was doubtful. The missile was considered inaccurate and its warhead too small to cause much damage. Military analysts studied the effects of the Iraqi missiles during the famous "War of the Cities," in which Iraq launched 177 *Scud* missiles against Teheran, and the average number of casualties per missile was 15. Finally, it was assumed that if war broke out, one of the first missions of the international coalition air forces would be to destroy all the deployed Iraqi SS missiles.

Reliance on deterrence and, failing that, assumptions of minimal loss as a result of missile attacks, led to self assurance about the probability of damages and casualties. At the same time, however, the Israeli defense establishment, cautious and responsible, did take steps to strengthen civil defense and introduce passive countermeasures such as the distribution of gas masks to the entire population. Nevertheless, expectations were that at most, only a few missiles would be launched at Israel and that their effectiveness would be extremely limited. Only as January 15 drew close and the crisis entered its climactic stage, did a few strategists outside the political and military leadership begin to doubt Israel's ability to deter Iraqi missile attacks on Israel.[50]

Failure of Israeli deterrence

Once war erupted, Iraq, true to her word, initiated the missile campaign against Israel. The *al-Hussein* missiles were targeted primarily at Tel Aviv and its environs, and to a lesser extent at Haifa and its environs. The clear objective of the attacks was political—to drag Israel into the war, thus disrupting the political and strategic cohesion of the Arab grouping within the international coalition. The launching of these missiles ostensibly demonstrated the failure of Israeli deterrence threats.

There may be several explanations for this apparent failure. The simplest and most logical is, as indeed has already been alluded to, that Iraq sought the threatened Israeli retaliation precisely in order to drag Israel into the war which would lead to the disintegration of the coalition and to an early termination of the war.[51] The Iraqi leadership probably welcomed the severe Israeli warnings of retaliation and believed in their validity. In other words, it was precisely the high credibility of these warnings which encouraged Iraq to launch the attacks. Paradoxically, therefore, Israel's repeated threats, along with its well-known historical inclination to retaliate, fitted in well with general Iraqi political strategy. In this sense, Israeli deterrence did not fail, since deterrence was not relevant to the political strategic relationship between Israel and Iraq. It has been argued that the best Israeli strategy would have been to make no threats of retaliation at all, thus convincing Iraq that Israel would not retaliate.[52] Once the rationale for provocation (viz. inviting Israeli retaliation) had disappeared, Iraq would not have attacked. This reasoning, however, is probably too extreme. First, even if Israel had not signaled her deterrence commitment, Iraq could have relied on the historical experience, according to which Israel would most likely retaliate. Second, faced with a threat to their country, decision-makers would find it difficult not to communicate deterrent threats.

The Iraqi missile campaign against Israel was probably designed not only to provoke Israel into retaliation but to serve other political objectives as well. Baghdad may have calculated that such attacks, even if they did not result in the prime objective, Israeli retaliation, would substantially enhance Iraq's position in the Arab world. If Israel retaliated, all the better. If it did not, then Iraq could present herself as a champion of Arab causes—a champion that did not back down even in the face of Israeli threats and which attacked the "Zionists" without fear. Iraq would be the first Arab state to do that since 1973. All this fitted nicely into Saddam Hussein's overall Arab strategy.

In passing, it should be added that this strategy was based on a series of misconceptions: that Arab states are motivated primarily by Pan-Arab concerns and considerations; that the Arab "masses" in each state can force its respective decision-maker elites to change policy in accordance with Iraq's priorities. In fact, Arab governments chose to oppose Iraqi ambitions and power as strongly as possible. The Israeli–Arab conflict assumed smaller proportions when compared to the Iraqi threat. In Egypt, the most important Arab country, most of the public backed the regime in its policy vis-à-vis Iraq, while in Syria, the regime was easily capable of repressing any public opposition that might occur. Except for Jordan with its specific position resulting from the linkages to the Palestinian problem, all the Arab states treated Iraq according to only one criterion—their potential vulnerability to Iraqi power. The further removed they were from Iraq geographically, the more likely they were to back her position (usually only rhetorically). The closer they were, the more likely they were to oppose her.

Turning back to Israel, what then were the reasons for her nonaction? First and foremost, Israel understood that retaliation would indeed serve Iraqi purposes, that it could lead to the breakdown of the international coalition and consequently to paralysis and even a halt in military operations. Clearly, from the Israeli point of view, the destruction of the Iraqi war machine was the main objective. If retaliation might hamper that objective, then it should be avoided.[53] In addition, there were two possible types of conventional counteractions: to inflict considerable punishment on the Iraqi population or other civilian assets, or to attempt damage limitations, viz. strikes at missile bases. A rational calculation here, however, would have led to the conclusion that the scale of punishment inflicted on Iraq by coalition air forces (primarily American) was so considerable that Israeli conventional retaliation in the punishing mode would have added only an incremental element to it. As for damage limitation, here again it was doubtful whether the Israeli air force would have been significantly more effective in destroying missile sites than the coalition air forces. Then again, American diplomatic pressure against action coupled with extensive economic and military aid, also served as an important factor in Israeli calculations. Finally, the number of casualties was so low (only one killed by direct hit) that even the extensive damage caused by the *Scud* attacks did not appear to justify the potential political and strategic costs resulting from retaliation.

An additional question presents itself: why did Iraq desist from using chemical warheads during the war? There are several possible answers. First, the reluctance to use chemical warheads did not result from a strategic decision but from technical or physical limitations. Three different explanations fall within this category. Iraq may not have had the technical ability to fit the chemical warheads on her SS missiles. This explanation is strengthened by the poor quality of the conversion of *Scud* missiles (which Iraq received from the USSR) to the *al-Hussein* version assembled by the Iraqis and used against Israel and Saudi Arabia. In addition, in the last phases of the war, when the possibility of this use became more relevant, the ability to transfer chemical warheads from storage sites near Baghdad to missile sites became extremely difficult and hazardous. Finally, there is the version that, toward the end of the war, in an act of desperation, Iraq was indeed planning to launch missiles carrying chemical warheads against Israel, but these plans were never carried out as a result of the activity of American and British special commando units.

Another set of possible explanations perceives Saddam Hussein as a rational leader who differentiated between the uses of various types of weapons.[54] Accordingly, Iraq was aware of the specific nature of chemical weapons and was conscious of the implications of their use. Saddam Hussein and his advisers purposefully tried to present chemical weapons as a special category, as a deterrent or balancer to Israel's nuclear weapons. It was logical to conclude, therefore, that they would use these weapons only in special circumstances. As against this it could be persuasively argued that they did not always emphasize this distinction. Thus, they invoked the threat of chemical weapons for contingencies short of the extreme as well. We are thus left with open questions as to the specific threshold the Iraqi leadership had delineated for the use of chemical weapons. Moreover, under conditions of great stress and in the midst of a terrible war (from the Iraqi standpoint), it is doubtful that erstwhile definitions of tolerance thresholds for the use of weapons would hold.

It has been argued that Israeli nuclear threats played an important role in deterring Iraqi use of chemical weapons against Israel. According to this theory, Saddam Hussein realized that the use of chemical weapons might trigger an Israeli nuclear response. In other words, he was able to distinguish between the various Israeli threats and to "decipher" the specific deterrent threats against the use of chemical weapons. Thus, a rational deterrence dialogue ensued in which Israeli nuclear threats successfully deterred chemical attacks.[55]

The first problem with this theory is that throughout the crisis and war, Israel had been ambiguous about what Iraqi moves would trigger retaliation. It had also been ambiguous about the nature of its retaliation. Indeed, no Israeli leaders ever referred explicitly to nuclear retaliation. They did maintain the ambiguous posture. International observers, however, interpreted much of Israel's rhetoric to mean that Israel would retaliate with nuclear weapons in response to both conventional and chemical attack on Israeli centers of population. As we know, this did not deter Iraq from attacking Israeli cities. The second problem with this theory is that if rational criteria are applied, Iraq might have reached the conclusion that since Israel did not respond at all to conventional attacks, it was unlikely to take the quantum leap and retaliate with nuclear weapons to say a limited use of chemical weapons. Then again, if the criterion of proportionality applies, viz. the retaliation must be in some proportion to the scope of provocation and the damage it causes, then clearly, nuclear retaliation would have been out of all proportion to the possible expected damage which might have been caused by a chemical weapons attack on Israel. The Iraqis were clearly aware of the extensive civil defense measures Israel undertook to protect her population against chemical attacks, and could have calculated that the number of casualties would be relatively small. Nuclear retaliation under these circumstances would have appeared completely out of proportion.

All these doubts need not necessarily undercut the nuclear deterrent argument, but they do demonstrate that this theory is not necessarily valid. Moreover, there are other explanations for Iraqi restraint. First, as already noted, there may have been physical or technical reasons that prevented the Iraqis from launching SS missiles carrying chemical weapons. As previously mentioned, according to one version, Iraq did plan to launch a large salvo of missiles, possibly carrying chemical warheads, against Israel in the final phase of the war, but this was preempted by coalition action. There is, however, an additional important reason to doubt the validity of the Israeli nuclear deterrence theory. Iraq not only desisted from using chemical weapons against Israel, it also desisted from using them against coalition forces during the ground operations. It is logical to assume that the reasons for this caution on both fronts are the same. It is clear that Israeli threats could not have served that purpose. On the other hand, there had been another set of deterrence warnings to Iraq which came from the United States and which covered both Israel and the coalition forces. According to that version,[56] the United States warned Iraq that any use of chemical weapons against any party, including Israel, would result in dreadful punishment. Indeed, it was clear that the United States had at its disposal at least two options, the exercise of which would have been catastrophic to the Iraqi regime. First, the coalition forces could have carried out an indiscriminate bombing of Baghdad, completely destroying the city with conventional bombs. The second option could have been an American ground operation up to Baghdad, with the total collapse of the regime as the specific and determined objective of the war.

Finally, there is the haunting question of the rationality of the Iraqi decisions. Assuming that Saddam Hussein was the main decision-maker in Baghdad before and during the war, we can assess the quality of his decisions based on his overall performance throughout his tenure in office. On the one hand, he has demonstrated considerable rationality in many of his moves. On the other, he has exhibited elements of gross misperception and miscalculation. Twice in his career he committed enormous blunders: initiating the war against Iran and the invasion of Kuwait. Each almost cost him his political position and even his life, to say nothing of the incalculable hardships they caused the Iraqi people. Moreover, in his handling of the Gulf Crisis he demonstrated total misunderstanding of American behavior and miscalculation of the reactions of other Arab states. Finally, during the war itself he again and again committed grave strategic and tactical mistakes. It is, therefore, very difficult to attribute to him necessarily a clear-headed process of decision-making during the war.

To sum up, the actual events of the war show that Israeli deterrent threats, some of which were widely interpreted as threatening nuclear retaliation for *any* Iraqi attack against its population centers, failed to deter such attacks. We can still only speculate on the Iraqi calculations that led to this failure. We know that restraint was employed in the use of chemical weapons, but since we do not know the reasons for this restraint, we can only posit several alternative explanations. What is clear, though, is that the Israeli nuclear deterrent explanation is certainly not the only explanation, and there may have been better ones.

It is interesting to note, however, that while the Israeli implied nuclear threats were probably not the cause of Iraqi restraint, the possibility of an Israeli nuclear reaction, became salient in discussions in the international and Israeli Media. In 1973, so the story goes (see Chapter 2), Moshe Dayan felt that a "last resort" situation had arisen and raised the possibility of an Israeli nuclear threat. Although the situation was grave, nevertheless, the Israeli "Kitchen Cabinet" completely rejected his plea. In 1991, Israeli leaders issued warnings which could have been interpreted as referring to the use of nuclear weapons for a much more moderate contingency.

Clearly we do not know to what extent these warnings reflected a coherent policy. They did, in part, however, reflect a measure of impatience with the possibility that the Israeli civilian infrastructure would be exposed and vulnerable to Iraqi attacks. The tenor of part of the media changed during the war and became more nuclear-prone than at any time previously. Several Israeli journalists and observers referred specifically to the need to retaliate with nuclear weapons to Iraqi provocations. One even went so far as to suggest that Israel should have struck at Baghdad and "destroyed it completely" even before Iraq launched the first missiles at Israel. In addition to all else, there was a feeling of frustration that Israel possessed so destructive a capability and could not even successfully deter with it. To be sure, Israeli policy makers would have been more cautious than the media. Yet the saliency of the nuclear issue certainly increased dramatically during the war.[57]

Thus, while implied nuclear threats did not deter Iraq from antipopulation attacks and may not have been relevant to deterrence or the nonuse of chemical weapons against Israel, the possibility of using nuclear weapons in retaliation assumed more realistic proportions. SS missiles, possibly carrying chemical agents, the low tolerance of Israel to attacks on population, and the nuclear weapons potential, is certainly an extremely dangerous combination. And this indeed underlines the general explosive situation in which the Middle East may find itself in future military confrontations.

7

ISRAEL'S STRATEGIC ALTERNATIVES

In earlier chapters in this book, the focus of our attention has been the dangers inherent in the proliferation of nuclear weapons in the Middle East. As was reviewed in Chapter 5, there are ways to moderate some of these dangers, but such measures, vital as they would be were nuclear weapons to be introduced into the region, would not eliminate the dangers that would threaten Israel and the other countries in a nuclear Middle East. Thus, Israel must make every effort to prevent regional nuclearization, and in this context, she ought to refrain from adopting a nuclear strategic doctrine. In the present chapter we will deal more specifically with Israel's security problems and with the strategic threats that are directed against her. We will examine the ways in which she might deal with these threats by comparing two alternative strategies: conventional and nuclear. The conventional alternative may also comprise an ambiguous nuclear posture whose nature will be discussed later on in the chapter.

A main theme of this book has been the inseparable relationship between the military, strategic, and political factors in assessing escalation, conflict and deterrence—conventional and nuclear. Hence, the discussion of Israel's preferred strategy is presented within a political context. The main body of the discussion will relate to a situation in which no Arab state possesses nuclear weapons. But in the course of the discussion we will also analyze specific situations given the assumption of nuclearization of the Middle East. This assumption will be explicitly noted whenever it is applicable.

The discussion of the conventional balance of forces and of the ways to improve it, relates to the present situation in which there remains a measure of ambiguity surrounding Israel's nuclear capability. While the threshold posture probably already serves a certain deterrence function (I shall refer to this when discussing notions such as a general deterrence against a general Arab coalition and the "last resort weapon"), in the analysis of the balance of power, the discussion focuses only on conventional arms.

Israel is confronted by a spectrum of potential military threats, from a general war against all or some of the Arab states, to limited wars of various types. These threats and their relative cost to Israel and the Arab states will be examined using the standard analytic tool—the balance of military power. We will first deal with the quantitative balance of power, and this will be followed by some comments on various qualitative factors and possible future developments. The military balance will be examined in terms of various political configurations. It should be emphasized, however, that an assessment of the balance of power and its significance—particularly when it involves future projections—is a very problematic undertaking. While the past and the present seem to be plausible indicators of certain future developments, our analysis must remain somewhat schematic and tentative, but this is a necessary function of the immense complexities and multiple uncertainties that attend our topic.

The Gulf War and the revelations about the extent of the clandestine Iraqi nuclear effort, analyzed in Chapter 6, highlighted two elements related to Israel's strategic alternatives: first, the potential threat to Israel involved in the massive use of surface-to-surface missiles armed with conventional or chemical munitions, launched from distant hostile countries, and second, the possibility of near-term nuclearization of the Middle East. Israeli strategy to counter both threats should involve military, political and arms control steps. These are discussed in detail in the latter part of this chapter.

THE QUANTITATIVE BALANCE OF POWER – PRELIMINARY COMMENTS

Analysis of the relationship between the military balance and possible war options is dependent on certain basic assumptions. A widely accepted assumption of military thought is that in order to ensure combat success, the attacking side must have a supremacy of at least 3:1 in the assault zone. Indeed, as was mentioned earlier, Soviet military thinking stressed the need for a supremacy ratio of between 5:1 and 10:1 in favor of the attacker, at least in the major assault zone.

In order to achieve local supremacy, it is necessary to achieve superiority across the entire front, although this does not require the ratio proposed by the Soviets for the assault zone. It is customary, however, to speak of a requisite power ratio of 3:1 in favor of the attacker, taking account of the overall military power of both sides, and assuming qualitative equality. (Nonetheless, there are certain situations in which the attacker triumphs with a lower superiority ratio, and *vice-versa:* he is defeated with a higher ratio than prescribed. In such cases, victory is a result of qualitative factors, or better operational and strategic planning.)[1]

The analysis of military power relationships is of necessity not very detailed. First, the determining factor on the modern battlefield is not necessarily manpower, but firepower—its volume, precision, and operational flexibility. The primary components of firepower are aircraft, attack helicopters, tanks, armored combat vehicles, artillery, and defensive antitank and antiaircraft missile systems.

On the modern battlefield, armored ground systems occupy the central role, and it is these systems that will be the initial focus of our attention in analyzing the balance of land power in the Middle East. Increasingly, various systems of Precision Guided Munitions (PGM) carried on various platforms will have their effect on the battlefield.

Let us begin by adopting an extreme assumption: the establishment of a general Arab coalition against Israel. In this case, the firepower count includes all the forces of Egypt, Syria and Jordan, plus expeditionary forces from other Arab states. Since Iraq is unlikely to take part in such a campaign in the short and mid-term range, her forces are not included in this count.

An examination of power ratios for armored divisions (not including mechanized and infantry divisions) yields the following picture:[2] Israel (in 1991) has 12 armored divisions, while the combined forces of Egypt, Jordan and Syria comprise 13 armored divisions. The ratio changes if we add all mechanized divisions to the above calculation, to obtain a combined ratio of armored and mechanized power. The general Arab coalition will comprise a total of some 25 divisions,[3] against approximately 12 Israeli divisions. This is a ratio of about 2:1.

The same ratio obtains when infantry divisions are added to the equation. Assuming that single brigades join the divisions schematically at the ratio of three brigades per division, the overall armored, mechanized, and infantry power of a general Arab coalition (including also expeditionary forces from Saudi Arabia, Morocco, and Libya) against Israel would compromise approximately 38–39 divisions, against approximately 20 on the Israeli side. This is a ratio of 1.9:1.

Leaving aside the question of the quality of weaponry, the Arab quantitative advantage is conditioned by an additional factor: it is plausible to assume, based on the experience of the past 40 years, that there will be little coordination between the various Arab armies. It would appear then, that the quantitative supremacy of Arab land forces is possibly less than that expressed schematically in the formal power ratios. Taking no account of the qualitative superiority of the Israeli Defense Forces against the Arab armies, the ratio does not appear to ensure the superiority requisite for a successful Arab land attack.

Therefore, assuming the stability of the conventional land forces ratio in the coming years, and even given the extreme political assumptions (which appear to be unrealistic at present) of Arab unity and the establishment of a general war coalition, the Arab side will not be possessed of a certain decisive quantitative military superiority. At the same time, it should be recognized that such a war coalition would pose a tremendous threat to Israel, and one can never predict with certainty the outcome of major military campaigns.

In turning to the rather thankless task of evaluating future developments, the principal question is whether the Arab states will be able to continue to establish new military formations that might alter the existing power ratio. In this connection it should be noted that the Arab states have also been affected by shortages of skilled manpower. Thus, for example, the enlargement of military structures has slowed due to a lack of manpower. The slowdown is not an outgrowth of actual population shortages in the Arab states; rather it derives from a lack of skilled manpower capable of operating the sophisticated equipment and technology used in a modern army. Equally important are the economic constraints.

Excepting Syria and Iraq, in the past 20 years (until 1992) the major Arab armies have registered only a small increase in the number of divisional frameworks. For example, in the 1973 War the Egyptian army comprised 10 divisional frameworks (excluding various types of independent brigades) while in 1992 it comprised 12 divisions. Indeed, in the same period, in terms of manpower alone the Egyptian order of battle in all the armed forces showed a net decrease from approximately 800,000 regulars in 1973 to approximately 435,000 regulars in 1991 (in addition there were 691,000 reservists). On the other hand, the Egyptian army underwent major qualitative structural changes. Whereas in 1973, it comprised two armored, three mechanized infantry, and five infantry divisions, by 1990 it comprised four armored, seven mechanized, and one infantry divisions.

Jordan did not increase the number of her divisions between 1973 and 1990–1991. However, the Jordanian army has undergone a process of transition to armored and mechanized divisions of high quality. Syria has increased only somewhat her order of battle between 1973 and 1982: from five divisions in 1973 to six divisions in 1982. However, during that period Syria underwent a far more vigorous transition to armored and mechanized divisional frameworks than Egypt. Syrian concern regarding the possibility of her isolation in a war against Israel, the situation in which she found herself in 1982, has further accelerated her military growth. Today, the Syrian ground forces comprise ten armored and mechanized divisions. It is still difficult to measure to what extent this rapid growth has affected the quality of the Syrian army.

Before moving to the Iraqi situation, the question of economic constraints must be weighed. Inter-Arab state politics is a major consideration here. The rich Gulf states extended generous financial assistance in order to bolster their military establishments of their other poor Arab countries. Their aid to Iraq during the Iraq–Iran War demonstrated that this generosity was much greater if there was an Iranian-Shiite threat, which could also be directed at them, than it was if the threat was an Israeli threat, the latter being far removed and indirect. Today with the extensive burdens of rebuilding Kuwait, falling oil prices, and the defaulted Iraqi debt to them (reaching neighborhood of U.S. $40 billion), it is unlikely that the Gulf states will offer Egypt, Jordan, and Syria the kind of financial support they did during the 1980s. Moreover, the Saudi decision not to accept the continued deployment of Egyptian and Syrian forces in Saudi Arabia and consequently to scale down the assumed financial support to these states further underlines the possible limits of the Gulf aid. Finally, the Gulf states' horrendous experience with Saddam Hussein would certainly inhibit their readiness to allow the restrengthening of Iraq.

The significant strengthening of the Iraqi armed forces during the war with Iran, did demonstrate that if financial constraints are removed, a leading Arab country may be able to raise a substantial military machine. However, even then the remarkable increase in military capabilities was skewed to a large extent. Most of the new military formations were infantry divisions (some 39–40 in number), which were primarily designed and trained for stationary defensive warfare.

But looking into the future, the destruction visited on the Iraqi forces and on the country's infrastructure during the Gulf War, coupled with the political constraints which are likely to persist for at least a few years, all but rule out any major rebuilding of the Iraqi army.

Two general conclusions emerge from this brief analysis. First for the present, even given the most arduous of political environments, the establishment of a general Arab coalition able to mobilize all the forces of the neighboring Arab countries, the quantitative balance of military power between the major ground formations does not yet represent an assured critical threat to Israel's existence.

Let us consider the case in the most extreme terms: ignoring for the moment any qualitative factors, we will take as our starting point the assumption that the Arab states cannot entertain the possibility of total victory over Israel, without the 3:1 superiority ratio accepted in the common strategic wisdom. Even then, total victory would remain an uncertain prospect. Nevertheless, in order to obtain the said ratio, the Arab states would have to reach an order of battle comprising some 36–40 armored and mechanized divisions; today, they would be able to deploy about 25 such divisions for a war. In other words, the Arab states must increase the number of their armored and mechanized divisions by 50–70 percent, an addition of 12–16 divisions. The second conclusion to be drawn from this analysis relates to future developments. The central question is whether the Arab states are capable of extensive military growth. Today, such an effort would appear to be of low probability, considering the various political and economic constraints operating in the Arab world. Thus, in a major drive from 1973 to 1985, which had an impoverishing effect on some of the countries, Egypt, Syria, Jordan, and Iraq managed to increase their armored and mechanized divisions as follows: by 1982 Syria had transformed three infantry divisions into armored and mechanized divisions, and had added another mechanized division. Since then she has formed two additional mechanized divisions, partly composed of existing independent armored brigades. It should be remembered that this effort focused primarily on the conversion of infantry forces into mechanized forces, and mechanized forces into armored forces. Iraq set up between four to five armored and mechanized divisions. Jordan established two divisional frameworks, as did Egypt. The combined results of this effort yields a total increase of 10–12 divisions, and this was probably achieved partly by the conversion of high-level infantry into armored forces. It may, therefore, be assumed that the skilled manpower capable of fulfilling jobs in a modern army has to a certain extent been strained. In order to reach a total of 36–40 divisions, the Arab military growth rate must exceed that of the previous decade and a half.

Manpower and economic constraints are likely to impose limitations also on Israel's ability to increase significantly her order of battle. Manpower constraints have eased of late due to the high-quality, highly skilled Soviet immigration and the rate of natural growth. Economic constraints, however, are likely to increasingly sharpen the dilemmas involved in choices between size of the standing army and continued investment in more advanced weapons systems. Altogether it is likely that the strengthening of Israel's ground forces will depend primarily on continued qualitative improvements and on the adoption of the right strategic and operational doctrines. Because of the relative easing of manpower constraints, however, in the coming decade Israel should be able to count on her ability not to lose in the competition for conventional capabilities were the Arab states to try and accelerate their military effort.

In summary then, at present and in the near future, it seems unlikely that the ratio of conventional ground forces could be altered to the extent that it would, for the first time, represent a credible threat to Israel's very existence. The development of such a situation would be dependent on a series of preconditions:

1 The complete collapse of the Israel–Egypt peace agreement, and Egypt's joining a war coalition against Israel.
2 The resolution of the various conflicts among the Arab states, such as between Egypt and Syria, Syria and Iraq, between the conservative and

the radical states, and even more importantly, the decision to establish a general Arab *coalition for war* against Israel.

3 The maintenance of such a coalition over a certain period of time, and the effecting of substantive cooperation in the military sphere.

4 The addition of 12–16 Arab divisions, most of them armored and mechanized, while Israel fails to increase her order of battle.

The recreation of a large Iraqi army of a size similar to the one existing before the Gulf War and a commitment of a large part of it for a battle against Israel, may fulfill part of condition 4.

However, bearing in mind the constant uncertainties attendant on the outcomes of conventional campaigns, these conclusions should naturally be treated with caution. Moreover, the costs involved in general war against a grand Arab coalition, even if all the mentioned conditions are not met, may be very high for Israel even if Arab objectives were denied. Furthermore, the quality of weapons available to the two sides has an important bearing on the outcomes of specific battles. If Israel were to lose the qualitative edge, the balance might turn against her. Also, even a smaller increase in the overall Arab order of battle than stated here, might increase the Israeli costs beyond an acceptable level.

Before turning to an analysis of the qualitative balance of power, mention should be made of the short internal lines that contributed to Israel's conventional advantage in all wars up to and including 1967. The shortness of the lines enabled the rapid transfer of mobilized forces from one front to another, and simplified logistics. Thus, the short lines allowed Israel efficiently to conduct a differentiated strategy of attack on one front, while running a holding operation on other fronts. This advantage was lost with the territorial expansion of 1967. The ill-effects were felt in the 1973 War, in which the distance from the Golan to Suez prevented the conduct of an integrated strategy on two fronts. Such a strategy would have required the swift transfer of forces from the southern to the northern front, or vice versa, in order rapidly to establish an overwhelming preponderance on one of the fronts. It was only during the final stages, when the result of the war had already been determined, that detachments were transferred from the north to the south. But this had no major influence on the course of the war. With the evacuation of Sinai, Israel was freed of the burden of long internal lines, and her advantage in this respect over a hypothetical Arab war coalition was restored. The Arab armies, on the other hand, are bound to the use of long, external lines. Indeed, the Arab states are unable to adopt strategies involving the differentiated concentration of forces on different fronts. Each front must be conducted independently, and this obviously simplifies Israeli planning for deployment and operations.

THE QUALITATIVE BALANCE

It is difficult to assess the qualitative components of a balance of power. The primarily qualitative components include morale and motivation; an effective strategic and operational doctrine; battle experience at the various levels from the troops to the higher echelons of command; intellectual flexibility and the ability to respond to changing conditions; and technical skill. Many of these factors depend on the general level of society; others depend on the army itself—on the levels of its training, its experience, and the structure and adaptability of the command system.

Thus, for example, technical skill and certain aspects of morale depend on the general character of the society. This is reflected in education at the various levels, and in the sociological and political structure of the society. Intellectual flexibility depends, on the one hand, on social and educational factors and, on the other hand, on the nature of the military structure and on the readiness of the higher levels of command to encourage the advancement of officers who are intellectually open and alert.

From all these perspectives, it seems that any basic change in the qualitative components to Israel's detriment is, in turn, dependent on the ensuance of fundamental changes in the character of Arab and Israeli societies. In both these societies, certain limited changes are occurring which will tend to work against Israel, but in the foreseeable future they will have no tangible impact on the abovementioned qualitative components.

As stated previously, it is difficult to assess the weight of qualitative factors; the most propitious analytical tool is past experience. Recent military history in the Middle East has evidenced Israeli superiority in two qualitative dimensions: in the air and in mobile and armored battle. In both these areas, the determining factor—aside from the quality of the weapons systems themselves—is flexibility in the activation of forces when confronted by rapidly changing tactical situations. It is conceivable that with the continued influx into the region of sophisticated weaponry which demands the ability to rapidly master a range of different weapons and to supervise complex and dynamic command systems, the qualitative balance of power will continue to improve in Israel's favor. Nevertheless, it must be noted that Israel's air superiority is liable to be impinged by the introduction of American aircraft into Arab air forces. Israeli superiority could also be eroded by the continued infusion of modern surface-to-air systems into Arab states, including Jordan.

It is hardly necessary to add that past and present experience is not the only key to future expectations: unpredicted changes are always liable to occur. However, since qualitative change is, to a certain extent, a function of change in the social and educational spheres of Arab society, it can be concluded with reasonable certainty that qualitative improvement will be slow, and that dramatic changes will not take place in the coming decade.

Another qualitative component is morale and motivation for war. The 1973 and 1982 Wars seem to have provided clear proof that when the vital interests of the Arab states are threatened, the motivational level of the fighting army is as high, or almost as high, as the motivational level of the Israeli army. Thus, should the interests of the respective Arab states be threatened, the morale of the combat troops (which depends partially on motivation) will be high. However, if the objective of the Arab forces is not to defend their own countries but to destroy the state of Israel or even seriously to harm her, the balance of motivation will operate in Israel's favor.

Various innovations in military technology may also influence the balance of qualitative components, but in ways that are difficult to evaluate. Among these factors, the development of precision guided munitions is of particular relevance. There is a debate in the literature regarding the extent to which such antitank and antiaircraft weapons systems alter the balance between defense and offense. In the context of the Middle East, however, the question that demands attention is the extent to which these systems influence the qualitative gap between the Israeli and Arab armies. And again, this is a difficult issue to assess. On the one hand, the new generations of some of these systems (particularly in the area of antitank weapons) are characterized by the relative ease of their operation; from this perspective the qualitative gap is likely to be reduced. On the other hand, given the widespread proliferation and integration of these systems into existing weapons systems, the level of coordination and command required is bound to rise. This aspect is likely to reflect and perhaps even widen Israel's qualitative advantage.

Definitive assessments of the impact of future technologies are, then, fraught with difficulty; but in general, it is unlikely that they will alter the qualitative balance to Israel's detriment. Nonetheless, the hypothetical proliferation of precision guided systems in the Arab armies, in quantities far exceeding those possessed by Israel, is liable to undermine the general balance of military power. It should be emphasized that were Israel to lose ground in this area, it could seriously damage the said balance. The opposite is also true: Israel's rapid advance in this area, in conjunction with sophisticated acquisition, command, and control systems, would significantly improve the balance of power in her favor.

Another issue located at the junction of the qualitative and quantitative aspects of the balance of power relates to the extreme intensification of firepower; indeed, it is possible to talk of the firepower "saturation" of the future battlefield. In Israel's northern and eastern sectors, some 7,000–8,000 tanks from both sides are likely to be concentrated along a number of relatively narrow axes. Such a density of armor is unprecedented in military history. The impact of this concentration on the balance of power is not clear. Nonetheless, it seems that in the eastern and northern sectors, where the number of passages which allow for the easy movement of tanks is limited, the concentration of forces will, in the final analysis, lend an advantage to the defense and will handicap the attacker from whatever side he may be. A limited partial example of this may be taken from the Lebanese war. During the armored battle in the Beqah valley, it emerged that at any one time only a relatively small proportion of all the armored forces could be advanced to the front line: in such circumstances, a determined, well-equipped and well trained defender is better able to block an attack. The defender's hand is strengthened further when he possesses a large quantity of firepower with substantial reserves, as will be the case for both sides on Israel's northern and eastern fronts.

The tentative conclusion that emerges from this analysis is as follows: should Israel be forced to adopt an offensive strategy against the combined concentrated forces of Syria, Jordan, and—if recovered militarily—Iraq, she will be confronted by a task of great difficulty. In such circumstances, Israel would be unable to utilize the advantages of her rapid battle mobility until after the opening assault and breakthrough, and this initial stage would demand a relatively high price in comparison to previous wars. The corollary is, of course, that it will be immensely difficult for the Arab forces to achieve any major breakthrough of the Israeli lines. The danger of a major defeat for Israel is thus low. The campaign, however, might degenerate into a stationary attrition situation. If Iraqi forces are not included in the calculation, then an offensive mission would be easier for the Israeli forces, though the costs involved may still be high.[4]

In this context it should be noted that the adoption of a strategic doctrine which permits a preemptive strike, for example in response to an infringement of Israel's *casus belli*, would underscore the possibility of an Israeli assault on the eastern front. Similarly, one can conceive of operational doctrines which would allow for Israeli offensive actions in the northern and northeastern sectors. In such circumstances, a flank attack might be adopted, perhaps in conjunction with air force operations against detachments. Such approaches may enable effective offensive operations in these sectors. It should be stressed that the development of such a doctrine would require considerable investments in various weapons systems, in particular the acquisition of advanced attack helicopters.

In Sinai, in contrast, the concentration of armored forces will be less significant from the perspective of firepower saturation. The expanses in Sinai provide options for battles based on rapid mobility and armor, together with operational or tactical flanking maneuvers. In Sinai, thus, the considerable growth in armored power and firepower does not change the essential nature of the battlefield. There Israel can exploit her superiority in battle mobility and flanking movements. In the same arena Israel is capable, in principle, of achieving victory against the Egyptian armored forces, even when the power ratio of armored forces is 1:1, and possibly even when Israeli forces are numerically inferior. The experience of the 1973 War should be mentioned again here. Three armored divisions and, in addition, another reduced division stopped, and then successfully counterattacked, 9–10 Egyptian armored, mechanized, and infantry divisions; this occurred on a battlefield with which it was difficult for Israel to contend – the battle involved crossing the Suez Canal in order to break through the Egyptian army. During the initial phase of the campaign, October 6–14, Israel fought in a narrow area, thus unable fully to exploit her superior capabilities. The Israeli advantage in flanking movements and mobile battles was only manifest in the final stages of the war, on the western side of the Canal.[5]

Thus it appears that the saturation of the battlefield resulting from increase in firepower, particularly in terms of the number of tanks and precision guided antitank weapons, combines to form the following scenario: in the case of a general war against a broad Arab coalition, Israel will be able, in principle, to conduct a stable defense in the northern and eastern sectors, while efficiently defeating the Egyptian army in the expanses of Sinai. Under such conditions Israel could manage with a substantially inferior general power ratio in the northern and eastern sectors, and an equal ratio for armored forces in Sinai. After defeating the Egyptian forces, Israel could direct her forces from the southwestern sector in an attempt to penetrate either or both the northern and eastern fronts, either by a frontal assault or by using flanking techniques.

Given the present quantitative power ratios, Israel can permit a more comfortable allocation of forces than described in the scenario above, and in doing so, preserve for herself additional options. Moreover, even were the quantitative power ratios to deteriorate to a situation of 1:3 in the armored and mechanized divisions, Israel would not be obliged to alter her strategy. Nevertheless, a deterioration of the power ratios would exact a high, possibly unacceptable, cost were Israel to attempt a penetration in fire-saturated sectors in which the number of traversable axes is limited. The option of an assault and penetration on the eastern and northern sectors would essentially be negated. Israel would be forced to adopt an essentially defensive strategy or, alternatively, if Iraqi forces were to join the campaign, a preventive operation prior to the concentration of the combined Syrian, Jordanian, and Iraqi forces.

To summarize the issue of power ratios: the foregoing analysis assumed the most extreme possible scenario from the political-strategic perspective, that is the establishment of a broad Arab coalition, not including Iraqi in the short- and mid-range terms, aimed at a general war of destruction against Israel. The analysis revealed that according to the current ground force power ratios, such a coalition is incapable of deploying armored and mechanized divisions in a quantity that meets the ratio requisite for offensive success. This is the case even excluding account of the various qualitative components in which, at least until now, Israel has demonstrated a substantial superiority. If it is the intention of the Arab states to change these power ratios, they will be obliged to increase their land forces considerably, and this without any growth whatsoever on Israel's behalf—something that would appear of low probability. An Arab military expansion of this magnitude would involve an investment of effort exceeding that of the previous decade and a half. Even then, however, the Arab states will have obtained a ratio which is a necessary, but not sufficient, condition for victory.

It would appear then that in a conventional military environment, Israel's very existence is at present secure. The evolution of the extreme political-strategic situation described above, which in itself is very unlikely, might however, create uncertainties about the outcome of a military campaign. It appears that even in such circumstances Israel's very existence would be assured, but given the uncertainties attendant on conventional campaigns, this can not be stated unequivocally. Moreover, the continuation of the arms race in the Middle East with further qualitative improvements in Arab arms, might exacerbate Israeli strategic uncertainties.

A general Arab war against Israel will probably not constitute a threat to Israel's existence, but it could exact a very high cost. Given the present power ratios, it appears probable that Israel could successfully contend with a broad Arab coalition by concentrating her forces at one front while maintaining defensive operations at another. It seems that it would be easier to contend first with the Egyptian army in the Sinai, while running holding operations on the other fronts. Following the completion of the Sinai offensive, Israel would be free to launch attacks elsewhere. However, were the quantitative power ratio to deteriorate in the coming years, while a strategy of movement and destruction in Sinai would still be possible, an offensive strategy on the northern or northeastern fronts, and conceivably even on the eastern front, may involve unacceptable costs for Israel. Israel would be at risk of being drawn into a war of attrition on all or some of these fronts; while such a war would not constitute a military threat to Israel's existence, it would have substantial erosive military, economic and social effects and, as such, would also pose a major threat to morale.

In this context, mention should be made of the 1973 War. While Israel defeated the armies of Egypt and Syria, together with the substantial Iraqi expeditionary forces, the war caused an erosion of the economic and social fabric of Israeli society.

LIMITED WAR SCENARIOS

An analysis of the above power ratios does not indicate that limited wars of various types are beyond the realm of possibility. On the contrary, such wars are much more probable than a general war, and some scenarios are even liable to impose very heavy costs on Israel.

There is a great number of possible limited war scenarios, and it is difficult to anticipate the entire range of the possible variations. We will deal here with only two situations that would involve the use of ground forces, the first of which appears quite possible under the political conditions to be described below, while the second is less probable although not impossible. In addition, we have to mention a third scenario involving the use of surface-to-surface missiles targeted on the civilian population, either in conjunction with ground operations or by itself. The Gulf War, discussed in Chapter 6, could serve as an example for such a situation. Because of the specific characteristics of such a scenario, we shall discuss it in greater detail later in this chapter.

We will begin with a possible long-range scenario, viz. one that follows an Iraqi recovery from the Gulf War. Let us assume that a positive political solution has been found neither for the problem of the West Bank (and consequently the Palestinian issue also remains unresolved), nor for the problem of the Golan. Let us also assume that political relations along the Syrian–Iraqi–Jordanian axis have improved. The combination of these two conditions, along with an additional deterioration of political relations between Israel and Egypt (albeit without the total annulment of the peace agreement) create a backdrop for the establishment of a Syrian–Iraqi–Jordanian military coalition. The leaders of this coalition might even assume that should they initiate war, that Egypt—even if she does not join the war effort—will tie down a sizable Israeli force, exceeding the latter's peacetime deployment of forces in the south. Israel would be compelled to allocate even more forces were Egypt to violate certain of the clauses regarding the demilitarization of Sinai; that is, by her deployment of additional forces in the limited military zone adjacent to the Suez Canal, while refraining from penetrating into the fully demilitarized areas of Sinai. In this case, it is possible that Israel would prefer not to respond militarily although she would be compelled to further strengthen her southern forces. Under these conditions the balance of power would yield an approximate ratio between Israel and her opponents of 1.8:1; on the eastern and northeastern fronts.[6] Moreover, given the effective saturation of defensive firepower, it seems that Israel would be hard-pressed to adopt an offensive doctrine on these fronts. The war would most likely begin with a Syrian–Iraqi attempt to conquer the Golan Heights, or an Iraqi–Jordanian attempt to invade via the West Bank.

Once these attacks are blocked by Israel, there is some chance that the campaign would deteriorate into an ongoing war of attrition. Another possibility would include a successful Israeli assault in one of the sectors and the destruction of some of the Arab forces; Israel, however, would have to pay a high price for this assault. Moreover, it is likely that such an assault would not be fully realized: the United States, probably with Russian support, would likely intervene and enforce a cease fire.

The second scenario is that of war initiated by Syria alone with the objective of regaining the Golan Heights. The Syrian operation could take the form of either a surprise attack or a static war of attrition. It may be assumed that the probability of such a war will increase as political conditions become more favorable to the Syrian leadership—for example, should Arab frustration rise regarding the failure to find a solution to the Palestinian problem or should Israeli–Egyptian relations deteriorate. In such a case, Israel could concentrate greater forces against Syria than in the first scenario, thus weakening Syria's ability to block an Israeli attack. The probability for such a scenario is low, but it will rise as Syria's perception of political conditions changes—that is, when the Syrian leadership believes that additional Arab states will actively join the war.

In summary, it appears that at present neither a general or limited war represent a threat to Israel's existence. Moreover, because of the neutralization of the Iraqi military capability in the short and medium run, the likelihood of limited wars initiated by Arab states in the next few years has declined even beyond that obtaining since 1973. Nevertheless, various types of limited wars, and certainly general wars, will impose heavy costs on Israel and are liable to cause her considerable harm. In addition, according to past experience, there is little chance that a general or limited Israeli victory will bring any positive political dividends to Israel. Finally, every war contributes to a further escalation of the arms race in the region, which poses an economic burden on Israel. Thus, Israel must pursue the deterrence of all types of wars, and particularly a war involving all the regional Arab states. Israel must develop a strategic doctrine which will diminish her adversaries' ability to inflict high costs on her in the event that a war should break out. However, such a doctrine cannot stand alone—it must form part of an integrated *political* and strategic approach, and it is to the shape of such a scheme that we now turn.

CONVENTIONAL DETERRENCE AS A PREFERRED STRATEGY

The underlying assumption of the following analysis is that, for the present and if conditions do not change, for the foreseeable future, Israel will be able to continue to follow a strategy based primarily on conventional arms. This strategy will be directed first and foremost toward "general" deterrence. The strategy will also manifest elements of "specific" deterrence, strictly linked to *casus belli*. Should conventional deterrence fail, Israel would still be able to successfully defend herself against any actual military aggression that she might conceivably confront. Nevertheless, in the case of a general war coalition, the costs for Israel may be extremely high and there are some uncertainties regarding the outcomes. Even if limited wars break out the costs for Israel may be high. Hence, Israel should further enhance her overall strategic situation, and should also pursue ways to diminish the likelihood of war and overall stability.

The success of deterrence, and if the need should arise, of defense, are tightly linked to a complex, integrated web of politico-strategic factors. The discussion that follows will examine these factors. First, however, note should be taken of the integrated nature of these factors; Israeli strategic policy must comprise a "package," combining military strategy with political and security arrangements which can collectively reinforce general and specific deterrence while maintaining a favorable balance of power. The following are the basic assumptions of an integrated general strategy: Israel has a continuing need to make every effort possible to prevent the formation of a grand Arab coalition against her, because of the enormous costs she would incur in a war against such a coalition. Israel must also reduce the motivation of individual Arab states to initiate war against her for their own particular reasons.

In Chapter 2 we noted the relative success, over an extended period, of Israeli conventional deterrence. Note was made of the complexity of the deterrence process, and of the existence of three axes of equilibria which comprise this process: the balance of military power, the balance of interests, and the balance of resolve, with emphasis on the first two axes. An understanding of these three balances and the interaction between them is critical to the analysis of Israeli conventional deterrence. Reducing the motivation for war as the result of political arrangements will contribute to stabilizing politico-strategic relations, and this in turn will intensify the effect of conventional deterrence.

The analysis presented in this book concerning the processes of escalation and crisis, that have preceded and eventually led to the outbreak of the various Israeli–Arab wars, is indicative of the direct correlation that exists between the level of readiness to go to war, and the degree of political grievance felt by different Arab states in their interaction with Israel. Indeed, prior to the 1967 War, while the Arab states were adamant in their refusal to accept the territorial status quo, they nevertheless refrained from initiating war with Israel. War was not at the top of their respective priorities. Moreover, war with Israel would have involved the Arab states in very high costs, and threatened to expose them to the danger of severe punishment. Since 1967, the political grievance arising from the damage to the particular interests of Egypt and Syria—the loss of Sinai and the Golan—has caused the War of Attrition of 1969–1970, and the 1973 War. These two wars resulted therefore, not from the traditional causes of the Arab–Israeli conflict, but rather from specific grievances relating to the particular interests of the respective states. It is, therefore, highly probable that the relief of this grievance will improve the balance of interests, which is fundamental to the effectiveness of the deterrence process. Let us now turn to an elaboration of the specific strategic problems confronted by Israel in respect to each of her various neighbors.

Egypt

The nurturing of the peace between Israel and Egypt is critical to Israel's general security. Furthermore, the stability of the peace with Egypt is largely dependent on Israeli policy. Egypt's task in upholding her end of the peace would be simplified were Israel to refrain from attempts to create a military hegemony in parts of the Middle East (an ambition which was apparently one of the goals of the 1982 Lebanese War), as well as by the rendering of a solution to the problem of the West Bank, probably through an Israeli–Jordanian–Palestinian agreement. Egypt is also deeply interested in an Israeli–Syrian agreement. Significantly Egypt's increased active involvement in the Arab world since the mid-1980s, has not affected her commitment to the peace with Israel. Beyond its impact on the peace process, Egypt's abstention from a military coalition against Israel is in itself an important strategic factor for Israel, both in terms of deterrence, and in terms of her ability to deal militarily with any Arab threat using conventional weapons.

In the foreseeable future, the probability that Egypt would be ready to join a war coalition against Israel, except under extreme provocation, is very low. The Egyptian preference for peace with Israel is a reflection of several factors: first, the recognition of the extremely high cost of the conflict with Israel. This position voiced repeatedly by Sadat expressed feelings widely held among the Egyptian elite, the military and civil bureaucracies, and some intellectuals. The same point has been manifest in Egyptian public debate since Sadat's trip to Jerusalem. Indeed, even most of those opposed to Sadat's peace initiative emphasize that they do not want to cancel the 1979 peace treaty, and most certainly desire no return to a state of war with Israel. Rather, they oppose "normalization" with Israel, and criticize the peace treaty for having left out the solution of the Palestinian problem. Yet, as stated, they do not call for the treaty's complete annulment. Indeed, the Gulf Crisis strengthened the position of the groups which backed the peace. Even members of the opposition have of late come out and recognized the importance of the peace treaty.[7] The most extreme and radical of all opposition groups in Egypt, which is connected with fundamentalist terror organizations, focuses its main attention on Egypt's internal problems and religion–state relations. The Israeli–Arab conflict and opposition to the Camp David peace agreement play a secondary role in the policies of these organizations.[8] Nonetheless, it should be borne in mind that these radical organizations do in fact demand cancellation of the peace agreement.

Second and most important, for many years Egypt has pondered her national identity, vacillating between a strictly "Egyptian orientation," and an emphasis on a more general Arab identification. In the 1920s, for example, a specifically Egyptian territorial orientation—interposed even by Pharoahnic elements—was predominant. This notion was integrated within a secular liberal trend, whose proponents had been active in Egyptian politics since the late 19th century.[9] During the period of King Farouk and President Nasser—that is, from the 1930s to the 1960s the "Arab" dimension became more prominent. During this period, an Arab-Muslim orientation became the major component of the Egyptian national consciousness.[10] The "Egyptian" orientation did not disappear, but it occupied a markedly less central position. (It can be argued that the "Arab" orientation, which in the period under Nasser developed into a full-blown pan-Arab approach, was primarily a mechanism for the advancement of particularistic Egyptian goals.)[11] Since the 1967 War, and certainly from the time of Sadat's ascension to the national leadership, this approach has changed. The Arab element in the makeup of Egyptian political identity has become less important, and especially marked has been the demise of pan-Arab views.[12] Egypt's desire of late to strengthen her ties with the Arab world do not necessarily reflect any change in this "Egyptianist" trend: it could be interpreted as a pragmatic turn in Mideast politics, or perhaps as the creation of a new balance between the "Egyptian" and "Arabist" poles of national identity. In the latter case, the policy direction initiated by Sadat can be perceived as not merely rooted in immediate instrumental needs, but in fundamental requirements of national identity. In this regard, it should be noted that the closure of the breach with the Arab world did not lead to the breaking of the peace agreement with Israel. Quite the opposite has been the case: Arab states such as Jordan, Syria and Saudi Arabia, appear ready to accept the Egyptian position on peace with Israel. The PLO has also joined the peace process.

Another factor bearing on Egyptian policy is its change of orientation toward the United States since 1973. Washington–Cairo relations continue to improve, with substantial benefits accruing to the latter. In the area of economic and technological aid, the United States and the West in general demonstrated their marked ascendancy over the USSR. The latter was unable to meet the demands of its clients in the Third World. Any Egyptian regime interested in economic and technological development therefore preferred a Western orientation. Moreover, the Egyptian army is in the process of conversion to American arms, a process which will take many years. As long as this process continues, it is difficult to imagine the occurrence of any sudden drastic change in Egypt's international orientation. Finally, Egypt's bitter experience during the period of her cooperation with the USSR was felt at all levels—personal, organizational, and national—and brought about a crisis in relations between the two states. In addition, given the existence of strong ties with the United States, it will be very difficult for Egypt to cancel the peace agreement with Israel, in the attainment of which the United States was so deeply involved.

In the unlikely event of Egypt cancelling the peace treaty, it remains highly improbable that she would rejoin the circle of military confrontation and war against Israel. Active belligerence against Israel would involve, first and foremost, Egyptian military penetration into Sinai. However, the Sinai is patrolled by American units responsible for its demilitarization. That is, the Egyptian military penetration into Sinai would involve her, at the very least, in a diplomatic confrontation with the United States. Needless to say this would have critical implications for Egypt, and it can be assumed that she would refrain from such an act. The gradual removal of American forces from Sinai, at the request of Egypt, is perhaps a more conceivable scenario, but it is fair to assume that such a process would be difficult and crisis-bound.

Another factor preventing Egypt from entering into a state of belligerence with Israel relates to the political status of Sinai. In the 15 years between 1967 and 1982, the liberation of Sinai was the principal focus of Egyptian political aspirations. The efforts to recover Sinai involved two wars—the War of Attrition, and the 1973 War—and also led to the reversal of the Egyptian position regarding Israel and a peace treaty. From the Egyptian point of view, the process was brought to a satisfactory conclusion in 1982. After the expense of such immense efforts, it is difficult to conceive of Egypt endangering its sovereignty over Sinai by means of an ill-considered military-political operation. Entry into a state of belligerence, an attempt to violate the demilitarization of the Sinai, and military acts against Israel, would expose Egypt to the danger of a military setback. The result of this might be a retreat from all of Sinai and the loss of Egyptian sovereignty—in short, the loss of all that was achieved with such great effort in the peace agreement.

As was argued in the previous chapter, the failure to lower the profile of the Palestinian problem by means of some settlement of the West Bank problem, is liable, in the long run, to damage the Israeli–Egyptian peace agreement. It might also provoke an Israeli–Egyptian crisis under conditions of general escalation throughout the region. Nevertheless, the development of a belligerent confrontation between Egypt and Israel remains highly improbable. All this is, of course, not to discount the possibility of tension and political-strategic discomfort impinging on relations between the two states.

An additional and critical issue relates to the demilitarization of Sinai, as was required in the peace agreement. The demilitarization of Sinai, aside from a narrow strip along the Suez Canal in which Egypt is permitted limited forces, greatly improves Israel's strategic position. This factor alone ought to reduce Egyptian readiness to engage in military actions in or via Sinai, since her ability to defeat Israel in such circumstances compares unfavorably with the situation preceding 1973, in which the IDF was strung across the entire peninsula. From the Israeli military point of view, the demilitarization of Sinai is preferable to her own military presence there.[13] This was demonstrated in the contrast between the elegant Israeli victory of 1967, and the imbroglio of 1973.

This contrast was not a function of the way in which the two wars were conducted, but rather reflects deeper, structural factors. In order to further the analysis we will now focus attention on a number of points of comparison between the demilitarization and the Israeli occupation of Sinai in the period 1967–1973. First in the 1967–1973 situation, Israel was faced with serious dilemmas of deployment. The Egyptian army was concentrated adjacent to the canal, waiting for an opportune moment to strike. Israel, dependent mostly on reserve forces, was able to deploy only a limited regular force in Sinai. This factor lent a massive advantage to the Egyptians, as was reflected in the 1973 War, in which the tactic of a surprise attack was used, enabling the Egyptian army to attack before Israeli reserve forces could arrive to reinforce the regular army. Were it not for the demilitarization, the possibility of surprise attack would remain, given the inability of Israel to consistently identify Egyptian preparations for a surprise attack, and this despite major advances in the efficiency of her early warning systems. Moreover, Egypt could occasionally adopt the familiar tactic of fabricating "noises" as though she were preparing for attack and thus force Israel to mobilize her forces again and again. This would create an insufferable drain on Israeli resources, would dull the sensitivity of the Israeli early warning system, and would eventually enable Egypt to implement a surprise attack after all.

An additional reason for preferring demilitarization over an Israeli presence in Sinai stems from the structure of the Israeli Defense Forces (IDF). The IDF's land force is chiefly organized around armored and mechanized units. Armor is emphasized more strongly in the IDF than in any other army in the world, except perhaps for Syria. As such, the IDF is most suited for battle involving rapid movement over considerable distances—and in that respect Sinai is an ideal battle zone. On the other hand, the IDF is not suited for static battle in defense of a fixed line. Attempting to hold such a line in Sinai was a major error for Israel. It should be added that the structure of the IDF is a necessary function of manpower constraints. The use of tanks, armored personnel carriers, and attack helicopters elicits the most efficient ratio of manpower to firepower. As a result, any change in this structure could have a negative impact on the overall balance of power. In this sense, it is better for Israel that her forces are not deployed in Sinai. If Egypt were to attempt the deployment of forces there, Israel could carry the battle to them. Indeed, that was precisely the situation during 1957–1967. When the Egyptian army was deployed in Sinai in the 1967 crisis, Israel was able to attack and use its superior capability in movement and maneuvers.

Indeed, the history of Israeli–Arab wars indicates that the qualitative superiority of the IDF is most clearly manifest in battles involving rapid armor movements. This is a function of the intellectual flexibility characteristic of the Israeli officer corps. To this must be added the ability of the IDF in the quick ad hoc organization of units taken from various parent units, in response to the dynamics of battle. Again, this advantage is most markedly apparent in an expansive arena, in which the impact of infantry is neutralized. All this leads to the conclusion that in Sinai the IDF is better placed to conduct battle against the Egyptian Army than in a forward deployment in the region of the Canal.

A third matter that arises in this context, relates to Israel's possible goals in a war on the Southern Front. Should there be another Israeli–Egyptian war, the only goal that Israel could consider would be the destruction of the threat of Egyptian military force against Israel. The experience of previous Israeli–Arab wars confounds any expectation that military accomplishments will be translated into political gains. The only conceivable strategic goal is the destruction of the enemy army, in order to remove the immediate threat to Israel, and thus to attain temporary relief. The ideal arena for the destruction of the Egyptian army is Sinai, because it readily accommodates operations of flanking and circling. In a war conducted near the Suez Canal, the IDF will be unable to destroy the Egyptian army, and the war could deteriorate into a static war of attrition, which is a major irritation for Israel.

Let us now examine this last claim in the light of the 1967 and 1973 wars. In the 1967 War, the collapse of the Egyptian army was brought about by Israeli flanking and encircling operations which had either been completed or were verging on completion. This campaign successfully combined a *blitzkrieg* strategy, involving a rapid thrust into the enemy's rear, and thereby putting him off balance, and a strategy of encirclement. All this was achieved while the strategic goal was not the conquest of the Sinai Peninsula, but the collapse of the Egyptian Army. With its back to the Canal, the Egyptian army succumbed quickly. In 1973, Israel wanted to deliver a devastating blow to the Egyptian army, so as to prevent the outbreak of a war of attrition. The means to this end was an integrated strategy of *blitzkrieg* and encirclement, and it was only possible to conduct such an operation by crossing the canal. The only force that Israel successfully besieged was the Egyptian Third Army, which had crossed to the eastern side of the Canal. On the western side of the Canal, Israel managed to besiege very few Egyptian forces. Furthermore, the crossing of the Canal, which was intended to tip both the military and strategic scales, was the most difficult and bloody battle throughout the entire southern campaign, far more so than the first failure-filled days of the war. But, as we have stated, crossing the canal was a necessary step under the conditions prevalent in 1973, which involved the deployment of the IDF in Sinai. Had she not crossed the Canal, Israel would have been unable to win a decisive victory. Needless to say, Israel was nevertheless unable to earn political dividends from her military achievements, particularly where such dividends would have involved the contradiction of Egyptian political interests. Israel was unable to force Egypt into a political agreement that did not include the restoration of Egyptian sovereignty to Sinai.

A fourth military advantage for Israel of the demilitarization, relates to the interface between air and land battles. When Egyptian forces were concentrated in a static deployment on either side of the Canal, as was the case in 1967–1973, they could relatively easily deploy a dense web of antiaircraft systems. When operated in an integrated manner, such systems can impede the free movement of the Israeli air force. Mobile antiaircraft defense is much less effective as an integrated system, as would necessarily be the case in a war that ranged over the expanses of Sinai. The ability of the Egyptian antiaircraft systems to provide effective cover for the Egyptian forces would be substantially restricted. Another advantage accruing to the IDF from the return to the pre-1967 southern border, is the shortening of her internal lines. This factor has three different aspects. The first factor reflects the expedience of short lines for the logistics of a motorized attack force. The longer the line the more difficult the supply: consequently the army is forced to allocate more manpower and resources to second and third echelon units. Israel's deployment in Sinai after 1967 required a substantial allocation of resources for the development of a supply base network throughout Sinai. Apart from the waste of resources and additional burden that these tasks involved, the flexibility of the Israeli forces in Sinai was also affected due to requirements for the defense of the various supply bases. This problem will recur in the future, should Israel redeploy in Sinai.

The third, but perhaps most important aspect, is that short lines enable the speedy transfer of the main attack effort from one front to another. Long lines stretching from the Egyptian side of the Suez Canal, on the one hand, and into Lebanon, on the other, make the swift transfer of forces very difficult. This factor is of importance, not only in a war situation, but also for its impact on the strategic considerations made by Israel and her enemies. Thus, for example, it is plausible to assume that were Syria, Iraq, and Jordan to plan an attack against Israel, the knowledge that part of the Israeli regular army is deployed opposite Egyptian forces in the distant reaches of western Sinai, would reduce their apprehension of possible Israeli military opposition against them. It is not only that the southern placed forces would be situated far from the arena of the planned war, but also that Israel would be forced to send part of her reserve forces to reinforce the southern front, even in the absence of an Egyptian attack. Israel has much greater flexibility with the IDF situated in the northeastern side of the international boundary with a demilitarized Sinai separating the Israeli and Egyptian armies. This configuration allows for the more rational allocation of forces in response to actual Egyptian movements, and enables the rapid transfer of forces to other fronts according to changes in conditions.

To summarize, the demilitarization of the Sinai prevents the possibility of an Egyptian surprise attack on a sparsely manned Israeli forward line; it makes possible the most effective use of Israeli land forces, viz. in battles of mechanized armor over the expanses of the peninsula; it exposes the Egyptian army advancing into Sinai to Israeli air attack; it enables Israel to destroy the Egyptian army without having to become embroiled in a complicated and expensive process of crossing the Suez Canal; and finally, it provides Israel with optimal operational flexibility.

Jordan[14]

From the Israeli point of view, the demilitarization of Sinai is strategically and militarily preferable to deployment there. The same cannot be said of an Israeli military withdrawal from the West Bank. The demilitarization of the West Bank together with certain security arrangements, would be necessary conditions of Israel's conceding the territories as part of a peace agreement. However, in comparison with present conditions, a demilitarization clause, while it would not necessarily compromise Israel's military posture, would not represent a net strategic gain. In this respect, the demilitarization of the Sinai differs from the demilitarization of the West Bank. The improvement of Israel's strategic situation on the eastern front will require a more comprehensive security settlement than was achieved with Egypt.

What is the primary military threat that would arise from Israel's restoration of Arab sovereignty to the West Bank? The main danger would derive from major concentrations of Arab armor in the West Bank, which could be used in a surprise attack against the soft underbelly of Israel.

However, this danger should not be stated categorically. The West Bank is an enclave which, by means of a north–south pincer movement into the Jordan Valley, can quite easily be cut off from the East Bank, thus facilitating an encirclement action. The demilitarization of the West Bank would diminish the possibility of an enemy force being concentrated there. But even were the demilitarization violated, the relative ease with which it is possible to isolate the West Bank from the East, would enable the destruction of the enemy concentrations.

Indeed, it is quite conceivable that acting alone, Jordan would be reluctant to violate the demilitarization, unless backed by the deployment of major additional Arab forces on the East Bank. And the probable condition of such a Jordanian action would be the staging of attacks on the Syrian, and possibly Lebanese fronts, by a preponderant concentration of Arab forces.

However, such a concentration of force would constitute a threat to Israel, even were there no possibility of transferring troops and armor to a West Bank under Arab sovereignty. Indeed, such a troop concentration constitutes the real threat from the east. Therefore, the concentration of Arab forces along the Jordan, exceeding the limited Jordanian order of battle, should constitute a *casus belli* for Israel.

This combination of factors makes it possible to develop a "package of security measures," which Israel would have to demand in return for granting Jordanian or Palestinian–Jordanian sovereignty over the West Bank. First, the absolute demilitarization of the West Bank, with the exception of internal security forces for the maintenance of order. Second, the continuation of an Israeli presence, over a trial period, in a limited number of important strategic positions that control the main approaches from the east of the Jordan to the West Bank, and which could also serve as bases for Israeli forces in an operation to cut off the West Bank in the event that the demilitarization agreement be violated. To meet the latter requirement, it would be sufficient to have military control over just a few strong points in the north and south of the Jordan Valley. Finally, it would be desirable to include in such an agreement a requirement for a number of intelligence outposts, for early warning purposes,[15] although probably most of the information could be gathered through airborne surveillance.

From a strategic and military point of view, the critical Israeli requirement is not sovereignty over territory, nor even Israeli military control over the entire Jordan Valley, but an Israeli presence in a number of vital outposts in the north and south of the valley, and on the road from Jericho to Jerusalem. For this purpose neither sovereignty nor civilian settlements are required. All that is necessary is a certain military presence in a limited number of strategic points.

Beyond this security "package," Israel could significantly improve her security posture by the formulation of a general political-strategic agreement with Jordan. Such an agreement would only be possible following the return of the West Bank to Palestinian–Jordanian sovereignty (together with the institution of the abovementioned security arrangements). This arrangement would comprise two major elements: first, a bar on the entry of foreign Arab forces to Jordan on the east side of the river, and second, a strategic understanding between Jordan and Israel regarding potential threats to both countries. It must be emphasized that such an arrangement is not a pipe dream, but is rooted in the security interests of Jordan and, in particular, in the history of the security interests she has shared with Israel.[16] These two matters require further elaboration.

Since the mid-1950s, Jordan has been involved in a constant search for allies that might prevent her being conquered by other Arab states. This quest derives from Jordan's intrinsic weakness relative to her powerful neighbors. One such attempt was initiated by Egypt under Nasser by means of an internal overthrow of the Hashemite Kingdom under external pressure. Since 1967, the primary threats have had their source in Syria and Iraq. The most extreme manifestation of these threats was the Syrian invasion in 1970. Jordan has acquired assistance from various sources, both from within the Middle East and from without. In the 1950s, for example, Britain lent assistance, and since then the United States has stood behind her. During the Middle East crisis in July 1958, following the Qassim Revolution in Iraq, the Lebanese Civil War, and the fear of a Nasserite conspiracy in Jordan, British units were sent to Jordan at the request of King Hussein to defend his regime. It is interesting to note that Israel was involved even then, in that the British air shuttle to Jordan flew over Israeli air space.[17] Jordan was later aided by various Arab states.

In 1970, at the time of the attempted Syrian invasion, Jordan turned to the United States and Israel for help. Israel transmitted implicit threats to Syria by means of force concentrations and by placing its air force on alert. In this way, Israel contributed to the deterrence of Syrian air attacks against Jordanian ground forces. It must be added that by defining the introduction of foreign Arab forces into Jordan as a *casus belli*, Israel had, prior to 1967, indirectly contributed to the deterrence of actors intending damage to the Jordanian regime. The confluence at this point of Jordanian and Israeli interests holds even today.

The Jordanian request in 1970 for indirect Israeli assistance was the reflection of an ongoing situation, albeit rife with contradictions for Jordan. Israel's control of the West Bank makes it difficult for Jordan to accept aid from Israel, even in secret or indirectly. Were this stumbling block removed, it seems plausible to assume that a marked change would occur in Jordanian readiness to accept Israeli aid, even on an explicitly formal basis. Thus, in such an environment, shared Israeli–Jordanian interests might enable the signing of an agreement, including an explicit clause prohibiting the introduction of foreign Arab forces into Jordan, and defining this as a situation justifying Israeli military intervention.

Israel's most severe response to a violation of the agreement, either because of a Jordanian invitation for the introduction of foreign Arab armies, or due to some other significant violation of the agreement by Jordan, would be the reoccupation of the West Bank. The occupation of a demilitarized West Bank would present no serious military problem to Israel. It is, therefore, clear that Jordan would have a deep-seated interest in preventing any violations of the agreement with Israel—the upshot of such violations would be the loss of Jordanian or Palestinian–Jordanian sovereignty over the West Bank. It is, of course, also possible that other Arab states would attempt the military penetration of Jordan against her will, as was the case in 1970. In such circumstances, Israel and Jordan could cooperate militarily to combat the invasion.

It appears then, that an Israeli–Palestinian–Jordanian agreement,[18] which would include demilitarization of the West Bank and the abovementioned package of security provisions, in conjunction with an agreement preventing the introduction of foreign Arab armies into the territory east of the Jordan River, could, in fact, radically improve Israel's strategic position. First, this arrangement would reduce the Jordanian motivation to join a belligerent Arab coalition: Jordanian political grievance would have been relieved by her acquisition of the West Bank. Moreover, any violation of the security agreement would result in her losing it again. Second, shared Israeli–Jordanian interests would be created, enabling the two states' cooperation against the introduction of foreign forces into Jordanian territory. This confluence of security interests will create, in effect, a shared Israeli–Jordanian defense zone. This, in itself, would represent a considerable improvement in Israel's strategic posture, while benefiting Jordanian strategic interests.

An Israeli–Jordanian agreement would inhibit the realization of three strategic threats to Israel: a massive concentration of Arab armor on the West Bank; the concentration and threatening deployment of a Jordanian force on the East Bank as part of a general or partial Arab war coalition; the merging of large Iraqi or Syrian forces with the Jordanian army, and their concentration along the length of the Jordan River.

At this point, it is important to make explicit an assumption that underlies the foregoing argument. In the absence of an Israeli–Jordanian agreement, Israel is unable to create a credible deterrence threat against the introduction of substantive Iraqi or Syrian forces into Jordan. In order to lend credence to such a deterrent threat, it must, in turn, be related to some form of credible political association. Present conditions, in which Israel occupies the West Bank, and has not reached political

agreement with Jordan, is not the appropriate environment for the prom-
ulgation of an Israeli threat of a preemptive strike against Iraqi or Syrian
forces located in Jordan. Such a threat and its definition as a *casus belli*
will not be credible, and will not deter the entry of Syrian or Iraqi forces
into Jordan if the action is undertaken with Jordanian agreement. The
same applies from the Israeli point of view: it is difficult to conceive of
Israel responding violently to Syrian or Iraqi acquiescence to a Jordanian
request of this nature. Indeed, Israel refrained from such action despite
the extended presence of two Iraqi divisions in Jordan between 1967 and
1971. During the Gulf Crisis and War, Israel sent deterrence signals
threatening to retaliate if Iraqi forces penetrated Jordan. These warnings
reflected a serious Israeli concern and a readiness to act in case deterrence failed. It is not clear, however, whether these warnings actually were
a factor that inhibited Iraq from sending troops into Jordan. So the
success of deterrence in that particular instance cannot be proven. For
its part, Jordan did not invite Iraqi forces on its soil; quite the contrary,
Jordan repeatedly warned against such action. In that respect Israeli and
Jordanian interests coincided and the Israeli warnings served an important Jordanian foreign policy objective.

In any case, an Israeli–Jordanian strategic agreement such as the one
proposed here, would constitute a firm basis upon which to attach the
terms of the formal peace agreement itself. This holds, whether the strategic agreement be formal or informal, public or secret, or even partially
implicit. The paramount motivation for Jordanian adherence to such an
agreement would be her interest in dealing with foreign threats. In
addition, the sanction of possible Israeli reoccupation of the West Bank
should she violate the peace or security agreements, is a risk Jordan would
be unwilling to flaunt. And thus, with both Egypt and Jordan unwilling
to join a war coalition against Israel, the latter's strategic position would
be very comfortable.

The focus of the discussion will return now to the question of the
balance of power. In a political context characterized by a highly salient
peace with Egypt, and the abovementioned security arrangements with
Jordan, Israel's security situation would be most opportune. Consider the
quantitative balance of land forces: our basic assumption is that Israel
would need to allocate only minimal forces to the defense of its southern
and eastern borders. Moreover, due to the demilitarization of the West
Bank, and the absence of any foreign Arab military presence in Jordan,
Israel would be able to depend on non-armored forces for the ongoing
security needs of its eastern border. Thus, she would be able to concentrate her principal armored forces and all her air force, against Syria.
Under such conditions, Syria would be liable to absorb a severe blow in
any confrontation with Israel and, indeed, it is possible that Israel would
be able to bring a war with Syria to a rapid conclusion. This military-

strategic configuration would therefore generate a strong deterrent effect vis-à-vis Syria.

Looking into the more distant future, it should be added that Iraqi cognizance of this power balance, and her recognition of the possibility that Israel might activate her air force against Iraqi forces moving toward Syria, or attempting to penetrate into Jordan, would also have a deterrent effect on Iraqi forces were Iraq to return as an effective military power to the Arab–Israeli confrontation. It is possible that Iraqi readiness to send expeditionary forces to Jordan in 1967, and to Syria in 1973, stemmed from her perception of a favorable balance of land forces. In 1967, Egypt, Jordan and Syria participated in the war, and in 1973, Egypt and Syria. The Iraqis might be more reluctant were Syria the sole combatant, and were there the threat of Jordanian military opposition to the influx of Iraqi troops into Jordan.

It seems not unrealistic to picture an even more optimistic scenario, in which Syria would be forced to consider the possibility of actual military cooperation between Jordan and Israel, following the signing of a peace agreement. This does not lie beyond the realms of possibility. After all, a few years before it would have been difficult to imagine that the conflict-ridden relations between Israel and Egypt would improve to the extent that even prior to the signing of the Camp David agreement, Egypt would be able to react with understanding to a major Israeli military initiative. Indeed, during this operation—the 1978 Litani Operation—Israel provided Egypt with a constant flow of information regarding the campaign.[19] Furthermore, at the time of the Lebanese War in 1982, an event that caused Egypt extreme political discomfort, Egypt was still able to "accept" the war, without attempting to cancel the peace agreement. As for Jordan, in the past, when confronted by threats to her independence and security, she has acted in defense of her interests, even if these actions required the attainment of tacit understandings with Israel. Given conditions of peace between Israel and both Egypt and Jordan, it is therefore quite reasonable to assume, that in cases in which Jordanian interests would be served, such as during a war with Syria, or with a Syrian–Iraqi coalition, Jordan would be willing to accept Israeli aid either directly or indirectly.

For example, the transfer of Israeli forces through Jordanian territory in order to carry out a deep flanking attack against Syria, illustrates the kind of Israeli–Jordanian cooperation that would improve Israel's strategic ability, and would create serious difficulties for Syria. Such a scheme would not require the activation of any Jordanian forces against another Arab army, and would be of major assistance to Israel. In the absence of a Jordanian–Israeli peace agreement, a deep flanking operation of this nature would raise the specter of war between Israel and Jordan. This strategic cost would clearly outweigh operational military benefits that the operation might furnish.

Syria

A detailed discussion of the political context of Israeli–Syrian relations is beyond the scope of this book. Suffice to say that there are indications of Syrian readiness to agree to a system of "peaceful coexistence" with Israel, if the Golan Heights is returned to Syrian sovereignty. Public pronouncements by Syrian leaders refer to this as an agreement for "non-belligerence." At the time of writing, in connection with the bilateral negotiations in Washington Syrian spokesmen have raised the possibility of full peace with Israel if the Golan Heights are returned to Syria and Israel withdraws from the other territories conquered in 1967. Indeed, one of them even went so far as to suggest a full peace agreement in return for only the Golan Heights. In any case Syrian acceptance of full peace with Israel, against the background of her deep involvement in Lebanon, may serve as part of a stable basis for future Israeli–Syrian relations. However, this must be accompanied by credible security measures. But these will be much more difficult to achieve than in the Sinai or in the Israeli–Palestinian–Jordanian context. The first measure must be complete demilitarization of the Golan Heights. Because the Heights are a high plateau with easy access from the Syrian side, Syria is in a much better position to reoccupy it in a surprise move. A necessary additional measure would be to demilitarize the size of Syrian forces beyond the demilitarized zone. However, using forces deployed in other parts of the country, Syria would still be in a position to move into the area. Thus, such restrictions could serve only as a partial measure. They would become more credible only if the overall size of Syrian forces is reduced and its offensive capability considerably blunted. Thus, an Israeli withdrawal from the Golan should be connected with an overall reduction in Syrian military capability.

Equally important may be American guarantees for the demilitarization of the Golan, backed by the deployment of American forces there. In any case, because of the serious security difficulties Israel faces in the Golan, any withdrawal from there should be spread over a long period of time during which the strategic threats must be carefully weighed, and should ideally be linked to a broad system of arms control and confidence-building measures to be applied to Syria and Israel.

THE NUCLEAR ALTERNATIVE

The foregoing analysis is by way of a preliminary to a comparative assessment of the efficacy of Israeli nuclear and conventional doctrines. The following comparison will be conducted across different political contexts, ranging from Arab–Israeli peace agreements to continued belligerence.

The starting point of the discussion is the assumption, developed in

Chapter 3, that the nuclearization of the Middle East would be dangerous for both Israel and the region as a whole, and thus, that Israel would do best by refraining from the adoption of a nuclear doctrine, and maintaining a low profile on her threshold capability. On the other hand, an explicit Israeli nuclear doctrine and the removal of official ambiguity, would probably motivate Arab states to opt for quick nuclear developments.

The analysis presented so far in this chapter has yielded the following conclusions:

1 Under the present balance of military forces, and in the context of the current political situation, there is no threat to the very existence of Israel. Even the formation of a broad Arab war coalition would probably not alter this situation. However, in the latter case, and especially with a further widening of the quantitative gap between the sides, there would be uncertainty about the course and outcome of a war.
2 The formation of such a coalition and the launching of a general war against her—even if not posing an existential threat—would be extremely costly for Israel.
3 In the absence of a broad Arab coalition, the spectrum of threats against Israel, and their potential costs, are accordingly circumscribed. Nevertheless, even limited or partial wars by a number of Arab states, or one large Arab state (such as Syria), may exact considerable costs from Israel.
4 The Israeli conventional deterrent effect against possibility 3 will be more effective than in the case of possibility 1.
5 The maintenance of the peace agreement between Israel and Egypt renders unlikely the scenario described in 1 and constrains the probability of 3.
6 A Jordanian–Israeli–Palestinian peace agreement would increase the durability of the Egyptian–Israeli agreement, and would further restrict the possibilities given in 3. An agreement with Jordan would also raise the effect of Israel's general and specific deterrent postures. Moreover, a peace agreement with Jordan would guarantee that even in the event of the failure of Israeli deterrence against one of the possibilities in 3, Israel would nevertheless be able to deal with the military challenge with acceptable costs. Similarly, a political accommodation with Syria, which is quite possible, would further diminish the threat of war.
7 The ambiguous Israeli nuclear posture probably serves as an additional deterrent—beyond conventional deterrence—against the threat involved in possibility 1.

Against the background of these conclusions, and in view of the high costs involved in proliferation, the main policy question to emerge is the following: Is the need for nuclearization of Israeli strategy so paramount that it should be adopted despite the cost? It may of course be argued that even if Israel did adopt a fully fledged nuclear doctrine no Arab state could follow suit. However, this appears rather unlikely. As argued in previous chapters, under such conditions, intensified Arab motivations on the one hand, and in particular the diminishing constraints on the nuclear suppliers on the other, will converge to fuel general proliferation in the region.

In the second part of this chapter we shall discuss the preferred nature and the uses of the ambiguous posture. We now focus on the extent to which the nuclear alternative may improve Israel's strategic position under the different contexts listed above.

At the outset, note should be taken of a number of basic assumptions:

1 If the Arab states arm themselves with nuclear weapons, Israel will have no choice but to adopt a doctrine of nuclear deterrence. In this case, the Middle East will become a nuclear region—a most disconcerting prospect, replete with dangers for all regional states. The implications of this situation are dealt with in Chapter 3.

2 Deterrence must be conceived of as a continuum ranging from its total absence to absolute deterrence. Israel's adoption of a doctrine of explicit nuclear deterrence will surely advance Israel's deterrent effect along this continuum. Nonetheless, the effect of Israeli nuclear deterrence will not be unqualified; conceivably, it will fall out somewhere near the halfway point between Israel's conventional general deterrence and absolute deterrence.

Generally speaking, the impact of the nuclearization of the Israeli deterrence system will vary from threat to threat: it will be stronger against a general Arab war aimed at the destruction of Israel, less strong against the various types of limited wars, and almost irrelevant against guerrilla and terrorist activities. (As for its possible deterrent effect against attacks with chemical weapons, see below.) Moreover, in certain situations, the nuclear deterrent effect will be even weaker than the conventional deterrent effect. These points will be elaborated upon in the following discussion.

3 An Israeli nuclear doctrine, were it adopted, should be tailored to one objective: the general deterrence of a general war initiative posing an existential threat to Israel. In earlier chapters we pointed out that a nuclear doctrine intended to achieve objectives additional to deterrence will be both ineffective and dangerous.

4 The experience of the superpowers indicates that they have tended to conduct their military policy with caution. This applies both to their direct conflictual interactions, as well as to their activity vis-à-vis non-nuclear powers. In the first place this resulted from their mutual concern about the reactions of the nuclear adversary, as well as from a

general attitude dictated by the enormous power under their control. It is likely that were a nuclear Israel to behave in a similar way, her military activity would be constrained even were she to maintain a nuclear monopoly in the Middle East. This would be emphasized if one or more Arab adversaries were also to become nuclear.

For the sake of the present analysis, consider the following three categories of threats arranged in ascending order of gravity:

1 Guerrilla and terrorist activities.
2 Static war of attrition conducted by one or more than one Arab state.
3 Mobilized offensive war conducted by one or more than one Arab state.
4 Offensive war conducted by an Arab grand coalition with unlimited objectives.

Israeli nuclear threats will be of no relevance whatsoever to guerrilla and terrorist activities. The disproportion between the stimulus and the response would be so immense that the threat of a nuclear response to terrorist activity would hold no credibility. This straightforward observation is accepted by all observers and researchers in the field, and requires no supportive evidence. And an additional variant: even were the terrorist or guerrilla activities inspired or supported by any particular Arab state, nuclear threats against this state would also lack all credibility. Once again, the imbalance of stimulus and response undermines the credibility of the threat. In these strategic circumstances, in which deterrence is relatively more effective against larger-scale military activities, Arab states committed to conflict with Israel may perhaps tend to increase their guerrilla and terrorist activities.

Furthermore, precisely the existence of the nuclear factor will constrain Israeli use of conventional military power in response to terrorist and guerrilla activities. Large scale operations are liable to trigger a process of escalation which is difficult to curb. For example, an operation such as the Litani Campaign might not have been implemented had Israel and Syria been nuclear. Even more limited operations would be ridden with dangers. Consequently, precisely an explicit nuclear Israel will face greater constraints in effecting military operations against the low-level Arab operations.

The credibility level of a nuclear deterrent threat would be relatively higher if the objective was the prevention of wars of attrition such as those in which Israel was involved with Egypt between 1969 and 1970, or the limited war of attrition on the Golan Heights in 1974. But here too deterrence would be far from absolute, and it is unlikely that it would much exceed Israel's conventional deterrent effect. Indeed, under certain conditions, it might even be lower.

First, in these circumstances too, the credibility of the nuclear threat would be undermined by the stimulus–response gap. In the final analysis, static battles along the border constitute no threat to Israel's survival, and generally do not involve unacceptable losses. The activation of nuclear weapons would be irrelevant and completely unjustified. From Israel's point of view, the cost of such a war is largely economic, to which can be added the corrosive effect it has on the participant troops. These costs do not justify invoking nuclear threats even if Israel maintains a nuclear monopoly. If the Arab adversary were nuclear, then the Israeli threat would be countered by a reciprocal Arab nuclear threat.

Second, it is possible that a war of attrition situation might develop from limited military clashes along the border. Such clashes would certainly not be deterred by nuclear threats. The escalation of these confrontations into a comprehensive, static attrition situation would be a gradual process, and it would be difficult to determine salient turning points that could bear the burden of being the justification of a nuclear threat.

Finally, and paradoxically, it is also possible that an Arab decision to initiate campaigns of military attrition, or to permit a gradual escalation from limited operations to a major campaign of attrition, could be made somewhat easier by Israeli adoption of a nuclear doctrine. The Arab calculation might run as follows: under conditions of conventional deterrence and the non-use of nuclear weapons, Israel is likely to pursue a doctrine of deliberate escalation, which would result from a campaign of attrition on a specific front, such as the Golan. The very risk of such an escalation, even in the absence of an explicit threat, is itself likely to effectively deter a war of attrition. In a nuclear environment, however, Israel may find that nuclear escalation in response to a war of attrition is excessively dangerous; escalation is liable to lead to the use of nuclear weapons, and a continued war of attrition would, of course, be preferable to such a development.

Thus, in both the cases of terrorist or guerrilla activity and static wars of attrition, one of the paradoxes of nuclear weapons is evident: precisely the enormous destructiveness of nuclear weapons leads to self-imposed limitations on the readiness for violent escalation.

By contrast, it may be assumed that in the case of a mobile attack on the part of one or more Arab states, a nuclear deterrent will be more relevant although probably remaining secondary to conventional deterrence. Here too, the effect of the nuclear threat would be far from absolute, and would not match the level of superpower deterrence. There are a number of reasons for this: first, the balance of interests will influence the decision to initiate such a major military action. This is recognized even by some of those who call for a nuclear deterrence doctrine.[20] Should the level of Arab grievance be intense, even nuclear weapons could not decisively reduce the probability of war. Second, given

246

the present balance of power, a campaign of this nature constitutes no threat to Israel's existence. Under such conditions, the credibility level of a nuclear threat would be limited, although it would be more effective than in the case of a war of attrition. The credibility of nuclear deterrence would increase were the balance to change. Indeed, to the extent that the outcome of a major conventional campaign involving a broad Arab war coalition, is uncertain, nuclear deterrence becomes more relevant. However, such a campaign might develop gradually, with no prior planning. In this case, the Israeli nuclear threats may not be able to deter the initial phase of war. Their efficacy in deterring additional escalation would probably be high, but, coming in the middle of an ongoing war, would involve uncertainty.

Moreover, in a conflict system involving proximate regional states, and between which the level of military friction is high, the existence of a mixed nuclear–conventional environment creates problems of a new sort. Due to the high probability that conventional confrontations will escalate into nuclear confrontations, it becomes difficult to distinguish between conventional and nuclear deterrent threats. Every conventional deterrent is liable, if realized, to rapidly lead to a nuclear confrontation. It follows from this that a nuclear deterrent threat may be formulated only against a direct, well-defined military attack, which poses critical dangers to the deterring side, and when the threatened activation of nuclear weapons is perceived as credible.

"Specific Deterrence" and Casus Belli

As detailed in Chapter 2, casus belli once served an important function in Israeli security policy. Indeed Israel will probably have to recreate such a system in order to enhance her deterrence within the various military-political "packages" outlined in this chapter. However, in a nuclear environment this would involve additional complexities. The foregoing discussion considered a situation of intense conflict between regional countries sharing a common border, between whom the level of military friction is high and that operate in a mixed conventional–nuclear environment. Two general conclusions emerged from the analysis of that situation:

1 At the level of deterrence threats, it may be difficult to differentiate between conventional and nuclear casus belli. These casus belli, if explicated, would have a relatively low credibility, and would also be replete with risks arising from the possibility of rapid escalation from the conventional to the nuclear level.

2 This being the case, it becomes difficult to formulate casus belli

247

regarding possible future developments that precede the actual initiation of hostilities.

From here certain analogies can be drawn regarding Israel. In Israel's situation, there are two hostile strategic developments that are replete with danger, which in a conventional environment could be prevented by deterrent threats, but which, in a nuclear environment are difficult to define as *casus belli*: first, the breach of the Sinai demilitarization agreement by the massive influx of Egyptian troops into Sinai, and their concentration along Israel's southern border, but without actually attacking Israel, or second, the joint deployment of a large Iraqi expeditionary force with the Jordanian army along Israel's eastern border.

Indeed, it is even possible to conceive of a scenario in which Israel's strategic situation would worsen as a result of the introduction of nuclear weapons into the Middle East and regional nuclearization. This may even be the case were Israel to maintain a nuclear monopoly. Before presenting the relevant scenario, two prior considerations should be added here. First, the credibility of a *casus belli* as a deterrent, depends on the challenging side recognizing that violation of the delineated threshold does indeed constitute a serious threat to the security of the deterrers. Second, in the particular case of Israel and the Middle East, the *casus belli* should be acceptable *politically* to the international community (primarily the United States) as well as to the Arab countries. Both conditions are predicated on the *casus belli* being logical and not infringing on the vital interests of Arab states. Under nuclear conditions, Arab states, as well as external powers, may consider that Israel's nuclear capability provides her with sufficient security under any conditions. The *casus belli* would then appear superfluous.

Now we can turn to the relevant scenario. It would require two Arab actions in parallel: the movement of massive Iraqi forces into Jordan, and the annulment of the Sinai demilitarization agreement by the massive introduction of Egyptian forces into Sinai, but with no actual attack on Israel. In a conventional environment, Israel could predefine these actions as *casus belli*, and thus initiate a series of preemptive strikes. In contrast, in a nuclear environment Israel would find herself in serious trouble. It would be difficult for her to define those actions as pretexts for nuclear war. The mere entry of Iraqi forces into Jordan, particularly if at Jordanian bequest, would not justify a nuclear operation (assuming no prior political and strategic agreement between Israel and Jordan as detailed earlier in this chapter). Therefore, even the definition of this development as a *casus belli* under nuclear conditions would not be credible. The breach of the Sinai demilitarization agreement by Egypt and the influx of her forces into Sinai would create a very serious strategic threat to Israel, that would justify military action. However, it is difficult to imagine that a nuclear threat could appear credible under such conditions. After all, the Egyptian action, as defined, does not involve the firing of a single shot at an Israeli soldier; it is also carried out in a region under Egyptian sovereignty. Moreover, in a nuclear environment, there will be serious constraints on exercising a conventional response to the Iraqi and Egyptian actions. The constraints on conventional action are due to the fact that in a nuclear environment any massive conventional military operation could rapidly deteriorate into a nuclear confrontation. This, of course, may act as an additional constraint on Arab behavior. However, were deterrence to fail, Israel would find it difficult to apply a conventional response.

The upshot of the foregoing analysis is, then, that in a nuclearized Middle East any hostile strategic event short of outright military attack on Israel, would make a conventional preemptive response difficult to undertake politically. This would certainly be the case regarding developments occurring beyond her borders in which no fire was directed against Israeli forces. Thus, Israel could not play an active role in her strategic environment even in the face of events that represented a serious threat to her security.

It follows from this that under nuclear conditions, Israel would be divested of the rational option of a preemptive strike, linked to a set of "reasonable" *casus belli*. This would be a strategic concession of the first order and one which would also reduce the effectiveness of Israeli deterrence against limited attacks.

In summary, the most serious threat confronting Israel, and which it is supposed that nuclear deterrence would counter—that of an attack by a broad-based Arab coalition subsequent to a major alteration in the balance of conventional forces to Israel's detriment—is currently low. This may change, however, if there are negative political processes and if the current arms race continues and Israel loses the qualitative edge in armaments. Moreover, certain political and strategic processes and initiatives as detailed in this chapter, could reduce even further the probability of this threat being realized. Israel must also contend with other less extreme threats, such as a unilateral Syrian military initiative. To be sure, the level of Israeli general deterrence against such threats will be improved by the adoption of a nuclear doctrine. But the level of deterrence would not match the profile of global deterrence between the superpowers. Concerning an additional group of threats—the various modes of static wars of attrition and erosion—the improvement of the deterrence effect in a nuclear context would be marginal at best, and under certain conditions, deterrence may even be weakened. Nuclear deterrence is virtually irrelevant to the threat of terrorist and guerrilla activities. The final category of threats comprises actions that represent a major potential strategic menace: specifically, the violation of the Sinai demilitarization agreement or the introduction of Iraqi troops into Jordan or Syria, and the border deployment of the two states' joint forces. The adoption of a nuclear doctrine might have the effect of lowering the Israeli deterrent effect below its present level, and most certainly below the level that would develop were the political-strategic means detailed at the beginning of this chapter applied.

In short, the Israeli system of *specific deterrence*, which is framed within the context of a set of *casus belli*, would not be enhanced by a nuclear doctrine; indeed it might even be weakened. *General deterrence* would in certain circumstances be strengthened, but it would probably not attain the level of effective deterrence obtaining between the superpowers. In other cases the level would remain unchanged, while in still other circumstances it is possible that it would even be lowered.

From this analysis it may be tentatively concluded that in a nuclear Middle East, and similarly in a situation where only Israel has a nuclear capability but chooses to adopt an explicit nuclear strategy, and given further deterioration in the Arab–Israeli relationship, the Arab states would choose a strategy that inflicts maximum harm to Israel at the minimum cost, but which does not cause a nuclear war. The guiding assumption of this Arab strategic choice would presumably be that Israel would refrain from all nuclear activity unless absolutely desperate. The strategy that most adequately meets these requirements is a prolonged static war of attrition, that would involve Israel in continued casualties, and would impose a heavy economic and social burden on Israeli society. Israel could not respond in a conventional offensive manner, lest this lead to a nuclear holocaust. Moreover, should an attack nonetheless be contemplated, the loss of the conventional preemptive attack option formulated within the context of a system of *casus belli* is liable to place Israel in a difficult situation from a conventional military point of view.

THE USES OF THE UNDECLARED POSTURE

In Chapter 1 we discussed the debate surrounding the emergence of the Israeli strategy of ambiguity which ultimately enabled Israel to attain a threshold status. It should be stressed that the strategy of ambiguity was not a calculated policy. Rather it emerged gradually as a result of political compromises. But once it had emerged, it seems that Israeli decision-makers realized its utility. The following discussion is an attempt to analyze the rationale of this policy, as it emerged, and specifically to identify the intentions of decision-makers concerning the possible "uses" of the strategy. In the absence of clear-cut, hard evidence, the discussion is of necessity partly speculative, although it is in part based on certain later public comments. Furthermore, the discussion will focus on various hypothetical uses of an ambiguous posture. During the Gulf Crisis and War, the Israeli threshold status was possibly invoked as a deterrent. This was discussed in Chapter 6 and will be further treated below.

Israeli–American relations

In Chapter 4 we discussed the possible American reactions to an Israeli decision to violate the nuclear threshold. Here we shall briefly discuss the possible diplomatic uses of the threshold status itself.[21] It is likely that Israel has never actually mentioned the possibility of "going nuclear" in its negotiations with the USA about the transfer of conventional weapons to Israel.[22] However, a rational analysis of the security dilemmas confronting Israel, and the persistent Israeli inclination to maintain the widest possible security margins, suggest that if Israel were to perceive the conventional balance as tilting against it, then it would seek an alternative to conventional arms. This situation has not escaped the attention of American officials. Thus, given the Israeli security dilemma, the nuclear option gradually became a tacit bargaining card in its arms transfer negotiations with the United States. To be sure, the United States would almost certainly have supplied Israel with the required conventional arms, in any case. Nevertheless, the nuclear option had apparently played some role in the interagency debate in the U.S. administration regarding arms transfer policy towards Israel.[23] Needless to say, in the event that Israel violates the threshold, her ability to use this bargaining card, even tacitly, would diminish.

Looking to the future, one may speculate about still another use: the threat to cross the threshold if Israel were to perceive an impending major adverse change in U.S. policy. This would constitute a diplomatic use of the nuclear option, par excellence. However, it is highly doubtful whether Israel would invoke a component of security as a means for purely diplomatic ends. Moreover, such a move could result in even more damaging changes in U.S. policy. If that were the case, the credibility of such a threat would be found lacking.

Deterring the Arab World from Acquiring a Nuclear Capability

This "use" developed only gradually, but was apparently actively sought by Israel. This is probably the explanation of Allon's statement that: "Israel will not be the first to introduce nuclear weapons into the Middle East, nor will it be the second".[24] This phrase encapsulated both promise and threat.

As analyzed in Chapter 1, Israeli nuclear developments, rather than deterring the Arab states from acquiring a nuclear capability, served as a catalyst for several Arab states to seek an independent nuclear infrastructure. Nevertheless, they have not set this objective at the top of their priorities. This, together with their lack of scientific and technological resources, has inhibited the Arab states—with the exception of Iraq, from developing a meaningful weapon-related nuclear infrastructure.

To Cross the Threshold Were an Arab State to Become a Nuclear Power

Two general scenarios for the Arab development of nuclear weapons are possible. First, there is the likelihood that such a progression to nuclear weapon capability by an Arab state would occur gradually and could be monitored by Israel. In the absence of any arms control agreement preempting the nuclearization of the Middle East, Israel will have to define her nuclear policy: this could take place at any time close to production of Arab weapons. In the second scenario, an Arab country would acquire nuclear weapons suddenly through the secret transfer of weapons from a nuclear power. The only counter to this situation is an undeclared Israeli capability already in place which would become public in parallel with the acquisition of the Arab capability.

Another question pertains to the possibility of the emergence of another threshold state in the region. Is a stable relationship between two, or more, opposing threshold states realistic? This question requires detailed treatment beyond the scope of this chapter. However, the ambiguity surrounding such an adversarial relationship may engender mistaken decisions, even more than a clear-cut nuclear balance of deterrence.

A Compellent Use—To Force the Arab World to Accept Israel Politically

In Chapter 2 we noted that very probably the Israeli nuclear posture did not play a role in changing Arab political positions. It is unlikely that this will change in the future. Thus, for example, it appears unreasonable to assume that the Arab states, within the framework of the peace negotiations, would give up the basic demand of territory for peace, because of Israeli nuclear capabilities. If at all, two of the Arab parties, viz. Jordan and the Palestinians, do not insist on any steps on the part of Israel toward denuclearization. Quite the contrary, in informal contacts they argue that the main problem is territory, and if Israel feels more secure by maintaining her overall military capabilities, including the nuclear one, they are not opposed to it.[25] The position of Egypt and Syria is, of course, different (see below).

In Chapter 3 we noted that the superpowers' experience suggests that compellent nuclear threats aimed at accomplishing political objectives have been ineffective. Indeed, this experience supports the theoretical formulation that compellence, by nuclear or conventional threats, is more difficult to achieve than deterrence.[26] Past experience in the Middle East further validates this thesis.[27] In Chapter 3 we also cautioned against

252

attempting to pursue nuclear compellent and coercive strategies in a nuclear Middle East; first because they are basically ineffective, and second, because they might lead to dangerous escalations. The analysis presented in Chapter 2 and here of the Israeli–Arab situation illustrates the first point, viz. the ineffectiveness of compellence based on ambiguous nuclear threats, even in a situation in which Israel holds a monopoly status. One may only add that compellent nuclear threats aimed at political objectives which do not enjoy wide international legitimacy, apart from lacking credibility, and consequently of doubtful effectiveness, may very probably lead to harsh international reactions.

Deterrence Against Conventional Arab Attacks

In Chapter 2 we argued that in the past the Israeli nuclear development has been essentially irrelevant to processes of war initiation in the Middle East. In the first half of this chapter we discussed the extent to which an *explicit* Israeli nuclear capability and doctrine may serve as a deterrent to an Arab initiated attack on Israel. We noted the various constraints on the effectiveness of Israeli nuclear deterrence and pointed out that the credibility of explicit nuclear deterrent threats can be scaled in descending order.

In turning to an analysis of the present situation, a general comment can be made: the overall deterrent effect of a threshold posture is lower than that of an explicit capability and doctrine. Basically, this is due first to the political constraints imposed on Israel's ambiguous posture. Israel's inhibitions on using her nuclear capability are augmented by her recognition that such a use would incur tremendous international consequences. Second, the absence of definition of the threats that are subject to nuclear deterrence is also an important factor. Finally, although in the past few years there is less doubt among Arabs about Israel's capability, a measure of uncertainty may still persist. Nevertheless, it appears that the effectiveness of this deterrent increases as we progress up the scale, starting from guerrilla attacks and moving up through different limited war scenarios, through to the most extreme case of an unlimited general war with unlimited objectives. Thus, it may be argued that the threshold posture hardly has any credibility as a deterrent against all types of limited or attrition wars fought for limited political objectives (such as the liberation of territories occupied in 1967). But the same posture, albeit burdened with uncertainties, nonetheless plays a role in deterrence of a war launched by a grand Arab coalition against Israel. According to conventional wisdom, Arab leaders may probably remember that, in launching a general unlimited war against Israel, they may encounter Israeli nuclear retaliation. Whereas in 1973 the nuclear issue appears to have been entirely absent from Arab calculations, by 1992, given the publicity now attending the possibility (many observers say certainty) of Israel's nuclear capability, this dimension may have gained sufficient salience to enter into Arab strategic calculations. If deterrence is viewed as a continuum, rather than a polarized dichotomy, it is conceivable that Israel's threshold status plays a partial role (secondary to conventional deterrence), in deterring some Arab leaders from contemplating a general attack with unlimited objectives.

Even this scenario must be qualified. It is not at all clear that nuclear deterrence can deter the very initiation of hostilities. It may become much more credible if the fortunes of such a war turn against Israel. This particular variant will be discussed below in the section on "weapon of last resort". In such a scenario, the credibility of the threshold posture is equivalent to that of an explicit doctrine.

In any case, the deterrence effect against a general war is of largely theoretical interest. In the current situation in the Middle East, as was discussed earlier in this chapter, the formation of a grand Arab war coalition aimed at the destruction of Israel appears to be unlikely. At present, the only real threats are for limited military confrontations, and of the various possible configurations, the most likely is a war between Syria and Israel. Such a war would be fought for limited objectives, and it is unlikely that a threshold status could deter such an eventuality.

In this context, a general comparison may be relevant. That nonnuclear states are ready to initiate hostilities, or to defend themselves against nuclear or threshold powers is, of course, not new. The record begins with the Chinese intervention in the Korean War, and since then has included several instances, of which perhaps the most notable has been the Vietnam War. Apart from guerrilla wars as in Afghanistan, the four most recent instances of military confrontation between nonnuclear and nuclear or threshold countries have been the Chinese–Vietnamese encounter in 1979, the Falklands War, the Lebanon War of 1982, and the Gulf War of 1991. These cases represent archetypal examples. In the first case, the nuclear power (China) initiated the encounter, but was rebuffed. In the second, the nonnuclear power (Argentina) attacked a nuclear power (Britain) and ultimately lost in a test of will based on conventional arms. In the third case, a threshold country (Israel) initiated the encounter, and the nonnuclear power (Syria) took up the challenge, fighting a defensive and retreating campaign. In the fourth case, the nonnuclear power (Iraq) triggered the crisis and the nuclear power (the United States and, one might add, Britain and France) initiated hostilities and won with conventional arms. In each of these encounters, the nuclear issue was never invoked, and the two sides fought under the assumption that conventional arms should decide the outcome of the campaign.

To be sure, all four campaigns were fought for limited objectives. Moreover, in the Falklands, in Lebanon, and in the Gulf, the nuclear powers and the threshold state (Israel) managed to win with only conventional arms. Finally, where the nonnuclear power (Vietnam) won local victories, the nuclear power (China) may have partly been deterred from escalating to nuclear weapons because of Vietnam's alliance with the Soviet Union. However, the fact emerges that in these cases, as well as in previous ones, there remains the possibility of military encounters between nuclear or threshold powers, and nonnuclear powers, sometimes even initiated by nonnuclear powers and sometimes—as in Vietnam— won by them. It is in this light that one must relate to the potential uses of ambiguous or threshold postures in deterring wars, or in limiting wars after they have begun.

"Weapon of Last Resort"

The use of nuclear arms as a weapon of last resort in order to prevent national destruction, has been proposed by various observers as a rationale for developing an explicit nuclear doctrine.[28] Although upon close consideration, there are difficulties in the application of this use, it appears nevertheless to be rational. It would be argued here that the effectiveness of such a "use" is as strong if the nuclear threat remains ambiguous within a threshold posture, as when it is part of an explicit open doctrine.

The "last resort" option refers primarily to a hypothetical scenario in which Israeli conventional forces are defeated (or about to be defeated) on the battlefield, presumably in the face of a concentrated Arab attack by a general Arab war coalition, and the very existence of Israel is threatened.

The notion of a "last resort" has a double aspect—deterrence and actual use. The deterrence aspect, in turn, is also twofold. First, there is deterrence against the very initiation of a certain type of war which I shall define as first-type deterrence. Second, deterrence may apply midwar, such as in threats to use nuclear weapons against attacking Arab states if the war is not terminated immediately.

Deterrence against the very initiation of war is similar to the case discussed above of deterrence of a general war. It may, however, be characterized by difficulties peculiar to the case. For example, in planning a general war Arab leaders are likely to assume that in the case of an Israeli victory, or even a stalemate, Israel would have no need for nuclear weapons. Therefore, the nuclear issue may not appear to be relevant to their calculations; hence its effectiveness as a deterrent may be circumvented. In this context it may be added that Arab leaders might contemplate launching war against Israel even in the face of estimates of their likely military defeat. As was assumed, and rightly so, by Egypt in 1973, Arab leaders are liable to assume that an Arab military defeat, and certainly a stalemate, might nevertheless bear political dividends, or at least inflict major costs on Israel. On the other hand, it is possible that a general Arab attack although not calculated to be successful, could succeed, posing dangers to Israel's very existence. This threat would emerge, however, only *during* the course of a war. In terms of deterrence—which is operative *prior* to war—this final possibility is only one of a spectrum of possibilities regarding which the effectiveness of the nuclear deterrent effect would be limited.

Another example of a war which a "weapon of last resort" doctrine may not be able to deter, although it involves a great threat to Israel, is a limited war launched initially by only a partial Arab coalition with apparent limited objectives but which escalates midway into a general unlimited war. Here again, only the second type of deterrence—midwar deterrence—is relevant.

Indeed, it appears that altogether, midwar deterrence is the more relevant variant of "last resort" deterrence. A relevant scenario is a situation in which Israel's military defence has collapsed, the army is beating a retreat, and massive numbers of Arab forces are penetrating beyond the "Green Line." Before the actual use of nuclear weapons, and in an attempt to prevent the total collapse of the army and the subsequent dissolution of the state, a threat is issued, warning that nuclear weapons will be used if the Arab attack is not halted. Midwar deterrence may, of course, on its own part, somewhat enhance first-type deterrence.

Midwar deterrence has its own inherent difficulties. First, it is possible that the situation at the conventional military level will be marked by uncertainties: the uncertainties may relate to the actual developments in the field, to the scope of Arab reserves, or to the intentions of the Arab states. It is possible that Israel, while forced to retreat from certain sectors, will be holding her ground in others. Similarly, the level of military and political coordination between the various Arab states will in all probability be unclear. In such circumstances, viz. when the military situation can be stabilized, a nuclear threat may appear to be too extreme. An additional possibility may be that the threat is misdirected—it may be issued against one Arab state while it should have been directed against another.

It seems, however, that the principal problems will be in the area of command and control, rather than with the credibility of Israel's deterrent threat. Given the difficulties, intensity, and uncertainty of a conventional war conducted in parallel in a number of sectors, and in which many of the respective armies' communication and control systems have been damaged, the probability of disruptions in the channels of command is considerable. Thus, for example, Israel's deterrent threats may indeed result in an Arab decision to cease the attack. However, the orders to effect this decision may not be transmitted down the various military command channels in an orderly fashion.

Similarly, in he heat of battle that promises victory, field officers may tend to ignore the order to halt. Moreover, it is possible that the various Arab political leaderships will issue different and possibly even contradictory commands to their armies. The history of Arab–Israeli wars is replete with incidents testifying to deficiencies in the horizontal coordination between the different Arab states, and to the many shortcomings in the vertical coordination between each leadership and its armed forces. In the case of the first Arab victory following decades of military failure—a situation which would elicit widespread euphoria—these shortcomings might be intensified. It should be added that in the literature written during the Cold War on a possible war in Europe, in which use would be made of both conventional and nuclear weapons, much is made of the imposing dilemmas that would be faced by the strategic leaderships. In the case of the Middle East the problems would be even more complex, and this is for three reasons: first, the narrow geographical margins that separate Israel from military defeat; second, the inherent lack of coordination between the different Arab armies (as opposed to the situation in Europe, in which the principal attacker would have been only or primarily the Soviet army), and finally, the Israeli perception that a military defeat would signify the destruction of the state and her populace.

These problems would also complicate any process of strategic bargaining, conducted by means of signals using limited and controlled nuclear attacks. For example, one can conceive of the dispatch of one nuclear warhead with a low destructive effect to a desolate region, with the intention of demonstrating the credibility of Israel's deterrent threats. It may be assumed that this would immediately raise the deterrent effect of the "weapon of last resort." However, the decision-making process is bound to be so complex and intricate, and carried out under conditions of such uncertainty and distress, that in many cases it is unlikely to be rational. In other words, it is possible that the nuclear attack will be unjustified, or it may be carried out against the state that does not represent the major threat. It is also possible that a decision will be made to attack an Arab city as a first step, in order to raise the deterrence profile. Such an action is liable to have major long-term ramifications.

Aside from deterrence, the "weapon of last resort" doctrine relates primarily to the actual combat use of nuclear weapons under conditions in which Israel stands on the threshold of destruction. In this respect, there are two possible perspectives: preventing the state's ultimate destruction, or apocalyptic revenge along the lines of "let me die with the Philistines."

The second perspective, involving an act of revenge, has no rational significance and, in essence, is indicative of the irrelevance of nuclear weapons to Israel security. It is possible, of course, to attribute a deterrence function to the threat of apocalyptic revenge. The significance of this category of threat was discussed previously. We shall turn now to the first perspective.

Battlefield Uses

Of late a limited debate began in the Israeli media about the advisability of Israel developing an option for battlefield weapons and incorporating them in its operational doctrine. One of the arguments was to view such weapons—if developed—as part of a "last resort" doctrine.[29]

In Chapter 5, I have pointed out the dangers and difficulties involved in the proliferation of tactical nuclear weapons and doctrines for their use in the Middle East. Some of the arguments mentioned there are relevant also to our discussion here.[30]

First, and in very general terms, the development of tactical weapons and doctrines for their use would tend to lower the threshold for the use of nuclear weapons. This is so precisely because the battlefield use of nuclear weapons may appear to be initially less frightening and less catastrophic than their use in a strategic mode. In fact, once used (except perhaps in Sinai), their impact would be tantamount to a strategic use.

Second, the introduction of tactical weapons and the doctrine for their battlefield use would increase the saliency and visibility of nuclear weapons, thus increasing motivations for general proliferation in the Middle East. It is one thing for Arab states to assume that Israel may have a limited nuclear capability for strategic deterrence against the most existential contingency. It is quite another for them to suspect that a threshold posture may also comprise tactical weapons, and that the threshold for their use may be quite low.

Third, turning to the operational level, within a context of the "last resort" doctrine, the use of battlefield weapons relates to the hypothetical situation in which Israel is faced with probable and imminent destruction; enemy forces have invaded or are within reach of territories vital to the state, while engaged in short-range battles with Israeli forces. In such circumstances, the use of tactical nuclear weapons on the battlefield is liable to inflict losses on Israeli civilians and combat units.

Fourth, because of the possibility of casualties caused to Israeli civilians, there would be a strong motivation to use tactical weapons *before* a "last resort" situation. This would again lower the threshold for their use.

Finally, as noted before in this book, if Arab states indeed equip themselves with tactical weapons, the overall balance may in several respects turn against Israel. In addition, there is the issue of sensitivity to casualties. The use of tactical weapons may increase both sides' casualties on the battlefield manifold compared to a conventional battlefield. In a competition of sensitivity to casualties, the Arab side may have an advantage.

To sum up, scenarios of last resort appear largely irrelevant to the current situation in the Middle East and also for the foreseeable future. The likelihood of Israel having to confront a general war against a broad coalition with unlimited objectives now appears extremely unlikely. Moreover, were such a conflict to occur, Israel could probably successfully defend its existence with conventional arms. At the same time, such an eventuality cannot be completely ruled out, specially if we are to consider possible long-term developments. Against this background, it appears that a small nuclear arsenal with very low profile and shrouded with ambiguity, designed exclusively for strategic deterrence in very extreme existential situations, is a rational choice for Israel. Such a posture may even be acceptable to some Arab states, and would not serve as a catalyst for the development of a nuclear capability. I shall return to this again later in this chapter.

THE LESSONS OF THE GULF WAR AND THE PROSPECTS FOR ARMS CONTROL

The Gulf War (analyzed in Chapter 6) as well as the extent of the Iraqi nuclear effort revealed after the war, have highlighted three important issues relevant to the themes of this chapter.

First, Arab behavior during the Gulf Crisis and War clearly demonstrated that competition between Arab states for influence and hegemony is more important for Arab decision-makers than the conflict with Israel. Egypt, Syria, and the Gulf states perceived the Iraqi threat as much more critical and dangerous than the Israeli one. It was understandable for Egypt to have these preferences, as since the peace treaty she has had no remaining conflicts of state interests with Israel. But even Syria, with the Golan Heights question still unsettled, adopted a similar strategy. Although this preference was not an entirely new phenomenon (one previous example was Arab behavior during the Lebanon War in 1982), the readiness of these states to endorse this policy openly and without rhetorical hesitation signaled an important departure from past Arab behavior. This pattern of behavior underlines the change that has taken place in Arab attitudes toward Israel, namely their readiness to accept her existence. It also demonstrated yet again that the pattern of inter-Arab competition is robust and fundamental to their behavior. The main policy implication of all this for Israel is that, since Arab attitudes toward Israel have changed, and since their interstate competition for influence and hegemony has been maintained, peace settlements with specific Arab states (comprising the elimination of political grievances resulting from the 1967 War) can reduce considerably the likelihood of these states joining a grand war coalition against Israel. This general conclusion reconfirms the analysis presented earlier in this chapter. Such peace agreements, therefore, will continue to ensure a positive balance of conventional forces for Israel.

Second, American readiness to intervene militarily against Iraq bolstered the credibility of American power in general. It also signaled that in future regional wars the United States is likely to intervene militarily on the side of its allies. The very close American–Israeli relations make such an intervention very probable whenever Israel finds herself hard-pressed militarily. While such an intervention is very likely even in the absence of a formal defense treaty between the two countries, the signing of such a treaty would also considerably enhance deterrence against general Arab attacks.

Third, the introduction of SSM in large numbers into the arsenals of Arab states creates a significant security problem for Israel. To be sure, these weapons cannot pose an existential threat and they are not capable of determining the fortunes of war. They can, however, when used against population centers, assume the proportions of a strategic threat. Needless to say, the use of SSM with chemical warheads would exacerbate the situation. Because of the complexity of this issue, we shall discuss it at greater length below. Suffice it to say here that this threat underlines yet again the themes stressed in this chapter, namely the need to combine strategic, military and political steps in order to lessen the security threats that Israel faces. But in addition, this particular threat can be reduced if appropriate arms control measures are introduced into the region. We shall return to this issue below.

Finally, the revelations about the extent of the Iraqi nuclear effort that surfaced after the war, and the Iraqi ability to pursue it clandestinely, have impressed upon Israel the dangers involved in nuclear proliferation. This has become of late a major subject of discussion and debate in Israel. Again, one of the main themes developed in this chapter is underlined: the need to secure, through political agreements and security measures, a more stable environment in the Arab–Israeli region so as to preempt processes of nuclearization. In addition, as in the case of the SSM and the use of chemical agents, the need for regional arms control is relevant here. We shall return to these issues below.

THE MISSILE AND CHEMICAL MUNITIONS THREAT

Neither surface-to-surface missiles nor chemical munitions in Arab arsenals are a new phenomenon. The Iraqi use of the latter is well known. But it should be remembered that the Egyptian air force used (on a very limited scale) chemical agents already during the civil war in Yemen in the 1960s, and both Egypt and Syria equipped their forces with surface-to-surface missiles in the 1970s. Indeed, the Egyptians even fired some of them during the 1973 War. Israel, however, was not unduly concerned about these weapons until the late 1980s. By that time Syria had begun the deployment of accurate surface-to-surface missiles and also armed part of her overall SSM arsenal with chemical warheads. Two Israeli concerns surfaced at the time: first, the possibility that accurate SSM with conventional (or chemical) warheads would be used against sensitive Israeli military targets; and second, that SSM with chemical warheads would be used against Israeli population centers.[31]

It appears that the Israeli counterstrategy to both threats was multi-faceted. It combined an emphasis on deterrence with, as it were, damage-limitation and warfighting strategies. When the threat became more apparent, Rabin, then defense minister, warned that the use of chemical weapons against Israel would lead to terrible devastation in Damascus.[32] This threat was interpreted at the time in two ways: first, as implying the use of nuclear weapons; second, as referring to heavy attacks with conventional arms. Indeed, in view of the Israeli air force's clear-cut superiority, and its ability to deliver vast amounts of ordnance, the second interpretation seemed credible. This warning constituted the deterrence element.

Second, bearing in mind the Israeli air superiority, it is likely that at least part of the Syrian SSM could be destroyed by air-to-surface munitions. This could serve as an active damage-limitation strategy.

During the Gulf War and the experience the Israel public had with the Iraqi SSM, Rabin reflected on Israeli plans during his tenure as defense minister from 1984 to 1991. He noted that Syrian SSM (with conventional or chemical warheads) attacks on Israeli population centers had been discussed. If deterrence failed, the Israeli strategy would be to achieve a quick and decisive termination of the war through ground operations. Thus, maximum effort would be invested in warfighting.[33]

Turning to passive damage-limitation measures, Rabin recalled plans to minimize civilian casualties: centers of population would be evacuated, and large shelters could accommodate part of the population for several days until the war was over.[34] Thus, if deterrence failed, a combination of warfighting and active and passive measures would limit the extent of damage to the civilian base of the country.

It was clear that the Israeli planning put the emphasis on warfighting, and considered the possible damage to population as secondary to the main objective of winning a quick and decisive victory. The contradiction between planning active and passive defensive measures and relying on deterrence is apparent. One might reach the conclusion that the actual use of nuclear weapons, in case deterrence failed, did not play a salient role in the Israeli strategy of the time. Conventional retaliation appears to fit more with that planning.

Needless to say, Israel's overall military superiority vis-à-vis Syria turned this planning into a credible deterrence strategy. Altogether, then, it has been Israel's conventional superiority that has constituted the main deterrent against any form of military action by Syria, including also the use of SSM (both conventionally and chemically armed) against population centers.

It should be noted in this context that the very deployment of Syria's SSM, armed either by conventional or chemical warheads, was probably designed primarily to serve a deterrent strategy. Syria's recognition of Israel's overall military superiority, and in particular her air force's superiority, dictated to Syria the need to search for a credible deterrent. The deployment of SSM could pose, so the Syrians reckoned, a capability that might deter Israel from massive use of her air force against Syrian cities and infrastructure. Indeed, the threat implied in the development of chemical warheads may have been perceived by Syria as even better serving the same purpose.[35]

Although the introduction of chemical weapons into the Middle East has received considerable attention, the actual consequences of their use remain a debatable issue. There is a consensus that their military impact is limited and that passive countermeasures can make their impact on the battlefield against well-prepared forces rather small. Their effect is primarily psychological, and assuming troops learn how to react and are equipped with the necessary defensive gear, chemical munitions are becoming less effective than many conventional armaments.[36] Indeed, the decision not to use poison gas in World War II resulted not only from the possible retaliation in kind, but also from its relative lack of effectiveness coupled with the difficulty of controlling it.

On the other hand, the use of chemical agents against population can have a strong psychological effect. Here again, defensive measures can vastly diminish the effects of these agents. Nevertheless, their use in a surprise attack (for example, when they are carried by SSM), before part of the population could protect itself, can increase the number of casualties.

As analyzed in Chapter 6, it is not clear what has deterred Iraq from the use of chemical agents against Israel (if indeed deterrence was the reason for nonuse). Moreover, if indeed it was the implied Israeli nuclear threat that deterred the Iraqis, it is not clear at all whether one could generalize from that particular episode to other possible future scenarios.

THE ACTUAL USE OF NUCLEAR WEAPONS: THE PROBLEMS OF PROPORTIONALITY

In Chapter 6 we have already addressed the problem of proportionality in the more limited context of implied Israeli nuclear threats against

Iraq. But the possible implications of the actual use of nuclear weapons by Israel, if indeed she has this capability, require more extensive discussion. It appears that there are enormous potential costs involved in such a use. To begin with, in a world in which the "nuclear taboo" has become so entrenched and in which, if anything, the trend is toward partial nuclear disarmament and toward making nuclear weapons less and less relevant to strategy,[37] the first use of a nuclear weapon since World War II could carry tremendous international political costs. Apart from anything else, the permanent members of the Security Council are bound by Resolution 255, which forms a security guarantee against nuclear threats or the actual use of nuclear weapons against nonnuclear weapon states which are party to the NPT. To be sure, the conditions under which such a use is decided would be critical for assessing the costs involved for Israel. But it appears likely that if these conditions appear to involve less than an existential threat to Israel, the political costs for her may be extreme. It is possible that after such a use, enormous international pressure would be put on Israel to forgo her nuclear capability altogether. In addition, there may be other international political costs in terms of her relationship with the United States and the other leading powers. It is likely that the powers, with the United States leading them, would assess that nonaction against Israel would lead to the total collapse of the nonproliferation regime and to nuclear anarchy. Indeed, were the latter to happen, or even something short of this, it is likely that the constraints on some of the nuclear suppliers against delivery of nuclear technology or even nuclear weapons to Arab states would disappear following the actual use of an Israeli weapon. Finally, an enormous Arab motivation to respond in kind would probably emerge, and this— in conjunction with the diminishing constraints on the suppliers and on Arab states themselves to produce nuclear weapons—could lead eventually to a revenge nuclear strike on Israel.

These potential catastrophic outcomes of the first use of nuclear weapons since 1945 may undercut the credibility of implied Israeli nuclear threats in situations short of existential threats. But Israeli dilemmas in deterring lesser—yet very painful—threats, especially to civilian population, may increase were the source of the threat more remote than Israel. As analyzed earlier, if the threat emanates from Syria, Israel can rely on deterrence, and, if that fails, on other measures as well as on quick termination of hostilities. But if the source is a remote country such as Iran, Iraq or Libya, the possibility to cause great pain and damage by conventional means in retaliation for a large-scale SSM attack armed with chemical warheads targeted on civilian population, is more limited. Similarly, the use of ground operations in order to destroy the SSM bases is difficult, though not entirely impossible.[38] Finally, the option for terminating the war through decisive ground operations hardly exists.

Under such conditions nuclear deterrence may reemerge as a possible strategy, with a potential readiness by Israel to exercise the threat were deterrence to fail. This possible readiness to exercise nuclear threats may be the outcome of assessments that the use of chemical arms against Israeli population centers causing many casualties would constitute a real threat to the social fabric of Israeli society and, hence, an existential threat. Indeed, theoretically, the use of hundreds of SSM—even with conventional warheads—against the urban metropolitan areas of Israel may also lead to leadership assessments that the cost for Israel would be unacceptable. Thus, although, as I argued earlier, such a use would be irrational and highly counterproductive from Israel's point of view, one can envisage conditions under which such use could seriously be contemplated.

These potential threats underline yet again the dangers involved for the whole region in the introduction of great numbers of SSM into the arsenals of countries throughout the region, especially those armed with chemical warheads. Israel's recent agreement to join the chemical weapons convention was, therefore, logical from her point of view.[39] Similarly, her agreement to accede by the rules of the MTCR system also reflects a similar attitude.

Finally, in addition to arms control agreements (to be briefly discussed below) and Israel–Arab peace agreements which could minimize the general danger of instability in the Middle East, there are two political-strategic measures that could minimize the danger of escalation to the nuclear threshold: first, an American–Israeli defense agreement (to be briefly discussed below); and second, security arrangements between Israel and her neighboring Arab countries with which she signed peace treaties, which could allow her access to hostile peripheral Arab countries from which missile attacks may be targeted at Israel.

Proliferation Threats

The disclosures about the Iraqi clandestine nuclear developments highlighted the dangers posed by the lack of an effective regime to preempt proliferation in the Middle East. This concern, coupled as it were with the disintegration of the Soviet Union and the possibility that nuclear materials and even weapons might find their way from there to Middle Eastern countries, impressed upon Israel the dangers of proliferation. As pointed out in Chapter 1, successive Israeli leaderships have rejected the notion that proliferation in the Middle East could stabilize this region and have viewed proliferation to Arab countries as a major existential threat to Israel.

Following the attack on Osiraq in 1981 Israel adopted what came to be known as the Begin Doctrine, according to which Israel would seek to destroy emerging nuclear-weapon capabilities in Arab countries. Would it be possible politically and operationally to implement that doctrine at present? There are operational and political factors affecting such an implementation. The lessons of the Iraqi nuclear effort demonstrated a major operational limitation on this doctrine: as Iraq did, a future Arab country seeking to develop a nuclear-weapons capability, could implement the building of its infrastructure on a wide front, dispersing, hiding and hardening her nuclear facilities and concentrating extensive defensive assets around them.

It is probable, on the other hand, that the political constraints on the application of the "Begin Doctrine" are not considerable. In a world in which the United States and most of the international community strongly oppose proliferation, an attack on clandestine nuclear facilities, especially those of states such as Iran, Iraq or Libya, that are considered anti-status quo, will not be perceived as an unacceptable aggressive act. It is likely, however, that such Israeli activity—if operationally possible—would be more acceptable were Israel herself to accept some confidence-building measures in the nuclear field. The subject of such CBM will be discussed, in any case, below.

As mentioned, most Israeli leaders have sincerely doubted that proliferation could lead to stability in the Middle East. But following the Gulf War, some Israeli decision-makers may have reached the conclusion that proliferation was bound to occur in any case. Thus, Defense Minister Moshe Arens (since retired) of the Likud Party, stated explicitly that within ten years the Middle East would be nuclearized.[40] He proposed two strategies to counter this emerging threat: first, the quick development and deployment of the antiballistic missile system currently under development (with heavy American financial backing) in Israel, the ARROW; and second, deterrence (most probably meaning nuclear deterrence).

The idea that the nuclear threat to Israel could be dealt with by active defensive measures such as the ARROW raises, of course, many problems, some of them reminiscent of the great SDI debate in the United States. Suffice it to say here that it is unlikely that such a defensive system, if indeed its development is successfully completed, could be counted on for absolute defense against incoming nuclear warheads. The penetration of even one nuclear warhead targeted on population centers is, of course, sufficient to cause enormous damage. In addition, if indeed nuclear weapons were to proliferate in hostile countries, they might be delivered to Israel by other means than SSM. Altogether, then, the notion that the ARROW could serve as Israel's main counterstrategy to the threat of nuclear weapons appears at best problematic.

The ARROW could, however, become an important system limiting the damage to Israel resulting from strikes by chemical weapons and by massive SSM armed with conventional warheads. In these cases there is no need for absolute successful defense. Even if a high proportion of the incoming missiles is destroyed, the damage-limitation effect would be considerable. This would diminish the probability that Israel may be pushed to the irrational decision actually to use nuclear weapons. But the problem with the ARROW would then be the question of cost-effectiveness. Were its development and deployment to be fully or mostly covered by the United States, then it would become an important contribution to Israel's defenses. However, if Israel would have to cover its development and deployment from her own limited resources, the price may become prohibitive.

Similarly, if the planned American global antiballistic defense system were to be deployed, it would be highly beneficial for Israel to join it, as an important damage-limitation measure. This system would ideally limit potential costs involved in chemical or conventional attacks on Israel. However, because of the considerations noted above in relation to the ARROW, it is unlikely that it would resolve completely the potential nuclear threat.

It appears that the new government in Israel has approached the nuclear threat in a different way from that suggested by Arens. First, it does not regard proliferation as an unavoidable certainty. Second, in order to lessen the probability of proliferation, it emphasizes the need to press ahead with the peace process. The success of this process would presumably diminish motivations for proliferation throughout the region. Similarly, the task of the United States in halting proliferation in the region would become less difficult. Indeed, even if nuclear weapons were to proliferate in the Middle East, peace settlements would stabilize the region and consequently make war less likely altogether. It was very significant that in his first speech to the Knesset in presenting his new government, Prime Minister Rabin, when elaborating on his strategy for peace, stressed the nuclear threat in the Middle East, and cited it as one of the main reasons for his decision to hasten and deepen the peace process.[41]

Although political settlements would most probably lessen the threat of proliferation, additional measures in the area of arms control are necessary. This would depend primarily on an internationally concerted effort, led by the United States—a subject to which we shall now turn.

An American–Israeli Defense Treaty[42]

The main thrust of this chapter is to consider alternative strategies that Israel could adopt, and assess their benefits and costs. The formation of a defense treaty with the United States depends in the first instance on American preferences and therefore is not discussed here in any detail.

However, the potential impact of such a treaty on Israel's security could be considerable and therefore it merits a brief reference here. Moreover, it is likely that were Israel to insist on it as a *quid pro quo* for major political concessions within the peace process, the United States would be quite willing to seriously consider it. In any case, it is very probable that some of the potential security threats to Israel discussed in this book could be deterred were such a treaty to be endorsed.

As mentioned before in this chapter, it is very likely that in case Israel finds herself in a desperate military situation, the United States would extend to her substantial military support. This could come in several different ways, probably in the first instance by the use of the U.S. Air Force. But a formal defense treaty would certainly further enhance and deepen the American commitment to such an intervention, and would also considerably enhance Israeli deterrence.

Apart from deterrence against large-scale conventional attacks on Israel, a formal defense guarantee could be effective in changing the costs calculus of states distant from Israel which might consider launching long-range strikes against her with SSM. As mentioned before, such attacks, specially when armed with chemical warheads, might pose very difficult dilemmas for Israel. The American guarantee could be viewed as a useful deterrent against them.

Clearly, an American readiness to enter into such a formal guarantee, would depend on developments in the peace process and might be linked to arms control and CBM agreements concerning both conventional arms and nuclear ones. I shall not elaborate on these here. Suffice it to say, that such a defense treaty should be considered by Israel when she makes her overall decision on the political process as well as on arms control agreements concerning her nuclear posture.

The Prospects for Nuclear Arms Control

In Chapter 4, I argued that the changes in the international system that have taken place since the late 1980s will, on the whole, provide a conducive context for the application of a more stringent nonproliferation regime. Indeed, it appears that, following the Gulf Crisis, the leading global power, the United States, has become much more aware of the dangers involved in proliferation in general and in the Middle East in particular. This analysis also indicates that physical controls on the transfer of sensitive materials and technology are important in the prevention of proliferation but, because of the ability of regional powers such as Iraq to develop clandestine facilities for uranium enrichment, they are far from sufficient to stem proliferation. Consequently, the current safeguards system attached to the NPT regime is unable to fully verify nuclear weapons developments. Only a more stringent and intrusive verification system imposed on the NPT parties will halt proliferation. Indeed, the first steps in this direction have already taken place (and see on this Chapter 4), and more steps are most probably going to be endorsed in the coming Review Conference of the NPT in 1995. However, although physical and technological inspections are extremely important, political and security arrangements that supplement technological and physical ones are as important.

While universal measures are important and could apply in principle to the Middle East, more specific arrangements tailored to meet Middle Eastern conditions are required. A crude application of universal principles may miss the specific regional conditions. Moreover, the Middle East regional system of states is characterized by specific features which make it unique in certain respects. Most relevant are the high level of persistent conflicts and the extremely high rate of arms acquisitions, both of which result in an environment of insecurity. More specifically, in the Arab–Israeli conflict, the basic asymmetry in resources favoring the Arab states neighboring Israel may enable them, in the long run if they so decide, to mobilize overpowering conventional capabilities against Israel. On the other hand, Israel is presumably the only country at present to have an inventory of nuclear weapons. Thus, any treatment of the problem of nuclear proliferation in the region must also tackle these two asymmetries.

Throughout this chapter I have elaborated on the need for Israel to continue to rely primarily on a conventional deterrent and, should deterrence fail, on the ability to defeat her adversaries with conventional capabilities only. I have also pointed out, however, that in view of the basic asymmetries existing between Israel and the Arab world, Israel's security in "last resort" situations will have to depend on the existence of an inventory of nuclear weapons designed specifically for strategic deterrence. Consequently, such a capability should be maintained until basic conditions in the Middle East and the "rules of the game" of Israel's relations with its neighbors are transformed. I have also suggested several security and political "packages" which would reduce Arab political grievances while either positively affecting Israeli security problems, or, at least, not aggravating them further.

In addition, as elaborated earlier, the introduction of SSM in large numbers into the arsenals of Arab states creates a major security problem for Israel. As the Gulf War has demonstrated, the indiscriminate use of such weapons against population centers in Israel could become a major strategic threat to Israel. Needless to say, the use of SSMs with chemical warheads would exacerbate the situation. All these considerations increase the need for a broad spectrum of arms control agreements which would comprise not only restrictions on nuclear weapons but also on other armaments. With the evolving political process aimed at achieving peace treaties between Israel and her neighbors, there is now greater scope for combining a comprehensive package of arms control with peace developments.

Although regional powers have been alert to the dangers of nuclear proliferation for quite some time, they have naturally approached the problem with their respective national interests in mind, trying to maximize their own security. Following a brief description of the arms control postures of the main regional actors and the new initiative proposed by the United States, I shall conclude by proposing some tentative ideas about preferred Israeli postures.

The Israeli position[43]

Since the 1960s, Israel has publicly adhered to the following principles: first, concern about the dangers involved in proliferation in the Middle East, and, second, concern about the conventional regional arms race and the need for constraint. Indeed, since the 1960s, decision-makers and officials have argued that limitations on conventional arms should precede discussions of limitations on proliferation. Third, in response to international demand that Israel become party to the NPT, Israel has argued that since the treaty applies to conditions of peace between states, it is not applicable to the Middle East. It will become applicable only after peace is achieved. Fourth, Israel has raised the idea of a regional agreement for the denuclearization of the Middle East, similar in some respects to the Tlatelolco Treaty. In response to the Iranian–Egyptian UN proposal for the creation of a Nuclear Weapons Free Zone (NWFZ) in the Middle East (see below), Israel has insisted that the initiative originate within the region and that the regional powers negotiate it directly among themselves. The agreement, if reached, should be signed by all regional powers and be binding on them. Fifth, although Israel has refused to express readiness to join the NPT, since 1980 she has, nevertheless, been ready to join the UN consensus on the Egyptian draft resolutions for the establishment of a NWFZ in the Middle East. These draft resolutions included references to the NPT. Sixth and last, Israel is ready to accept a nuclear weapons free zone in the Middle East provided it is part of a regional agreement (and not the NPT), on condition that the final phase of such a regime, including the denuclearization of Israel, would apply after all the countries of the region had signed peace treaties with each other. Finally, Israel insists on mutual inspection and verification systems among the Middle Eastern states.

It is difficult to assess whether, and to what extent, the official Israeli position was defined for purely diplomatic and public relations purposes. It could be argued that the Israeli formulation was designed so as to allow Israel the freedom to pursue her nuclear activity without interference. In the seventies, at the time of its initial formulation, direct negotiations between the Arab states and Israel appeared so remote that the Israeli position could have been interpreted as a recipe for nonaction altogether. But by the early 1990s, the prospects for such negotiations have become much more realistic. Thus, even if Israel's position was initially primarily a tactical diplomatic step, she must now consider more seriously the possibility that at least some initial steps toward nuclear arms control may have to be taken. Of late, it appears more likely that part of the Israeli establishment is not entirely unreceptive to ideas of gradual denuclearization once peace treaties have been signed.

The Egyptian position[44]

Egypt joined the Iranian proposal for the creation of a NWFZ in the Middle East in 1974 and, since then, has been its main sponsor in the UN. Her posture stemmed from two strategic assessments: first that Israel leads in nuclear development, and second that Egypt does not wish to invest the required resources to compete with Israel in that field. In addition, Egypt was concerned lest other Arab countries join the nuclear race and produce their own capabilities. Given the tense relations within the Arab world, such a race would have turned into a strategic and political threat to Egypt. Moreover, the nuclearization of another leading Arab state might strengthen its claim for a hegemonic position in the Arab world, thus challenging the central position which Egypt presently enjoys.

The formal Egyptian position envisaged the creation of the NWFZ as an addition to, and not a replacement for, the NPT. The successive Egyptian draft proposals, therefore, called upon all the regional parties to join the NPT as an essential component of the NWFZ.

Several factors gradually affected the Egyptian position and led to the introduction of new variations. To begin with, the Camp David Accords as well as the peace treaty that followed in 1979, allowed for more flexibility in the Egyptian position in regard to direct negotiations between Israel and the Arab countries concerning the NWFZ. The second important political element during much of the 1980s was Egypt's isolation in the Arab world and the process of fragmentation in the Arab state system. These factors contributed to some reduction in Egyptian anxiety vis-à-vis nuclear developments in Israel, and simultaneously increased Egyptian suspicions about nuclear developments in other Arab states.

Egypt's inclination toward a peaceful resolution of regional conflicts, which became apparent during the late 1970s and the 1980s, served as a background for renewed attempts at arms control. By the late 1980s, Cairo, cognizant of Israel's growing concern about chemical weapons in Arab arsenals, advanced the notion of a treaty banning all types of weapons of mass destruction. While Syria and Iraq advanced this notion in order to fend off international demands that they join the newly evolving treaty prohibiting chemical weapons, Egypt appeared to have become genuinely interested in a ban on all types of such weapons.

Both the Egyptian political elite's deepening understanding of Israeli security concerns, and the traumatic experience of the Gulf Crisis and War, appear to have introduced an additional variation into the Egyptian position. Since 1991 Egyptian officials and arms control experts have been suggesting that the process leading to the denuclearization of the Middle East could be gradual.[45] The elements of this new policy are: first, a freeze on all nuclear activities in the Middle East; second, simultaneously with the commencement of peace negotiations between Israel and the Arab states, Israel discloses information about her nuclear arsenal; third, as the peace process progresses, Israel gradually cuts back her nuclear capabilities. With Israeli security concerns in mind, the Egyptians emphasize that the process could be slow and that it should be linked to political developments.

The Syrian position

Contrary to the situation in Egypt where, for quite some time officials have been conscious of the need for arms control and where academics have been both interested and active in international security issues, Syria has remained silent on questions of arms control.

In response to international demands that Syria become party to the expected treaty banning the production and stockpiling of chemical weapons, the standard Syrian response has been that its becoming a party to this treaty must be linked to denuclearization in Israel. This position has been maintained since then. Beginning in 1990, however, American visitors to Damascus learned that Syria has begun considering the possibility of unlinked arms control negotiations.[46] The Syrian position in the multilateral negotiations on arms control (conducted within the framework of the "Madrid" peace process) has been that political agreements are the precondition for any arms control agreement.

The American position[47]

By late May 1991, President Bush initiated a new comprehensive program for arms control in the Middle East.[48] Regional denuclearization formed an important part of this program.

The new initiative placed the nonproliferation element within a broad arms control plan that comprised such elements as the elimination of nonnuclear weapons of mass destruction as well, along with the control of conventional weapons. This broad approach indicated that the U.S.

271

administration realized that nonproliferation cannot be treated independently of other factors, such as security and arms control factors. The plan calls for a freeze as an initial step toward denuclearization on the production and acquisition of weapons-grade plutonium and uranium. It also invites all regional powers to join the NPT and defines a NWFZ in the Middle East as the final objective. All these elements— treating nonproliferation as part of a more comprehensive arms control policy, perceiving it as part of broader issues of security, the call for a freeze on nuclear activity as the initial phase toward a gradual process of regional denuclearization—were already formulated in an earlier document that was the result of a UN study group.[49]

While the United States clearly perceived of nonproliferation in the Middle East as a very important element in its regional policy, it appears that in terms of time priorities, it preferred, until the present, to concentrate on the political aspects of the Arab–Israeli peace process and give it priority over arms control. There are two reasons for that: first, the Arab states emphasize that political developments have precedence over arms control negotiations. While they would welcome pressure on Israel in the specific issue of nuclear proliferation, they recognize that this is linked to other arms control issues, something which they prefer to postpone. Second, the immediate operational step in the American initiative has to do with the freeze on the production of fissionable materials, namely, a halt to the Dimona activity. This may invite strong Israeli opposition and may complicate the peace process.

Israeli dilemmas

One of the propositions presented in this book is that the proliferation of nuclear weapons in the Middle East would not significantly stabilize the region and, with some probability, might result in the actual use of these weapons. Proliferation, therefore, poses tremendous risks to all countries in the Middle East. From the Israeli point of view, it probably comprises the greatest existential threat. Therefore, any measure designed to halt proliferation is important, and probably crucial. *In a situation where the alternatives are either a nuclearized Middle East or a Middle East in which no state (including Israel) has nuclear capability, the latter is preferable.*

Another of the propositions discussed in this book is the effect of ambiguity on deterrence and on Arab state's assessments whether to "go nuclear". Although the ambiguity surrounding the Israeli posture has considerably diminished over the years, nevertheless some of its dimensions had been maintained. And it should be borne in mind that an ambiguous posture does have advantages in a nonproliferation posture. An explicit doctrine would actually force Arab states to choose a nuclear path. It wold also place the United States in a very difficult situation. The

United States is committed to nonproliferation, both by policy as well as by law. A disclosure of proliferation might force the United States to act against Israel or, short of this, to undermine her overall antiproliferation policy. Then again, a disclosure by Israel would be an irreversible act. It is difficult to imagine that any Israeli government would be willing to forgo the capability or means of production Israel might have. Once things become explicit, attitudes and interests tend to coalesce around them and create a powerful lobby which would most probably preempt any move toward denuclearization. Then again, as a result of the above, a feedback process would probably be set in motion. Israeli disclosure would force some Arab governments to invest greater resources in nuclear developments. This, in turn, would tend to convince Israel of the necessity to increase rather than limit, her nuclear effort. As mentioned, recent ideas presented by Egyptian scholars, which probably reflect official views, refer to a graduated approach which would begin with an Israeli disclosure coupled with a freeze on activity, followed by a gradual reduction of Israeli capabilities tied to progress in the peace process. But this brings us back to the point that disclosure would be an irreversible act. A breakdown in the peace process following disclosures would create a political stalemate and would increase pressure on Arab states to develop their own capabilities. Moreover, the Israeli disclosure would make it virtually impossible for the United States to apply pressure on Arab states—even those friendly to America—to desist from producing their own capabilities. Similarly, nuclear weapons states and in general, the nuclear suppliers, would feel free to transfer know-how and components of nuclear technology, and possibly even the complete weapons, to Arab states. There is, therefore, a whole series of arguments on why the abandonment of the ambiguous posture would backfire in terms of nuclear arms control. Indeed, apparently both the UN document, as well as the American position, probably for the reasons mentioned above, have not called for a disclosure by Israel of her capability (whatever it may be).

While a move toward an explicit nuclear doctrine, especially if coupled with a disclosure of capabilities, would pose extremely difficult dilemmas for the Arab states and for the United States, probably leading to further proliferation in the region, it is unlikely that under present conditions an ambiguous posture by itself could, for the long term, stem the processes of regional nuclearization. The erosion of Israeli ambiguity as a result of the Vanunu revelations and the further erosion brought on by the Gulf Crisis, as discussed in this chapter, necessitate the adoption by Israel of confidence-building measures in the nuclear field which would strengthen tendencies against nuclearization. The idea of a freeze on future activities could serve as a very important step in that direction.[50]

At the time of this writing, it is difficult to predict Israel's reaction to the idea of a freeze. One problem might be that such a freeze could affect not only the production of future weapons capabilities, but could, for technical reasons, also gradually and over time, affect present capabilities. Another problem has to do with the kinds of *quid pro quo* which Arab states will have to provide. A much more stringent inspection and verification system of nuclear activities in the Arab world and in Iran would, naturally, be a necessary measure. But beyond that, Israel may find it necessary to insist on other measures in the area of conventional arms control and in the area of chemical and biological agents.

While such Israeli demands are consistent with Israeli strategic preferences and therefore have an internal logic, it is doubtful that the Arab states would be ready to accept them. From their point of view, regional freeze on the production of fissionable materials which is not followed by concrete steps designed to reverse the Israeli capability might leave them in a permanent inferior position. Israel would be left with its current capabilities, while they would not be able to develop even a nuclear option. There is, of course, from their point of view, one major redeeming feature, namely that the Israeli capability would cease to expand. It is possible that because of this the Arab states may after all be inclined to accept this particular measure. Indeed, Egypt appears in any case likely to welcome the idea of a freeze.

It is more doubtful whether the linkage of the freeze to a ban on chemical and biological weapons would be acceptable to the Arab states. They view this latter capability as a counter to Israel's nuclear one and as long as the latter remains intact, they would probably find it difficult to forgo their chemical weapons option.

Bearing in mind the critical importance of nonproliferation, it would probably be in Israel's interests not to link the nuclear freeze with agreements on the banning of other weapons of mass destruction.

But such a linkage may be formed through developments in the peace process. As Syria's overbearing interest is to get back the Golan Heights, Israel could link a political agreement on the Golan with different types of arms control and arms reductions (see also the discussion above in this chapter on such possible arms control agreements with Syria). One of these could be the accession of Syria to the Chemical Weapons Convention.

Another confidence-building measure, and one which might match the deterrence dimension of the assumed Israeli nuclear capability, refers to the missions of that capability. As argued before in this book, the two rational functions of Israeli nuclear capability are deterrence of "last resort" contingencies, and a deterrent of an Arab nuclear capability. Further clarifying these missions may be an important measure in restraining proliferation. One of the ways to go about it is through a declaration of "no first use" of weapons of mass destruction by all regional powers, which Israel would join. That would maintain the Israeli ambiguous posture, yet at the same time would contribute to the delineation of the limits of such use. Sheer declarations may have only a limited effect, yet they do have some efficacy. Furthermore, the possibility that the United States might play a role in underwriting such an undertaking should be weighed and considered.

Still another measure could be the undertaking by all regional powers to refrain from using threats of utilizing weapons of mass destruction for political purposes. Again, the United States could play a role in making such an undertaking more binding.

An ambiguous posture, under conditions of a freeze, coupled with several confidence-building measures, would be sufficient to enable the United States and an international coalition led by it, to apply stringent inspection and verification systems on other Middle Eastern countries. Whether such a "package" would be sufficient in the very long run is difficult to assess. In any case, the current official Israeli position is that once Israel and all the Arab countries have signed peace treaties Israel would be ready for complete denuclearization. It is likely that Israel would insist that Iran is included in the nuclear free zone. As such a prospect lies in the more distant future, it appears in general, not very relevant to immediate steps.

In summary, the Israeli approach to arms control should be based on a realistic assessment of the potential contribution of her ambiguous nuclear posture to her security, and the dangers involved in nuclear proliferation in the Middle East. Thus, the dimensions of deterrence and arms control should fit. The ambiguous Israeli nuclear posture provides her with an important security option in a region characterized by instability, in which a mere change in the structure of interstate coalitions could adversary impact the balance of conventional forces. However, bearing in mind the narrow contribution of the nuclear option to Israel's current security concerns, arms control agreements should allow Israel to maintain the two rational uses of the ambiguous posture—"last resort" strategic deterrence and a deterrent against a Middle Eastern state acquiring a nuclear capability. An ambiguous posture coupled with a freeze and an understanding of the only two missions for which this capability is designed, may possibly be sufficient to enable the evolution of effective arms control agreements prohibiting the production or retention of weapons of mass destruction in the Arab world. A change in the "rules of the game" of the Middle East state system toward the emergence of a region committed to economic and social development may, in the long run, bring complete denuclearization in the Middle East.

Finally, it should be stressed again, that in a situation where the alternatives are either a nuclearized Middle East or a Middle East in which no state (including Israel) has nuclear capability, the latter is preferable. Therefore, Israel should seek political strategic and arms control agreements to limit any move toward further proliferation in the Middle East. This should also affect her approach to her own nuclear posture.

NOTES

1 THE NUCLEAR STATUS OF THE MIDDLE EAST STATES

1 For a survey of the publicly available literature and documentation, see Peter Pry, *Israel's Nuclear Arsenal* (Boulder, CO: Westview Press, 1984). A useful account is provided in the volumes by Leonard Spector, *Nuclear Proliferation Today* (New York: Vintage Books, 1984); *The Undeclared Bomb* (Cambridge: Ballinger, 1988); and Leonard Spector and Jacqueline Smith, *Nuclear Ambitions* (Cambridge: Ballinger, 1990). It should be noted that none of the details appearing in either of these two books have received any official confirmation on the part of the Israeli government. Another addition to the literature is Frank Barnaby, *The Invisible Bomb*.

2 Recent books using already the Vanunu story include Barnaby, *ibid.*, Leonard Spector, *The Undeclared Bomb, ibid.* and Leonard Spector and Jacqueline Smith, *Nuclear Ambitions, ibid.*

3 Detailed accounts of the negotiations between Israel and France, and of the background to the 1957 agreement, can be found in Matti Golan, *Shimon Peres* (Hebrew) (Jerusalem: Shoken, 1982); Michael Bar-Zohar, *Ben-Gurion* (Hebrew) (Tel Aviv: Am Oved, 1977); and Pierre Pean, *Les deux bombes* (Paris: Fayard, 1982).

4 The claim regarding the establishment of a plutonium separation facility, is forwarded by Pean, *ibid.*, and also by Steven Weissman and Herbert Krosney, *The Islamic Bomb: The Nuclear Threat to Israel and the Middle East* (New York: Times Books, 1981) especially pp. 110–113. Weissman and Krosney base their claim on an interview with Françoise Peran, the former head of the French Atomic Energy Commission. Peran even claims that the French reached a decision on nuclear aid to Israel in September 1956, prior to the Suez Campaign (p. 111).

5 Spector, *op. cit.*, 1984, pp. 119–120.

6 Bar-Zohar, *op. cit.*, p. 1373, and also Charles De Gaulle, *Renewal and Endeavor* (New York: Simon and Schuster, 1971), p. 266.

7 Bar-Zohar, *op. cit.*, p. 1384.

8 Golan, *op. cit.*, p. 102.

9 Bar-Zohar, *op. cit.*, p. 1388.

10 *Ibid.*, p. 1389. American search for information began earlier. See, for example, the cable from Houghton in the Embassy in Paris, to Washington on November 22, 1960, describing a meeting with a member of the French Atomic Agency Commission concerning French–Israeli atomic cooperation (Kennedy Library).

This dispatch came as a response to queries sent from the American Atomic Energy Commission on October 19, 1960.

11 *New York Times,* December 10, 1960; *Time,* December 12, 1960.

12 *Daily Express,* December 16, 1960; *Washington Post,* December 18, 1960.

13 Bar-Zohar, *loc. cit.*

14 Yair Evron, "Israel and the Atom: The Uses and Misuses of Ambiguity", 1957–1967, *Orbis* Vol. 17, no. 4 (Winter 1974).

15 On this point, I differ from the thesis developed by Shlomo Aronson, in his book *Conflict and Bargaining in the Middle East* (Baltimore: Johns Hopkins University Press, 1978).

16 On the development of the debate in Israel on the question of the nuclear option, see Uri Bar-Joseph, "The Hidden Debate: The Formation of Nuclear Doctrines in the Middle East," *The Journal of Strategic Studies,* Vol. 5, No. 2, June 1982.

17 Upon the signing of the secret agreement with France, all the members of the Atomic Energy Commission resigned, with the exception of the commission's chairman, Prof. A. D. Bergman. Two of the members that resigned joined the Committee for a Nuclear-free Middle East.

18 Aronson, *op. cit.,* p. 51.

19 Spector, *op. cit.,* 1984, p. 375, footnote 39. Spector's source is information received from a member of the American administration. This assessment of the motives behind the American decision was first mooted in Israel in 1969, by Arnan Azaryah.

20 This account is based on Leonard Spector, *Nuclear Ambitions, op.cit.,* pp. 149–170. As long as Israel has not disclosed her nuclear status all such accounts are speculative. As I have no inside information about Israel's capability this account should not be seen as an "informal" validation of Spector's account.

21 For a categorization of threshold states, see Lewis A. Dunn, "Dealing with the Threshold Countries: Old Problems, Emerging Challenges and New Approaches," (Paper Presented at UCS Workshop, June 1991). For discussions of the concept of opaque proliferation as preferable to either an "ambiguous" posture or a threshold posture, see some of the contributions in Benjamin Frankel (ed.) *Opaque Nuclear Proliferation: Methodology and Policy Implications;* (London: Frank Cass, 1991); see especially Avner Cohen and Benjamin Frankel, "Opaque Nuclear Proliferation."

22 For a detailed discussion of the question whether Israel has or has not conducted a nuclear test jointly with South Africa, see Spector, *op. cit.,* 1988, p. 384 f.n. 5. For a reference to the question of whether test is essential for the development of fusion weapons within the Israeli context, see Spector, *op. cit.,* 1988, p. 166.

23 See Asher Arian, Ilan Talmud, Tamar Herman, *National Security and Public Opinion in Israel.* (Tel Aviv: Jaffee Center for Strategic Studies, Tel Aviv University, 1988).

24 See *Yedioth Ahronot,* 2/16/1991.

25 See Barnaby, *op. cit.;* Spector, *op. cit.,* 1988.

26 For example, Barnaby mentions it in his book. Also, the authoritative *Military Balance 1993/94* makes his statement about Israel's nuclear capacity as follows: "It is widely believed that Israel has a nuclear capability . . ."

27 On the development of Arab positions during this period, see Yair Evron, "The Arab Position in the Nuclear Field: A Study of Policies up to 1967," *Cooperation and Conflict,* No. 7, 1973.

28 *Ibid.*

29 *Middle East Record,*, p. 288.

30 Evron, *op. cit.*, p. 22.

31 *Ibid.*, pp. 22–23.

32 *Ibid.*, p. 24.

33 *Ibid.*, p. 28.

34 Shai Feldman, *Israeli Nuclear Deterrence: A Strategy for the 1980s*, (New York: Columbia University Press, 1982).

35 Feldman, *op. cit.*

36 *Ibid.*, p. 12.

37 *Loc. cit.*

38 *Loc. cit.*

39 *al-Qabas*, Kuwait, 9/13/1980.

40 Quoted in the Israeli daily newspaper *Ma'ariv*, 3/24/1983, from an interview published in the Japanese newspaper *Meinitze*.

41 The themes appear in the following: See, inter alia, *Alf Ba'a* (Iraq) 10/22/ 1986; *Al Anba* (Kuwait) 11/2/1986; *Al-Ahli* (Egypt) 12/10/1986; *Al-Tiasah al-Bulia* (Egypt) April 1987.

42 Interview in *Die Welt*, 11/19/1987.

43 The exception, as described in Chapter 6, is Iraq, which until the war enjoyed very extensive financial resources *and* vast energy resources.

44 See Roger F. Pajak, "Nuclear Status and Policies of the Middle East Countries," *International Affairs*, Vol. 59, No. 4, 1983, pp. 589, 594–596.

45 *Ibid.*, and also Joseph Yager (ed.), *Nonproliferation and US Foreign Policy* (Washington: Brookings Institute, 1980).

46 Pajak, *op. cit.*, pp. 595–596.

47 *Ha'aretz* (Israeli Hebrew newspaper), 1/30/1985.

48 For an overview of Egypt's nuclear power plans, see Leonard Spector, *Nuclear Ambitions, op. cit.*; *World Business Weekly* (London), 3/2/1981, p. 18.

49 On the Libyan attempts to acquire ready-made nuclear weapons from China, see, among others, Rodney W. Jones, *Nuclear Proliferation: Islam, the Bomb and South Asia*; The Washington Papers no. 82, Sage Policy Papers, 1981; S. Weissman, H. Krosney, *op. cit.*, pp. 55–57; and Pajak, *op. cit.*, pp. 600–601. For a comprehensive discussion of the Libyan search for nuclear weapons technology, see Leonard Spector, *op. cit.*, 1988, pp. 196–204.

50 Pajak, *op. cit.*, pp. 600–601.

51 *Loc. cit.* According to Spector, *ibid.*, the agreement was for the construction of two reactors, each of 440 megawatts.

52 See the reports by Paul Lewis in the *International Herald Tribune*, 11/20/1984 and 11/21/1984.

53 *Loc. cit.*

54 See, for example, Weissman and Krosney, *op. cit.*

55 This part will deal with developments in Iraq only until the destruction of Osiraq. Later developments are dealt with in Chapter 6.

56 The improvement of international status and the strengthening of political influence as elements in the spectrum of interests motivating various states to acquire nuclear weapons, have been noted by a number of observers. This phenomenon has been visible, for example, in the nuclear efforts of France and India. On Iraq's nuclear program as a vehicle for hegemony in the Arab world, see also Spector, *op. cit.*, 1988, p. 208, and Spector and Smith, *op. cit.*, 1990, p. 187.

57 On the negotiations that led to the establishment of "Osiraq," see, among others, Pajak, *op. cit.*, and also Haim Shaked, "The Nuclearization of the

Middle East: The Israeli Raid on Osiraq," *Middle East Contemporary Survey*, vol. 5, 1980–1981, pp. 182–183.

58 See, for example, *Nucleonic Week*, 1/19/1978, p. 10.

59 According to an official French announcement on 6/17/1981; see the *New York Times*, 6/18/1981.

60 *Christian Science Monitor*, 6/24/1981, and quoted in Pajak, *op. cit.*, p. 599.

61 See Spector, *op. cit.*, 1988, p. 208.

62 *Washington Post*, 6/18/1981.

63 The following presentation is based on among others, Spector, *op. cit.*, 1988; Spector and Smith, *op.cit.*; Rodney Jones, *op. cit.*; Weissman and Krosney, *op. cit.*; Z. M. Khalizad, "Pakistan," and A. Kapur, "Pakistan," in J. Goldblatt (ed.), *Non-proliferation: The Why and the Wherefore*, (London and Philadelphia: Taylor and Francis 1985), Chapters 7 and 7A; Praful Bidawi and Ackin Vanaik, "India and Pakistan" in C. R. Karp (ed.) *Security with Nuclear Weapons* (Oxford: Oxford University Press; 1991).

64 In the case of China, her position has traditionally been that nuclear proliferation constitutes no danger when confined to "peace-loving" states (namely, China's allies and friends). It should be noted that China was ready to transfer sensitive nuclear technology to Pakistan but she has never transferred the actual weapons. In the past few years the Chinese position has developed in two contradictory ways: on the one hand, she began exporting sensitive nuclear technology and know-how to additional states, viz. Iraq and Iran. On the other hand, she has recently joined the NPT (and see below in Chapter 4).

65 This, for example, is the assessment of the well-known Arab military commentator Hittam el Ayabi, as expressed in the Syrian newspaper, *al-Thaura*, 10/8/1975. He argues that Arab uncertainty as to the existence of Israeli nuclear weapons has prevented them from requesting nuclear weapons from states friendly to them. A similar case is made in another Syrian newspaper, *Alard*, 8/21/1976.

66 Private information received by the author in the United States.

2 THE DYNAMICS OF THE CONFLICT: ISRAEL'S POSTURE OF CONVENTIONAL DETERRENCE AND THE LIMITED RELEVANCE OF A NUCLEAR CAPABILITY

1 As Alexander George and Richard Smoke have pointed out when referring to "limited wars." See their *Deterrence in American Foreign Policy: Theory and Practice* (New York: Columbia University Press, 1974), p. 49.

2 Contributions to the definition and discussion of the concept were made by many. The following list refers to many of the main contributors: Bernard Brodie, Thomas Schelling, Alexander George, Glen Snyder, Bruce Russett, Morton Kaplan, Richard Rosecrance, George Quester, Thomas Milburn. For a comprehensive contribution, see Patrick Morgan, *Deterrence: A Conceptual Analysis* (Beverly Hills: Sage Publications, 1977).

3 For a discussion of the various definitions of deterrence see Morgan *op. cit.*, Chapter 1.

4 This incorporates an important political component into the deterrence equation. Indeed, the literature on deterrence has given some attention to different aspects of the political factor. For example, Alexander George discusses the necessity for adjusting deterrence (and coercion) to various foreign policy goals; see Alexander George, David Hall and William Simons, *The Limits of Coercive Diplomacy* (Boston: Little Brown, 1971). Bruce Russett is also concerned

with the political interests under contention in deterrence situations. See his "The Calculus of Deterrence," *Journal of Conflict Resolution*, Vol. 7, No. 2 (March 1963) and "Pearl Harbor: Deterrence Theory and Decision Theory," *Journal of Peace Research*, No. 2 (1967). Richard Rosecrance points to the centrality of political constraints in *Strategic Deterrence Reconsidered*, Adelphi Papers No. 116 (London: International Institute for Strategic Studies, 1975). Patrick Morgan refers to it in *op cit.*, Chapters 6 and 7. See also Steven Maxwell, *Rationality in Deterrence*, Adelphi Papers No. 50 (London: International Institute for Strategic Studies, 1975); Robert Jervis, "Deterrence Theory Revisited," *World Politics*, Vol. 30, No. 2 (Jan. 1979), pp. 322–324, and also ch. 3 of his *Perception and Misperception in International Politics* (Princeton: Princeton University Press, 1976). See also the various contributions by Robert Jervis, Janice Stein and Richard Ned Lebow in their *Psychology and Deterrence* (Baltimore: Johns Hopkins University Press, 1989).

5 Robert Jervis, *op. cit.*, 1979, p. 314.

6 The issue of resolve has been mentioned by many writers, usually as part of the issue of credibility. Oran Young discusses resolve and defines it as "intensity of feeling"; see his *The Politics of Force: Bargaining During International Crisis* (Princeton: Princeton University Press, 1978), pp. 33, 177–216. Jervis, *op. cit.*, 1979, when discussing "strategic interests" as distinguished from "intrinsic interests", refers to values which are related to the issue of resolve.

7 See his *Arms and Influence* (New Haven: Yale University Press, 1972), Chapter 3.

8 See Morgan *op. cit.*, pp. 25–43.

9 The distinction was first suggested by Glen Snyder, *Deterrence by Denial and Punishment* (Princeton: Princeton University Center of International Studies, 1959). His definition is somewhat different from the one used in my work.

10 To be sure, tactical nuclear weapons might be used within the framework of deterrence by denial, and deterrence by punishment might be exercised by conventional means (in the case of strategic bombardment with conventional bombs). However, in most cases the distinction between the two types of deterrence parallels the distinction between threats to use nuclear or conventional arms.

11 For a criticism of deterrence theory emphasizing among other things, psychological constraints on the calculations of decision-makers, see Richard Ned Lebow, Janice Gross Stein, "Beyond Deterrence," *Journal of Social Issues*, No. 4, 1987. See also the special edition of *World Politics*, January, 1989, featuring a general debate on the assumptions of deterrence theory.

12 For some of these "spiral" theories, see among others, Kenneth Boulding, "National Images and International Systems," *Journal of Conflict Resolution* 3, No. 3, 1959; Charles Osgood, *An Alternative to War or Surrender* (University of Illinois Press, 1962). For a critical appraisal see Jervis, *op. cit.*, 1976, Chapter 3.

13 It is difficult to identify a defined Israeli "strategic" let alone "deterrence" doctrine. Israeli strategic policy has remained flexible, without being fully defined or organized. For this reason I have preferred the looser term "deterrence posture". For studies of the Israeli strategic "doctrine" see Yoav Ben Horin and Barry Posen, *Israel's Strategic Doctrine* (Santa Monica: Rand Corporation R–2845–NA, Sept. 1981); Michael Handel, *Israel's Political-Military Doctrine*; Dan Horowitz, *Israel's Concept of Defensible Borders* (Jerusalem Paper on Peace Problems No. 16, Jerusalem, 1975); Dan Horowitz, "The Israeli Concept of National Security and the Prospects of Peace in the Middle East," in G. Sheffer (ed.) *Dynamics of a Conflict: A Re-examination of the Arab–Israeli Conflict* (New York: Humanities Press, 1975); Dan Horowitz, "The Constant and the

Changing in Israeli Strategic Thought" (Hebrew) in *Milchemet Breira* (Tel Aviv: Hakaibbuitz Hameuchad Press, 1985); Dan Horowitz, "The Control of Limited Military Operations: The Israeli Experience" in Y. Evron (ed.) *International Violence: Terrorism, Surprise and Control* (Jerusalem: 1979); Nadav Safran, *Israel, The Embattled Ally* (Cambridge: Harvard University Press, 1978); Ephraim Inbar, *Israeli Strategic Thought in the Post 1973 Period* (Jerusalem: IRICS, 1982); Avner Yaniv, *Deterrence Without the Bomb* (Lexington, MA: D.C. Heath, 1987); Yair Evron, *War and Intervention in Lebanon: The Israeli–Syrian Deterrence Dialogue* (London: Croom Helm and Baltimore: Johns Hopkins, 1987).

14 The Israeli strategy of retaliation and its effectiveness has been analyzed by several academic observers. See for example, the discussion by Horowitz *op. cit.*, 1979; Shlomo Aronson and Dan Horowitz, "The Strategy of Controlled Retaliation: The Israeli Example" *Medina Umimshal*, Vol. 1, No. 1 (Summer 1971); Barry M. Blechman, "The Impact of Israel's Reprisals on the Behavior of the Bordering Arab Nations at Israel," *Journal of Conflict Resolution*, Vol. 16, No. 2 (June 1972). For a recent detailed and thoughtful study concentrating on the deterrence aspect of the retaliation strategy see Jonathan Shimshoni, *Israel and Conventional Deterrence: Border Warfare from 1953 to 1970* (Ithaca: Cornell University Press). There are several disagreements about this strategy's objectives and functions.

15 This concept has not as yet been suggested in the literature. Although this behavior has an element of compellence, it nevertheless serves primarily as an instrument of deterrence.

16 The Fedayeen units which were sent on murder missions into Israel, had been organized by Egypt following and as a reaction to the Israeli raid on an Egyptian military installation near Gaza in late February 1955. Shimshoni argues that Nasser was in any case committed to a process of escalation with Israel. I disagree with his contention.

17 Janice Stein, in an excellent analysis, "Calculation, Miscalculation and Conventional Deterrence I: The View From Cairo," in *op. cit.*, 1985 analyzes thirteen cases of deterrence situations between Israel and Egypt during 1967–1973. In some of these Israel was the challenger, in others Egypt. As the focus of this chapter is on Israel's deterrence posture and its effectivity, only the more outstanding cases of successful Egyptian challenges of the status quo are considered—these took place in 1967 (failure of specific deterrence) in 1969/70 and in 1973. The more extensive discussion is focused only on the 1967 and 1973 Wars.

18 See *Ma'arachot* Nos. 191/192.

19 See "Army and State" (in Hebrew), *Ma'arachot*, 279–280, May–June 1981.

20 For images of the Israeli decision-makers during that period see Michael Brecher, *Decisions in Israel's Foreign Policy* (London: Oxford University Press, 1974), Chapter 6. On Ben-Gurion's assessment of the future of the military balance see specially pp. 245–247.

21 According to a well known distinction, "preventive war" is a war which seeks to prevent a long-term change in the balance of power; whereas "preemptive strike" refers to the preemption of an imminent attack by the opposing side. For references to the 1956 War and the processes leading to it, see Brecher *ibid.*, and the extensive bibliography listed in it. In addition see *inter alia* Moshe Dayan, *Story of My Life* Part III (Jerusalem: Edanim, 1976); Michael Bar-Zohar, *Ben-Gurion* (Tel Aviv: Am Oved, 1977), Vol. III, Parts 1 and 2.

22 Yigal Allon, *Curtain of Sand* (Tel Aviv: Hakibutz Hameuchad, 1984) and "Active

Defense as a Guarantee for our Existence", 1967; Shimon Peres, *The Next Phase* (Hebrew) (Tel Aviv: Am Oved, 1965), and in *Ma'arachot* No. 146 (1962).

23 Michael Brecher, *The Foreign Policy System of Israel* (London: Oxford University Press, 1972), pp. 51 and specially 67, and Allon and Peres *ibid.* See also some of the works cited in note 13. See also Yair Evron, *The Role of Arms Control in the Middle East*, Adelphi Papers No. 138 (London: IISS, 1977).

24 Brecher, *ibid.*, p. 67.

25 Egypt, by far the strongest Arab state, most probably viewed Israeli military superiority as very considerable. Hence the Egyptian persistent refusal to allow Syria to push her into an escalatory process with Israel. See, for example, Nadav Safran, *From War to War* (Indianapolis: Bobbs-Merrill, 1969). For a detailed analysis of Nasser's position in this context see Benjamin Geist, *The Six Day War: A Study in the Setting and the Process of Foreign Policy Decision Making Under Crisis Conditions* (Ph.D. Thesis, Hebrew University of Jerusalem, 1974), Chapter 13, specially p. 599 and fn. 31, and Ch. 4. On the intensive competition in the Arab world during the first half of the sixties, see *inter alia* Malcolm Kerr, *The Arab Cold War: Gamal Abdal Nassir and his Rivals, 1958–1970* (London: Oxford University Press, 1970).

26 The problem of resolve also arises in connection with the hypothetical possibility of a direct limited nuclear attack on the opposing nuclear power. The question is whether such a strike would lead to a response in kind by the attacked party, thus risking a second and catastrophic nuclear strike.

27 The balance of resolve remains important in extended deterrence in nuclear environments. This has already been argued by several authors. For another contribution in this general direction, see Paul Huth and Bruce Russett, "What Makes Deterrence Work: Cases from 1900 to 1980," *World Politics*, Vol. 36, No. 4, July 1984.

28 For analytical treatments of the complex relationship between inter-Arab relations and the Arab–Israeli conflict, see *inter alia* Gabriel Ben-Dor, "Inter-Arab Relations and the Arab–Israeli Conflict," *Jerusalem Journal of International Relations* (Summer 1976) and *State and Conflict in the Middle East* (New York: Praeger, 1983), Chs. 4 and 5; Yair Evron and Yaacov Bar-Simantov, "Coalitions in the Arab World", *Jerusalem Journal of International Relations* (Summer 1976).

29 The clearest statement of the Egyptian deterrence intentions in the first phase of the 1967 crisis was given by Nasser in an interview published in *Look* (New York) March 19, 1968, quoted in Geist *op. cit.*, ch. 13, fn. 31. Most observers, including Israelis, concur that deterrence was indeed Egypt's strategy in her initial move into Sinai in 1967. For a contrary argument see, *inter alia*, Theodor Draper, *Israel and World Politics: Roots of the Third Arab–Israeli War* (New York: Viking Press, 1968).

30 Stein, *op. cit.*, cites several cases of Egyptian contemplation of launching an attack during the period 1967–1973 and the success of Israeli deterrence. The success was due primarily to Egyptian recognition of Israeli military superiority. One may add that this was really the reason for their caution even when Egyptian decision-makers argued that they refrained from military operations due to the American role. For a detailed account of the process leading to the War of Attrition see Shimshoni *op. cit.*

31 See their "Beyond Deterrence", *op. cit.*

32 On this particular dimension see Stein, *op. cit.*

33 Indeed, Sadat had tried to secure a political solution but failed. He did it first during the negotiations in 1971–1972 on an interim agreement regarding the withdrawal of Israeli forces from the Suez Canal and its reopening. He also

sent feelers toward the United States in 1972 and 1973. Apparently Kissinger misunderstood these feelers and in fact, turned them down. For an initial treatment of the Egyptian "political grievance" as the main cause for the 1973 War, see Yair Evron, *op. cit.*, 1977, pp. 12–13.

34 Stein, *op. cit.*

35 The possibility of heavy air bombing of Egypt as a deterrent was implicitly signaled during the "deep penetration" bombing of 1970. Egypt partly neutralized it by the introduction of some surface-to-surface *Scud* missiles. These, however, were of very limited capability. One may conclude that prior to the war, the Egyptian leadership was ready *in extremis* to absorb an Israeli campaign of air bombing.

36 Rabin, in interview with Dov Goldstein, *Ma'ariv*, September 25, 1974. Peres also talked about the emphasis on a fast decisive victory rather than deterrence, *Ha'aretz*, September 29, 1974. One might, of course, argue that such an emphasis on a decisive victory projects an element of deterrence by denial. It appears, however, that this notion was not shared by the decision-makers themselves.

37 For Sharon's so-called *casus belli* see below.

38 For details see Evron, *op. cit.*, 1987.

39 *Ibid.*

40 See Inbar, *op. cit.*, p. 14.

41 For works discussing the effects of proliferation on the structure of the international system, see *inter alia* Alastair Buchan "Introduction,", Stanley Hoffmann, "Nuclear Proliferation and World Politics" in Buchan (ed.) *A World of Nuclear Powers?* (Englewood Cliffs, NJ: Prentice Hall, 1966); Richard Rosecrance, "Introduction" and "International Stability and Nuclear Diffusion" in his "Problems of Nuclear Proliferation," *Security Studies Papers*, No. 7, University of California, 1966; Erasmus, "Polycentrism and Proliferation," *Survey*, No. 58, Jan. 1966. For works emphasizing the stabilizing effect of proliferation on world order see, *inter alia*, Pierre Gallois, *The Balance of Terror: Strategy for the Nuclear Age* (Boston: Houghton Mifflin, 1961); Kenneth Waltz, "The Spread of Nuclear Weapons: More May Be Better," Adelphi Papers, No. 171, Autumn 1981).

42 This is one of the themes in Shlomo Aronson, *Conflict and Bargaining in the Middle East* (Baltimore: Johns Hopkins University Press, 1978).

43 All these explanations appear in the literature on the 1967 War. The volume of literature on the War is quite extensive. For a very extensive and detailed account of the events and processes leading to the crisis and war, which also discusses in great detail the inter-Arab competition, see Benjamin Geist, *op. cit.*, 1974. On inter-Arab states competition in the first half of the 1960s, see Malcolm Kerr, *op. cit.*, 1971.

For an analysis of the crisis and war which focuses primarily on the decision-making process in Israel, see Michael Brecher and Benjamin Geist, *Decisions in Crisis: Israel, 1967* (Berkeley: University of California Press, 1980). And see also footnotes 28 and 29 above.

44 This argument is developed in Shlomo Aronson, "The Nuclear Dimension of the Arab–Israeli Conflict," *The Jerusalem Journal of International Relations*, Vol. 7, Nos. 1–2, 1984.

45 On the War of Attrition, see, *inter alia*, Yaacov Bar-Simantov, *The Israeli–Egyptian War of Attrition: A Case Study of Limited Local War*, William Quandt, *Decade of Decisions* (Berkeley and London: University of California Press, 1977); Nadav Safran, *op. cit.*, 1978; Yair Evron, *The Middle East: Nations, Superpowers and*

Wars (London and New York: Elek and Praeger, 1973); Yonatan Shimshoni, *op. cit.*, 1988.

46 See, *inter alia*, the articles by Hasenin Heikal on the Israeli security doctrine and the need to destroy it, which appeared in *al-Ahram* on 3/7/1969 and on 4/12/1969, and also his book, *The Road to Ramadan* (New York: Quadrangle Books, 1975). See also below in the discussion of the 1973 War and Egyptian objectives in it.

47 On Hafez Ismail's mission to the United States and on his meetings with Henry Kissinger, see Henry Kissinger, *Years of Upheaval* (Boston and Toronto: Little Brown, 1982), Chapter 6. On the gradual change in the Egyptian orientation toward the United States, and on its significance as an additional instrument for a resolution of the conflict with Israel, see Shimon Shamir, *Egypt Under Sadat Leadership* (in Hebrew) (Tel Aviv: Dvir, 1978).

48 See Kissinger, *op. cit.*, Chapters 11–13.

49 On the Israeli conventional deterrence posture, see Chapter 3 in this book. On the Israeli–Egyptian conventional deterrence posture, see Janice Stein, "Calculation, Miscalculation and Conventional Deterrence II: The View from Jerusalem", in R. Jervis, R. N. Lebow, N. Richard and J. Stein (eds.) *Psychology and Deterrence* (Baltimore: Johns Hopkins, 1985). See also Jonathan Shimshoni, *op. cit.*

50 Much of the analysis of Egypt's political and strategic objectives in the 1973 War, and all the details about the military planning of the war are derived from an article published in *Ma'archot* (The Journal of the IDF) authored by Colonel "Avi Shai". This article, apart from relying on many of the available public sources, made extensive use of Egyptian classified military documents which fell into the hands of Israel during the 1973 War. It probably made use of much other classified material. Because of the extensive use of this classified material, which is corroborated in many instances by the public evidence, this article is surely the most reliable open source on Egyptian military planning. On the need to break the political status quo as the main objective of the war, there is unanimity among all the Egyptian writers. See Avi Shai, "Egypt Towards the Yom Kippur War: The War's Objectives and the Attack Plan" (in Hebrew), *Ma'arachot* 250, July 1976.

51 See *al-Ahbar*, 10/3/1975, quoted by Shai, *ibid.*, p. 16.

52 See Ismail Fahmy, *Negotiating for Peace in the Middle East* (London: Croom Helm, 1983); Mahmud Riad, *The Struggle for Peace in the Middle East* (London: Quartet, 1981); Anwar Sadat, *In Search of Identity* (New York: Harper and Row, 1978); Saad el-Shazli, *The Crossing of the Suez* (San Francisco: American Mideast Research, 1980). The only one referring to the possible connection between the nuclear issue and the 1973 War, is Heikal in one of his many articles on the Israeli nuclear issue. But even then, he does not refer to the assumed Israeli capability as a factor in the Egyptian planning of the war. It is also interesting that in his main work on the 1973 War, *The Road to Ramadan, op cit.*, he does not make any reference to the nuclear issue.

53 For example, his reference in *al-Usbu al-Arabi*, 7/2/1976.

54 See al-Ahbar, 10/3/1975 (fn. 11).

55 Interview with Heikal, *Al-Anwar*, 11/8/1973, quoted by Shai, *op. cit.*

56 Quoted by Shai, *ibid.*, fn. 11. Sadat's references to this subject appear in various places. See also in his interview with the editor of *al-Nahar*, brought in *The Middle East News Agency*, 9/7/1974.

57 See Shai, *op. cit.*, fn. 12 quoting Sadat's interview with Dr. Takala and Dr. Darwish, authors of the book *The Six Hours War* (in Arabic).

58 This detailed account is based primarily on various statements by Sadat, quoted in Shai, *op. cit.*, p. 17.

59 See *Ibid.*

60 *Ibid.* See also Avraham Adan, *Al Shtei Gdot Ha Suez* (in Hebrew) (Jerusalem: Edanim, 1979); John Mearsheimer, *Conventional Deterrence* (Ithaca and London: Cornell University Press, 1983); Hasan el-Badri, Taha el-Magdoub and Muhammad Diam el-Din Zhody, *The Ramadan War* (Dunn Loming, VA: T. N. Dupuy Associates, 1978).

61 On the Egyptian order of battle, see Shai, *ibid.*, and Adan, *ibid.*

62 Fahmi, *op. cit.*

63 Riad, *op. cit.*

64 For details of the actual attack, see, *inter alia*, Adan, *op. cit.*; Mearsheimer, *op. cit.*; Badri, Magdoub and Zhodi, *op. cit.* Haim Herzog, *The War of Atonement.*

65 The Egyptian War Minister Ahmed Ismail Ali opposed the decision on military grounds while the Chief of Staff Shazli pushed for it. For their discussions see Adan *ibid.*

66 See Seymour Hersh, *The Samson Option* (London and Boston: Faber and Faber, 1991) pp. 225–227.

67 It is surprising that Heikal has not referred to this information in any of his earlier writings. It is also interesting that he claimed in this interview that the Soviet intelligence relayed to Egypt referred also to Dayan's "scary report" from the Egyptian front which he communicated to the Israeli Cabinet on October, 8. One has the feeling that Heikal's account was already based on the literature he read after the war.

68 It is interesting to note that the first international public account of the nuclear-related events of October 8–9, was published in *Time* on April 12, 1976. The *Time* report suggested that Dayan gave orders for arming several nuclear weapons and the Israeli Cabinet cancelled the order.

69 See Herzog, *op. cit.* (Hebrew Edition), pp. 113–114.

70 See Sadat's interview in *al-Usbu al-Arabi*, 10/8/1974/

71 See Mearsheimer, *op. cit.*

72 See Fahmi, *op. cit.*, pp. 25–26. For a different account see Patrick Seale, *Asad* (Berkeley: University of California Press, 1988). However, in view of the overall lack of credibility in many of Seale's accounts of Asad's behavior, especially after 1970, I tend to lean more toward Fahmi's description.

73 See Shlomo Aronson, *op. cit.*, 1984. For a much more cautious variant of this general thesis, see George Quester, "The Middle East: Imposed Solutions or Imposed Problems" in M. Leitenberg and G. Shaffer (eds.) *Great Power Intervention in the Middle East* (New York: Pergamon, 1979). Ezer Weitzman relates to this subject in an oblique way, but from what he quotes from Egyptian statesmen it is difficult to conclude that the nuclear issue was really an important factor in Sadat's peace initiative. See Weitzman's *The Battle for Peace* (in Hebrew) (Jerusalem: Edanim, 1981), pp. 85–87.

74 See Fahmy, *op. cit.*, p. 33.

75 *Ibid.* That the nuclear issue played no role in Sadat's peace initiative was strongly emphasized by one of his closest aides during the peace negotiations, Tahsin Bashir, in an interview with me on 12/18/1990 in Cairo. A leading Egyptian diplomat, Muhamed Shaker expressed total surprise when he was asked by me (on November 13, 1991) whether in his view the nuclear issue played any role in Sadat's initiative. He emphasized that in his view and the consensus in the Egyptian government, this had no relevance.

76 In a conference on *Arms Control and Security in the Middle East*, The American Academy of Arts and Sciences, June 1991.

77 See Kissinger, *op. cit.*, 1982, pp. 481–482.

78 On the quest for "strategic parity" and its analysis, see *inter alia*, the analysis in Itamar Rabinovich, "The Syrian–Israeli Deterrence Relationship—The Syrian Perspective"; Patrick Seale, *op. cit.*, pp. 346–349; Michael Eisenstadt, *Arming for Peace? Syria's Elusive Quest for Strategic Parity* (Washington, D.C.: The Washington Institute for Near East Policy, 1992).

79 See *inter alia, Middle East Contemporary Survey*, Vol. XI, 1987, p. 654.

80 See his interview in *al-Qabas*, 1/24/1987.

3 NUCLEAR WEAPONS IN THE MIDDLE EAST: THE CONSEQUENCES FOR STRATEGY AND POLICY

1 Some of the arguments that appear in this chapter were originally developed in my "Some Effects of the Introduction of Nuclear Weapons in the Middle East", 1979; "Letter to the Editor", *Commentary*, February 1976; "Israel and Nuclear Weapons"; "The Middle East and the Atomic Bomb", *Skirah Hodshit.*

2 For works on the likely effects of proliferation in the Middle East, see *inter alia*, Y. Evron, "Israel and the Atom: The Uses and Misuses of Ambiguity, 1957–1967," *Orbis*, vol. 17, No. 4 (Winter 1974); Alan Dowty, "Nuclear Proliferation: The Israeli Case,", *International Studies Quarterly*, Vol. 22, 1978; Robert Harkavy, *Specter of a Middle Eastern Holocaust: The Strategic and Diplomatic Implications of the Israeli Nuclear Weapons Program* (Denver: University of Denver Press, 1977); Faud Jabber, *Israel and Nuclear Weapons* (London: Chatto and Windus, 1971); the various contributors in Louis Beres (ed.), *Security of Armageddon: Israel's Nuclear Strategy* (Lexington, MA: Lexington Books, 1986) especially Avner Yaniv and Allan Dowty; and Frank Barnaby, *The Invisible Bomb: The Nuclear Arms Race in the Middle East* (London: I. B. Taurts, 1989).

3 For the discussion on the Middle East as a subsystem (or subordinate system) see, among others, Leonard Binder, "The Middle East Subordinate International System," *World Politics*, Vol. 10, No. 3, April 1958; Michael Brecher, "The Middle East Subordinate System and its Impact on Israel's Foreign Policy," *International Studies Quarterly*, Vol. 13, No. 2, June 1969; Michael Brecher, *The Foreign Policy System of Israel* (London: Oxford University Press, 1972), ch. 3; Yair Evron, *The Middle East: Nations, Superpowers and Wars*, (London and New York: Elek and Prager, 1975), ch. 6; William Zartman, "Military Elements in Regional Unrest" in J. C. Hurevitz, *Soviet–American Rivalry in the Middle East* (New York: Prager, 1969); Yair Evron and Yaacov Bar Simon Tov, "Coalitions in the Arab World," *Jerusalem Journal of International Relations* (Summer 1976); L. Cantori, S. Spiegel, *The International Politics of Regions* (Englewood Cliffs, NJ: Prentice Hall, 1970); T. Y. Ismael, "A Subordinate System in Global Politics: The Middle East" in T. Y. Ismael (ed.) *The Middle East in World Politics* (Syracuse: Syracuse University Press, 1974); J. Lebovic, "The Middle East, The Region as a System", *International Interactions* Vol. 1, No. 3, 1986.

4 In Egypt, on the contrary, the military regime has undergone a thoroughgoing "civilianization."

5 In both countries the military is a powerful constituency and in Syria the main leader is an ex-military man. In Iraq, the Ba'ath Party and the various security services are also strong political constituencies (comparatively more so than in Syria).

6 George F. Kennan, *The Nuclear Delusion: Soviet–American Relations in the Atomic Age*, (New York: Parthenon Books, 1982), p. xii.

7 The most useful surveys of the development of nuclear strategy are by Lawrence Freedman, *The Evolution of Nuclear Strategy* (London: Macmillan, 1981), and McGeorge Bundy, *Danger and Survival: Choices about the Bomb in the First Fifty Years* (New York: Vintage Books, 1980). For an excellent brief study of the factors determining the evolution of American nuclear strategy, see Robert Art, "The United States: Nuclear Weapons and Grand Strategy" in R. C. Karp (ed.) *Security with Nuclear Weapons?* (Oxford: Oxford University Press, 1991).

8 "Implications for Military Policy," in Bernard Brodie (ed.), *The Absolute Weapon: Atomic Power and World Order* (New York: Harcourt Brace, 1946), p. 76. It is interesting to note that similar ideas were expressed by Ernst L. Woodward, in a public lecture entitled "The Development of the International Society: An Approach Using Law and Institutions," quoted in Barry H. Steiner, *Using the Absolute Weapon: Early Ideas of Bernard Brodie on Atomic Strategy* (Los Angeles: UCLA Center for International and Strategic Affairs, 1984).

9 On this see Lawrence Freedman, *op. cit.*; Richard Rosecrance, *Defence of the Realm*, (New York: Columbia University Press, 1968).

10 Needless to say, the doctrine of massive retaliation made the use of nuclear weapons more immediate, and thus, paradoxically, was distanced from a pure notion of deterrence.

11 In this respect, there are differences between the two superpowers: the United States is surrounded by seas. In contrast, on the borders of the former Soviet Union, or in their vicinity, there are a number of states allied with the United States, such as Turkey and Pakistan.

12 Hedley Bull, "Future Conditions of Strategic Deterrence," in Cristoph Bertram (ed.), *The Future of Strategic Deterrence* (London: Macmillan, 1981).

13 See Bruce Russett, *World Politics: The Menu for Choice* (New York: W. H. Freeman, 1985, 1989), p. 311, n. 16.

14 For rules of crisis prevention see Alexander George, *Managing US–Soviet Rivalry: Problems of Crisis Prevention* (Boulder, CO: Westview Press, 1983), and the contributions by Alexander George, Philip Farley, Alexander Dallin, in their edited volume, *US–Soviet Security Cooperation* (Boulder, CO: Westview Press, 1988). For various mechanisms to prevent nuclear war see the various contributions in Barry Blechman (ed.), *Preventing Nuclear War*.

15 On the use of the term "crisis stability," see for example, Richard Garwin, "Weapon Developments and the Threat of Nuclear War." It is also referred to with some elaboration and a definition by Daniel Frei, *Risks of Unintentional Nuclear War* (Totowa, NJ: Bowman and Allanbeld, 1983) p. 10. For a different definition, see Holst Afheldt, "Tactical Nuclear Weapons and European Security" in SIPRI (ed.) Tactical Nuclear Weapons: European Perspectives (London: SIPRI, 1979).

16 Needless to say, there is a considerable body of literature emphasizing the constraints—cognitive and others—on the rationality of leaders in general and in the superpower context as well. See for some obvious examples (among many) Robert Jervis, *Perception and Misperception in International Politics* (Princeton: Princeton University Press, 1976); John D. Steinbruner, *The Cybernetic Theory of Decision Making*; and in particular in relation to the question of rationality in deterrence see *inter alia* Robert Jervis, Richard Ned Lebow, and Janice Gross Stein, *Psychology and Deterrence* (Baltimore: Johns Hopkins University Press, 1985) and Richard Ned Lebow and Janice Stein "Beyond Deterrence—Building Better Theory", *Journal of Social Issues*, No. 4, 1987. However,

the overal behavior of the superpowers' leaderships throughout the period since the 1940s, though not the epitomization of caution and sensibility, was still sufficiently rational to overcome a whole series of severe crises.

17 Among many others, note the studies by Bernard Brodie, Stanley Hoffman, Richard Rosecrance, Robert Jervis, and Robert Art. See also Michael Mandel-baum, *The Nuclear Question: The United States and Nuclear Weapons, 1946–1976* (Cambridge: Cambridge University Press, 1979).

18 See, for example, Patrick Morgan, "Towards a Political Science Theory of Deterrence," (Unpublished Manuscript), p. 32.

19 Defined by J. Hertz in "Idealist Internationalism and the Security Balance." For the interesting distinction between the "power dilemma" and the security dilemma, see B. Buzan, *People, States and Fear: The National Security Problem in International Relations* (Chapel Hill: University of North Carolina Press, 1983).

20 McGeorge Bundy, "To Cap the Volcano", *Foreign Policy* (October 1969), p. 10.

21 For an analysis of the basic assumptions behind the two strategies, see Robert Jervis, "Why Nuclear Superiority Doesn't Matter," *Political Science Quarterly,* Vol. 94, No. 4, Winter 1979–1980. And see his detailed critique of the "countervailing strategy" in *The Illogic of American Nuclear Strategy* (Ithaca, N.Y.: Cornell University Press, 1984).

22 Robert McNamara, *The Essence of Security: Reflection in Office* (New York: Harper and Row, 1968); Geoffrey Kemp, *Nuclear Forces for Medium Powers* (London: Institute for Strategic Studies, 1974).

23 To be sure, in order to fulfill the requirements of MAD the amount of EMT had to be increased in order to account, in the first place for the effects of a Soviet strike, and in addition, for such factors as targeting errors, device failures, and the "fracticide effect." But even accounting for all these, the level of EMT each side had is several times that required.

24 On the size of EMT possessed by the two superpowers, see *The Military Balance 1982/83*, p. 141.

25 Another method for examining strategic requirements is by counting warheads. Geoffrey Kemp, for example (see *op. cit.*, Part II, p. 9, table 2, and p. 5, table 1), has estimated that to destroy the fifty largest cities in the former Soviet Union (the effective result is roughly equivalent to McNamara's definition) the United States requires 541 nuclear warheads, each of 50 kiloton. This estimate takes account of targeting errors and other possible failures, and also of the effect of Soviet ABM defense systems. On current figures, the United States has 6,656 nuclear warheads stationed on submarines alone, all 40–100 kiloton. As stated earlier, the submarine fleet was virtually immune to a Soviet first strike. Thus, according to this most conservative estimate, and taking no account of warheads on ICBMs or those carried on strategic bombers, the United States had an absolutely invulnerable nuclear force that exceeded fivefold McNamara's requirements for assured destruction. According to one estimate, the American inventory of strategic nuclear weapons in 1988 numbered 14,637 warheads, while the Soviet inventory numbered 11,694. This quantity is ten times what might be defined as a very high level of nuclear deterrence based on a counter-city strategy. For estimates of the nuclear inventories of the superpowers, see the recent issues of the IISS, *Strategic Survey* and *The Military Balance.* It should be noted that according to the START "counting rules", the United States had 9,789 warheads, whereas the USSR had 10,595. On this, see *The Military Balance, 1988–1989*, p. 230. These figures remained roughly through 1992.

26 On the "conventionalization" of nuclear weapons, see Robert Jervis (referring to Hans Morgenthau), *The Illogic of American Nuclear Strategy*, 1984, pp. 56–63.

27 John D. Steinbruner and Thomas M. Garwin, "Strategic Vulnerability: The Balance Between Prudence and Paranoia," *International Security*, Vol. 1, No. 4, 1976.

28 See an elaboration on this point in *Strategic Survey 1987–1988*, p. 40.

29 Admittedly, the total megatonnage of both sides diminished since the 1950s (in the case of the United States) and the 1960s (in the case of the USSR). These reductions, however, derived not from a basic change in perceptions, but from major improvements in technology, primarily in accuracy. Thus, the overall destructive power has not declined but rather has increased. See, on this, Fred Iklé and Albert Wolstetter, *Discriminate Deterrence*.

30 The "usability" in principle of nuclear weapons has been part of various counterforce strategies. It has been emphasized in *ibid.*

31 This part was initially written in the mid-1980s and somewhat updated in 1989. The Gulf Crisis and War do not appear to invalidate the basic analysis contained in it. Indeed, they only further reaffirmed the depth of inter-Arab conflicts and tensions. A possible "New Order" in the Middle East, if emerging, may limit the anarchical dimension of the Middle East. It would, however, most probably include more stringent measures against proliferation (see, for further discussion, below in Chapters 4 and 6).

32 See, on this, Louis R. Beres, "Introduction", in Beres (ed.) *Security or Armageddon*.

33 Michael Mandelbaum, *op. cit.*

34 For a useful study of these issues, see *inter alia*, Glen Snyder and Paul Diesing, *Conflict Among Nations: Bargaining, Decision-Making and System Structure in International Crisis* (Princeton: Princeton University Press, 1977). Richard Betts has argued that nuclear weapons do serve a useful coercive role in superpower crises; see his "Conventional Deterrence: Prediction, Uncertainty and Policy Confidence," *World Politics*, Vol. 35, No. 2, 1985. However, a careful study in the cases he refers to demonstrates that at least in the 1973 case, the role of the American implied nuclear threat was really as a deterrent and not as a compellant.

35 For the initial theoretical discussion of this point, see Thomas Schelling, *Arms and Influence* (New Haven: Yale University Press, 1972), pp. 78–86.

36 See, *inter alia*, Snyder and Diesing *ibid.*, and see the critique of the "Countervailing Strategy" in Robert Jervis, *The Illogic of America Nuclear Strategy*.

37 See, for example, Seweryn Bialer, "New Thinking and Soviet Foreign Policy".

38 An outstanding formulation of this viewpoint was given in the famous article by McGeorge Bundy, George F. Kennan and Gerard Smith, "Nuclear Weapons and the Atlantic Alliance," *Foreign Affairs*, Vol. 60, No. 4. Spring 1982. See also Robert McNamara, *The Military Role of Nuclear Weapons* (Los Angeles: ACIS Working Paper No. 46, UCLA, 1984). This school of thought opposed the early use of nuclear weapons against a conventional Soviet attack on Western Europe.

39 These views have been discussed in Yair Evron, "Israel and the Atom: The Uses and Misuses of Ambiguity 1957–1967," *Orbis*, Vol. 17, No. 4 (Winter 1974).

40 Shai Feldman, *Israeli Nuclear Deterrence: A Strategy for the 1980s*, (New York: Columbia University Press, 1982) pp. 149–151.

41 *Ibid.*, p. 92.

42 See *The Middle East Military Balance*, Annual, and the *Military Balance*, Annual.

43 Feldman, *op. cit.*, p. 101.

44 *Ibid.*, pp. 101–102.

45 *Loc. cit.*,

46 *Ibid.*, pp. 99–100.

47 This description is largely based on Paul Bracken, *The Command and Control of Nuclear Forces* (New Haven: Yale University Press, 1983).

48 Herman Kahn, *Thinking About the Unthinkable* (New York: Horizon Press, 1962), p. 40.

49 See Bracken, *op. cit.* For a more extreme view see Louis Beres, *Apocalypse: Nuclear Catastrophe in World Politics* (Chicago: Chicago University Press, 1980). Beres argues that no mechanical system is completely error-free. Daniel Frei, in *Risks of Unintentional Nuclear War* (Totowa, NJ: Rowman and Allanberd, 1983), p. 159, following a survey of the literature up to then, concludes that the technical risks are limited, but not so in regard to the human factor.

50 For discussion see Bracken *ibid.*, and Frei *ibid.*, pp. 159–160.

51 See Barry M. Blechman (ed.) *Preventing Nuclear War.*

52 *The Middle East Military Balance*, Annual.

53 At the request of Senator Nunn, General Richard Ellis, former commander of SAC, studied the possibility of a catalytic action by third parties. This SAC evaluation "showed that there are real and developing dangers in this area," see Blechman (ed.), *op. cit.* in fn. 44, p. 168.

54 See, *inter alia*, Anita Shapria, *From the Expulsion of the "Rama" to the Dissolution of the "Palmach"* (in Hebrew) (Tel Aviv: Hakibutz Hameuchad, 1985); Yoav Gelber, *Why Did the "Palmach" Dissolve?* (in Hebrew) (Jerusalem: Shoken, 1986).

55 On the general question of relations between the army and the Israeli political establishment, see *inter alia*, Yoram Peri, *Between Battles and Ballots: Israeli Military in Politics* (Cambridge: Cambridge University Press, 1983).

56 Lewis Dunn, *Controlling the Bomb: Nuclear Proliferation in the 1980s* (New Haven and London: Yale University Press, 1982).

57 Feldman, *op. cit.*, pp. 166–167.

58 Thomas Schelling, "Who Will Have the Bomb?" *International Security*, Vol. 1, No. 1 (Summer 1976) p. 88.

59 On this see Yair Evron and Yaacov Bar-Simon Tov, "Coalitions in the Arab World," *Jerusalem Journal of International Relations* (Summer 1976); Gabriel Ben Dor, "Inter-Arab Relations and the Arab–Israeli Conflict," *Jerusalem Journal of International Relations* (Summer 1976); Ali Hillal Dessouki, "The New Arab Political Order: Implications for the 1980s," in Malcolm Kerr and Sayed Yassin (eds) *Rich and Poor States in the Middle East: Egypt and the New Arab Order* (Boulder, Colorado: Westview Press, 1982); Faud Ajami, "The End of Pan Arabism". For an excellent and comprehensive study of the sources of Arab and other Middle Eastern coalitions, see Stephen Walt, *The Origins of Alliances* (Ithaca: Cornell University Press 1987).

4 INTERNATIONAL REACTIONS TO NUCLEAR PROLIFERATION IN THE MIDDLE EAST

1 Strategic nuclear forces are still deployed in Ukraine, Kazahkstan and Belarus, and would be finally dismantled within the process of START. However, it is unlikely that these states could play an independent role in facilitating proliferation (but see below in this chapter). On nuclear developments in the former

Soviet Union, see *inter alia*, Steven Miller, "Western Diplomacy and the Soviet Nuclear Legacy," *Survival*, Autumn 1992.

2 American policy on proliferation after the end of bipolarity and the Cold War is dealt with separately below.

3 Among the early important contributions, see Albert Wohlstetter, "Nuclear Sharing: Nato and the N+ Country" *Foreign Affairs*, Vol. 39, No. 3 (April 1961); Leonard Beaton and John Maddox, *The Spread of Nuclear Weapons* (London: Chatto and Windus, 1962); Alastair Buchan (ed.), *A World of Nuclear Powers?* (Englewood Cliffs, NJ: Prentice Hall, 1966).

4 This "international regime" refers to sets of rules of behavior, policies, and interational expectations as well as the formal instruments such as the NPT. On the concept of "international regimes" see *inter alia*, the basic set of articles included in *International Organization*, Spring 1982, and the book based on it edited by Stephen Krasner, *International Regimes* (Ithaca: Cornell University Press, 1983). On the various nonproliferation policies and norms as an international regime, see *inter alia* Roger Smith, "The Non-Proliferation Regime: Anomalies for Contemporary International Relations Theory," *International Organization*, 41 (Spring 1987); Roger Smith, "Opaque Proliferation and the Non-Proliferation Regime" in Benjamin Frankel (ed.), *Opaque Nuclear Proliferation: Methodological and Policy Implications* (London: Frank Cass, 1991); Jed Snyder, "The Non-Proliferation Regime: Managing the Impending Crisis," *Journal of Strategic Studies*, Vol. 8 (December 1985); Joseph S. Nye, Jr., "Maintaining the Non-Proliferation Regime", *International Organization*, 35, 1, Winter, 1981; Joseph S. Nye, "The Superpowers and the Non-Proliferation Treaty" in A. Carnesale and R. Haas (eds.) *Superpower Arms Control: Setting the Record Straight* (Cambridge: Ballinger, 1987); Joseph S. Nye, Jr., "US–Soviet Cooperation in a NonProliferation Regime" in Alexander Geroge (ed.) *US–Soviet Security Coopeartion* (Boulder Co: Westview Press, 1988).

5 Seymour M. Hersh, *The Price of Power: Kissinger in the Nixon White House*, 1983, p. 178.

6 Stated in his evidence before the Senate Committee. Quoted in Leslie Gelb, "The Atom is a Constant in U.S. Foreign Policy," *New York Times*, 3/14/1975.

7 For a detailed account, see Leonard Spector, *Nuclear Proliferation Today* (New York: Vintage Books, 1984).

8 See the article by Lawrence Scheinmann, "The Case for a Comprehensive U.S. Nonproliferation Policy" in C. S. Snyder, S. Wells (eds.) *Limiting Nuclear Proliferation* (Cambridge: Ballinger, 1985). For additional sources on American policy on nonproliferation during the 1970s, see *inter alia*, Joseph A. Yager (ed.) *Nonproliferation and United States Foreign Policy* (Washington: Brookings Institute, 1980); James E. Katz and Onkar S. Marwak, (eds.) *Nuclear Power in Developing Countries* (Lexington, MA: Lexington Books, 1982).

9 *Ibid*, in Lawrence Scheinmann.

10 See for example the article by Richard Burt, "U.S. Will Press Pakistan to Halt A-Arms Project," *New York Times*, 8/7/1979. Quoted in Spector, *op. cit.*, p. 84.

11 See for instance the White House statement of September 1982, in which it is emphasized that it is necessary to prevent "troublesome nations" from obtaining sensitive technologies. On this issue, see Caesar Merlini, "Nuclear Non-proliferation: After the Pause What?" *The International Spectator*, April–June 1984.

12 On the question of Reagan's policy, see the article by Robert Goheen, "Problems of Proliferation: U.S. Policy and the Third World," *World Politics*, Vol. 35, No. 2, 1983. Goheen distinguishes between a strategy of "control and denial"

and a strategy of "cooperation and persuasion." The latter strategy he identi-
fies with the Reagan administration.

13 See, for example, the reports in the *International Herald Tribune*, 11/7/1984;
Los Angeles Times, 12/4/1984.

14 There are many documents recording the disengagements between the two
countries regarding the nuclear issue. See, for example, the testimony of
Secretary of State Christian Herter before the Senate Foreign Relations Committee on January 6, 1961 (made public in April 1964). See *Historical Series of
the Senate Foreign Relations Committee*, Vol. XIII, Part 1, pp. 7–8. The nuclear
issue remained a constant major topic in many meetings between the Administration and Israeli officials. See, *inter alia*, conversation between Mordechai
Gazit, Consul, Israeli Embassy in Washington, and R.W. Komer, White House
on May 15, 1963 (Kennedy Library); meeting between then Secretary of State
and Abba Eban, then Israel's Minister of Education, on April 25, 1963
(Kennedy Library).

15 See "Framework and Tactics for Negotiations" attached to "Memorandum for
the President" of May 16, 1963, classified as "top secret" (Kennedy Library).

16 These Israeli demands appear in all the documents listed in footnotes 14
and 15.

18 This is based on the report given by Allon to the Israeli government. The
author was allowed to see the report.

17 See on America's positions vis-à-vis Israel's nuclear development *inter alia* in
Richard N. Haas, "South Asia: Too Late to Remove the Bomb."

19 See the testimony given by Richard Kennedy before the Senate committee, as
of 2/26/1987.

20 This division of Soviet policy into periods follows the article by William C.
Potter, "Soviet Nuclear Export Policy" in C. J. Snyder and S. Wells (eds.)
Limiting Nuclear Proliferation (Cambridge: Bullinger, 1985).

21 *Ibid.*, and Gloria Duffy, "Soviet Nuclear Exports," *International Security*, Vol. 3,
No. 1 (Summer 1978).

22 *Ibid.*

23 *Arms Control Today*, January 1985, p.11; Leonard Spector, *Nuclear Ambitions*
(New York: Vantage Books, 1984), p. 176.

24 Shai Feldman, *Israeli Nuclear Deterrence: A Strategy for the 1980s* (New York:
Columbia University Press, 1982).

25 On these developments see Steven E. Miller, *op. cit.*

26 *Ibid.*

27 See on this *inter alia*, *Newsbrief*, No. 19 (Programme for Promoting Nuclear
Non-Proliferation, University of Southampton) Autumn 1992, p. 11.

28 One estimate puts Russian U–235 stockpile as high as 1050 metric tons, while
PU–239 stockpiles are estimated to be in the range of 150 metric tons. See
ibid., p. 9.

29 *Ibid.*

30 See Benjamin Frankel, "An Anxious Decade: Nuclear Proliferation in the
1990s" in B. Frankel (ed.) *Opaque Nuclear Proliferation: Methodology and Policy
Implications* (London: Frank Cass, 1991) and *idem*, "The Brooding Shadow:
Structural Changes and Nuclear Proliferation" (forthcoming). But for a bal-
anced view about inbuilt restraints to proliferation see George Quester,
"Nuclear Proliferation and the Elimination of Nuclear Weapons," in Regina
Karp (ed.) *Security Without Nuclear Weapons?* (Oxford: Oxford University Press,
1992).

31 The most extreme formulation of this approach is, of course, Francis

Fukuyama, "The End of History," *The National Interest,* No. 16 (Summer 1989). For an interesting current assessment of global trends, see "A New World Order," *The Economist,* 9/28/1991–10/9/1991. For various discussions of different aspects of the emerging of new, more cooperative and peaceful rules of behavior in the international system which would substitute for the current ones, see Brian Urqhart, "The UN: From Peace-Keeping to Collective Security," Chan Hung Chee, "The UN: From Peace-Keeping to Peace-Making?" both in *Adelphi Papers* No. 265 (Winter 1991/92); Adam Roberts, "International Law and the Use of Force," and Richard Gardner, "International Law and the Use of Force," both in *Adelphi Papers* No. 266, (Winter 1991/92); Richard Gardner, "Practical Internationalism"; John Barton, Barry Carter, "The Uneven but Growing, role of International Law"; and Michael Doyle, "An International Liberal Community," all in Graham Allison and Gregory Treverton (eds.) *Beyond Cold War to New World Order.* See also Michael Doyle, "Kant, Liberal Legacies and Foreign Affairs," *Philosophy and Public Affairs,* Vol. 12 (Summer 1983).

32 John Mearsheimer, "Back to the Future: Instability in Europe After the Cold War,"*International Security,* Vol. 15, No. 1 (Summer 1990). For a theoretical discussion on the likelihood of proliferation in the post bipolar system, see Kenneth Waltz, "The Emerging Structure of International Politics" (unpublished manuscript presented APSA Meeting, August 1990).

33 For a clear and sound argumentation why nonproliferation should serve as a major American national interest in the post Cold War era, see Robert Art, "A Defensible Defense: America's Grand Strategy After the Cold War," *International Security,* Vol. 15, No. 4 (Spring 1991).

34 See *Newsbrief* (Program for Promoting Nuclear Non-Proliferation) No. 19, Autumn 1992.

35 *Ibid.,* p. 3.

36 See President Bush's speech at the Air Force Academy, Colorado Springs, May 29, 1991.

37 See the Report of the UN Secretary General, *Establishment of a Nuclear-Weapon-Free Zone in the Region of the Middle East* (A/45/435, October 10, 1990).

38 For these activities in Iraq during 1991, see the *Second Report by the Special Commission on Council Resolution 687.* For activities of the UN Commission during 1992, see *Newsbrief* (Program for Promoting Nuclear Non-Proliferation), Colorado Springs, Summer and Autumn 1992.

39 *Ibid.,* Spring 1992, p. 12.

40 See Shai Feldman *op. cit.,* pp. 211–233.

41 *Ibid.,* pp. 230–235.

42 *Ibid.,* p. 178.

5 MANAGEMENT OF A NUCLEAR MIDDLE EAST

1 One of the main criticisms of the initial assumptions of deterrence theory is that it focused primarily on the calculus and motivations of the deterrer, and ignored the calculus of the challenger. For the challenger, however, an intense political grievance may become an overriding consideration. This is one of the points elaborated upon in R. Jervis, N. Lebow and J. Stein (eds) *Psychology and Deterrence* (Baltimore: Johns Hopkins University Press, 1985). The same point has been referred to by earlier and subsequent writers, including both theorists of deterrence as well as some of its critics.

2 See Shai Feldman's *Israeli Nuclear Deterrence: A Strategy for the 1980s* (New York: Columbia University Press, 1982).

3 For further discussion of the security implications of such a plan, see Y. Evron, *Israeli–Palestinian–Jordanian Security Relations: The Idea of a Security Zone*, (Cambridge, MA; Emerging Issues, Occasional Papers of the American Academy of Arts and Sciences, 1990).

4 See a discussion of this issue in my *War and Intervention in Lebanon: The Israeli–Syrian Deterrence Dialogue* (London: Croom Helm and Baltimore: Johns Hopkins University Press, 1987).

5 See Stanley Hoffman's "Nuclear Proliferation and World Politics" in A. Buchan (ed.) *A World of Nuclear Powers* (Englewood Cliffs, NJ: Prentice Hall, 1966).

6 During the Cold War the two superpowers did in fact coordinate in crisis management in the Middle East. Their cooperation however, was limited and tacit. Moreover, simultaneously with management strategies they tried to utilize the regional crises in order to advance their respective competing objectives. See Yair Evron "Great Powers Military Intervention in the Middle East." On "crises prevention" between the superpowers see *inter alia* Alexander George, "Crisis Prevention reexamined," in his *Managing U.S.–Soviet Rivalry: Problems of Crisis Prevention* (Boulder, Co: Westview Press, 1983), and Part V of Alexander George, Philip Farley, Alexander Dallin *US–Soviet Security Cooperation* (Boulder, CO: Westview Press, 1988). International events have of course gone far beyond the policy recommendations included in the latter works. In the post Cold War era we may move into a systemic situation to which the concept of "concert" of great powers is more applicable.

7 See, for example, some of the ideas included in Richard Betts, "A Joint Nuclear Risk Control Center," 1985.

8 See John Weltman, "Nuclear Devolution and World Order," *World Politics*, Vol. 32, No. 2 (Jan. 1980) on the idea of transferring "stabilizing" nuclear weapons. Lewis Dunn, in *Containing Nuclear Proliferation*, Adelphi Papers No. 263 (London: International Institute for Strategic Studies, 1991), proposes similar ideas in addition to advise on how to develop doctrines for stable nuclear relations. But he also points out the difficulties in some of these ideas.

9 These arguments had essentially been developed in my book *Israel's Nuclear Dilemma* (in Hebrew) 1987; and cf. Lewis Dunn, *op. cit.*

10 The precedents created in the Helsinki and Stockholm Conferences on Confidence- and Security-Building Measures may serve as one source of inspiration for similar measures in the Middle East; the other source being precedents in the Middle East itself. There are, of course, major differences between the European and Middle Eastern environments.

11 For discussions of the possible role of CBM in the Arab–Israeli context, see Geoffrey Kemp, "The Middle East Arms Race: Can it be Controlled?," *Middle East Journal*, Vol. 45, No. 3, Summer 1991; Thomas Hirschfeld, "Mutual Security Short of Arms Control," and Yair Evron, "Confidence Building in the Middle East," in Dore Gold, (ed.) *Arms Control in the Middle East* (Tel Aviv: Jaffee Center for Strategic Studies, 1990). In the second work, there is also a discussion of some historical examples of CBMs which had been tacitly accepted by conflicting states in the Middle East.

12 See Paul Bracken's *The Command and Control of Nuclear Forces* (New Haven: Yale University Press, 1983).

13 There are already several examples of the immense pressures on decision-makers in the realm of air-battles, both at the operative and tactical levels. Those pressures have led to mistakes in the Israeli command system. One

example was the interception of the Libyan passenger carrier in 1973, and another was the downing of two Syrian interceptors in 1985. In both cases the mistakes resulted from time pressures in a situation of profound uncertainty, against the background knowledge of the possible high costs involved in not shooting first.

14 See Yair Evron, "Confidence Building in the Middle East," *op. cit.*, and Yair Evron, *War and Intervention in Lebanon: The Israeli–Syrian Deterrence Dialogue* (London: Croom Helm and Baltimore: Johns Hopkins University Press, 1987).

15 For an extensive discussion of this point, see Chapter 7.

6 THE NUCLEAR DIMENSION OF THE GULF CRISIS AND WAR

1 This account is based primarily on Marvin Miller, *The Iraqi Nuclear Program* (typed memorandum, July 31, 1991). The Miller memorandum describes already the three enrichment routes which Iraq adopted and the findings of the first three IAEA inspection teams. Other sources which by now are dated but nevertheless useful, are: Leonard Spector and Jacqueline Smith, *Nuclear Ambitions*, (Cambridge: Ballinger, 1990) Avner Cohen and Marvin Miller, *Nuclear Shadows in the Middle East*, (Cambridge: DAC, MIT, December 1990); David Albright and Mark Hibbs, "Iraq and the Bomb: Were They Even Close?" *The Bulletin of the Atomic Scientists*, No. 1, 1991 and their "Hyping the Iraqi Bomb," *The Bulletin of the Atomic Scientists*, No. 1, 1991.

2 See, in particular, David Albright and Mark Hibbs, *ibid.*

3 Thus Marvin Miller, *op. cit.*, estimated that each one of the EMIS plants (two were in the process of being built) would have cost several billion dollars.

4 See, for example, Albright and Hibbs, *op. cit.*

5 See Marvin Miller, Note 3, *op. cit.*

6 Many newspaper reports beginning in mid 1990 pointed out that involvement.

7 See, for example, Avner Cohen and Marvin Miller, Note 1, *op. cit.*

8 See Marvin Miller, Note 1, *op. cit.*

9 See Miller, *Ibid.*

10 *Ibid.*

11 *Ibid.*

12 There are two types of nuclear fission weapons that use U-235: first, the more primitive "gun" model, which requires at least 50 kilograms of enriched uranium as a critical mass. The second is the "implosion" type which can use either plutonium or enriched uranium. This more sophisticated type requires only about 20 kilograms of enriched uranium. Advances in nuclear-weapons technology since 1945 make it possible to assemble bombs using less enriched uranium. From documents apprehended by the IAEA team in Iraq it appears that Iraqi scientists have already been working on the design of an implosion bomb before the Gulf War broke out.

13 See *Al-Usbu Al-Arabi* 10/17/1977.

14 Saddam Hussein's speech was reproduced by the Iraqi News Agency on June 23, 1981.

15 For example *Al-Jumhuriyya* 4/3/1989 and *Al-Thawra*, 4/15/1989.

16 *Al-Jumhuriyya* 6/7/1989.

17 An Iraqi upgrading of the Soviet *Scud* B. Whereas the scud, carrying a warhead of approximately one ton, has a range of 300 kilometers, the *al-Hussein* version has a longer range—600 kilometers—but carries a warhead of approximately 250 kilograms of explosives.

18 See Spector and Smith, *op. cit.*, *Nuclear Ambitions*, pp. 192–193.

19 For accounts of the use of surface-to-surface missiles during the Iran–Iraq War see Thomas McNaughton "Missiles and Chemical Weapons: The Legacy of the Iran–Iraq War," *International Security*, Vol. 5, No. 2 (Fall 1990); Seth Carus, "Missiles in the Middle East,." *Policy Focus* (Washington, 1988).

20 See, for example, James A. Markham, "Arabs Link Curbs on Gas and A-Arms," (*The New York Times*, January 9, 1989).

21 See, for example, the warnings by Israeli officials referred to by Glenn Frankel, "Iraq said Developing A-Weapons" (*The Washington Post*, March 31, 1989). See also "Government Reacts to Iraqi Missile Threat: Called Serious Matter," (*Ma'ariv*, December 8, 1989).

22 See Cohen and Miller, *op. cit.*, pp. 6–7, quoting "Press comments on 1981 Israeli raid on Reactor," Baghdad INA (in English) JPRS–TND–89–013, *Nuclear Developments*, June 28, 1989, p. 19.

23 This was published in *Al-Jumhuriyya*, 1/6/1990.

24 See Cohen & Miller, *op. cit.*, p. 7. This was first reported in March 1990.

25 The speech was recorded by Baghdad Domestic Service in Arabic 1030 GMT, April 2, 1990. For the full text see Ofra Bengio, *Saddam Speaks on the Gulf Crisis*, (Tel Aviv: The Dayan Center for Middle Eastern and African Studies, 1992).

26 See Allan Cowell, "Egypt Says Israel Vows No First Strike" (*New York Times*, May 20, 1990); Ze'ev Schiff, "The Power of Silence" (*Ha'aretz*, July 6, 1990); and "The Weight of Miscalculation" (*Ha'aretz*, July 13, 1990).

27 See Saddam Hussein's address to a group of U.S. Senators, 12 April 1990. Ofra Bengio, *op. cit.*, pp. 71–84.

28 Interview with Dianne Sawyer, *ABC*, June 1990.

29 *Ibid.*

30 See note 14.

31 See *The Middle East Military Balance, 1989–1990.*

32 On the Iraqi situation following the Iran–Iraq War see *inter alia* Roland Dannrenther, *The Gulf conflict: A Political and Strategic Analysis* (London: The International Institute for Strategic Studies, Winter 1991/1992). The nuclear program by itself has been estimated to have cost 5–10 billion dollars.

33 The Iraqi defense budget during the year previous to the invasion of Kuwait has been estimated to run as high as 12.5 trillion dollars. See the Pentagon Report, p. 3. The overall GNP of Iraq in 1990 was about 55 billion dollars.

34 Iraq's main weakness lies in the lack of societal cohesion. Cleavages between Sunnis, Shi'is and Kurds are deep and in times of crisis threaten to break the unity of the state.

35 For a good analysis of Iraq's decision to invade Iran see Sharam Chubin and Charles Tripp, *Iran and Iraq at War* (London: K.I.B. Taurus, 1988).

36 For one analysis of this, see Samir al-Khalil, *The Republic of Fear: Saddam's Iraq* (London: Hutchinson Radius, 1989).

37 For a useful analysis of developments in the Arab world and Iraq's role in them during that period and up to the Gulf Crisis and War see Bruce Maddy-Weitzman, *The Inter-Arab System and the Gulf War: Continuity and Change* (Atlanta: The Carter Center of Emory University, 1991).

38 For the text of Saddam speeches at the ACC meeting and at the summit conference see Ofra Bengio, op. cit., pp. 34–49 and 84–98. For analysis of these conferences see, *inter alia*, Maddy-Weitzman, *op. cit.*, and Roland Dannreuther, *op. cit.*, f.n. 29.

39 See Ofra Bengio, *op. cit.*, p. 20 for references to Saddam's speeches in regard to Israel during late April, May and June 1990.

40 FBIS NCS 90–118, *Daily Report,* June 19, 1990, p. 21.

41 Saddam's attacks on the Gulf countries began already in early 1990. For analyses of the Iraqi strategy see *inter alia* Roland Dannrenther, *op. cit.* Bruce Maddy-Weitzman, *op. cit,* Lawrence Freedman and Ephraim Karsh, *The Gulf War* (Princeton, N.J.: Princeton University Press, 1993).

42 On Iraq's claim for Kuwait see Richard Schofield, *Kuwait and Iraq: Historical Claims and Territorial Disputes* (London: Royal Institute of International Affairs, 1991). For an analysis refuting the historical and ethnic claims of Iraq, see Uriel Dann "The Iraqi Invasion of Kuwait: Historical Observations," The Dayem Center for Middle Eastern and African Studies, Tel Aviv University, August 1990.

43 For a discussion of the Iraqi threats during that period, see Amatzia Baram, "Iraq Imaging and Success of Non-Conventional Deterrence vis-à-vis Israel" (Paper presented at *Conference on Deterrence in the Middle East,* United States Institution of Peace, June 1991).

44 See David E. Sanger, "Hussein Warns He'll Attack Saudis and Israelis if Iraq is Strangled by Embargo" (*New York Times,* September 24, 1990); and see Amatzia Baram, *op. cit.*, pp. 24–25.

45 See *IHT,* January 8, 1991.

46 This obvious objective was recognized as such in Israel during the war and played a central role in the Israeli decision *not* to retaliate. And cf. Shai Feldman, "Israeli Deterrence and the Gulf War" (Paper presented at *Conference on Deterrence in the Middle East,* United States Institute of Peace, June 1991).

47 See, for example, Ze'ev Schiff, "Take Him Seriously" (*Ha'aretz,* November 2, 1990).

48 See, for example, *The Economist,* 9/20/1990.

49 Prime Minister Shamir in interview on Israeli television, as quoted in *Ha'aretz* (August 13, 1990).

50 See, for example, the advice given by Aharon Yariv in an interview in *Ha'aretz* (January 7, 1991).

51 Cf. Shai Feldman, *op. cit.*

52 *Ibid.*

53 See clear reference to it in Chief-of-Staff Dan Shomron interview in *Davar* (2 August 1991).

54 Shai Feldman, *op. cit.*

55 Shai Feldman, *op. cit.*

56 I personally heard from State Department officials that such a warning had been communicated directly to Saddam Hussein during the war.

57 Another demonstration of the increase in the saliency of the nuclear issue could be found in a public opinion poll conducted immediately after the Gulf War (late March 1991). In contrast to previous polls (mentioned in Chapter 1), 88 percent of those asked saw circumstances which would justify the use of nuclear weapons by Israel (assuming Israel had them). Most of these thought it was appropriate to use nuclear weapons in response to a nuclear attack or chemical and biological attacks. Only about 50 percent supported such use in a desperate situation or in order to save a large number of casualties. Only a small percentage supported such a use in order to save a small number of casualties or instead of the use of conventional weapons. See Asher Arian, "Security and Political Attitudes," in JCSS Study Group, *War in*

the Gulf: Implications for Israel (Tel Aviv: Jaffee Center for Strategic Studies, Tel Aviv University, 1991).

7 ISRAEL'S STRATEGIC ALTERNATIVES

1 The complexities of power ratios are fully discussed in the literature. On the requirement for the classical 3:1 ratio in favor of the assaulting side, at least in the attack sector, see for example, John Mearsheimer, *Conventional Deterrence* (Ithaca and London: Cornell University Press, 1983), and David Eggenberger, *A Dictionary of Battle* (New York: Thomas Crowell, 1967). This is the basis of current American military doctrine. On this matter, see the official U.S. Army publication, *Operations: FM 100–5*. A side's ability to achieve a superior power ratio in the assault sector, despite equilibrium across the overall front, depends, of course, on the planning and strategic and operative capabilities of the two parties to the battle. Frequently, the attacker is able to achieve a breakthrough in the assault sector despite an equality of forces By contrast, the defensive side is sometimes able to stop the attacking force, even when the power ratio is far less favorable than 3:1. Thus, for example, the German army successfully withstood Soviet assaults when the power ratio was much worse than 3:1. In fact, the German army was able to maintain its defense lines on the Soviet front, while delivering successful counterattacks under conditions of 8:1 in favor of the Soviets.

Another crucial factor is the strategic doctrine employed by the adversaries. Equipped with a superior strategy, the German army was capable of defeating the French and British armies in France in 1940 while having, in fact, fewer tanks. For a detailed account stressing the central importance of strategy, see Barry Posen *The Sources of Military Doctrine: France, Britain and Germany between the World Wars* (Ithaca: Cornell University Press, 1984). Another argument has been that the side that initiates aggressive action, particularly in chance encounters, has a certain advantage. See Simcha Maoz, "Power Ratios, Aggression and Chances for Victory in Battle", *Ma'arachot*, No. 225 (September 1972). On the issue of power ratios, see also the various articles in the collection edited by Zvi Ofer and Avi Kover, *Quality and Quantity: Dilemmas in Building a Military Force* (in Hebrew) (Tel Aviv: Ma'arachot, 1985).

2 *The Middle East Miltary Balance, 1990–1991*, Table 1. The following analysis is based on details presented in various places in the referenced book, and in previous annual editions of this publication.

3 In addition, there are five armored and mechanized independent brigades in the Arab armies referred to.

4 For an interesting discussion of the pros and cons of an adoption of a defensive strategy for Israel on the Syrian front, see Ariel Levite, *Offense and Defense in Israeli Military Doctrine.*

5 *The Military Balance in the Middle East*, 1983, p. 253 (Hebrew), and see also Avraham Adan, *Quality and Quantity in the Yom Kippur War* (in Hebrew).

6 This refers to armored and mechanized divisions, and also includes independent brigades, every three of which is counted here as a division.

7 This was evident, for example, in the contributions by Egyptian participants at the meeting held in Cairo in December 1990 by the Middle East Security Group under the auspices of the American Academy of Arts and Sciences.

8 For the position of the moderate opposition to Sadat's initiative see, for example, Ismail Fahmy, *Negotiating for Peace in the Middle East* (London: Croom Helm, 1983). For the position of the extreme Islamic groups see the in-depth

discussion of Immanuel Sivan, *Zealots of Islam* (in Hebrew) (Tel Aviv: Am Oved, 1986). See also Oded Granot and Jack Reineich, *The Day Sadat was Killed* (in Hebrew) (Tel Aviv: Ma'ariv, 1984).

9 See, among others, Shimon Shamir, *Egypt under Sadat's Leadership* (in Hebrew) (Tel Aviv: Dvir, 1978); Israel Gershoni, *The Revival of Islam as a Catalyst in the Rise of Abrabism* (in Hebrew) (Tel Aviv: Shiloh Center for Middle East and African Studies, Tel Aviv University, 1979); P. T. Vatikiotis, *The Modern History of Egypt* (London: Weidenfeld and Nicolson, 1969).

10 Gershoni, *op. cit.*, p. 4.

11 See for example, Adeed Dawisha, *Egypt in the Arab World* (London: 1976); Leonard Binder, *The Ideological Revolution in the Middle East* (New York: 1964). Gershoni, *op. cit.*, also points to the ideological-idealistic basis for this change in national identity in Egypt.

12 See Shimon Shamir, *op. cit.*, and Gershoni, *op. cit.*

13 For more detail on this point, see Yair Evron, *The Demilitarization of Sinai* (Jerusalem: The Leonard Institute for International Relations, The Hebrew University of Jerusalem, 1975); Yair Evron, *The Role of Arms Control in the Middle East* (London: International Institute for Strategic Studies, 1977).

14 The following discussion assumes that a settlement of the West Bank and Gaza Strip issues would be achieved only on the basis of Jordanian involvement. The most likely political scenario is that of an eventual Israeli withdrawal leading to the establishment of a Jordanian–Palestinian confederation.

15 On this, see Aryeh Shalev, *The Defense Line in Judea and Samaria* (in Hebrew), (Tel Aviv: Hakibutz Hameuchad, 1982).

16 For a comprehensive study of the early connections between Israel and Jordan see Avi Shlaim, *Collusion across the Jordan*; for another study covering a longer period see Dan Shiftan, *A Jordanian Option: Israel, Jordan and the Palestinians* (in Hebrew) (Tel Aviv: Yad Tabenkin and Hakibutz Hameuchad, 1986). For an in-depth study of the context of Israeli–Jordanian relations, see Aharon Klieman, *Coexistence without Peace*, (in Hebrew) (Tel Aviv: Ma'ariv, 1987).

17 For the discussions in Israel on this subject, see Michael Bar-Zohar, *Ben-Gurion* (Tel Aviv: Am Oved, 1971), pp. 1334–1335.

18 For further elaboration of such an agreement, see Yair Evron, *Israeli–Palestinian–Jordanian Security Relations: The Idea of a Security Zone*, (Cambridge, MA: Occasional Papers of the American Academy of Arts and Sciences, 1990).

19 On this, see Ezer Weitzman, *The Battle for Peace* (in Hebrew, (Jerusalem: Edanim, 1980).

20 Feldman, *op. cit.*

21 For an early discussion of these uses see Y. Evron, "Israel and the Atom: The Uses and Misuses of Ambiguity, 1957–1967," *Orbis*, Vol. 17, No. 4 (winter 1974).

22 Conversation with Mordechai Gazit, who served during parts of the 1960s and the 1970s, as Director General of the Foreign Ministry and at other times as Director General of the Prime Minister's Office.

23 See, for example, William Quandt, *Decade of Decisions*, (Berkeley and London: University of California Press, 1977).

24 See Yair Evron, *op. cit.*, 1974.

25 This has been suggested by various Palestinians in international conferences on security in the Middle East. For example, in some of the conferences on security and arms control in the Middle East, organized by the American Academy of Arts and Sciences, in Cambridge, MA, during 1989–1991, as well

as in two conferences on arms control in the Middle East held under the auspices of the Quakers United Nations Office in Switzerland during 1991.

26 See Thomas Schelling, *Arms and Influence* (New Haven: Yale University Press, 1972); Alexander George, David Hall, William Simon, *The Limits of Coercive Diplomacy* (Boston: Little Brown, 1971).

27 Thus, the American compellent threats against Iraq during the Gulf Crisis aimed at forcing Iraq to withdraw from Kuwait, failed completely.

28 For a discussion of this use see Y. Evron, "Israel", in Regina Cowen Karp (ed.), *Security with Nuclear Weapons? Different Perspectives on National Security* (Oxford: Oxford University Press, 1991).

29 See for example Meir Stieglitz, "Israel's Nuclear Doctrine: The Amount of Necessary Evil" (in Hebrew) *Politika*, No. 13 (March–April 1987).

30 Cf. the discussion in Frank Barnaby, *The Invisible Bomb: The Nuclear Arms Race in the Middle East* (London: I. B. Tauris, 1989), pp. 64–66.

31 On the implications of the introduction of SSM, see, *inter alia*, Martin Havias, *Missile Proliferation in the Middle East*, Adelphi Paper No. 252, (London's International Institute for Strategic Studies, summer 1990).

32 During the Gulf War, Rabin discussed the issue in a meeting of Labor members of Knesset. He reportedly mentioned the Syrian SSM threat and reminded his audience of the Israeli deterrent threats communicated to Damascus in the late 1980s. See Dan Margalit, "Rabin: 'For Israel This Is a Deluxe War; the Next Ones Will Be More Painful" ' (*Ha'aretz*, February 19, 1991).

33 *Ibid.*

34 *Ibid.*

35 On Syrian strategy, see *inter alia*, Ahmed Khalidi and H. J. Agha, "The Syrian Doctrine of Strategic Parity" (1990); On Syria's perceptions of her security concerns, see Bassma Kodmani-Darwish, "Security in the Middle East as Viewed from Syria" (Paper presented to the conference on a *New Security Order for the Middle East* (Almeria 1991). For a solid Israeli assessment of Syria's strategic objectives, see Dov Tamari, "The Syrian–Israeli Balance of Forces and Strategic Parity" in Joseph Alpher, Zeev Eitan, Dov Tamari (eds.) *The Middle East Military Balance 1989–1990* (Tel Aviv: Tel Aviv University, 1990).

36 For discussions of chemical arms and their effects, see, *inter alia*, Mathew Meselson, "The Role of Chemical Defense in Chemical Warfare: Chemical Deterrence and Chemical Disarmament," Working Paper delivered for Paguash Meeting No. 181, El Escoval, August 1991; see also Peter Herby, *The Chemical Weapons Convention and Arms Control in the Middle East* (Oslo: International Peace Research Institute, 1992, pp. 17–20).

37 And see, *inter alia*, the discussion in Carl Kaysen, Robert McNamara, and George Rathjens, "Nuclear Weapons After the Cold War", *Foreign Affairs*, Vol. 70, No. 4 (Fall 1991).

38 Indeed, during the Gulf War, Israel apparently planned such ground operations. These were, however, called off because of the considerations discussed in Chapter 6. See interview with the retired commander of the Israeli Air Force Avihu Ben-Nun, *Yedioth Aharonot* (December 25, 1991).

39 The Israeli condition for ratifying the chemical weapons convention is that the Arab states join as well.

40 See interview with Moshe Arens (*Ma'ariv*, March 8, 1991).

41 See *Divrei Haknesset*, first session of the 13th Knesset, July 13, 1992, pp. 9–10.

42 For in-depth studies of an American–Israeli defense treaty see Yair Evron, *An American–Israeli Defense Treaty*, 1981; and Yair Evron, "Some Political and Strategic Implications of an American–Israeli Defense Treaty", 1980.

43 For a description of the evolvement of the Israeli official position, see Shalhevet Freier, "The Nuclear Non-Proliferation Policy of Israel" (August 1991) to be published in the collection in honor of Jorma K. Miettineu); Ran Marom, *Israel's Position on Non-Proliferation* (Jerusalem: The Leonard Davis Institute of International Relations, 1986). See also, Mahmoud Karem, *A Nuclear Weapon Free Zone in the Middle East.*

44 See Karem, *ibid.*

45 For example, in several international academic conferences on arms control in the Middle East which were held during 1991.

46 This was disclosed by Cyrus Vance at a meeting at Tel Aviv University in February 1992 when he visited Israel following a visit to Damascus.

47 And see also Chapter 4.

48 See President Bush's speech at the Air Force Academy, Colorado Springs, May 29, 1991.

49 See the Report of the UN Secretary General, *Establishment of a Nuclear-Weapon-Free Zone in the Region of the Middle East* (A/45/435, October 10, 1990).

50 And see the ideas contained in Avner Cohen and Marvin Miller, "Facing the Unavoidable: Israel's Nuclear Monopoly Revisited."

BIBLIOGRAPHY

BOOKS AND MONOGRAPHS

Adan, Avraham, *Al Shtei Gdot HaSuez* (in Hebrew) (On Both Banks of the Suez) (Jerusalem: Edanim, 1979).

al-Khalil, Samir, *The Republic of Fear: Saddam's Iraq* (London: Hutchinson Radius, 1989).

Allison, Graham and Treverton, Gregory (eds.), *Rethinking America's Security: Beyond Cold War to New World Order* (London: W. W. Norton, 1992).

Allon Yigal, *Masach Shel Chol* (in Hebrew) (Curtain of Sand) (Tel Aviv: Hakibutz Hameuchad, 1984).

Alpher, Joseph, Eitan, Ze'ev and Tamari, Dov (eds.) *The Middle East Military Balance 1989–1990* (Tel Aviv: Tel Aviv University, 1990).

Arian, Asher (ed.) *Israel–A Developing Society* (Netherlands: Van Gorcum, 1980).

Arian, Asher, Talmud, Ilan and Herman, Tamar, *National Security and Public Opinion in Israel* (Tel Aviv: Jaffee Center for Strategic Studies, Tel Aviv University, 1988).

Aron, Raymond, *The Modern Strategists: Problems of Modern Strategy*, Adelphi Papers No. 54 (London: International Institute for Strategic Studies, 1968).

Aronson, Shlomo, *Conflict and Bargaining in the Middle East* (Baltimore: Johns Hopkins University Press, 1978).

el Badri, Hasan, el-Magdoub, Taha and el-Din Zhody, Muhammad Dian, *The Ramadan War* (Dunn Loming, VA: T. N. Dupuy Associates, 1978).

Barnaby, Frank, *The Invisible Bomb: The Nuclear Arms Race in the Middle East* (London: I. B. Tauris, 1989).

Bar-Simantov, Yaacov, *Linkage Politics in the Middle East: Syria Between Domestic and External Conflict 1961–1970* (Boulder, CO: Westview, 1983).

——, *The Israeli–Egyptian War of Attrition* (New York: Columbia University Press, 1980).

Bar-Tov Hanoch, *Arbaim Veshmone Shaot veod Esrim Yom* (in Hebrew) (48 Hours and another 20 Days) (Tel Aviv: Ma'ariv, 1978).

Bar-Zohar, Michael, *Ben-Gurion* (Tel Aviv: Am Oved, 1977).

Beaton, Leonard and Maddox, John, *The Spread of Nuclear Weapons* (London: Chatto and Windus, 1962).

Ben-Dor, Gabriel, *State and Conflict in the Middle East* (New York: Praeger, 1983).

Bengio, Ofra, *Saddam Speaks on the Gulf Crisis* (Tel Aviv: The Dayan Center for Middle Eastern and African Studies, 1992).

Ben Horin, Yoav, Posen, Barry, *Israel's Strategic Doctrine* (Santa Monica: Rand Corporation R–2845-NA, September 1981).

Beres, Louis Rene, *Apocalypse: Nuclear Catastrophe in World Politics* (Chicago: Chicago University Press, 1980).

——, (ed.) *Security or Armageddon: Israel's Nuclear Strategy* (Lexington, M.A.: Lexington Books, 1986).

Bertram, Christoph (ed.), *The Future of Strategic Deterrence* (London: Macmillan, 1981).

Binder, Leonard, *The Ideological Evolution in the Middle East* (New York: 1964).

Blechman, Barry N. (ed.), *Preventing Nuclear War*, (Bloomington: Indiana University Press, 1985).

Bracken, Paul, *The Command and Control of Nuclear Forces* (New Haven: Yale University Press, 1983).

Brecher, Michael, *The Foreign Policy System of Israel* (London: Oxford University Press, 1972).

——, *Decisions in Israel's Foreign Policy* (London: Oxford University Press, 1974).

—— with Geist, Benjamin, *Decisions in Crisis: Israel, 1967, 1973* (Berkeley: University of California Press, 1980).

Brodie, Bernard (ed.), *The Absolute Weapon: Atomic Power and World Order* (New York: Harcourt Brace, 1946).

Buchan, Alastair (ed.), *A World of Nuclear Powers?* (Englewood Cliffs, NJ: Prentice Hall, 1966).

Bundy, McGeorge, *Danger and Survival: Choices About the Bomb* (New York: Vintage Books, 1990).

Buzan, Barry, *People, States and Fear: The National Security Problem in International Relations* (Chapel Hill, NC: University of North Carolina Press, 1983).

Cantori, Leonard and Spiegel, Steven, *The International Politics of Regions* (Englewood Cliffs, NJ: Prentice Hall, 1970).

Carnesale, Albert and Haas, Richard (eds.), *Superpower Arms Control: Setting the Record Straight* (Cambridge: Ballinger, 1987).

Chubin, Sharam and Tripp, Charles, *Iran and Iraq at War* (London: K.I.B. Tauris, 1988).

Cochran, Thomas, Arkin, William M., Hoening, Milton, *US Nuclear Forces and Capabilities* Vol. I (Cambridge, MA: Ballinger, 1984).

Cohen, Avner and Miller, Marvin, *Nuclear Shadows in the Middle East* (Cambridge: DAC, MIT, December 1990).

Dannreuther, Roland, *The Gulf Conflict: A Political and Strategic Analysis*, Adelphi Papers, No. 264 (London: The International Institute for Strategic Studies, winter 1991/92).

Dawisha, Adeed, *Egypt in the Arab World* (London: 1976).

Dayan, Moshe, *Avnei Derech* (in Hebrew) (Story of My Life) (Jerusalem: Edanim, 1976).

De Gaulle, Charles, *Renewal and Endeavor* (New York: Simon and Schuster, 1971).

Draper, Theodor, *Israel and World Politics: Roots of the Third Arab–Israeli War* (New York: Viking Press, 1968).

Dunn, Lewis, *Controlling the Bomb: Nuclear Proliferation in the 1980s* (New Haven and London: Yale University Press, 1982).

——, *Containing Nuclear Proliferation*, Adelphi Papers No. 263 (London: International Institute for Strategic Studies, 1991).

Eggenberger, David, *A Dictionary of Battle* (New York: Thomas Crowell, 1967).

Eisenstadt, Michael, *Arming for Peace? Syria's Elusive Quest for Strategic Parity* (Washington, D.C.: The Washington Institute for Near East Policy, 1992).

Evron, Yair, *The Middle East: Nations, Superpowers and Wars* (London and New York: Elek and Praeger, 1973).

——, *The Demilitarization of Sanai*, Jerusalem Papers on Peace No. 16 (Jerusalem: The Leonard Institute for International Relations, The Hebrew University of Jerusalem, 1975).

——, *The Role of Arms Control in the Middle East*, Adelphi Papers No. 138 (London: International Institute for Strategic Studies, 1977).

—— (ed.), *International Violence: Terrorism Surprise and Control* (Jerusalem: Leonard Davis Institute for International Relations, 1979).

——, *An American–Israeli Defense Treaty*, (1981).

——, *War and Intervention in Lebanon: The Israeli-Syrian Deterrence Dialogue* (London: Croom Helm; and Baltimore: Johns Hopkins University Press, 1987).

——, *Israeli–Palestinian–Jordanian Security Relations: The Idea of a Security Zone* (Cambridge: Emerging Issues, Occasional Papers of the American Academy of Arts and Sciences, 1990).

Fahmy, Ismail, *Negotiating for Peace in the Middle East* (London: Croom Helm, 1983).

Feldman, Shai, *Israeli Nuclear Deterrence: A Strategy for the 1980s* (New York: Columbia University Press, 1982).

——, *Harta'a Garinit Le Israel* (in Hebrew) (Israel Nuclear Deterrence) (Tel Aviv: Hakibutz Hameuchad, 1983).

Frankel, Benjamin (ed.), *Opaque Nuclear Proliferation: Methodological and Policy Implications* (London: Frank Cass, 1991).

Freedman, Lawrence, *Britain and Nuclear Weapons* (London: Macmillan Press, 1980).

——, *The Evolution of Nuclear Strategy* (London: Macmillan Press, 1981).

——, and Karsh, Ephraim, *The Gulf War* (Princeton, N.J.: Princeton University Press, 1993).

Frei, Daniel, *Risks of Unintentional Nuclear War* (Totowa, NJ: Rowman and Allanbeld, 1983).

Gallois, Pierre, *The Balance of Terror: Strategy for the Nuclear Age* (Boston: Houghton Mifflin, 1961).

Geist, Benjamin, *The Six Day War: A Study in the Setting and the Process of Foreign Policy Decision Making Under Crisis Conditions* (Ph.D. Thesis, Hebrew University of Jerusalem, 1974).

Gelber, Yoav, *Lama Pirko Et Hapalmach?* (in Hebrew) (Why the "Palmach" was Dissolved?) (Jerusalem: Soken, 1986).

George, Alexander, *Managing US–Soviet Rivalry: Problems of Crisis Prevention* (Boulder, Colorado: Westview Press, 1983).

——, Hall, David, Simons, William, *The Limits of Coercive Diplomacy* (Boston: Little Brown, 1971).

——, Smoke, Richard, *Deterrence in American Foreign Policy: Theory and Practice* (New York: Columbia University Press, 1974).

——, Farley Philip, Dallin Alexander, *US–Soviet Security Cooperation* (Boulder, CO: Westview Press, 1988).

Gershoni Israel, *Tchiat Ha'Islam Kemanof Le'alyat Haraviot* (in Hebrew) (The Revival of Islam as a Catalyst in the Rise of Arabism) (Tel Aviv: Shiloh Center for Middle East and African Studies, Tel Aviv University, 1979).

Golan, Mati, *Shimon Peres* (Jerusalem: Shoken, 1982).

Gold, Dore (ed.) *Arms Control in the Middle East* (Tel Aviv: The Jaffee Center for Strategic Studies, 1990).

Goldblat, Jozef, *Non-Proliferation: The Why and Wherefore*, Published for SIPRI (London and Philadelphia: Taylor and Francis, 1985).

Granot, Oded and Keineich, Jack, *Hayom Bo Nirtzach Saadat* (in Hebrew) (The Day Sadat was killed) (Tel Aviv: Ma'ariv, 1984).

Griffith, Franklyn and Polonyi, John (eds.), *The Dangers of Nuclear War* (Toronto: University of Toronto Press, 1973).

Handel, Michael, *Israel's Political Military Doctrine*, Occasional Papers No. 30 (Cambridge: Harvard Center for International Affairs, July 1973).

Harkavy, Robert, *Spectre of a Middle Eastern Holocaust: The Strategic and Diplomatic Implications of the Israeli Nuclear Weapons Program* (Denver: University of Denver Press, 1977).

Hart, David, *India's Attitudes towards Nuclear Weapons Proliferation* (Center for European Studies, 1986).

Havias, Martin, *Missile Proliferation in the Middle East*, Adelphi Paper No. 252. (London: International Institute for Strategic Studies, 1990).

Heikal, Muhamad Hassenin, *The Road to Ramadan* (New York: Quadrangle Books, 1975).

Heller, Mark, Tamari, Dov, Eitan, Ze'ev, *Hama'azan Hatzvai* (in Hebrew) (The Military Balance) (Tel Aviv: The Jaffee Center for Strategic Studies, 1983).

——, Levran, Aharon, Eitan, Ze'ev, *The Military Balance in the Middle East*, 1985 (Tel Aviv: The Jaffee Center for Strategic Studies, 1986).

Herby, Peter, *The Chemical Weapons Convention and Arms Control in the Middle East* (Oslo: International Peace Research Institute, 1992).

Hersh, Seymour M., *The Price of Power: Kissinger in the Nixon's White House* (New York: Summit Books, 1983).

——, *The Samson Option* (London and Boston: Faber and Faber, 1991).

Herz, John, *Political Realism and Political Idealism* (Chicago: University of Chicago Press, 1951).

Herzog, Haim, *The War of Atonement* (Boston, M.A.: Little, Brown, 1975).

Horowitz, Dan, *Israel's Concept of Defensible Borders*, Jerusalem Papers on Peace Problems No. 16 (Jerusalem, 1975).

Hurevitz, Jacob, *Soviet–American Rivalry in the Middle East* (New York: Praeger, 1969).

Iklé, Fred and Wohlstetter, Albert, *Discriminate Deterrence*, Report of the Commission on Integrated Long-term Strategy (Washington, January 1988).

Inbar, Ephraim, *Israeli Strategic Thought in the Post 1973 Period* (Israeli Research Institute of Contemporary Society, Jerusalem, 1982).

Ismael, T. Y. (ed.) *The Middle East in World Politics* (Syracuse: Syracuse University Press, 1979).

Jabber, Faud, *Israel and Nuclear Weapons* (London: Chatto and Windus, 1971).

JCSS, *War in the Gulf: Implications for Israel* (Tel Aviv: Jaffee Center for Strategic Studies, 1992).

Jervis, Robert, *Perception and Misperception in International Politics* (Princeton: Princeton University Press, 1976).

——, Lebow, Richard Ned, Stein, Janice (eds.), *Psychology and Deterrence* (Baltimore: Johns Hopkins University Press, 1985).

——, *The Illogic of American Nuclear Strategy* (Ithaca, N.Y.: Cornell University Press, 1984).

Joeck, Neil, *The Strategic Consequences of Nuclear Proliferation in South Asia* (London: Frank Cass, 1986).

Jones, Rodney, W., *Nuclear Proliferation: Islam, The Bomb, and South Asia*, The Washington Papers No. 82 'Sage Policy Papers, 1981'.

Kahn, Herman, *Thinking About the Unthinkable* (New York: Horizon Press, 1962).

Karem, Mahmoud, *A Nuclear Weapons Free Zone in the Middle East* (Westport: Greenwood Press, 1988).

Karp, Regina Cowen (ed.), *Security with Nuclear Weapons? Different Perspectives on National Security* (Oxford: Oxford University Press, 1991).

Katz, James E. and Onkar, Marwah, S. (eds.), *Nuclear Power in Developing Countries* (Lexington, MA: Lexington Books, 1982).

Kemp, Geoffrey, *Nuclear Forces for Medium Powers*, Adelphi Papers No. 106, 107 (London: Institute for Strategic Studies, 1974).

——, "The Middle East Arms Race: Can it be Controlled?," *Middle East Journal* (Vol. 3, No. 3, Summer, 1991).

Kennan, George F., *The Nuclear Delusion: Soviet–American Relations in the Atomic Age* (New York: Partheon Books, 1982).

Kerr, Malcolm, *The Arab Cold War: Gamal Abd al Nassir and his Rivals, 1958–1970* (London: Oxford University Press, 1971).

Kissinger, Henry, *Years of Upheaval* (Boston and Toronto: Little Brown, 1982).

Klieman, Aharon, *Do-kyom Lelo Shalom* (in Hebrew) (Coexistence without Peace) (Tel Aviv: Ma'ariv, 1987).

Kordesman, Anthony, *The Iran–Iraq War and Western Security 1984–1987* (London: Jane's, 1987).

Krasner, Stephen, *International Regimes* (Ithaca: Cornell University Press, 1983).

Leitenberg, Milton and Sheffer, Gabriel (eds), *Great Power Intervention in the Middle East* (New York: Pergamon, 1979).

Levite, Ariel, *Offense and Defense in Israeli Military Doctrine* (Boulder, C.O.: Westview Press, 1990).

McNamara, Robert, S., *The Essence of Security: Reflection in Office* (New York: Harper and Row, 1968).

——, *The Military of Role of Nuclear Weapons Role* (ACIS Working Paper No. 46, UCLA, 1984).

Maddy-Weitzman, Bruce, *The Inter-Arab System and the Gulf War: Continuity and Change*, Occasional Paper Series, Vol. 2, No. 1 (Atlanta: The Carter Center of Emory University, 1991).

Mandelbaum, Michael, *The Nuclear Question: The United States and Nuclear Weapons, 1946–1976* (Cambridge: Cambridge University Press, 1979).

Marom, Ran, *Israel's Position on Non-Proliferation* (Jerusalem: The Leonard Davis Institute of International Relations, 1986).

Martin, Lawrence (ed.) *Strategic Thought in the Nuclear Age* (Baltimore: Johns Hopkins University Press, 1979).

Maxwell, Steven, *Rationality in Deterrence*, Adelphi Papers No. 50 (London: International Institute for Strategic Studies, 1968).

Mearsheimer, John J., *Conventional Deterrence* (Ithaca and London: Cornell University Press, 1983).

Miller, Marvin, *The Iraqi Nuclear Program* (typed Memorandum, July 1991).

Morgan, Patrick, *Deterrence: A Conceptual Analysis* (Beverly Hills: Sage Publications, 1977).

Nacht, Michael, *The Age of Vulnerability* (Washington: Brookings Institute, 1985).

Ofer, Zvi and Kover, Avi (eds.) *Eichot Vekamot: Dilemot Bebinyan Hakoch Hatzvai* (in Hebrew) (Quality and Quantity: Dilemmas in Building a Military Force) (Tel Aviv: Ma'arachot, 1985).

Osgood, Charles, *An Alternative to War or Surrender* (Urbana–Champaign, Il: University of Illinois Press, 1962).

Park, Jae Kyn (ed.) *Nuclear Proliferation in Developing Countries* (Seoul: The Institute for Far Eastern Studies, 1979).

Pean, Pierre, *Les deux bombes* (Paris: Fayard, 1982).

Peres, Shimon, *Hashlav Haba* (in Hebrew) (The Next Phase) (Tel Aviv: Am Oved, 1965).

Peri, Yoram, *Between Battles and Ballots: Israeli Military in Politics* (Cambridge: Cambridge University Press, 1983).

Posen, Barry, *The Sources of Military Doctrine: France, Britain and Germany between the World Wars* (Ithaca: Cornell University Press, 1984).

Pry, Peter, *Israel's Nuclear Arsenal* (Boulder, CO: Westview Press, 1984).

Quandt, William, *Decade of Decisions* (Berkeley and London: University of California Press, 1977).

Quester, George, *Nuclear Pakistan and Nuclear India*, Unpublished manuscript.

—— (ed.), *Nuclear Proliferation: Breaking the Chain* (Madison: University of Wisconsin Press, 1981).

Reis, Michael, *Without the Bomb: The Politics of Nuclear Nonproliferation* (New York: Columbia University Press, 1988).

Riad, Mahmud, *The Struggle for Peace in the Middle East* (London: Quartet Books, 1981).

Rosecrance, Richard, *The Dispersion of Nuclear Weapons* (New York: Columbia University Press, 1964).

——, *Strategic Deterrence Reconsidered*, Adelphi Papers No. 116 (London: International Institute for Strategic Studies, 1975).

——, *Defence of the Realm* (New York: Columbia University Press, 1968).

Russett, Bruce, *World Politics: The Menu for Choice* (New York: W. H. Freeman & Co., 1985, 1989.

El-Sadat, Anwar, *In Search of Identity* (New York: Harper and Row, 1978).

Safran, Nadav, *From War to War* (Indianapolis: Bobbs-Merrill, 1969).

——, *Israel, The Embattled Ally* (Cambridge, MA.: Harvard University Press, 1978, 1981).

Schelling, Thomas, *Arms and Influence* (New Haven: Yale University Press, 1972).

——, *Strategy of Conflict* (London: Oxford University Press, 1960).

Schofield, Richard, *Kuwait and Iraq: Historical Claims and Territorial Disputes* (London: Royal Institute of International Affairs, 1991).

Seale, Patrick, *Asad* (Berkeley: University of California Press, 1988).

Shalev, Aryeh, *Kav Hahagana Beyehuda Veshomron* (in Hebrew) (The Defense Line in Judea and Samaria) (Tel Aviv: Hakibutz Hameuchad, 1982).

Shamir, Shimon, *Mitzraiim Behanhagat Saadat* (in Hebrew) (Egypt under Sadat's Leadership) (Tel Aviv: Dvir, 1978).

Shapira, Anita, *Mepitore Harama ad Perok Hapalmach* (in Hebrew) (From the Expulsion of the "Rama" to the Dissolution of the "Palmach") (Tel Aviv: Hakibutz Hameuchad, 1985).

El-Shazli, Saad, *The Crossing of the Suez* (San Francisco: American Mideast Research, 1980).

Sheffer, Gabriel (ed.) *Dynamics of a Conflict: A Re-examination of the Arab–Israeli Conflict* (New York: Humanities Press, 1975).

Shiftan, Dan, *Optziyia Yardenit, Israel, Jordan Vehapalestinaim* (in Hebrew) (A Jordanian Option: Israel, Jordan, and the Palestinians) (Tel Aviv: Yad Tabenkin Vehakibutz Hameuchad, 1986).

Shimshoni, Jonathan, *Israel and Conventional Deterrence: Border Warfare From 1953 to 1970* (Ithaca: Cornell University Press, 1988).

Shlaim, Avi, *Collusion across the Jordan* (Oxford: Oxford University Press, 1987).

SIPRI (ed.), *Tactical Nuclear Weapons: European Perspectives* (London, 1979).

Sivan, Emanuel, *Kana'ey Ha'Islam* (in Hebrew) (Zealots of Islam) (Tel Aviv: Am Oved, 1986).

Snyder, Glen, *Deterrence by Denial and Punishment* (Princeton: Princeton University, Center of International Studies, Research Monograph No. 1, 1959).

Snyder, Glen and Diesing, Paul, *Conflict Among Nations: Bargaining, Decision-Making and System Structure in International Crisis* (Princeton: Princeton University Press, 1977).

Snyder, C. Jed and Wells, Samuel, *Limiting Nuclear Proliferation* (Cambridge: Ballinger, 1985).

Spector, Leonard, *Nuclear Proliferation Today* (New York: Vintage Books, 1984).

——, *The Undeclared Bomb* (Cambridge: Ballinger, 1988).

—— and Smith, Jacqueline, *Nuclear Ambitions* (Cambridge: Ballinger, 1990).

Steinbruner, John D., *The Cybernetic Theory of Decision* (Princeton: Princeton University Press, 1974).

Steiner, H. Barry, *Using the Absolute Weapon: Early Ideas of Bernard Brodie on Atomic Strategy* (ACIS Working Papers No. 44, Center for International and Strategic Affairs UCLA, 1984).

United Nations, Report of the Secretary-General, *Establishment of a Nuclear-Weapon-Free Zone in the Region of the Middle East* (A/45/435, 10 October, 1990).

United Nations, *Second Report by the Special Commission on Security Council Resolution 687.*

Vatikiotis, P. J., *The Modern History of Egypt* (London: Weidenfeld and Nicolson, 1969).

Walt, Stephen, *The Origins of Alliances*, (Ithaca: Cornell University Press, 1987).

Weissman, Steve and Krosney, Herbert, *The Islamic Bomb: The Nuclear Threat to Israel and the Middle East* (New York: Times Books, 1981).

Weitzman Ezer, *Hakrav Al Hashalom* (in Hebrew) (The Battle for Peace) (Jerusalem: Edanim, 1981).

Yager, Joseph (ed.), *Nonproliferation and US Foreign Policy* (Washington: Brookings Institute, 1980).

Yaniv, Avner, *Deterrence Without the Bomb* (Lexington, M.A.: D.C. Heath, 1987).

Young, Oran, *The Politics of Force: Bargaining During International Crisis* (Princeton: Princeton University Press, 1978).

ARTICLES AND CHAPTERS IN BOOKS (NOT INCLUDING ARTICLES IN DAILIES AND WEEKLIES)

Afheldt, Holst, "Tactical Nuclear Weapons and European Security" in SIPRI (ed.) *Tactical Nuclear Weapons: European Perspectives* (London, 1979).

Albright, David and Hibbs, Mark, "Iraq and the Bomb: Were They Even Close?", *The Bulletin of the Atomic Scientists* (No. 1, 1991).

——, "Hyping the Iraqi Bomb", *The Bulletin of the Atomic Scientists* (No. 1, 1991).

Ajami, Fuad, "The End of Pan-Arabism," *Foreign Affairs* (Winter, 1978–9).

Arian, Asher, "Security and Political Attitudes", in JCSS Study Group, *War in the Gulf: Implications for Israel* (Tel Aviv: Jaffee Center for Strategic Studies, Tel Aviv University, 1991).

Aronson, Shlomo, "The Nuclear Dimension of the Arab–Israeli Conflict", *The Jerusalem Journal of International Relations* (Vol. 7, No. 1–2, 1984).

—— and Horowitz, Dan, "The Strategy of Controlled Retaliation: The Israeli Example" (Hebrew) Medina Umimshal, (Vol. 1, No. 1 summer 1971).

Art, Robert, "The United States: Nuclear Weapons and Grand Strategy" in Regina

Cowen Karp, *Security with Nuclear Weapons?* (Oxford: Oxford University Press, 1991).

——, "A Defensible Defense: America's Grand Strategy After the Cold War", *International Security* (Vol. 15, No. 4 spring 1991).

Baram, Amatzia, "Iraqi Imagery and the Success of Non-Conventional Deterrence vis-à-viz Israel" (Paper presented at *Conference on Deterrence in the Middle East*, US Institute of Peace, June 1991).

Bar-Joseph, Uri, "The Hidden Debate: The Formation of Nuclear Doctrines in the Middle East", *The Journal of Strategic Studies*, (Vol. 5, No. 2, June 1982).

Barton, John and Carter, Barry, "The Uneven but Growing Role of International Law", in Graham Allison and Gregory Treverton (eds) *Rethinking America's Security: Beyond Cold War to New World Order* (London: W. W. Norton, 1992).

Ben-Dor, Gabriel, "Inter-Arab Relations and the Arab–Israeli Conflict", *Jerusalem Journal of International Relations* (summer, 1976).

Betts, Richard, "Conventional Deterrence: Prediction, Uncertainty and Policy Confidence", *World Politics* (Vol. 35, No. 2, 1985).

Bialer, Seweryn, "New Thinking and Soviet Foreign Policy", *Survival* (Vol. 30, No. 4, 1988).

Bidawi, Praful, Vanaik, Achin, "India and Pakistan" in Regina Karp, *Security with Nuclear Weapons? Different Perspectives on National Security* (Oxford: Oxford University Press, 1991).

Binder, Leonard, "The Middle East Subordinate International System", *World Politics* (Vol. 10, No. 3, April 1958).

Blechman, Barry M., "The Impact of Israel's Reprisals on the Behavior of the Bordering Arab Nations of Israel", *Journal of Conflict Resolution* (Vol. 16, No. 2, June 1972).

Boulding, Kenneth, "National Images and International Systems", *The Journal of Conflict Resolution* (3, No. 4, 1959).

Brecher, Michael, "The Middle East Subordinate System and its Impact on Israel's Foreign Policy", *International Studies Quarterly* (Vol. 13, No. 2, June 1969).

Brodie, Bernard, "The Continuing Relevance of *On War*" in the English translation by Michael Howard and Peter Paret of Karl von Clausewitz, *On War* (Princeton: Princeton University Press, 1976).

Bull, Hedley, "Future Conditions of Strategic Deterrence" in C. Bertram (ed.) *The Future of Strategic Deterrence* (London: Macmillan, 1981).

Bundy, McGeorge, "To Cap the Volcano", *Foreign Policy* (October 1969).

——, Kennan, George F., McNamara, Robert S. and Smith, Gerard, "Nuclear Weapons and the Atlantic Alliance", *Foreign Affairs* (Vol. 60, No. 4, spring 1982).

Carus, W. Seth, "Chemical Weapons in the Middle East", *Policy Focus* (Washington, 1988).

——, "The Genie Unleashed: Iraq's Chemical and Biological Weapons Program", *Policy Papers* (Washington, 1989).

——, "Missiles in the Middle East", *Policy Focus* (Washington, 1988).

Cohen, Avner, Benjamin, Frankel, "Opaque Nuclear Proliferation" in Benjamin Frankel (ed.), *Opaque Nuclear Proliferation: Methodological and Policy Implications* (London: Frank Cass, 1991).

—— and Miller, Marvin, "Facing the Unavoidable: Israel's Nuclear Monopoly Revisited" in Benjamin Frankel (ed.) *Opaque Nuclear Proliferation: Methodological and Policy Implications* (London: Frank Cass, 1991).

Dann, Uriel, "The Iraqi Invasion of Kuwait: Historical Observations" (The Dayan Center for Middle Eastern and African Studies, Tel Aviv University, August 1990).

Dessouki, Ali Hillal, "The New Arab Political Order: Implications for the 1980s," in Malcolm Kerr and Sayed Yassin, *Rich and Poor States in the Middle East: Egypt and the New Arab Order* (Boulder, C.O.: Westview Press, 1982).

Doyle, Michael, "An International Liberal Community" in Graham Allison and Gregory Treverton (eds), *Rethinking America's Security: Beyond Cold War to New World Order* (London: W. W. Norton, 1992).

——, "Kant, Liberal Legacies and Foreign Affairs", in *Philosophy and Public Affairs* (Vol. 12, summer).

Dowty, Alan, "Nuclear Proliferation: The Israeli Case", *International Studies Quarterly* (Vol. 22, 1978).

Duffy, Gloria, "Soviet Nuclear Exports", *International Security* (Vol. 3, No. 2 summer 1978).

Dunn, Lewis, "Dealing with the Threshold Countries: Old Problems, Emerging Challenges and New Approaches", (Paper presented at UCS Workshop, June 1991).

Erasmus, "Polycentrism and Proliferation", *Survey* (No. 58, January 1966).

Evron, Yair, "Israel and the Atom: The Uses and Misuses of Ambiguity, 1957–1967", *Orbis* (Vol. 17, No. 4, winter 1974).

——, "The Arab Position in the Nuclear Field: A Study of Policies up to 1967", *Cooperation and Conflict* (No. 1, 1973).

——, "Letter to the Editor", *Commentary* (February 1976).

——, "Israel and Nuclear Weapons" in Jae Kyn Park (ed.) *Nuclear Proliferation in Developing Countries* (Seoul: The Institute for Far Eastern Studies, 1979).

——, "Great Powers Military Intervention in the Middle East" in Milton Leitenburg and Gabriel Sheffer (eds) *Great Power Intervention in the Middle East* (New York: Pergamon, 1979).

——, "Some Effects of the Introduction of Nuclear Weapons into the Middle East" in Asher Arian (ed.) *Israel—A Developing Society*, (The Netherlands: Van Gorcum, 1980).

——, "Some Political and Strategic Implications of an American–Israeli Defense Treaty," 1980.

——, "The Middle East and the Atomic Bomb" (in Hebrew) *Skirah Hodshit* (Vol. 28, No. 7, July 1981).

——, "Opaque Proliferation: The Israeli Case", *The Journal of Strategic Studies* (Vol. 13, No. 3, September 1990).

——, "Israel" in Regina Cowen Karp, *Security with Nuclear Weapons? Different Perspectives on National Security* (Oxford: Oxford University Press, 1991).

——, "Confidence-Building in the Middle East" in Dore Gold (ed.) *Arms Control in the Middle East* (Tel Aviv: The Jaffee Center for Strategic Studies, 1990).

——, Bar Simantov, Ya'acov, "Coalitions in the Arab World", *Jerusalem Journal of International Relations* (summer 1976).

Feldman, Shai, "Israeli Deterrence and the Gulf War" (Paper presented to *The Conference on Deterrence in the Middle East*, US Institute of Peace, June 1991).

Frankel, Benjamin, "An Anxious Decade: Nuclear Proliferation in the 1990s" in Benjamin Frankel (ed.) *Opaque Nuclear Proliferation: Methodological and Policy Implications* (London: Frank Cass, 1991).

——, "The Brooding Shadow: Structural Changes and Nuclear Proliferation" (forthcoming).

Freier, Shalhevet, "The Nuclear Non-Proliferation Policy of Israel" (forthcoming).

Fukuyama, Francis, "The End of History", *The National Interest* (No. 16, summer 1989).

Gardner, Richard, "International Law and the Use of Force", *Adelphi Papers* No. 266 (London: International Institute for Strategic Studies, 1991/2).

——, "Practical Internationalism" in Graham Allison and Gregory Treverton (eds), *Rethinking America's Security: Beyond Cold War to New World Order* (London: W. W. Norton, 1992).

Garwin, Richard, "Weapon Development and the Threat of Nuclear War" in Franklyn Griffith and John Polony (eds) *The Dangers of Nuclear War* (Toronto: University of Toronto Press, 1979).

George, Alexander, "Crisis Prevention Reexamined" in Alexander George, *Managing U.S.–Soviet Rivalry: Problems of Crisis Prevention* (Boulder, Colorado: Westview Press, 1983).

Gilpin, Robert, "The Richness of the Tradition of Political Realism", in Robert O. Keohane (ed.), *Neorealism and its Critics* (New York: Columbia University Press, 1986).

Goheen, Robert, "Problems of Proliferation: US Policy and the Third World", *World Politics* (Vol. 35, No. 2, 1983).

Haas, Richard, "South Asia: Too Late to Remove the Bomb", *Orbis* (32, winter 1988).

Hartman, William, "Military Elements in Regional Unrest" in Jacob Hurevitz (ed.), *Soviet American Rivalry in the Middle East* (New York: Praeger 1969).

Hirschfield, Thomas, "Mutual Security Short of Arms Control" in Dore Gold (ed.), *Arms Control in the Middle East* (Tel Aviv: The Jaffee Center for Strategic Studies, 1990).

Hoffman, Stanley, "Nuclear Proliferation and World Politics" in Alastair Buchan (ed.) *A World of Nuclear Powers* (Englewood Cliffs, NJ: Prentice Hall, 1966).

Horowitz, Dan, "The Israeli Concept of National Security and the Prospects of Peace in the Middle East" in Gabriel Sheffer (ed.) *Dynamics of a Conflict: A Reexamination of the Arab–Israeli Conflict* (New York: Humanities Press, 1975).

——, "The Control of Limited Military Operations: The Israeli Experience" in Yair Evron (ed.) *International Violence: Terrorism, Surprise and Control* (Jerusalem: The Leonard Davis Institute for International Relations, 1979).

——, "The Constant and the Changing in Israel Strategic Thought" (Hebrew) in *Milchemet Breira* (Optional War) (Tel Aviv: Hakaibbutz Hameuchad, 1985).

Hung Chee, Chan, "The UN: From Peace-Keeping to Peace Making?" *Adelphi Papers* (No. 265).

Huth, Paul, Russet, Bruce, "What Makes Deterrence Work: Cases from 1900 to 1980", *World Politics* (Vol. 36, No. 4, July 1984).

Ismael, T. Y., "A Subordinate System in Global Politics: The Middle East" in T. Y. Ismael (ed.) *The Middle East in World Politics* (Syracuse: Syracuse University Press, 1974).

Jervis, Robert, "Cooperation Under the Security Dilemma", *World Politics* (January 1978).

——, "Deterrence Theory Revisited", *World Politics* (Vol. 30, No. 2, January 1979).

——, "Why Nuclear Superiority Doesn't Matter", *Political Science Quarterly* (Vol. 94, No. 4, 1979–1980).

Kapur, A., "Pakistan" in J. Goldblatt (ed.) *Non-proliferation: The Why and Wherefore* (London and Philadelphia: Taylor and Francis, 1985).

Kaysen, Carl, McNamara, Robert and Rathjens, George, "Nuclear Weapons After the Cold War," *Foreign Affairs*, Vol. 70, No. 4, Fall 1991).

Khalizad, K. M. "Pakistan" in J. Goldblatt *Nuclear Non-Proliferation: The Why and Wherefore* (London and Philadelphia: Taylor and Francis, 1985).

Lebovic, J., "The Middle East, The Region as a System", *International Interactions* (Vol. 1, No. 3, 1986).

Lawrence, Martin, "The Role of Military Force in the Nuclear Age", in Martin Lawrence (ed.) *Strategic Thought in the Nuclear Age* (Baltimore: Johns Hopkins University Press, 1979).

Lebow, Richard Ned, "Deterrence Reconsidered: The Challenge of Recent Research", *Survival* (Vol. 27, No. 1, January/February 1985).

—— and Stein, Janice, "Beyond Deterrence—Building Better Theory", *Journal of Social Issues* (No. 4, 1987).

McNaughton, Thomas, "Ballistic Missiles and Chemical Weapons: The Legacy of the Iran–Iraq War", *International Security* (Vol. 15, No. 2, Fall 1990).

Maoz, Simcha, "Power Ratios, Aggression and Chances for Victory in Battle" (Hebrew) *Ma'arachot* (No. 225, September 1972).

Mearsheimer, John, "Back to the Future: Instability in Europe After the Cold War", *International Security* (Vol. 15, No. 1, summer 1990).

Merlini, Cesare, "Nuclear Non-proliferation: After the Pause What?", *The International Spectator* (April–June 1984).

Miller, Steven, "Western Diplomacy and the Soviet Nuclear Legacy", *Survival* (Autumn 1992).

Morgan, Patrick, "Towards a Political Science Theory of Deterrence" (unpublished manuscript).

Nye, Joseph, "NPT: The Logic of Inequality", *Foreign Policy* (Vol. 35, No. 29, 1985).

——, "Maintaining the Nonproliferation Regime", *International Organization* (Vol. 35, No. 1, Winter, 1981).

——, "The Superpowers and the Non-Proliferation Treaty" in Albert Carnesale and Richard Haas (eds) *Superpower Arms Control: Setting the Record Straight* (Cambridge: Ballinger, 1987).

——, "US–Soviet Cooperation in a Non-Proliferation Regime" in Alexander George, *US–Soviet Security Cooperation* (Boulder, CO: Westview Press, 1988).

Pajak, F. Roger, "Nuclear Status and Policies of the Middle East Countries", *International Affairs* (Vol. 59, No. 4, 1983).

Potter, C. William, "Soviet Nuclear Export Policy", in C. Jed Snyder and Samuel Wells (eds) *Limiting Nuclear Proliferation* (Cambridge: Ballinger, 1985).

Quester, George, "The Middle East: Imposed Solutions or Imposed Problems", in Milton Leitenberg and Gabriel Sheffer (eds), *Great Power Intervention in the Middle East* (New York: Pergamon Press, 1979).

——, "Knowing and Believing about Nuclear Proliferation", *Security Studies* (Vol. 1, No. 2, Winter, 1991).

——, "Nuclear Proliferation and the Elimination of Nuclear Weapons", in Regina Cowen Karp (ed.), *Security Without Nuclear Weapons? Different Perspectives on Non Nuclear Security* (Oxford: Oxford University Press, 1992).

Rabinovich, Itamar, "The Syrian–Israeli Deterrence Relationship—The Syrian Perspective" (Paper presented to *The Conference on Deterrence in the Middle East*, U.S. Institute of Peace, June 1991).

Roberts, Adam, "International Law and the Use of Force", *Adelphi Papers* (No. 266).

Rosecrance, Richard, "Problems of Nuclear Proliferation", *Security Studies Papers* (No. 7, University of California, 1966).

Russet, Bruce, "The Calculus of Deterrence", *Journal of Conflict Resolution* (Vol. 7, No. 2, March 1963).

—— "Pearl Harbor: Deterrence Theory and Decision Theory", *Journal of Peace Research* (No. 2, 1967).

Scheinman, Lawrence, "The Case for a Comprehensive U.S. Nonproliferation Policy" in C. Jed Snyder and Samuel Wells (eds) *Limiting Nuclear Proliferation* (Cambridge: Ballinger, 1985).

Schelling, Thomas, "Who Will Have the Bomb?", *International Security* (Vol. 1, No. 1, summer 1976).

Shaked, Haim, "The Nuclearization of the Middle East: The Israeli Raid on Osiraq", *Middle East Contemporary Survey* (Vol. 5, 1980–81).

Smith, Roger, "The Non-Proliferation Regime: Anomalies for Contemporary International Relations Theory", *International Organization* (41, spring 1987).

—— "Opaque Proliferation and the Fate of the Non-Proliferation Regime", in Benjamin Frankel (ed.), *Opaque Nucleaer Proliferation: Methodological and Policy Implications* (London: Frank Cass, 1991).

Snyder, Jed, "The Non-Proliferation Regime: Managing the Impending Crisis", *Journal of Strategic Studies* (No. 8, December 1985).

Stein, Janice, "Calculation, Miscalculation and Conventional Deterrence: The View from Jerusalem" in Robert Jervis, Richard Ned Lebow and Janice Stein, *Psychology and Deterrence* (Baltimore: Johns Hopkins University Press, 1985).

—— "Calculation, Miscalculations and Conventional Deterrence: The View from Cairo" in *Psychology and Deterrence* (Baltimore: Johns Hopkins University Press, 1985).

Steinbruner, John D., Garwin, Thomas M., "Strategic Vulnerability: The Balance Between Prudence and Paranoia", *International Security* (Vol. 1, No. 4, 1976).

Stieglitz, Meir, "Israel's Nuclear Doctrine: The Amount of Necessary Evil" (Hebrew), *Politika* (No. 13, March–April 1987).

Tamari, Dov, "The Syrian–Israeli Balance of Forces and Strategic Parity" in Joseph Alpher, Ze'ev Eitan and Dov Tamari (eds) *The Middle East Military Balance 1989–1990* (Tel Aviv: Tel Aviv University, 1990).

Urqhart, Brian, "The UN: From Peace-Keeping to Collective Security", *Adelphi Papers* No. 265, (Winter 1991/92).

Vanaik, Achin and Praful, Bidwai, "Security without Nuclear Weapons? South Asia Case Study" in *Security with Nuclear Weapons* (Oxford: Oxford University Press, 1991).

Waltz Kenneth, "The Spread of Nuclear Weapons: More May be Better", *Adelphi Papers* (No. 171, autumn 1981).

—— "The Emerging Structure of International Politics" (unpublished manuscript presented at *APSA* Meeting, August 1990).

Weltman, John, "Nuclear Devolution and World Politics", *World Politics* (Vol. 32, No. 2, January 1980).

Wohlstetter, Albert, "Nuclear Sharing: Nato and the N+ Country", *Foreign Affairs* (Vol. 39, No. 3, April 1961).

Zartman, William, "Military Elements in Regional Unrest" in J. C. Hurevitz (ed.) *Soviet–American Rivalry in the Middle East* (New York: Praeger, 1969).

INDEX

Achdut Ha'avodah party 6, 7
Afghanistan, Soviet invasion of 146
Agranat Commission, on 1973 war 129
air battles, effect of demilitarization of
  Sinai on 235, 236
Algeria: and Syria 57; war with France 2
Allon, Yigal 9, 43; Allon Plan 8; on
  Israeli adoption of nuclear weapons
  251; and nonproliferation 150; and
  "nuclear" decision during
  Israel–Egypt war (1973) 71, 72; and
  nuclear strategy 6, 8
ambiguity of Israeli nuclear capability
  215; and deterrence 243; effects of
  disclosure 273; effects of 250–1,
  272–3; rational uses of 259, 275–6
ambiguity of Israeli nuclear posture 7;
  see also threshold status
anarchy: influence of religious
  fundamentalism on 103; in
  international relations 93, 94–5, 100;
  and Middle East conflict 100–4
Arab League 198
Arab states: acceptance of existence of
  Israel 259; attitude to territorial-
  state 101–2; authority to activate
  nuclear weapons 129–32;
  competition and conflict between
  83–4, 178, 259–60; current attitudes
  to Israel 79; deterrence of
  nuclearization of 251–2; division
  among on nuclear development 33;
  effects on of possible Israeli
  adoption of nuclear doctrine 34;
  financial assistance from Gulf states
  for military development 218–19;
  military regimes 102; morale and
  motivation for war 223, 229–30;

nuclear options 20; pan-Arabism 79,
  101, 208, 210; perceptions of Israeli
  nuclear capacity 13, 14–20, 32–4;
  possible coalitions of 132–8, 215,
  217–18, 220–1, 254; power ratio of
  217–18; relations with U.S.S.R. 154,
  171; shortages of skilled manpower
  218, 220; use of long external lines
  221; *see also under individual countries*
Arab–Israeli conflict: 1956 war 40–2;
  1967 war 150, 184; 1973 war 109,
  225, 226–7, 230, 232, 233, 234–5;
  costs of 230; effect on decision-
  makers 108–9; extent of 108;
  Palestinian issue underlying 175–6;
  and possible coalition of Arab states
  132–8, 215, 217–18, 220–1, 254; War
  of Attrition (1969–70) 40, 52, 64,
  230, 232, 245
Arens, Moshe: on nuclearization of
  Middle East 265, 266
Argentina: and Non-Proliferation
  Treaty (NPT) 142; as threshold state
  142, 161
armour, concentrations of: tactical
  nuclear weapons and 190–1
armoured ground systems, Precision
  Guided Munitions (PGM) 217
arms control agreements 264, 267–76;
  connection of nonproliferation with
  security factors 271–2; effect of Gulf
  Crisis and War on prospects for
  259–60; Egyptian position 270–1;
  INF treaty 155; Israeli position
  269–70; new U.S. plan 162–3; Non-
  Proliferation Treaty (NPT) *see* Non-
  Proliferation Treaty (NPT); SALT-1
  agreement 179; SALT-II 95–6;

battlefield uses 257, 258–9;
deterrent effect 255–7; lack of
relevance to current Middle East
situation 259; and midwar
deterrence 256; as revenge 257–8;
use of nuclear arms in 255–8
weapons systems: anti-tank and antiaircraft systems 223; ARROW
(antiballistic missiles) 265–6; cruise
missiles 125; fission bombs 188;
Precision Guided Munitions (PGM)
217; SSM *see* surface-to-surface
missiles (SSM) 260; strategic 188,
189; tactical 188; theater 188; V/
STOL aircraft 186
Weizmann Institute, nuclear research 2
Weltman, John: on transfer of nuclear
materials 180, 182

West Bank: demilitarization of 236–7,
239; and limited war scenario 227,
228; as source of conflict 175–7; and
terms for peace treaty between
Jordan and Israel 79
White Papers on defense 89
"window of vulnerability" argument
97–8
World War II, influence on superpower
nuclear strategy 113

Yadin, Yigael, Israeli Chief of Staff 40–1
Yemen: civil war 86; confrontations
between North and South 183;
Egyptian use of chemical weapons in
war in 260; military clashes in 109;
as part of Middle East 82
Yugoslavia, disintegration of 159